# The Haskell School of Expression

## LEARNING FUNCTIONAL PROGRAMMING THROUGH MULTIMEDIA

**PAUL HUDAK**

*Yale University*

**CAMBRIDGE**
UNIVERSITY PRESS

PUBLISHED BY THE PRESS SYNDICATE OF THE UNIVERSITY OF CAMBRIDGE
The Pitt Building, Trumpington Street, Cambridge, United Kingdom

CAMBRIDGE UNIVERSITY PRESS
The Edinburgh Building, Cambridge CB2 2RU, UK      http://www.cup.cam.ac.uk
40 West 20th Street, New York, NY 10011-4211, USA  http://www.cup.org
10 Stamford Road, Oakleigh, Melbourne 3166, Australia
Ruiz de Alarcón 13, 28014 Madrid, Spain

First published 2000

Printed in the United States of America

*Typeface* Lucida Y&Y 9.25/13 pt. and Optima      *System* $\text{\LaTeX}\,2_\varepsilon$   [TB]

*A catalog record for this book is available from the British Library.*

*Library of Congress Cataloging in Publication Data*
Hudak, Paul.
    The Haskell school of expression: learning functional programming through
multimedia / Paul Hudak
        p.   cm.
    ISBN 0-521-64338-4 (hardback) – ISBN 0-521-64408-9 (pbk.)
    1. Functional programming (Computer science)   2. Multimedia systems.   I. Title.
QA76.62 H83   2000
005.1′14 21 – dc21                                                    99-045529

ISBN 0 521 64338 4 hardback
ISBN 0 521 64408 9 paperback

*This book is dedicated to*
*Cathy, Cristina, Jennifer, and Rusty*

# Contents

# Preface

The first high-level languages developed for general purpose programming were *Fortran* (Backus, 1978) and *Lisp* (McCarthy, 1978), developed in the late 1950s by John Backus and John McCarthy, respectively. From Fortran grew many of today's modern *imperative* languages, most of which did not improve significantly on the fundamental ideas found in the language *Algol* (de Morgan, Hill and Wichmann, 1976), which shortly followed Fortran. The Lisp family was less fecund, perhaps because it was so far ahead of its time, but was the seed for the family of *functional* languages about which this textbook was written. The most radical in this class of languages is probably *Haskell*, originally designed in the late 1980s (Hudak, Wadler, 1988) based on, at that point, a good ten years of experience designing and implementing similar languages, most notably a series of languages developed by David Turner in the late 1970s and early 1980s (Turner, 1976; 1985). Although research continues on the design of Haskell, the version used in this textbook, *Haskell 98* (Augustsson, et al., 1999), is the latest and most stable version of the language and its libraries.

Haskell was named after the logician Haskell B. Curry who, along with Alonzo Church, established the theoretical foundations of functional programming back when computers themselves were only a gleam in researchers' eyes. A curious historical fact is that Haskell Curry's father, Samuel Silas Curry, helped to found and direct a school in Boston called the *School of Expression*.[1] Because pure functional programming centers around the notion of an *expression*, I thought that *The Haskell School of Expression* would be a good title for this book.

---

[1] This school eventually evolved into what is now called *Curry College* (see `www.curry.edu:8080/history/history.html` for a brief history of the college).

## A Brief Account of Language Success Stories

It's hard to predict just how it is that a language becomes popular. Fortran became popular because it was the first high-level language and a welcome alternative to assembly language, and ultimately because it was a good vehicle for coding numerical algorithms in the domain of scientific computing. C (Kernighan and Ritchie, 1978) was not revolutionary by any means, often being described as a high-level assembly language. But it found a niche in Unix and systems-level programming, and from there to other operating system platforms. Cobol (Cobol, 1968) was designed from day one for business applications, and so made its mark. Java's (Gosling, Joy and Steele, 1996) recent astonishing rise in popularity is rather perplexing on one hand, yet quite understandable on another. As a language, it is simple and elegant, but certainly not revolutionary. Yet it found a niche in its use on the world-wide-web, which at the time was (and still is) a phenomenon in its own right. Lisp and Scheme (Rees and Clinger, 1986) for AI, Ada (Ada,79) for real-time applications, VHDL and Verilog for digital hardware design, and the list goes on.

From this discussion it appears that for a language to become popular it needs an application – a *niche* – in which it excels, or in which it at least was the first to arrive. Curiously, for most language designers, this is the *opposite* of what is desired. Most language designers would like their languages to be truly general purpose, able to solve all of the world's problems with great succinctness, clarity, and efficiency. As a result, many excellent languages out there, some with very decent implementations, will probably forever remain in obscurity because they never found their niche.

Although the designers of Haskell exhibited no exception to this ambitious approach to language design, in retrospect I wonder if there might be a plausible niche for Haskell. These sorts of things are mostly out of my control, of course, but I thought it would be fun to use *multimedia* – graphics, sound, and animation – as an underlying theme, embodied concretely through many examples and exercises, in this text. Multimedia is an application area that is certainly current and important, and one in which Haskell's advantages are highly visible.

In addition, one of the nice things about multimedia programming is that all of the really interesting (and hard!) problems faced by computer scientists over the past 30 years are found in the "virtual worlds" that we create. Nondeterminism, concurrency, state, time, efficiency, decidability, and others are all issues that must be addressed. Although I don't cover all of these issues in this text, multimedia programming nevertheless provides a good vehicle through which one could teach general topics in computer science.

I also hope that this text demonstrates the ease with which one can embed a *domain-specific language* in Haskell. In a more general sense, this might actually be the most profitable niche for Haskell, as there have been a number of success stories in this area already.

In any case, I hope that you enjoy working through the various multimedia programs as much as I have enjoyed creating them. At the same time, I hope that this text might help Haskell to find its niche and thus avoid the fate of obscurity described earlier. Haskell really is a beautiful language.

## Why I Wrote This Book, and How to Read It

At the time I began writing this book there were not many other books about programming specifically in Haskell. But that wasn't the main reason I decided to tackle this task. More importantly, there was a need for a book that described *how to solve problems using a functional language* such as Haskell. As with any major class of languages, there is a certain mind-set for contemplation, a certain viewpoint of the world, and a certain approach to problem solving that collectively work best. If you teach only Haskell language details to a C programmer, she is likely to write very ugly, incomprehensible functional programs. But if you teach her how to think differently, how to see problems in a different light, functional solutions will come easily, and elegant Haskell programs will result. That, in a nutshell, is my goal in this textbook. As Samuel Silas Curry once said:

> All expression comes *from within outward,* from the center to the surface, from a hidden source to outward manifestation. The study of expression as a natural process brings you into contact with cause and makes you feel the source of reality.
> (http://www.curry.edu:8080/history/history.html)

I encourage the seasoned programmer having experience only with conventional imperative and/or object-oriented languages to read this text with an open mind. Many things will be different, and will likely feel awkward. There will be a tendency to rely on old habits when writing new programs, and to ignore my suggestions about how to approach things differently. If you can manage to resist these tendencies, I am confident that you will have an enjoyable learning experience. Many of those who succeed in this process find that many of the things that they learn about functional programming can be applied to imperative and object-oriented languages – after all, most of these other languages contain a significant functional subset – and that their imperative coding style changes for the better as a result.

I also ask the experienced programmer to be patient while in the earlier chapters I explain things like "syntax," "operator precedence," and others because my goal is that this text should be readable by someone having only modest prior programming experience. With patience the more advanced ideas will appear soon enough.

If you are a novice programmer, I suggest taking your time with the book; work through the exercises, and don't rush things. If, however, you don't fully grasp an idea, feel free to move on, but try to reread difficult material at a later time when you have seen more examples of the concepts in action. For the most part this is a "show by example" textbook, and you should try to execute as many of the programs in this text as you can, as well as every program that you write. Learn-by-doing is the corollary to show-by-example.

Finally, although the text begins quite gently, it moves at a fairly rapid pace, and covers many advanced ideas in functional programming, some of which are not covered in any other text that I am aware of. So there is much here even for those who are already familiar with the basics of functional programming.

## Suggestions to Instructors

All of the material in this textbook can be covered in one semester as an advanced undergraduate course. For lower-level courses, including possible use in high school, some of the mathematics may cause problems, but for bright students I suspect most of the material can still be covered.

I strongly encourage sticking to the order of the chapters in the book, which introduces Haskell language features as they are demanded by the underlying application themes (generally the chapters alternate between "concepts" and "applications"). If you are an experienced functional programmer, you will see instances early in the book where a lambda expression here, or eta-conversion there, will simplify things, but I have chosen to delay such simplifications in most cases. Flooding the student with too many features early on can be overwhelming.

The only exception to following the given chapter order is that Chapters 20 to 22 provide a somewhat independent thread on computer music, and can be covered anytime after Chapter 11. The most difficult chapter is probably Chapter 15, and the most dispensible chapters are probably Chapters 17 and 22. Also, if you want to omit nonmultimedia applications you might consider skipping Chapter 6, although that chapter contains the first introduction to infinite lists. Finally, Chapters 23 and 24 are short "tours" of the PreludeList Module and Standard Type Classes, respectively, and could be assigned as auxiliary reading, or covered piecemeal as related topics are introduced.

The web page `http://haskell.org/soe` contains a great deal of useful information related to the text, including libraries, source code for each chapter, PowerPoint slides, and errata. You can send email to me at `paul.hudak@yale.edu` with feedback, questions, corrections, etc.

## Haskell Implementations

There are several good implementations of Haskell, all available free on the Internet through the Haskell home page at `http://haskell.org`. One that I especially recommend is the *Hugs* implementation, a very easy-to-use and easy-to-install Haskell interpreter. Hugs runs on a variety of platforms, including PC's (Windows 95/NT), various flavors of Unix (Linux, Solaris, HP), and Mac OS. The Glasgow Haskell Compiler (GHC) supports the same libraries as Hugs, and has the benefit of being a true compiler instead of an interpreter.

All of the code in the book is compliant with the Haskell '98 standard, and has been tested on the Hugs '98 implementation of Haskell. Unfortunately, the graphics and animation applications rely on a library that was originally developed only for Windows 95/NT. You should consult the SOE web page for the latest information regarding compatibility with other platforms.

## Acknowledgments

I learned that writing a textbook is not an easy task, and could not have been accomplished without the help of many friends and colleagues. I would especially like to thank Mark Jones, with whom I started this project, and who first suggested the use of the name *School of Expression*. I'd also like to thank John Peterson and Joe Fasel for help in writing *A Gentle Introduction to Haskell* (Hudak and Fasel, 1992), from which some of this text was adapted; Alastair Reid for help with the Hugs implementation and graphics libraries; Conal Elliott for many helpful suggestions and inspirations, especially concerning graphics and animation; Erik Meijer for feedback from using a previous version of this text in his class; Mark Tullsen for careful proofreading and tedious index generation; Tom Makucevich and John Garvin for help with computer music; Tim Sheard for feedback from using my book in teaching a functional programming course at Yale, and for creating great PowerPoint slides in the process; Zhanyong Wan for excellent feedback on the text as a Teaching Assistant in Tim's course; Sigbjorn Finne for writing the kaleidoscope program; Valery Trifonov for adapting the kaleidoscope program and other useful feedback; Linda Joyce for help with the indexing and excellent administrative support; Martin Sulzmann for help debugging graphics; Lauren Cowles, my editor, whose patience is extraordinary; and the many students in various classes at Yale who endured earlier versions of the text.

I would also like to thank the several United States funding agencies, most notably NSF and DARPA, who have provided considerable financial support for functional programming research at Yale and elsewhere.

Most of all, this work could not have been accomplished without the love and support of my family. Thank you Cathy, Cristina, and Jennifer.

Happy Haskell Hacking!

Paul Hudak
New Haven
June 1999

# CHAPTER ONE

# Problem Solving, Programming, and Calculation

Programming, in its broadest sense, is *problem solving*. It begins when we look out into the world and see problems that we want to solve, problems that we think can and should be solved using a digital computer. Understanding the problem well is the first – and probably the most important – step in programming, because without that understanding we may find ourselves wandering aimlessly down a dead-end alley, or worse, down a fruitless alley with no end. "Solving the wrong problem" is a phrase often heard in many contexts, and we certainly don't want to be victims of that crime. So the first step in programming is answering the question, "What problem am I trying to solve?"

Once you understand the problem, then you must find a solution. This may not be easy, of course, and in fact you may discover several solutions, so we also need a way to measure success. There are various dimensions in which to do this, including correctness ("Will I get the right answer?") and efficiency ("Will I have enough resources?"). But the distinction of which solution is better is not always clear, because the number of dimensions can be large, and programs will often excel in one dimension and do poorly in others. For example, there may be one solution that is fastest, one that uses the least amount of memory, and one that is easiest to understand. Choosing can be difficult and is one of the more interesting challenges that you will face in programming.

The last measure of success mentioned above – clarity of a program – is somewhat elusive, most difficult to measure, and, quite frankly, sometimes difficult to rationalize. But in large software systems clarity is an especially important goal, because the most important maxim about such systems is that they are never really finished! The process of continuing work on a software system after it is delivered to users is what software engineers call *software maintenance*, and is the most expensive phase of the so-called "software lifecycle." Software maintenance includes fixing bugs in programs, as well as changing certain functionality and enhancing the system with new features in response to users' experience.

Therefore, taking the time to write programs that are highly legible – easy to understand and to reason about – will facilitate the software maintenance process. It is important to realize that the person performing software maintenance is usually not the person who wrote the original program. Therefore, when you write your programs, write them as if you are writing them for someone else to see, to understand, and ultimately to pass judgment on!

In this book, I will often solve each example in several different ways (some of which are dead ends!), taking the time to contrast the style, efficiency, clarity, and functionality of the results.[1] I do this not just for pedagogical purposes. *Such reworking of programs is the norm*, and you are encouraged to get into the habit of doing so. Don't always be satisfied with your first solution to a problem, and always be prepared to go back and change parts of your program that you later discover do not satisfy your actual needs.

## 1.1  Computation by Calculation in Haskell

Discussions of program clarity bring us ultimately to the issue of our programming language choice. This choice determines how we express our solutions in such a way that a computer can understand them. Our programs embody our solutions – and our creativity, eloquence, and perseverance – for interpretation by the computer.

In this text I will use the programming language *Haskell* to address many of the issues discussed in the last section.[2] I have tried to avoid the approach of explaining Haskell first and giving examples second. Rather, I will walk with you, step by step, along the path of understanding an application, understanding the solution space, and understanding how to express a particular solution in Haskell. I want you to learn how to problem solve!

Along this path I will use whatever tools are appropriate for analyzing a particular problem domain, very often mathematical tools familiar to the average college student, indeed most to the average high school student. Concurrently, I will evolve our problems toward a particular view of computation that is especially useful: that of *computation by*

---

[1] At times I also explore different methods for proving properties of programs.

[2] If this were a text on software engineering, I would address many other issues as well. The methods that I describe are consistent with the principles of software engineering, but detailed discussion of those principles is beyond the scope of this textbook.

*calculation.* You will find that such a viewpoint is not only powerful, it is also *simple* (we won't shy away from difficult problems). Haskell supports well the idea of computation by calculation. Programs in Haskell can be viewed as *functions* whose input is that of the problem being solved, and whose output is our desired result; and the behavior of functions can be understood easily as computation by calculation.

An example might help to demonstrate these ideas. Suppose we want to perform an arithmetic calculation such as $3 \times (9 + 5)$. In Haskell we would write this as $3 * (9 + 5)$ because most standard computer keyboards and text editors do not recognize the special symbol $\times$. To calculate the result, we proceed as follows:

$$3 * (9 + 5)$$
$$\Rightarrow \quad 3 * 14$$
$$\Rightarrow \quad 42$$

It turns out that this is not the only way to compute the result, as evidenced by this alternative calculation:[3]

$$3 * (9 + 5)$$
$$\Rightarrow \quad 3 * 9 + 3 * 5$$
$$\Rightarrow \quad 27 + 3 * 5$$
$$\Rightarrow \quad 27 + 15$$
$$\Rightarrow \quad 42$$

Even though this calculation takes two extra steps, it at least gives the correct answer. Indeed, an important property of each and every program in this textbook – in fact every program that can be written in the functional language Haskell – is that it will always yield the same answer when given the same inputs, regardless of the order in which we choose to perform the calculations.[4] This is precisely the mathematical definition of a function: For the same inputs, it always yields the same output.

On the other hand, the first calculation above took fewer steps than the second, and so we say that it is more *efficient.* Efficiency in both space (amount of memory used) and time (number of steps executed) is important when searching for solutions to problems, but of course if we get the wrong answer, efficiency is a moot point. In general, we will search first for any solution to a problem, and later refine it for better performance.

---

[3] This assumes that multiplication distributes over addition in the number system being used, a point that I will return to later.

[4] As long as we don't choose a nonterminating sequence of calculations, another issue that we will return to later.

The above calculations are fairly trivial, of course. But we will be doing much more sophisticated operations soon enough. For starters – and to introduce the idea of a function – we could *generalize* the arithmetic operations performed in the previous example by defining a function to perform them for any numbers *x*, *y*, and *z*:

$$simple\ x\ y\ z\ =\ x * (y + z)$$

This equation defines *simple* as a function of three *arguments*, *x*, *y*, and *z*. In mathematical notation, we might see the above written slightly differently, namely:

$$simple(x, y, z) = x \times (y + z)$$

In any case, it should be clear that "*simple* 3 9 5" is the same as "3 * (9 + 5)." In fact the proper way to calculate the result is:

> *simple* 3 9 5
> ⇒  3 * (9 + 5)
> ⇒  3 * 14
> ⇒  42

The first step in this calculation is an example of *unfolding* a function definition: 3 is substituted for *x*, 9 for *y*, and 5 for *z* on the right-hand side of the definition of *simple*. This is an entirely mechanical process, not unlike what the computer actually does to execute the program.

When I wish to say that an expression *e* evaluates (via zero, one, or possibly many more steps) to the value *v*, I will write *e* ⟹ *v* (this arrow is longer than that used earlier). So we can say directly, for example, that *simple* 3 9 5  ⟹  42, which should be read "*simple* 3 9 5 evaluates to 42."

With *simple* now suitably defined, we can repeat the sequence of arithmetic calculations as often as we like, using different values for the arguments to *simple*. For example, *simple* 4 3 2  ⟹  20.

We can also use calculation to *prove properties* about programs. For example, it should be clear that for any *a*, *b*, and *c*, *simple a b c* should yield the same result as *simple a c b*. For a proof of this, we calculate *symbolically*, that is, using the symbols *a*, *b*, and *c* rather than concrete numbers such as 3, 5, and 9:

> *simple a b c*
> ⇒  *a* * (*b* + *c*)
> ⇒  *a* * (*c* + *b*)
> ⇒  *simple a c b*

The same notation will be used for these symbolic steps as for concrete ones. In particular, the arrow in the notation reflects the direction of our reasoning, and nothing more. In general, if $e1 \Rightarrow e2$, then it's also true that $e2 \Rightarrow e1$.

I will also refer to these symbolic steps as "calculations," even though the computer will not typically perform them when executing a program (although it might perform them *before* a program is run if it thinks that it might make the program run faster). The second step in the calculation above relies on the commutativity of addition (namely that, for any numbers $x$ and $y$, $x + y = y + x$). The third step is the reverse of an unfold step, and is appropriately called a *fold* calculation. It would be particularly strange if a computer performed this step while executing a program, because it does not seem to be headed toward a final answer. But for proving properties about programs, such "backward reasoning" is quite important.

When I wish to make the justification for each step clearer, whether symbolic or concrete, a calculation will be presented with more detail, as in:

> *simple a b c*
> $\Rightarrow$ { unfold }
> $a * (b + c)$
> $\Rightarrow$ { commutativity }
> $a * (c + b)$
> $\Rightarrow$ { fold }
> *simple a c b*

In most cases, however, this will not be necessary.

Proving properties of programs is another theme that will be repeated often in this text. As the world relies more and more on computers to accomplish not just ordinary tasks such as writing term papers and sending email, but also life-critical tasks such as controlling medical procedures and guiding spacecraft, then the correctness of programs gains in importance. Proving complex properties of large, complex programs is not easy, and is rarely if ever done in practice. However, that should not deter us from proving simpler properties of the whole system, or complex properties of parts of the system, because such proofs may uncover errors, and if not, at least help us to gain confidence in our effort.

If you are already an experienced programmer, the idea of computing *everything* by calculation may seem odd at best and naive at worst. How does one write to a file, draw a picture, or respond to mouse clicks? If you are wondering about these things, have patience reading the early chapters and find delight reading the later chapters where the full power of this approach begins to shine. I will avoid, however, most comparisons between Haskell and conventional programming languages such as C, C++, Ada, Java, or even Scheme or ML (two "almost functional" languages), because for those who have programmed in these other languages the differences will be obvious, and for those who haven't the comments would be superfluous.

In many ways this first chapter is the most difficult chapter in the entire text because it contains the highest density of new concepts. If you have trouble with some of the ideas here, keep in mind that we will return to almost every idea at later points in the text. And don't hesitate to return to this chapter later to reread difficult sections; they will likely be much easier to grasp at that time.

---

**Exercise 1.1**   Write out all of the steps in the calculation of the value of

*simple* (*simple* 2 3 4) 5 6

---

**Exercise 1.2**   Prove by calculation that *simple* $(a - b)$ $a$ $b$ $\implies$ $a^2 - b^2$.

---

> **DETAILS**
> In this text the need will often arise to explain some aspect of Haskell in more detail, without distracting too much from the primary line of discourse. In those circumstances I will offset the comments and precede them with the word "Details," such as is done with this paragraph, so that you know the nature of what is to follow. These details will sometimes concern the *syntax* of Haskell (i.e., the *notation* used to write Haskell programs) or its *semantics* (i.e., how to calculate with the language features).

## 1.2  Expressions, Values, and Types

In this section we will take a much closer look at the idea of computation by calculation. In Haskell, the objects that we perform calculations on are called *expressions*, and the objects that result from a calculation (i.e., "the answers") are called *values*. It is helpful to think of a value just as an expression on which no more calculation can be carried out.

Examples of expressions include *atomic* (meaning indivisible) expressions such as the integer 42 and the character '*a*,' as well as *structured* (meaning made from smaller pieces) expressions such as the list [1, 2, 3] and the pair ('*b*,' 4) (lists and pairs are different in a subtle way, to be described later). Each of these examples is also a value, because by themselves there is no calculation that can be carried out. As another example,

1 + 2 is an expression, and one step of calculation yields the expression 3, which is a value, because no more calculations can be performed on it.

Sometimes, however, an expression has only a never-ending sequence of calculations. For example, if $x$ is defined as:

$$x \ = \ x + 1$$

then here's what happens when we try to calculate the value of $x$:

$$x$$
$$\Rightarrow \ x + 1$$
$$\Rightarrow \ (x + 1) + 1$$
$$\Rightarrow \ ((x + 1) + 1) + 1$$
$$\Rightarrow \ (((x + 1) + 1) + 1) + 1$$
$$\cdots$$

This is clearly a never-ending sequence of steps, in which case we say that the expression does not terminate, or is *nonterminating*. In such cases, the symbol ⊥, pronounced "bottom," is used to denote the value of the expression.

Every expression (and therefore every value) also has an associated *type*. You can think of types as sets of expressions (or values) in which members of the same set have much in common. Examples include the atomic types *Integer* (the set of all fixed-precision integers) and *Char* (the set of all characters), as well as the structured types [*Integer*] (the set of all lists of integers) and (*Char, Integer*) (the set of all character/integer pairs). The association of an expression or value with its type is very important, and there is a special way of expressing it in Haskell. Using the examples of values and types above, we write:

$$42 \qquad :: \ Integer$$
$$'a' \qquad :: \ Char$$
$$[1, 2, 3] \ :: \ [Integer]$$
$$('b', 4) \quad :: \ (Char, Integer)$$

**DETAILS**

Literal characters are written enclosed in single forward quotes, as in $'a'$, $'A'$, $'b'$, $','$, $'!'$, $'\ '$ (a space), etc. (There are some exceptions, however; see the *Haskell Report* for details.)

The "::" should be read "has type," as in "42 has type *Integer*."

---

**DETAILS**

Note that the names of specific types are capitalized, such as *Integer* and *Char*, but the names of values are not, such as *simple* and *x*. This is not just a convention; it is required when programming in Haskell. In addition, the case of the other characters matters. For example, *test*, *teSt*, and *tEST* are all distinct names for values, as are *Test*, *TeST*, and *TEST* for types.

---

Haskell's *type system* ensures that Haskell programs are *well-typed*; that is, that the programmer has not mismatched types in some way. For example, it does not make much sense to add together two characters, so the expression *'a'* + *'b'* is *ill-typed*. The best news is that Haskell's type system will tell you if your program is well-typed *before you run it*. This is a big advantage, because most programming errors are manifested as typing errors.

The idea of dividing the world of values into types should be familiar to most people. We do it all the time for just about every kind of object. Take boxes, for example. Just as we have integers and reals, lists and tuples, etc., we also have large boxes and small boxes, cardboard boxes and wooden boxes, and so on. And just as we have lists of integers and lists of characters, we also have boxes of nails and boxes of shoes. And just as we would not expect to be able to take the square of a list or add two characters, we would not expect to be able to use a box to pay for our groceries.

Types help us to make sense of the world by organizing it into groups of common shape, size, functionality, and others. The same is true for programming, where types help us to organize values into groups of common shape, size, and functionality, among others. Of course, the kinds of commonality between values will not be the same as those between objects in the real world, and in general, we will be more restricted – and more formal – about just what we can say about types and how we say it.

## 1.3  Function Types and Type Signatures

What should the type of a function be? It seems that it should at least convey the fact that a function takes values of one type – $T1$, say – as input and returns values of (possibly) some other type – $T2$, say – as output. In Haskell this is written $T1 \rightarrow T2$, and we say that such a function "maps values of type $T1$ to values of type $T2$." If there is more than one argument, the notation is extended with more arrows. For example, if our intent is that the function *simple* defined in the previous section has type $Integer \rightarrow Integer \rightarrow Integer \rightarrow Integer$, we can declare this fact by including a *type signature* with the definition of *simple*:

*simple* :: *Integer* → *Integer* → *Integer* → *Integer*
*simple x y z* = *x* ∗ (*y* + *z*)

---

**DETAILS**

When you write Haskell programs using a typical text editor, you will not see nice fonts and arrows as in *Integer* → *Integer*. Rather, you will have to type `Integer -> Integer`.

---

Haskell's type system also ensures that user-supplied type signatures, such as this one, are correct. Actually, Haskell's type system is powerful enough to allow us to avoid writing any type signatures at all, in which case we say that the type system *infers* the correct types for us.[5] Nevertheless, judicious placement of type signatures, as we did for *simple*, is a good habit, because type signatures are an effective form of documentation and help bring programming errors to light. Also, in almost every example in this text, I will make a habit of first talking about the types of expressions and functions as a way to better understand the problem at hand, organize our thoughts, and lay down the first ideas of a solution.

The normal use of a function is referred to as *function application*. For example, *simple* 3 9 5 is the application of the function *simple* to the arguments 3, 9, and 5.

---

**DETAILS**

Some functions, such as (+), are applied using what is known as *infix syntax*; that is, the function is written between the two arguments rather than in front of them (compare *x* + *y* to *f x y*). Infix functions are often called *operators* and are distinguished by the fact that they do not contain any numbers or letters of the alphabet. Thus $^! and ∗#: are infix operators, whereas *thisIsAFunction* and *f9g* are not (but are still valid names for functions or other values). The only exception to this is that the symbol ' is considered to be alphanumeric; thus *f'* and *one's* are valid names, but not operators.

In Haskell, when referring to an operator as a value, it is enclosed in parentheses, such as when declaring its type, as in:

(+) :: *Integer* → *Integer* → *Integer*

---

[5] There are a few exceptions to this rule, and in the case of *simple* the inferred type is actually a bit more general than that written above. Both of these points will be returned to later.

Also, when trying to understand an expression such as $f\ x + g\ y$, there is a simple rule to remember: Function application always has "higher precedence" than operator application, so that $f\ x + g\ y$ is the same as $(f\ x) + (g\ y)$.

Despite all of these syntactic differences, however, operators are still just functions.

---

**Exercise 1.3** Identify the well-typed expressions in the following and, for each, give its proper type:

[(2, 3), (4, 5)]
['z', 42]
('z', −42)
*simple* 'a' 'b' 'c'
(*simple* 1 2 3, *simple*)

## 1.4 Abstraction, Abstraction, Abstraction

The title of this section answers the question: "What are the three most important ideas in programming?" Well, perhaps this is an overstatement, but I hope that I've gotten your attention, at least. Webster defines the verb "abstract" as follows:

> **abstract,** *vt* (1) remove, separate (2) to consider apart from application to a particular instance.

In programming we do this when we see a repeating pattern of some sort and wish to "separate" that pattern from the "particular instances" in which it appears. Let's refer to this process as the *abstraction principle* and see how it might manifest itself in problem solving.

### 1.4.1 Naming

One of the most basic ideas in programming – for that matter, in everyday life – is to *name* things. For example, because it is inconvenient to retype (or remember) the value of $\pi$ beyond a small number of digits, we may wish to give it a name. In mathematics the Greek letter $\pi$ in fact *is* the name for this value, but unfortunately we don't have the luxury of using Greek letters on standard computer keyboards and text editors. So in Haskell we write:

```
pi  ::  Float
pi  =  3.14159
```

to associate the name *pi* with the number 3.14159. The second line above is called an *equation*. The type signature in the first line declares *pi* to be a *floating-point number*, which mathematically, and in Haskell, is distinct from an integer.[6] Now we can use the name *pi* in expressions whenever we want; it is an abstract representation, if you will, of the number 3.14159. Furthermore, if we ever need to change a named value (which hopefully won't ever happen for *pi*, but could certainly happen for other values), we would only have to change it in one place, instead of in the possibly large number of places where it is used.

Suppose now that we are working on a problem whose solution requires writing some expression more than once. For example, we might find ourselves computing something such as:

$$x \ :: \ Float$$
$$x \ = \ f \ (a - b + 2) + g \ y \ (a - b + 2)$$

The first line declares $x$ to be a floating-point number, while the second is an equation that defines the value of $x$. Note on the right-hand side of this equation that the expression $a - b + 2$ is repeated – it has two instances – and thus, applying the abstraction principle, we wish to separate it from these instances. We already know how to do this – it's called *naming* – so we might choose to rewrite the single equation above as two:

$$c \ = \ a - b + 2$$
$$x \ = \ f \ c + g \ y \ c$$

If, however, the definition of $c$ is not intended for use elsewhere in the program, then it is advantageous to "hide" the definition of $c$ within the definition of $x$. This will avoid cluttering up the namespace, and prevents $c$ from clashing with some other value named $c$. To achieve this, we simply use a **let** expression:

$$x \ = \ \textbf{let } c \ = \ a - b + 2$$
$$\textbf{in } f \ c + g \ y \ c$$

A **let** expression restricts the *visibility* of the names that it creates to the internal workings of the **let** expression itself. For example, if we write:

$$c \ = \ 42$$
$$x \ = \ \textbf{let } c \ = \ a - b + 2$$
$$\textbf{in } f \ c + g \ y \ c$$

then there is no conflict of names; the "outer" $c$ is completely different

---

[6] I will have more to say about floating-point numbers later in this chapter.

from the "inner" one enclosed in the **let** expression. Think of the inner *c* as analogous to the first name of someone in your household. If your brother's name is "John" he will not be confused with John Thompson who lives down the street when you say, "John spilled the milk."

---

**DETAILS**

An equation such as $c = 42$ is called a *binding*. A simple rule to remember when programming in Haskell is never to give more than one binding for the same name in a context where the names can be confused, whether at the top level of your program or nested within a **let** expression. For example, this is not allowed:

$$a \;=\; 42$$
$$a \;=\; 43$$

nor is this:

$$a \;=\; 42$$
$$b \;=\; 43$$
$$a \;=\; 44$$

---

So you can see that naming – using either top-level equations or equations within a **let** expression – is an example of the abstraction principle in action. It's often the case, of course, that we *anticipate* the need for abstraction; for example, directly writing down the final solution above, because we knew that we would need to use the expression $a - b + 2$ more than once.

### 1.4.2 Functional Abstraction

Let's now consider a more complex example. Suppose we are computing the sum of the areas of three circles with radii $r1$, $r2$, and $r3$, as expressed by

$$totalArea \;::\; Float$$
$$totalArea \;=\; pi * r1\,\hat{}\,2 + pi * r2\,\hat{}\,2 + pi * r3\,\hat{}\,2$$

---

**DETAILS**

($\hat{}$) is Haskell's integer exponentiation operator. In mathematics we would write $\pi \times r^2$ or just $\pi r^2$ instead of $pi * r \,\hat{}\, 2$.

---

Although there isn't an obvious repeating expression here as there was in the last example, there is a repeating *pattern of operations*, namely, the operations that square some given quantity – in this case the radius – and then multiply the result by $\pi$. To abstract a sequence of operations such as this, we use a *function*, which we will give the name *circleArea*, that takes the "given quantity" – the radius – as an argument. There are three instances of the pattern, each of which we can expect to replace with a call to *circleArea*. This leads to:

$$
\begin{aligned}
circleArea & \;::\; Float \rightarrow Float \\
circleArea\ r & \;=\; pi * r\char`^2 \\
totalArea & \;=\; circleArea\ r1 + circleArea\ r2 + circleArea\ r3
\end{aligned}
$$

Using the idea of unfolding described earlier, it is easy to verify that this definition is equivalent to the previous one.

This application of the abstraction principle is sometimes called *functional abstraction*, because the sequence of operations is abstracted as a function, in this case *circleArea*. Actually, it can be seen as a generalization of the previous kind of abstraction: *naming*. That is, *circleArea r*1 is just a name for $pi * r1\char`^2$, *circleArea r*2 for $pi * r2\char`^2$, and *circleArea r*3 for $pi * r3\char`^2$. In other words, a named quantity, such as *c* or *pi* defined previously, can be thought of as a function with no arguments.

Note that *circleArea* takes a radius (a floating-point number) as an argument and returns the area (also a floating-point number) as a result. This is reflected in its type signature.

The definition of *circleArea* could also be hidden within *totalArea* using a **let** expression as we did in the previous example:

$$
\begin{aligned}
totalArea \;=\; & \textbf{let}\ circleArea\ r \;=\; pi * r\char`^2 \\
& \textbf{in}\ circleArea\ r1 + circleArea\ r2 + circleArea\ r3
\end{aligned}
$$

On the other hand, it is more likely that computing the area of a circle will be useful elsewhere in the program, so leaving the definition at the top level is probably preferable in this case.

### 1.4.3 Data Abstraction

The value of *totalArea* is the sum of the areas of three circles. But what if in another situation we must add the areas of five circles, or in other situations, even more? In situations where the number of things is not certain, it is useful to represent them in a *list* whose length is arbitrary.

So imagine that we are given an entire list of circle areas whose length isn't known when we write the program. What now?

I will define a function *listSum* to add the elements of a list. Before doing so, however, there is a bit more to say about lists.

Lists are an example of a *data structure*, and when their use is motivated by the abstraction principle, I will say that we are applying *data abstraction*. Earlier we saw the example [1, 2, 3] as a list of integers, whose type is thus [*Integer*]. Not surprisingly, a list with *no* elements is written [], and pronounced "nil." To add a single element $x$ to the front of a list $xs$, we write $x : xs$. (Note the naming convention used here; $xs$ is the plural of $x$, and should be read that way.) In fact, the list [1, 2, 3] is equivalent to $1 : (2 : (3 : [\,]))$, which can also be written $1 : 2 : 3 : [\,]$ because the infix operator (:) is "right associative."

---

**DETAILS**

In mathematics we rarely worry about whether the notation $a + b + c$ stands for $(a + b) + c$ (in which case + would be "left associative") or $a + (b + c)$ (in which case + would "right associative"). This is because in situations where the parentheses are left out the operator usually is *mathematically* associative, meaning that it doesn't matter which interpretation we choose. If the interpretation *does* matter, mathematicians will include parentheses to make it clear. Furthermore, in mathematics there is an implicit assumption that some operators have higher *precedence* than others; for example, $2 \times a + b$ is interpreted as $(2 \times a) + b$, not $2 \times (a + b)$.

In most programming languages, including Haskell, each operator is defined as having some precedence level and to be either left or right associative. For arithmetic operators, mathematical convention is usually followed; for $2 * a + b$ is interpreted as $(2 * a) + b$ in Haskell. The predefined list-forming operator (:) is defined to be right associative. Just as in mathematics, this associativity can be overridden by using parentheses: thus $(a : b) : c$ is a valid Haskell expression (assuming that it is well-typed), and is very different from $a : b : c$. I will explain later how to specify the associativity and precedence of new operators that we define.

---

Examples of predefined functions defined on lists in Haskell include *head* and *tail*, which return the "head" and "tail" of a list, respectively. That is, *head* $(x : xs) \Rightarrow x$ and *tail* $(x : xs) \Rightarrow xs$ (we will define these two functions formally in Section 5.1). Another example is the function (++), which *concatenates*, or *appends*, together its two list arguments. For example, [1, 2, 3] ++ [4, 5, 6] $\Rightarrow$ [1, 2, 3, 4, 5, 6] ((++) will be defined in Section 11.2).

Returning to the problem of defining a function to add the elements of a list, let's first express what its type should be:

*listSum* :: [*Float*] → *Float*

Now we must define its behavior appropriately. Often in solving problems such as this, it is helpful to consider, one by one, all possible cases that could arise. To compute the sum of the elements of a list, what might the list look like? The list could be empty, in which case the sum is surely 0. So we write:

*listSum* [ ] = 0

The other possibility is that the list *isn't* empty (i.e., it contains at least one element) in which case the sum is the first number plus the sum of the remainder of the list. So we write:

*listSum* (*x* : *xs*) = *x* + *listSum xs*

Combining these two equations with the type signature brings us to the complete definition of the function *listSum*:

*listSum*             :: [*Float*] → *Float*
*listSum* [ ]         = 0
*listSum* (*x* : *xs*) = *x* + *listSum xs*

---

**DETAILS**
Although intuitive, this example highlights an important aspect of Haskell: *pattern matching*. The left-hand sides of the equations contain *patterns* such as [ ] and *x* : *xs*. When a function is applied, these patterns are *matched* against the argument values in a fairly intuitive way ([ ] only matches the empty list, and *x* : *xs* will successfully match any list with at least one element, while naming the first element *x* and the rest of the list *xs*). If the match succeeds, the right-hand side is evaluated and returned as the result of the application. If it fails, the next equation is tried, and if all equations fail, an error results. All of the equations that define a particular function must appear together, one after the other.

Defining functions by pattern matching is quite common in Haskell, and you should eventually become familiar with the various kinds of patterns that are allowed; see Appendix B for a concise summary.

---

This is called a *recursive* function definition because *listSum* "refers to itself" on the right-hand side of the second equation. Recursion is a very powerful technique that will be used many times in this text. It is also an example of a general problem-solving technique where a large problem is broken down into many simpler but similar problems; solving these simpler problems one by one leads to a solution to the larger problem.

Here is an example of *listSum* in action:

*listSum* [1, 2, 3]
   ⇒  *listSum* (1 : (2 : (3 : [ ])))
   ⇒  1 + *listSum* (2 : (3 : [ ]))
   ⇒  1 + (2 + *listSum* (3 : [ ]))
   ⇒  1 + (2 + (3 + *listSum* [ ]))
   ⇒  1 + (2 + (3 + 0))
   ⇒  1 + (2 + 3)
   ⇒  1 + 5
   ⇒  6

The first step above is not really a calculation, but rather is a rewriting of the list syntax. The remaining calculations consist of four unfold steps followed by three integer additions.

Given this definition of *listSum* we can rewrite the definition of *totalArea* as:

*totalArea* = *listSum* [*circleArea* $r1$, *circleArea* $r2$, *circleArea* $r3$]

This may not seem like much of an improvement, but if we were adding many such circle areas in some other context, it would be. Indeed, lists are arguably the most commonly used structured data type in Haskell. In the next chapter we will see a more convincing example of the use of lists; namely, to represent the vertices that make up a polygon. Because a polygon can have an arbitrary number of vertices, using a data structure such as a list seems like just the right approach.

In any case, how do we know that this version of *totalArea* behaves the same as the original one? By calculation, of course:

*listSum* [*circleArea* $r1$, *circleArea* $r2$, *circleArea* $r3$]
   ⟹  { unfold *listSum* (four succesive times) }
*circleArea* $r1$ + *circleArea* $r2$ + *circleArea* $r3$ + 0
   ⟹  { unfold *circleArea* (three places) }
$pi * r1\hat{\ }2 + pi * r2\hat{\ }2 + pi * r3\hat{\ }2 + 0$
   ⇒  { simple arithmetic }
$pi * r1\hat{\ }2 + pi * r2\hat{\ }2 + pi * r3\hat{\ }2$

## 1.5 Code Reuse and Modularity

There doesn't seem to be much repetition in our last definition for *totalArea*, so perhaps we're done. In fact, let's pause for a moment and consider how much progress we've made. We started with the definition:

$$totalArea \ = \ pi * r1\hat{} 2 + pi * r2\hat{} 2 + pi * r3\hat{} 2$$

and ended with:

$$totalArea \ = \ listSum \ [circleArea \ r1, \ circleArea \ r2, \ circleArea \ r3]$$

But we have also introduced definitions for the auxiliary functions *circleArea* and *listSum*. In terms of size, our final program is actually larger than what we began with! So have we actually improved things?

From the standpoint of "removing repeating patterns," we certainly have, and we could argue that the resulting program is easier to understand. But there is more. Now that we have defined auxiliary functions, such as *circleArea* and *listSum*, we can *reuse* them in other contexts. Being able to reuse code is also called *modularity*, because the reused components are like little modules, or bricks, that can form the foundation of many applications.[7] We've already talked about reusing *circleArea*; and *listSum* is surely reusable: imagine a list of grocery item prices, or class sizes, or city populations, for each of which we must compute the total. In later chapters you will learn other concepts – most notably higher-order functions and polymorphism – that will substantially increase your ability to reuse code.

## 1.6 Beware of Programming with Numbers

In mathematics there are many different kinds of number systems. For example, there are integers, natural numbers (i.e., non-negative integers), real numbers, rational numbers, and complex numbers. These number systems possess many useful properties, such as the fact that multiplication and addition are commutative, and that multiplication distributes over addition. You have undoubtedly learned many of these properties in your studies and have used them often in algebra, geometry, trigonometry, and physics, among others.

Unfortunately, each of these number systems places great demands on computer systems. In particular, a number can in general require an

---

[7] "Code reuse" and "modularity" are important software engineering principles.

*arbitrary amount of memory* to represent it – even an infinite amount! Clearly, for example, we cannot represent an irrational number such as $\pi$ exactly; the best we can do is approximate it, or possibly write a program that computes it to whatever (finite) precision we need in a given application. But even integers (and therefore rational numbers) present problems, because any given integer can be arbitrarily large.

Most programming languages do not deal with these problems very well. In fact, most programming languages do not have exact forms of any of these number systems. Haskell does slightly better than most, in that it has exact forms of integers (the type *Integer*) as well as rational numbers (the type *Rational*, defined in the Ratio Library). But in Haskell and most other languages, there is no exact form of real numbers, for example, which are instead approximated by *floating-point numbers* with either single-word precision (*Float* in Haskell) or double-word precision (*Double*). What's worse, the behavior of arithmetic operations on floating-point numbers can vary somewhat depending on the CPU being used, although hardware standardization in recent years has lessened the degree of this problem.

The bottom line is that, as simple as numbers seem, great care must be taken when programming with them. Many computer errors, some quite serious and renowned, have been rooted in numerical incongruities. The field of mathematics known as *numerical analysis* is concerned precisely with these problems, and programming with floating-point numbers in sophisticated applications often requires a good understanding of numerical analysis to devise proper algorithms and write correct programs.

As a simple example of this problem, consider the distributive law, expressed here as a calculation in Haskell and used earlier in this chapter in calculations involving the function *simple*:

$$a * (b + c) \quad \Rightarrow \quad a * b + a * c$$

For most floating-point numbers, this law is perfectly valid. For example, in the Hugs implementation of Haskell, the expressions $pi * (3.52 + 4.75)$ and $pi * 3.52 + pi * 4.75$ both yield the same result: 25.981. But funny things can happen when the magnitude of $b + c$ differs significantly from the magnitude of either $b$ or $c$. For example, the following two calculations are from Hugs:

$$5 * (-0.123456 + 0.123457) \quad \Rightarrow \quad 4.99189e - 006$$
$$5 * (-0.123456) + 5 * (0.123457) \quad \Rightarrow \quad 5.00679e - 006$$

Although the error here is small, its very existence is worrisome, and in certain situations it could be disastrous. The nature of floating-point numbers will not be discussed much further in this text, but just remember that they are *approximations* to the real numbers. If real-number accuracy is important to your application, further study of the nature of floating-point numbers is probably warranted.

On the other hand, the distributive law (and many others) is valid in Haskell for the exact data types *Integer* and *Ratio Integer* (i.e., rational numbers). However, another problem arises: Although the representation of an *Integer* in Haskell is not normally something that we are concerned about, it should be clear that the representation must be allowed to grow to an arbitrary size. For example, Haskell has no problem with the following number:

```
veryBigNumber  ::  Integer
veryBigNumber  =  43208345720348593219876512372134059
```

and such numbers can be added, multiplied, etc., without any loss of accuracy. However, such numbers cannot fit into a single word of computer memory, most of which are limited to 32 bits. Worse, because the computer system does not know ahead of time exactly how many words will be required, it must devise a dynamic scheme to allow just the right number of words to be used in each case. The overhead of implementing this idea unfortunately causes programs to run slower.

For this reason, Haskell provides another integer data type called *Int*, which has maximum and minimum values that depend on the word size of the CPU. In other words, every value of type *Int* fits into one word of memory, and the primitive machine instructions for integers can be used to manipulate them very efficiently.[8] Unfortunately, this means that *overflow* or *underflow* errors could occur when an *Int* value exceeds either the maximum or minumum values. However, most implementations of Haskell (as well as most other languages) do not even tell you when this happens. For example, in Hugs, the following *Int* value:

```
i :: Int
i = 1234567890
```

works just fine, but if you multiply it by 2, Hugs returns the value −1825831516! This is because twice *i* exceeds the maximum allowed

---

[8] The *Haskell Report* requires that every implementation support *Int*s in the range $-2^{29}$ to $2^{29} - 1$, inclusive. The Hugs implementation running on a Pentium processor, for example, supports the range $-2^{31}$ to $2^{31} - 1$.

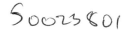

value, so the resulting bits become nonsensical[9] and are interpreted in this case as a negative number of the given magnitude.

This is alarming! Indeed, why should anyone ever use *Int* when *Integer* is available? The answer, as mentioned earlier, is efficiency, but clearly, care should be taken when making this choice. If you are indexing into a list, for example, and you are confident that you are not performing index calculations that might result in the above kind of error, then *Int* should work just fine, because a list longer than $2^{31}$ will not fit into memory anyway! But if you are calculating the number of microseconds in some large time interval or counting the number of people living on earth, then *Integer* would most likely be a better choice. Choose your number data types wisely!

In this text the data types *Integer*, *Int*, *Float*, and *Rational* will be used for a variety of different applications; for a discussion of the other number types, consult the *Haskell Report*. As I use these data types, I will do so without much discussion; this is not, after all, a book on numerical analysis. But I will issue a warning whenever reasoning about numbers in a way that might not be technically sound.

---

[9] Actually, they are perfectly sensible in the following way: The 32-bit binary representation of $i$ is 01001001100101100000001011010010, and twice that is 10010011001011000000010110100100. But the latter number is seen as negative because the 32nd bit (the highest-order bit on the CPU on which this was run) is a one, which means it is a negative number in "twos-complement" representation. The twos-complement of this number is in turn 01101100110100111111101001011100, whose decimal representation is 1825831516.

# CHAPTER TWO

# A Module of Shapes: Part I

In the previous chapter you learned quite a few techniques for problem solving via calculation in Haskell. It's time now to apply these ideas to a larger example, which will require learning even more problem-solving skills and Haskell language features.

Our job will be to design a simple module of geometric *shapes*, that is, a collection of functions and data types for computing with geometric shapes such as circles, squares, triangles, and others. Users of this module will be able to create new instances of geometric shapes and compute their areas. You will learn lots of new things in building this module, including how to design your own data types. Then in Chapter 4 we will extend this functionality with the ability to *draw* geometric shapes, and in Chapter 6 compute their *perimeters*.

In the description above I refer to the end product as a *module*, through which a user has access to certain well-defined functionalities. A module can be seen as a way to conveniently wrap up an application in such a way that only the functionality intended for the end-user is visible; everything else needed to implement the system is effectively hidden.

In Haskell we can create a module named *Shape* in the following way:

**module** *Shape* ( · · · ) **where**

   *...body-of-module...*

The "( · · · )" after the name *Shape* will ultimately be a list of names of the functions and data types that the end-user is intended to use, and is sometimes called the *interface* to a module. At the end of this chapter we will fill in the details of the interface once we know what they should be. The *...body-of-module...* is of course where we will place all the code developed in this chapter.

> **DETAILS**
> Module names must always be capitalized (just like type names).

A user of our shape module can later *import* it into a module that he or she is constructing, by writing:

**import** *Shape*

Indeed, we will do exactly this in later chapters where new modules will be created in which users will be able to draw shapes, compute their perimeters, combine them into larger "regions," color them, scale them, and place them on a "virtual desktop." This desktop will be displayed on your computer screen, and will be designed in such a way that regions will rise to the surface of the desktop when they are clicked, just like windows do in a windows-based user-interface.

## 2.1 Geometric Shapes

Our first job will be to design a single data type to represent all of the possible geometric shapes of interest to us. Aside from the fact that this is intuitively appealing, there are several pragmatic reasons for doing so. For example, in Section 1.4.2 we saw a function for computing the area of a circle, and later a function for computing the area of a square. If we were to define functions for computing the areas of, say, *n* different shapes, we would end up with *n* functions, each with a different name. Similarly, we would have *n* functions for drawing shapes and *n* functions for computing their perimeters. In contrast, if we had a single data type that captured *all* of the geometric shapes, we could (hopefully) define a single function for each of these tasks.

In Haskell, new data types such as this are defined using a **data** declaration:

**data** *Shape* = *Circle Float*
            | *Square Float*

This declaration can be read: "There are two kinds of *Shape*s: a *circle* of the form *Circle r* where *r* is a radius of type *Float*, and a *square* of the form *Square s* where *s* is the length (also of type *Float*) of one side." Because *Circle* and *Square* construct new values in this data type, they are called *constructors*.

> **DETAILS**
> All constructors in a **data** declaration must be capitalized. In this way they are syntactically distinguished from ordinary functions. This distinction is useful because only constructors can be used in the pattern matching that is part of a function definition, as will be described shortly.

Of course, there are more shapes than just circles and squares. And to complicate matters, squares are really rectangles, rectangles are really parallelograms, and parallelograms are just quadrilaterals (4-sided polygons). And, there are (right, equilateral, and isosceles) triangles, trapezoids, pentagons, hexagons, etc. Do we really want representations for all of them? If not, which ones do we choose? This is a difficult design decision that is dependent on the eventual use of the data type, which may be difficult to predict.

For mostly pedagogical purposes, let's settle on the following definition:

> **data** *Shape* = *Rectangle Float Float*
> | *Ellipse Float Float*
> | *RtTriangle Float Float*
> | *Polygon* [(*Float, Float*)]
> **deriving** *Show*

> **DETAILS**
> The phrase "**deriving** *Show*" is a way to tell the Haskell system that you are interested in printing out values of the data type that you are defining. Exactly how this is accomplished will be described in a later chapter.

This declaration defines a new data type called *Shape* in which:

- *Rectangle* $s1$ $s2$ is a rectangle with sides $s1$ and $s2$, both floating-point numbers.
- *Ellipse* $r1$ $r2$ is an ellipse with radii $r1$ and $r2$, both floating-point numbers.
- *RtTriangle* $s1$ $s2$ is a right triangle with sides of length $s1$ and $s2$, both floating-point numbers.
- *Polygon* [$v1, v2, \ldots, vn$] is an $n$-sided polygon whose vertices are $v1$ through $vn$, each vertex being represented by a pair $(x, y)$ of floating-point coordinates on a Cartesian plane. (Recall that (*Float, Float*) is the type of *pairs* of floating-point numbers; for example (1.0, *pi*) :: (*Float, Float*).)

One unfortunate aspect of this definition is that floating-point numbers are used to represent several different quantities, a fact only evident in the documentation of the code (such as we have written above). One way to improve on this is to create new names for the various uses of floating-point numbers, which in Haskell can be achieved using a **type** declaration:

```
data Shape   =  Rectangle Side Side
             |  Ellipse Radius Radius
             |  RtTriangle Side Side
             |  Polygon [Vertex]
     deriving Show

type Radius  =  Float
type Side    =  Float
type Vertex  =  (Float, Float)
```

**DETAILS**

Here the *Shape* declaration is really the same as before, except that we've used different names for the "constituent types," and the **type** declarations tell us what they really are. It is important to realize that, although a **data** declaration creates a completely new data type, a **type** declaration does not: it simply creates a new *name* for an *existing* type. Indeed, these are called *type synonyms* because the new name is just a synonym for the old one. The result is "self-documenting," and arguably easier to read.

This change can also be seen as another application of the abstraction principle. Note, for example, that if we decide to represent sides as double-precision floating-point numbers (which in Haskell have type *Double*), we could just change a single line:

```
type Side  =  Double
```

no matter how often we used the name *Side*. This is a good thing.

Returning to the design issue of deciding which shapes to choose for this data type, you might object to the fact that to create a square with side *s* you must now write something like *Rectangle s s*. It is easy to remedy this situation, however, by defining a function *square* as:

```
square s  =  Rectangle s s
```

Similarly, a *circle* function can be defined by:

```
circle r  =  Ellipse r r
```

But, you might point out, with the *Polygon* constructor we can create polygons with an arbitrary number of sides, each with an arbitrary length, so why include the special cases of rectangle and right triangle? In other words, why not just define functions *rectangle* and *rtTriangle* in terms of *Polygon*? Good question! One answer, as mentioned earlier, is in the interest of pedagogy: I am trying to illustrate a variety of programming techniques. Another answer is that the algorithms for computing the areas of rectangles and right triangles are simpler than the algorithm for computing the area of a general polygon. A final answer is that there may be lower-level graphics commands, say, that are more efficient at drawing rectangles and/or right triangles than general polygons. In any case, let's proceed with our design and investigate its consequences later.

---

**Exercise 2.1** Define functions *rectangle* and *rtTriangle* in terms of *Polygon*.

---

**Exercise 2.2** Define a function *regularPolygon* :: *Int* → *Side* → *Shape* such that *regularPolygon n s* is a regular polygon with *n* sides, each of length *s*. (Hint: Consider using some of Haskell's trigonometric functions, such as *sin* :: *Float* → *Float*, *cos* :: *Float* → *Float*, and *tan* :: *Float* → *Float*.)

## 2.2 Areas of Shapes

Returning to the problem in Section 1.4.2 of computing areas, we will define a function:

    *area* :: *Shape* → *Float*

by defining its behavior on each of the *Shape* constructors. We know how to do this for a rectangle:

    *area* (*Rectangle s1 s2*) = *s1 ∗ s2*

And the area of a right triangle is just as easy:

    *area* (*RtTriangle s1 s2*) = *s1 ∗ s2/2*

Before proceeding, note that this way of writing function definitions – by *pattern matching* on the arguments – is just like the way we defined the function *listSum* in Section 1.4.3. There, *listSum* was defined by its behavior on the two constructors in the list data types, [ ] and (:). In the case of the *Shape* data type, we happen to have four constructors to consider instead of two.

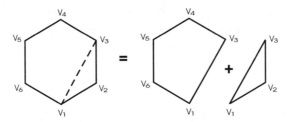

Figure 2.1. Computing the Area of a Convex Polygon

Moving on, a standard geometry text tells us that the area of an ellipse with radii $r_1$ and $r_2$ is just $\pi r_1 r_2$. It is easy to see that this reduces to $\pi r^2$ for a circle. Translated into Haskell, this becomes:

$$area\ (Ellipse\ r1\ r2)\ =\ pi * r1 * r2$$

What about the area of a general polygon? If the polygon is *convex* (meaning that all of its interior angles are less than 180°), its area can be computed fairly simply as follows (the case of concave polygons will be an exercise):

1. Compute the area of the triangle formed by the first three vertices of the polygon.
2. Delete the second vertex, forming a new polygon.
3. If there are at least three vertices in the new polygon, repeat this procedure, returning as the total area the sum of the areas of the individual triangles.

The intuition for this algorithm is shown pictorially in Fig. 2.1; it is another example of solving a problem by solving a smaller problem first, which at least slightly reduces the size of the larger one.

Although we haven't yet decided how to compute the area of a general triangle, we can write out the above algorithm in Haskell as follows:

$$area\ (Polygon\ (v1 : v2 : v3 : vs))$$
$$=\ triArea\ v1\ v2\ v3 + area\ (Polygon\ (v1 : v3 : vs))$$
$$area\ (Polygon\ \_)$$
$$=\ 0$$

**DETAILS**

The first line above is an example of a *nested pattern*; that is, the pattern $(v1 : v2 : v3 : vs)$ is nested within the pattern *Polygon* . . . .

The second equation uses an "underscore" character "_" as a pattern. This is called a *wildcard pattern*, and matches *any* argument. When more than one equation is used to define a function, Haskell will try them in the order that they appear. So in the case of *area*, an attempt is first made to match a list containing at least three elements. If that fails, then the second equation is tried, which of course succeeds immediately, yielding the value 0.

This version of the algorithm has a more "declarative" feel than the description given earlier and can be read: "The area of a (convex) polygon is the area of the triangle formed by its first three vertices, plus the area of the polygon resulting from deleting the second vertex." In general, we will try to write declarative definitions such as this directly.

However, note in the recursive call to *area* that the polygon is "reconstructed" using the *Polygon* constructor; so the polygon is taken apart and then put back together, so to speak, on each recursive call. Also note that the first vertex never disappears; it is always part of the reconstruction. We can avoid these slight inefficiencies by defining an auxiliary function *polyArea* that computes the area directly from a list of vertices, as follows:

$$
\begin{aligned}
\textit{area } (\textit{Polygon } (v1 : vs)) \;\; &= \;\; \textit{polyArea } vs \\
\textbf{where } \textit{polyArea} \qquad\qquad &:: \;\; [\textit{Vertex}] \to \textit{Float} \\
\textit{polyArea } (v2 : v3 : vs') \;\; &= \;\; \textit{triArea } v1\ v2\ v3 \\
&\qquad\quad + \textit{polyArea } (v3 : vs') \\
\textit{polyArea } \_ \qquad\qquad &= \;\; 0
\end{aligned}
$$

**DETAILS**

Note the use of a **where** expression. For the most part you can consider *exp* **where** *...equations...* to be equivalent to **let** *...equations...* **in** *exp*. The only difference is that a **where** expression is only allowed at the top level of a function definition, where its visibility rules are slightly different (see the *Haskell Report* for details).

What about *triArea*? Fortunately, there is a single formula for the area of an arbitrary triangle with sides of lengths *a*, *b*, and *c*, due to Heron:

$$
A \;\; = \;\; \sqrt{s(s-a)(s-b)(s-c)} \;\;\; \textit{where } s = \tfrac{1}{2}(a+b+c)
$$

or, in Haskell:

$$
\begin{aligned}
\textit{triArea} \quad &::\quad \textit{Vertex} \rightarrow \textit{Vertex} \rightarrow \textit{Vertex} \rightarrow \textit{Float} \\
\textit{triArea } v1\ v2\ v3 \quad &=\quad \textbf{let } a \ =\ \textit{distBetween } v1\ v2 \\
&\qquad\quad\ b \ =\ \textit{distBetween } v2\ v3 \\
&\qquad\quad\ c \ =\ \textit{distBetween } v3\ v1 \\
&\qquad\quad\ s \ =\ 0.5 * (a + b + c) \\
&\quad \textbf{in } \textit{sqrt } (s * (s - a) * (s - b) * (s - c))
\end{aligned}
$$

---

**DETAILS**

*sqrt* is Haskell's square root function.

Also, note that more than one equation is allowed in a **let** (or **where**) expression. The first characters of each equation, however, must line up vertically, and if an equation takes more than one line then the subsequent lines must be to the right of the first characters. For example, this is legal:

```
let a  =  aLongName
            +anEvenLongerName
    b  =  56
in ...
```

but neither of these is:

```
let a  =  aLongName
      +anEvenLongerName
      b = 56
in ...
```

```
let a  =  aLongName
            +anEvenLongerName
    b = 56
in ...
```

(The second line of the first example is too far to the left, as is the third line in the second example.)

Although this rule, called the *layout rule*, may seem a bit ad hoc, it avoids the use of special syntax to denote the end of one equation and the beginning of the next, thus enhancing readability. In practice, use of layout is rather intuitive. Just remember two things:

1.  The first character following either **where** or **let** (and a few other keywords that we will see later) is what determines the starting column for the set

of equations. Thus, we can begin the equations on the same line as the keyword, the next line, or whatever.

2.  Be sure that the starting column is further to the right than the starting column associated with any immediately surrounding clause (otherwise it would be ambiguous). The "termination" of an equation happens when something appears at or to the left of the starting column associated with that equation.

Here *distBetween* computes the difference between two vertices – that is, the length of each side of the triangle – and is defined by:

$$distBetween \quad :: \quad Vertex \rightarrow Vertex \rightarrow Float$$
$$distBetween \ (x1, y1) \ (x2, y2)$$
$$= \ sqrt \ ((x1 - x2)\hat{}2 + (y1 - y2)\hat{}2)$$

This definition is easy to see as an application of Pythagorean's theorem, as shown graphically in Fig. 2.2.

In summary, by collecting the four equations for *area*, we see that we have covered each of the constructors in the *Shape* data type:

$$area \qquad\qquad\qquad :: \quad Shape \rightarrow Float$$
$$area \ (Rectangle \ s1 \ s2) \quad = \quad s1 * s2$$
$$area \ (RtTriangle \ s1 \ s2) \quad = \quad s1 * s2/2$$
$$area \ (Ellipse \ r1 \ r2) \qquad = \quad pi * r1 * r2$$
$$area \ (Polygon \ (v1 : vs)) \quad = \quad polyArea \ vs$$

$$\textbf{where} \ polyArea \qquad\qquad\quad :: \quad [Vertex] \rightarrow Float$$
$$polyArea \ (v2 : v3 : vs') \quad = \quad triArea \ v1 \ v2 \ v3$$
$$+ polyArea \ (v3 : vs')$$
$$polyArea \ \_ \qquad\qquad\qquad\quad = \quad 0$$

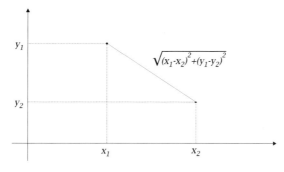

Figure 2.2. Computing the Distance between Two Vertices

We can also prove properties about our functions, subject to the limitations of reasoning with floating-point numbers discussed in Section 1.6. For example, it would be nice if *area* (*circle r*) yielded the same result as *circleArea r*, where *circleArea* was defined in Section 1.4.2. We can do this easily by calculation:

> *area* (*circle r*)
> $\Rightarrow$ { unfold *circle* }
> *area* (*Ellipse r r*)
> $\Rightarrow$ { unfold *area* }
> *pi* $*$ *r* $*$ *r*
> $\Rightarrow$ { fold (^) }
> *pi* $*$ *r*^2
> $\Rightarrow$ { fold *circleArea* }
> *circleArea r*

We can also prove more complex properties, such as:

> *area* (*RtTriangle s1 s2*)
> $\Longrightarrow$ *area* (*Polygon* [(0, 0), (s1, 0), (0, s2)])

To prove this particular property it's more natural to start with the right-hand-side and work backwards:[1]

> *area* (*Polygon* [(0, 0), (s1, 0), (0, s2)])
> $\Rightarrow$ *polyArea* [(0, 0), (s1, 0), (0, s2)]
> $\Rightarrow$ *triArea* (0, 0) (s1, 0) (0, s2) + *polyArea* [(0, 0), (0, s2)]
> $\Rightarrow$ *triArea* (0, 0) (s1, 0) (0, s2) + 0
> $\Rightarrow$ **let** *a* = *distBetween* (0, 0) (s1, 0)
>                 *b* = *distBetween* (s1, 0) (0, s2)
>                 *c* = *distBetween* (0, s2) (0, 0)
>                 *s* = 0.5 $*$ (*a* + *b* + *c*)
>         **in** *sqrt* (*s* $*$ (*s* − *a*) $*$ (*s* − *b*) $*$ (*s* − *c*))
> $\Rightarrow$ **let** *b* = *sqrt* (s1^2 + s2^2)
>                 *s* = 0.5 $*$ (s1 + *b* + s2)
>         **in** *sqrt* (*s* $*$ (*s* − s1) $*$ (*s* − *b*) $*$ (*s* − s2))      −− (1)

---

[1] From this point on I may skip a few of the more obvious steps in a calculation. If this is unclear, you should try filling in the missing steps yourself.

We can simplify this further in two steps. First note:

$s * (s - b)$
$\Rightarrow\ 0.5 * (s1 + b + s2) * (0.5 * (s1 + b + s2) - b)$
$\Rightarrow\ 0.5 * (s1 + b + s2) * (0.5 * (s1 - b + s2))$
$\Rightarrow\ 0.25 * (s1 + s2 + b) * (s1 + s2 - b)$
$\Rightarrow\ 0.25 * ((s1 + s2)\hat{}2 - b\hat{}2)$
$\Rightarrow\ 0.25 * ((s1 + s2)\hat{}2 - (s1\hat{}2 + s2\hat{}2))$
$\Rightarrow\ 0.25 * (s1\hat{}2 + 2 * s1 * s2 + s2\hat{}2 - (s1\hat{}2 + s2\hat{}2))$
$\Rightarrow\ 0.25 * (2 * s1 * s2)$
$\Rightarrow\ 0.5 * s1 * s2$

And further note:

$(s - s1) * (s - s2)$
$\Rightarrow\ (0.5 * (s1 + b + s2) - s1) * (0.5 * (s1 + b + s2) - s2)$
$\Rightarrow\ 0.5 * (b - s1 + s2) * (0.5 * (b + s1 - s2))$
$\Rightarrow\ 0.25 * (b\hat{}2 - (s1 - s2)\hat{}2)$
$\Rightarrow\ 0.25 * ((s1\hat{}2 + s2\hat{}2) - (s1 - s2)\hat{}2)$
$\Rightarrow\ 0.25 * ((s1\hat{}2 + s2\hat{}2) - (s1\hat{}2 - 2 * s1 * s2 + s2\hat{}2))$
$\Rightarrow\ 0.5 * s1 * s2$

Combining these and continuing from point (1), we get:

$sqrt\ (s * (s - s1) * (s - b) * (s - s2))$
$\Rightarrow\ sqrt\ ((0.5 * s1 * s2) * (0.5 * s1 * s2))$
$\Rightarrow\ 0.5 * s1 * s2$
$\Rightarrow\ area\ (RtTriangle\ s1\ s2)$

and we are done.

That was a lot of work! The primary reason for this is that Heron's general formula for the area of a triangle is subtle - and powerful. It is interesting to note, however, that if we were to carry out this proof in mathematics, we would reason in a very similar way, as follows. By Heron's formula, the area of a polygon with vertices $(0,0)$, $(s_1, 0)$, and $(0, s_2)$ is given as follows: Let $s = \frac{1}{2}(a + b + c)$, $a = |\ (0,0), (s_1, 0)\ |$, $b = |\ (s_1, 0), (0, s_2)\ |$, $c = |\ (0, s_2), (0, 0)\ |$ (where $|\ p_1, p_2\ |$ is the distance between vertices $p_1$ and $p_2$). Then the area is given by:

$$\sqrt{s(s - a)(s - b)(s - c)}$$

Simplifying $a$ to $s_1$ and $c$ to $s_2$ yields:

$$\sqrt{s(s - s_1)(s - b)(s - s_2)} \tag{2.1}$$

where $b = \sqrt{s_1^2 + s_2^2}$ and $s = \frac{1}{2}(s_1 + b + s_2)$.

We can simplify this further in two steps. First note:

$$
\begin{aligned}
s(s - b) &= \tfrac{1}{2}(s_1 + b + s_2)(\tfrac{1}{2}(s_1 - b + s_2)) \\
&= \tfrac{1}{4}(s_1 + s_2 + b)(s_1 + s_2 - b) = \tfrac{1}{4}((s_1 + s_2)^2 - b^2) \\
&= \tfrac{1}{4}((s_1 + s_2)^2 - (s_1^2 + s_2^2)) = \tfrac{1}{4}(s_1^2 + 2s_1 s_2 + s_2^2 - (s_1^2 + s_2^2)) \\
&= \tfrac{1}{4}(2 s_1 s_2) = \tfrac{1}{2} s_1 s_2
\end{aligned}
$$

And further note:

$$
\begin{aligned}
(s - s_1)(s - s_2) &= \tfrac{1}{2}(b - s_1 + s_2)(\tfrac{1}{2}(b + s_1 - s_2)) \\
&= \tfrac{1}{4}(b^2 - (s_1 - s_2)^2) = \tfrac{1}{4}((s_1^2 + s_2^2) - (s_1 - s_2)^2) \\
&= \tfrac{1}{4}((s_1^2 + s_2^2) - (s_1^2 - 2 s_1 s_2 + s_2^2)) \\
&= \tfrac{1}{2} s_1 s_2
\end{aligned}
$$

Combining these and continuing from point (1), we get:

$$
\begin{aligned}
&\sqrt{s(s - s_1)(s - b)(s - s_2)} \\
&= \sqrt{(\tfrac{1}{2} s_1 s_2)(\tfrac{1}{2} s_1 s_2)} \\
&= \tfrac{1}{2} s_1 s_2
\end{aligned}
$$

This last formula is just the area of a right triangle with sides $s_1$ and $s_2$. If you compare this mathematical proof with the corresponding proof by calculation in Haskell, you will find that they are almost identical, except for the notation used. So reasoning in Haskell is very often quite the same as reasoning in mathematics. Because we often use mathematics to *specify* the correct behavior of our programs, a proof by calculation in Haskell is a proof both *about the implementation and about the specification.* This is why Haskell is sometimes referred to as an "executable specification language."

Unfortunately, as discussed in Section 1.6, care must be taken when performing this kind of reasoning with floating-point numbers. As is often the case, numbers that do not approach the limits of floating-point precision work perfectly well:

$$area \; (RtTriangle \; 3.652 \; 5.126) \;\; \Rightarrow \;\; 9.36008$$
$$area \; (Polygon \; [(0, 0), \, (3.652, 0), \, (0, 5.126)]) \;\; \Rightarrow \;\; 9.36008$$

whereas ones that do can yield inconsistent results:

$$area\ (RtTriangle\ 0.0001\ 5.126)\ \Rightarrow\ 0.0002563$$
$$area\ (Polygon\ [(0, 0), (0.0001, 0), (0, 5.126)])\ \Rightarrow\ 0.000256648$$

---

**Exercise 2.3**  Prove the following property:

$$area\ (Rectangle\ s1\ s2)$$
$$\Rightarrow\ area\ (Polygon\ [(0, 0), (s1, 0), (s1, s2), (0, s2)])$$

---

**Exercise 2.4**  Define a function *convex :: Shape → Bool* that determines whether or not its argument is a convex shape (although we are mainly interested in the convexity of polygons, you might as well define it for each kind of shape).

---

**Exercise 2.5**  Here is an alternative way to compute the area of a polygon. Consider a polygon in quadrant 1 of the Cartesian plane (i.e., every vertex has positive $x$ and $y$ coordinates). Then every pair of adjacent vertices forms a trapeziod with respect to the $x$-axis. Starting at any vertex and working clockwise, compute these areas one-by-one, counting the area as positive if the $x$-coordinate increases, and negative if it decreases. The sum of these areas is then the area of the polygon.

It is easy to see that this algorithm is correct for a convex polygon by just looking at an example, as in Fig. 2.3. But the real beauty in this algorithm is that it works for *concave* polygons as well (see figure), and for a polygon located anywhere in the Cartesian plane. It is also more efficient than our previous algorithm. (Why?)

Write a Haskell function to compute polygonal areas in this way.

(Note: Polygons can not only be convex or concave, but also *self-crossing*. Consider, for example, the four-vertex polygon that outlines a "bowtie," or the five-vertex polygon that outlines a five-pointed star. What is the proper notion of area in this case, and do any of the algorithms discussed here compute it properly?)

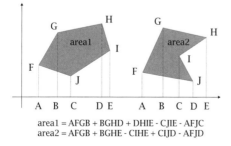

area1 = AFGB + BGHD + DHIE - CJIE - AFJC
area2 = AFGB + BGHE - CIHE + CIJD - AFJD

Figure 2.3.  Using Trapezoids to Compute Area of Polygon

## 2.3  Cleaning Up

Recall the discussion at the beginning of this chapter about modules and the desire to make visible only those named values that are of interest to the user of a module, thereby hiding irrelevant details of the implementation. We can now fill in the module declaration details to achieve this effect:

> **module** *Shape* (*Shape* (*Rectangle, Ellipse, RtTriangle, Polygon*),
>         *Radius, Side, Vertex*,
>         *square, circle, distBetween, area*
>      ) **where**
>
>    ...

The list of names above are those entities that are intended to be visible, or *exported*, from the module. These names come in three flavors:

1. Data types (in this case the data type *Shape*) that are listed with their constructors in parentheses.

> **DETAILS**
>
> A data type and its list of constructors may be abbreviated by just listing the name of the data type followed by (...). For example, the entire *Shape* data type may be exported using the form *Shape* (...). There are many other rules concerning the import and export of entities to and from modules. Some of these rules will be used later in the text, but you should consult the *Haskell Report* for all of the details.

2. Type synonyms (*Radius, Side,* and *Vertex*).
3. Ordinary values (in this case the functions *square, circle, distBetween,* and *area*).

So, for example, the function *triArea* is *not* exported from the *Shape* module, and thus is not available for use by someone importing the module.

> **DETAILS**
>
> It is sometimes desirable to export *everything* from a module. A shorthand way to express this is to simply write:
>
> **module** *Shape* **where**
>
>    ...
>
> (i.e., omitting the list of exports is equivalent to exporting everything).

# CHAPTER THREE

# Simple Graphics

In this chapter simple *graphics programming* in Haskell will be explained. Graphics in Haskell is consistent with the notion of computation via calculation, although it is special enough to warrant the use of special terminology and notation. In the next chapter we will use the techniques learned here to draw in a graphics window the geometric shapes defined in the last chapter. The ideas developed in this chapter will be put into a module called *SimpleGraphics*:

**module** *SimpleGraphics* **where**

There are many predefined functions and data types in Haskell, so many, in fact, that they demand some organization. Entities that are deemed essential to defining the fundamental nature of Haskell are contained in what is called the *Standard Prelude*, a collection of modules defining various categories of functionality. Entities that are deemed useful but not essential are contained in one of several *Standard Libraries*, also a collection of modules. The entire Standard Prelude is automatically imported into every program that you write, whereas the Standard Libraries need to be imported module-by-module.

Unfortunately, there is no standard graphics library for Haskell yet, although there is one in popular use on Windows machines called *Graphics*. The basic graphics functionality that we will use is defined in a library called *SOEGraphics*, which is very similar to *Graphics* but is guaranteed to work with this textbook, whereas the *Graphics* library may evolve over time. To use *SOEGraphics*, it must be imported into the module that is using it, as follows:

**import** *SOEGraphics*

Graphics is a special case of *input/output* (IO) processing in Haskell, and thus I will begin with a discussion of this more general idea.

## 3.1 Basic Input/Output

The Haskell Report defines the result of a program as the value of the name *main* in the module *Main*. On the other hand, the Hugs implementation of Haskell allows you to type whatever expression you wish to the Hugs prompt, and it will evaluate it for you. But in either case, the Haskell system "executes a program" by evaluating an expression, which (for a well-behaved program) eventually yields a value. The system must then display that value on your computer screen in some way that makes sense to you. Most systems will try to display the result in the same way that you would type it in as part of a program. So an integer is printed as an integer, a string as a string, a list as a list, and so on. I will refer to the area of the computer screen where this result is printed as the *standard output area*, which may vary from one implementation to another.

But what if a program is intended to write to a file or print a file on a printer or, the main topic of this chapter, draw a picture in a graphics window? These are examples of *output*, and there are related questions about *input*: For example, how does a program receive input from a keyboard or a mouse?

In general, how does Haskell's "expression-oriented" notion of "computation by calculation" accommodate these various kinds of input and output?

The answer is fairly simple: In Haskell, there is a special kind of value called an *action*. When a Haskell system evaluates an expression that yields an action, it knows not to try to display the result in the standard output area, but rather to "take the appropriate action." There are primitive actions – such as writing a single character to a file or receiving a single character from the keyboard – as well as compound actions – such as printing an entire string to a file. Haskell expressions that evaluate to actions are commonly called *commands*, because they command the Haskell system to perform some kind of action. Haskell functions that yield actions when they are applied are also commonly called commands.

Commands are still just expressions, of course, and some commands return a value for subsequent use by the program: keyboard input, for instance. A command that returns a value of type $T$ has type $IO\ T$; if no useful value is returned the command has type $IO\ ()$. The simplest example of a command is *return x*, which for a value $x :: T$ immediately returns $x$ and has type $IO\ T$.

---

**DETAILS**

The type () is called the *unit type*, and has exactly one value, which is also written (). Thus *return* () has type $IO\ ()$, and is often called a "noop" because it is an operation that does nothing and returns no useful result. Despite the negative connotation, it is used quite often!

Remember that all expressions in Haskell must be well-typed before a program is run, so a Haskell system knows ahead of time, by looking at the type, that it is evaluating a command, and is thus ready to "take action."

To make these ideas clearer, let's consider a few examples. A very useful command is the *putStr* command, which prints a string argument to the standard output area, and has type *String* → *IO* (). The () simply indicates that there is no useful result returned from this action; its sole purpose is to print its argument to the standard output area. So the program:

> **module** *Main* **where**
> *main* = *putStr* "Hello World\n"

is the canonical "Hello World" program, which is often the first program that people write in a new language.

**DETAILS**

Strings (i.e. sequences of characters) are written between double quotes in Haskell, as in **"Hello World"**. When typed on your computer, however, it will look a little different, as in **"Hello World"** (the double-quote character is the same at both ends of the string). Strings have type *String*. The "**\n**" at the end of the string above is a "newline" character; that is, if another string were printed just after this one, it would appear beginning on the next line, rather than just after "Hello World".

Suppose now that we want to perform *two* actions, such as first writing to a file named "testFile.txt", then printing to the standard output area. Haskell has a special keyword, **do**, to denote the beginning of a sequence of commands such as this, and so we can write:

> **do** *writeFile* "testFile.txt" "Hello File System"
> *putStr* "Hello World\n"

where the file-writing function *writeFile* has type:

> *writeFile* :: *FilePath* → *String* → *IO* ()
> **type** *FilePath* = *String*

**DETAILS**

A **do** expression allows us to sequence an arbitrary number of commands, each of type *IO* (), using layout to distinguish them (just as in a **let** or **where** expression). When used in this way, the result of a **do** expression also has type *IO* ().

So far we have only used actions having type *IO* () (i.e., output actions). But what about input? As above, we will consider input from both the user and the file system.

To get a line of input from the user (which will be typed in the *standard input area* of the computer screen, usually the same as the standard output area) we can use the function:

*getLine* :: *IO String*

Suppose, for example, that we wish to read a line of input using this function, and then write that line (a string) to a file. To do this we write the compound command:

**do** *s* ← *getLine*
   *writeFile* "testFile.txt" *s*

Note the syntax for binding *s* to the result of executing the *getLine* command; because the type of *getLine* is *IO String*, the type of *s* is *String*. Its value is then used in the next line as an argument to the *writeFile* command.

Similarly, we can read the entire contents of a file using the command *readFile* :: *FilePath* → *IO String*. For example:

**do** *s* ← *readFile* "testFile.txt"
   *putStr* *s*

There are many other commands available for file, system, and user IO, some in the Standard Prelude, and some in various libararies (such as *IO*, *Directory*, *System*, and *Time*). I will not discuss any of these here; rather, in the next section I will concentrate on *graphics IO*.

Before that, however, I want to emphasize that, despite the special **do** syntax, Haskell's IO commands are no different in status from any other Haskell function or value. For example, it is possible to create a *list* of actions, such as:

*actionList* = [*putStr* "Hello World\n",
          *writeFile* "testFile.txt" "Hello File System",
          *putStr* "File successfully written."]

However, a list of actions is just a list of values; they actually don't *do* anything until they are sequenced appropriately using a **do** expression, and then returned as the value *main* of the overall program. Still, it is often convenient to place actions into a list as above, and the Haskell Report and Libraries have some useful functions for turning them into commands. In particular, the function *sequence_* in the Standard Prelude, when used with IO, has type:

> *sequence_* :: [*IO a*] → *IO* ()

and can thus be applied to the *actionList* above to yield the single command:

> *main* = *sequence_ actionList*

Before I give you a more interesting example of this idea, I will tell you a secret (more secrets will be revealed later in the text):

> **DETAILS**
>
> Haskell's strings are really *lists of characters*. In other words, *String* is a shorthand – a type synonym – for a list of characters:
>
> > **type** *String* = [*Char*]
>
> However, because strings are used so often, Haskell allows you to write "*Hello*" instead of [*'H'*, *'e'*, *'l'*, *'l'*, *'o'*]. But keep in mind that this is just syntax – strings really are just lists of characters, and these two ways of writing this string are identical from Haskell's perspective.
>
> (Earlier the type synonym *FilePath* was defined for *String*. This shows that type synonyms can be made for other type synonyms.)

Now back to the example. From the function *putChar* :: *Char* → *IO* (), which prints a single character to the standard output area, we can define the function *putStr* used earlier, which prints an entire string. To do this, let's first define a function that converts a list of characters (i.e., a string) into a list of IO actions:

> | | | |
> |---|---|---|
> | *putCharList* | :: | *String* → [*IO* ()] |
> | *putCharList* [ ] | = | [ ] |
> | *putCharList* (*c* : *cs*) | = | *putChar c* : *putCharList cs* |

With this, *putStr* is easily defined:

> | | | |
> |---|---|---|
> | *putStr* | :: | *String* → *IO* () |
> | *putStr s* | = | *sequence_* (*putCharList s*) |

Note that the expression *putCharList s* is a list of actions, and *sequence_* is used to turn them into a single (compound) command, just as we did earlier. (The function *putStr* can also be defined directly as a recursive function, but I leave this as an exercise.)

IO processing in Haskell is consistent with everything you have learned about programming with expressions and reasoning through calculation, although that may not be completely obvious yet. Indeed, it turns out that a **do** expression is just syntax for a more primitive way of combining actions using functions. This secret will be revealed in full in Chapter 18.

## 3.2 Graphics Windows

Let's now look at the particulars of *graphics* IO. Graphics commands are no different in concept from those discussed earlier. However, there is no "standard graphics area" on which to draw things. Instead, we must create a fresh *graphics window*. Furthermore, because we may wish to create several such windows, we need a way to distinguish them once they are created, in order to specify in which window to draw at some particular point in a program. Haskell accomplishes this by returning a unique value of type *Window* at the time we create a window.

To see this concretely, let's look at the type of the *openWindow* command that (you guessed it) opens a window:

```
openWindow  ::  Title → Size → IO Window
type Title   =  String
type Size    =  (Int, Int)
```

The *Title* is a string displayed in the title bar of the new graphics window, and *Size* represents the size of the window as a pair of numbers indicating the width and height in *pixel coordinates*. A pixel is the smallest dot that can be displayed on a computer screen; usually 100 or so pixels can be lined up along one inch. The *Window* that returns from a call to *openWindow* is used in subsequent graphics commands to tell the computer within which window to perform its action. In other words, every call to *openWindow* creates a new, unique window, and the *Window* value provides a way to distinguish between them in the rest of the program.

Let's write our first graphics program:

```
main0
  =  runGraphics (
       do w ← openWindow
```

"My First Graphics Program" (300, 300)
*drawInWindow w* (*text* (100, 200) "Hello Graphics World")
*k ← getKey w*
*closeWindow w*
)

It's not hard to guess what this program does: A $300 \times 300$-pixel graphics window is opened, a greeting message is displayed in it, and the window remains open until the user types a character on the keyboard. The following five new functions are introduced by this example:

◼ *runGraphics* :: *IO* () → *IO* () runs a graphics "action." This is needed because of special operating system tasks that need to be set up to perform graphics IO.

◼ *drawInWindow* :: *Window* → *Graphic* → *IO* () draws a given *Graphic* value on a given *Window*.

◼ *text* :: *Point* → *String* → *Graphic* creates a *Graphic* value consisting of a *String* whose lower left-hand corner is at the location specified by the *Point* argument, in pixel coodinates:

    **type** *Point* = (*Int, Int*)

◼ *getKey* :: *Window* → *IO* () waits for the user to press (and release) a key on the keyboard. In the above example *getKey* is used to prevent the window from closing before the user has a chance to read what's on the screen.

◼ *closeWindow* :: *Window* → *IO* () closes the specified window.

You should know enough about IO at this point that these descriptions are sufficient to fully understand the sample program given above, except for one other detail: (0, 0) is the location of the *upper left-hand corner of the graphics window.* As the *x* coordinate increases, the position moves to the right, and as the *y* coordinate increases, the position moves downward. Thus, in the above program, the bottom right-hand corner of the graphics window is at coordinate (299, 299). I will have more to say about this in the next chapter.

For convenience, I will define the following command, which also demonstrates how to write a *loop* using command sequencing:

*spaceClose* :: *Window* → *IO* ()
*spaceClose w*
    = **do** *k ← getKey w*
        **if** *k* ==' ' **then** *closeWindow w*
                **else** *spaceClose w*

> **DETAILS**
> An expression **if** *pred* **then** *cons* **else** *alt* is called a *conditional expression*. If *pred* (called the *predicate*) is true, then *cons* (called the *consequence*) is the result; if *pred* is false, then *alt* (called the *alternative*) is the result. Thus, the second command in the **do** context above will either be *closeWindow w* or *spaceClose w*, depending on whether *k* is a blank space character.

Note that *spaceClose* is defined recursively, and it is precisely the recursion that achieves the desired looping behavior. This command reads a keystroke and sees if it is the space character (' '). If it is, the window is closed and the command is finished; if it is not, then the process is repeated. Because *spaceClose w* has type *IO* (), we can use it in a **do** expression like this:

> *main*1
>   = *runGraphics* (
>     **do** *w* ← *openWindow*
>         "My First Graphics Program" (300, 300)
>       *drawInWindow w* (*text* (100, 200) "Hello Graphics World")
>       *spaceClose w*
>   )

---

**Exercise 3.1** Rewrite the definition of *putStr* from Section 3.1 so that it does not use *sequence_* nor create a list of actions; rather, express it recursively, using the looping idea mentioned above. Similarly, define the function *getLine* (also from Section 3.1) recursively, using the more primitive function *getChar* :: *IO Char*.

Hint: To define these two functions in this way you will need to use the expressions *return* () :: *IO* () and *return* "" :: *IO String* (recall the earlier discussion about *return*).

### 3.3 Drawing Graphics Other Than Text

We have seen that the function *text* returns a *Graphic* value, and we used the function *draw* to turn that into an action. As it turns out, there are other functions besides *text* that create *Graphic* values, in particular ones for drawing certain kinds of geometric shapes:

> *ellipse*      :: *Point* → *Point* → *Graphic*
> *shearEllipse* :: *Point* → *Point* → *Point* → *Graphic*
> *line*         :: *Point* → *Point* → *Graphic*

*polyline*   :: [*Point*] → *Graphic*
*polygon*   :: [*Point*] → *Graphic*
*polyBezier* :: [*Point*] → *Graphic*

Here is a brief description of each of these:

1. *ellipse p1 p2* draws an ellipse that just fits into the rectangle whose upper left-hand vertex is at point *p1* and whose lower right-hand vertex is at point *p2*, using the graphics window coordinate system described earlier.
2. *shearEllipse p1 p2 p3* draws an ellipse that just fits into the parallelogram formed by the vertices *p1*, *p2*, and *p3*.
3. *line p1 p2* draws a straight line between points *p1* and *p2*.
4. *polygon pts* draws a closed polygon with vertices *pts*. The last point is connected back to the first, and thus the polygon can be filled with a color.
5. *polyline pts* connects each pair of successive points with a straight line, but does not connect the last point back to the first; thus it cannot be filled with a color.
6. *polyBezier* is like *polyline*, but uses *Bezier curves* to connect successive points, rather than straight lines.

If we draw figures and lines using the above primitive functions, the figures and lines will be white by default. To make the colors more interesting, we can use the graphics library function:

*withColor*   ::   *Color* → *Graphic* → *Graphic*

**data** *Color* = *Black* | *Blue* | *Green* | *Cyan*
            | *Red* | *Magenta* | *Yellow* | *White*

## 3.4  Some Examples

As a simple example, here is a program that draws a red ellipse and a blue outline of a rectangle.

*pic1* = *withColor Red*
            (*ellipse* (150, 150) (300, 200))
*pic2* = *withColor Blue*
            (*polyline* [(100, 50), (200, 50),
                    (200, 250), (100, 250), (100, 50)])

*main2*
  =  *runGraphics (*
     **do** *w* ← *openWindow*
              "`Some Graphics Figures`" (300, 300)
        *drawInWindow w pic*1
        *drawInWindow w pic*2
        *spaceClose w*
     )

For a more interesting example, let's draw a simple *fractal image*. A *fractal* is a mathematical structure that repeats itself infinitely often in successively finer detail (Barnsle, 1993). Using fractals is a popular method to simulate natural phenomena like skylines, leaves, and snowflakes. I am sure you have seen them in many computer-generated pictures found in calendars, animated movies, among others. A skyline, for example, has the property that as you "zoom in" on it, it looks approximately the same at each level of detail. Whereas this detail is somewhat random for skylines, for crystaline structures such as a snowflake, it is very regular. Both can be modelled using fractals.

The mathematics of fractals is beyond the scope of this textbook, but there are some simple fractal images that are pleasing to the eye yet very easy to describe and draw. One such image is called *Sierpinski's Triangle*, which can be described via successive drawings of a triangle (Fig. 3.1). The first drawing is a single triangle. The second drawing subdivides the first triangle into three triangles, each one-half the original in both length and height. The third drawing subdivides each of the triangles in the second drawing in a similar way. Now imagine doing this *ad infinitum*, and there you have Sierpinski's Triangle.

Of course, we cannot actually show this infinitely-dense triangle in a graphics window, because we are limited by pixel size (and our eyes would not be sharp enough to see the details). So to draw Sierpinski's Triangle we will stop subdividing the triangles when we reach some predetermined image size, and then just draw each tiny triangle completely at that point.

Figure 3.1: First Three Constructions of Sierpinski's Triangle

First I will define a function *fillTri* that draws a blue-filled triangle, given *x* and *y* coordinates and a size (all in pixel coordinates):

*fillTri* :: *Window → Int → Int → Int → IO* ()
*fillTri w x y size*
      = *drawInWindow w* (*withColor Blue*
          (*polygon* [(*x, y*), (*x* + *size, y*), (*x, y* − *size*), (*x, y*)]))

The rest of the algorithm is really very easy (and elegant), and is presented in one fell swoop:

*minSize*      :: *Int*
*minSize*      = 8

*sierpinskiTri* :: *Window → Int → Int → Int → IO* ()
*sierpinskiTri w x y size*
      = **if** *size* <= *minSize*
        **then** *fillTri w x y size*
        **else let** *size2* = *size* '*div*' 2
          **in do** *sierpinskiTri w x y size2*
                *sierpinskiTri w x* (*y* − *size2*) *size2*
                *sierpinskiTri w* (*x* + *size2*) *y size2*

---

**DETAILS**

*div x y* is the integer quotient of *x* and *y*. But sometimes it is desirable to use a function as if it were an infix operator. To do so in Haskell, just enclose it in backquotes, as in *size* '*div*' 2 above. The reason for doing this is purely aesthetic. In the case above, I chose to do so because division is normally done using an infix operator in mathematics, as in *size*/2. (The (/) operator in Haskell is reserved for floating-point and other *fractional* numbers, a concept to be explained much later in the text.)

---

Note the three recursive calls to *sierpinskiTri*; when the size drops to 8 or less, *fillTri* is called instead.

Using *sierpinskiTri* is easy enough; the only trickery is to use a number that is a power of two for the initial size, to make the subdivisions look most uniform by avoiding rounding errors.

*main3*
    = *runGraphics* (
      **do** *w* ← *openWindow* "Sierpinski's Triangle" (400, 400)
        *sierpinskiTri w* 50 300 256
        *spaceClose w*
      )

Fig. 3.2 is a snapshot of the actual output of this program.

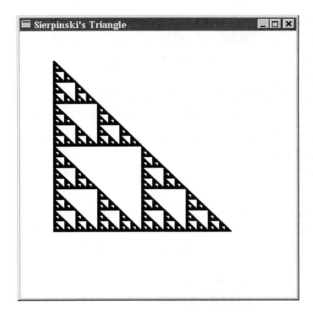

Figure 3.2: Snapshot of Sierpinski's Triangle

Figure 3.3: A Snowflake Fractal

I have shown this example primarily to illustrate how one can use the various graphics primitives in interesting ways. But ultimately we are trying to build higher-level ways to do this, starting with the ability to draw values of type *Shape* defined in Chapter 2. We will discuss this in the next chapter.

---

**Exercise 3.2** Draw a *snowflake fractal*. The idea is to draw an equilateral triangle, then another of the same size but rotated 180° (thus making a Star of David). This process is then repeated for each of the six corners, but now with triangles one-third the size. The process is repeated infinitely often in the abstract, but in reality is stopped at some suitably small triangle size, as for the Sierpinski triangle. Fig. 3.3 shows the result of a program that achieves this to four levels.

Use recursion to write your program, but note that the strategy is a bit different from that used with the Sierpinski triangle. With Sierpinski, no triangles are drawn until the very bottom of the recursion, whereas with the snowflake, triangles are drawn as you recurse, with each set being of a different size. For aesthetics, try coloring each level of triangles differently.

# CHAPTER FOUR

# Shapes II: Drawing Shapes

In Chapter 2 a shape data type and a function for computing the area of shapes were defined. In the last chapter you learned about basic graphics programming in Haskell. In this chapter I will define another function of shapes, namely one that converts a shape into a graphics value that can then be drawn in a graphics window. Conceptually, this function is no different from the *area* function defined in Chapter 2. In both cases, a shape is turned into some other kind of value; in the case of area, that value has type *Float*, and in the case of the function to be defined in this chapter, that value has type *Graphic*.

In order to perform graphics IO, we need to import the graphics library, as discussed in the last chapter. Additionally, we need to import the *Shape* module. Calling our new module *Draw*, we therefore write:

> **module** *Draw* (*inchToPixel*, *pixelToInch*, *intToFloat*,
>         *xWin*, *yWin*, *trans*, *shapeToGraphic*, *spaceClose*
>       ) **where**
>
> **import** *Shape*
> **import** *SOEGraphics*

where the list of names contains those functions and values, *inchToPixel*, *pixelToInch*, etc., that we choose to export from the module, and that are defined in the remainder of this chapter.

## 4.1 Dealing With Different Coordinate Systems

Before proceeding, let's define a couple of *coercion functions* that we will use to convert, or "coerce," the coordinates of a graphics window into ones that we are more familiar with (and *vice versa*).

In our discussions of shapes, we have always assumed floating-point numbers for all dimensions, presumably in inches or some similar dimensional units. But the Graphics Library uses pixel coordinates, so first we need a function to convert from the former to the latter. Let's assume that the floating-point numbers are in inches, and that there are 100 pixels per inch. Thus, to convert from inches to pixel coordinates, we can apply the following function:

$$
\begin{aligned}
inchToPixel \quad &::\quad Float \to Int \\
inchToPixel\ x \quad &=\quad round\ (100 * x)
\end{aligned}
$$

> **DETAILS**
> The value *round x* is *x* rounded to the nearest whole number.

---

**Exercise 4.1** Why is *inchToPixel x* not defined as $100 * round\ x$?

There will also be occasion to coerce in the other direction:

$$
\begin{aligned}
pixelToInch \quad &::\quad Int \to Float \\
pixelToInch\ n \quad &=\quad intToFloat\ n/100
\end{aligned}
$$

$$
\begin{aligned}
intToFloat \quad &::\quad Int \to Float \\
intToFloat\ n \quad &=\quad fromInteger\ (toInteger\ n)
\end{aligned}
$$

> **DETAILS**
> The function *intToFloat* converts an integer into a floating-point number, but to explain it adequately requires an understanding of Haskell's *type classes*, which is not covered until Chapter 12. For now, trust that *intToFloat* works properly.

---

**Exercise 4.2** Why is *pixelToInch n* not defined as $intToFloat\ (n/100)$?

Also, recall from the previous chapter that the point (0, 0) marks the upper left-hand corner of a graphics window. If we define some global names for our window size (in pixel coordinates):

$$
\begin{aligned}
xWin, yWin \quad &::\quad Int \\
xWin \quad &=\quad 600 \\
yWin \quad &=\quad 500
\end{aligned}
$$

then the coordinate of the lower right-hand corner is ($xWin - 1$, *yWin* − 1). Remember that increasing the *x* coordinate moves the position to the right, and increasing the *y* coordinate moves the position downward.

> **DETAILS**
> A type signature may contain more than one name if they all have the same type.

Unfortunately, this *graphics window coordinate system* is not the same as the one most of us are familiar with. Normally, we would expect (0, 0) to be in the center of the screen, increasing *x* to move to the right, and increasing *y* to move upward. So let's define another coercion function that translates "our" coordinates into those required by the graphics window:

$$
\begin{array}{lcl}
trans & :: & Vertex \rightarrow Point \\
trans\ (x, y) & = & (xWin2 + inchToPixel\ x, \\
& & \quad yWin2 - inchToPixel\ y)
\end{array}
$$

$$
\begin{array}{lcl}
xWin2,\ yWin2 & :: & Int \\
xWin2 & = & xWin\ `div`\ 2 \\
yWin2 & = & yWin\ `div`\ 2
\end{array}
$$

The values *xWin2* and *yWin2* are defined at the top-level to prevent them from being recomputed every time *trans* is called (although a good compiler may avoid recomputation in any case).

As a sanity check on this function, note that:

$$
trans\ (0, 0) \implies (xWin2, yWin2)
$$

as we would expect. Also note, assuming that *inchToPixel* and *pixelToInch* are inverses, that:

$$
\begin{array}{l}
trans\ (pixelToInch\ xWin2,\ pixelToInch\ yWin2) \\
\quad \Rightarrow\ (xWin2 + inchToPixel\ (pixelToInch\ xWin2), \\
\qquad\quad yWin2 - inchToPixel\ (pixelToInch\ yWin2)) \\
\quad \Rightarrow\ (xWin2 + xWin2,\ yWin2 - yWin2) \\
\quad \Rightarrow\ (xWin, 0)
\end{array}
$$

which, if you think about it, is also correct.

As a final preliminary task, let us define a function that translates a *list* of vertices into the points required by a graphics window:

$$transList \quad :: \quad [Vertex] \rightarrow [Point]$$
$$transList\,[\,] \quad = \quad [\,]$$
$$transList\,(p : ps) \quad = \quad trans\,p : transList\,ps$$

You should convince yourself that this recursive definition achieves the specified task.

## 4.2 Converting Shapes to Graphics

Our goal is to define a function:

$$shapeToGraphic \quad :: \quad Shape \rightarrow Graphic$$

that converts a *Shape* value into a *Graphic* value, which can then be drawn using *draw*. Let's consider each *Shape* constructor in turn. The first one, a rectangle, will be the hardest one to convert, but is nonetheless fairly straightforward:

$$shapeToGraphic\,(Rectangle\,s1\,s2)$$
$$= \; \textbf{let}\; s12 \; = \; s1/2$$
$$s22 \; = \; s2/2$$
$$\textbf{in}\; polygon\,(transList$$
$$[(-s12, -s22), (-s12, s22), (s12, s22), (s12, -s22)])$$

Note the use of *transList* to translate the four coordinates of a rectangle centered over the origin to the coordinates needed by the graphics window.

Converting an ellipse is even more straightforward:

$$shapeToGraphic\,(Ellipse\,r1\,r2)$$
$$= \; ellipse\,(trans\,(-r1, -r2))\,(trans\,(r1, r2))$$

A right triangle is handled similarly to a rectangle:

$$shapeToGraphic\,(RtTriangle\,s1\,s2)$$
$$= \; polygon\,(transList\,[(0, 0), (s1, 0), (0, s2)])$$

And a polygon simply requires translating the vertices:

$$shapeToGraphic\,(Polygon\,vts)$$
$$= \; polygon\,(transList\,vts)$$

Collecting the pieces, we arrive at:

$shapeToGraphic \ :: \ Shape \rightarrow Graphic$
$shapeToGraphic \ (Rectangle \ s1 \ s2)$
$$= \ \textbf{let} \ s12 \ = \ s1/2$$
$$s22 \ = \ s2/2$$
$$\textbf{in} \ polygon$$
$$(transList \ [(-s12, -s22), (-s12, s22),$$
$$(s12, s22), (s12, -s22)])$$
$shapeToGraphic \ (Ellipse \ r1 \ r2)$
$$= \ ellipse \ (trans \ (-r1, -r2)) \ (trans \ (r1, r2))$$
$shapeToGraphic \ (RtTriangle \ s1 \ s2)$
$$= \ polygon \ (transList \ [(0, 0), (s1, 0), (0, s2)])$$
$shapeToGraphic \ (Polygon \ vts)$
$$= \ polygon \ (transList \ vts)$$

## 4.3 Some Examples

For some examples, let's start by creating a variety of shapes:

$sh1, \ sh2, \ sh3, \ sh4 \ :: \ Shape$

| | | |
|---|---|---|
| $sh1$ | $=$ | $Rectangle \ 3 \ 2$ |
| $sh2$ | $=$ | $Ellipse \ 1 \ 1.5$ |
| $sh3$ | $=$ | $RtTriangle \ 3 \ 2$ |
| $sh4$ | $=$ | $Polygon \ [(-2.5, 2.5), (-1.5, 2.0), (-1.1, 0.2),$ |
| | | $(-1.7, -1.0), (-3.0, 0)]$ |

We can color and draw shapes one by one by doing something as simple as:

$main0$
$$= \ runGraphics \ ($$
$$\textbf{do} \ w \leftarrow openWindow \ \text{"Drawing Shapes"} \ (xWin, yWin)$$
$$drawInWindow \ w \ (withColor \ Red \ (shapeToGraphic \ sh1))$$
$$drawInWindow \ w \ (withColor \ Blue \ (shapeToGraphic \ sh2))$$
$$spaceClose \ w$$
$$)$$

which draws a red rectangle and a blue ellipse centered on the screen.

To make things more convenient, however, let's define a function that draws a whole list of color/shape pairs:

$\textbf{type} \ ColoredShapes \ = \ [(Color, \ Shape)]$
$shs \ :: \ ColoredShapes$
$shs \ = \ [(Red, sh1), (Blue, sh2), (Yellow, sh3), (Magenta, sh4)]$

Such a function is simple to define:

*drawShapes* :: *Window* → *ColoredShapes* → *IO* ()
*drawShapes w* [ ]
        = *return* ()
*drawShapes w* ((*c*, *s*) : *cs*)
        = **do** *drawInWindow w* (*withColor c*
            (*shapeToGraphic s*))
          *drawShapes w cs*

and can be used like this:

*main*1
  = *runGraphics* (
    **do** *w* ← *openWindow* "Drawing Shapes" (*xWin*, *yWin*)
      *drawShapes w shs*
      *spaceClose w*
    )

A snapshot of *main*1 is shown in Fig. 4.1, although the colors have been

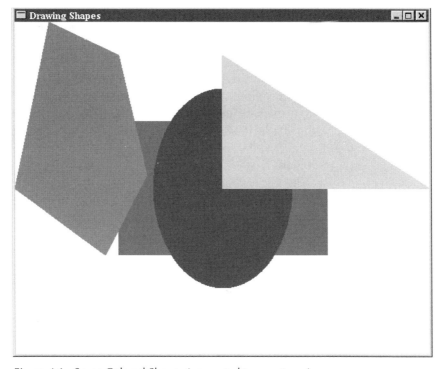

Figure 4.1: Some Colored Shapes (converted to grey tones)

converted to grey tones (as they have been for all of the figures in this text).

## 4.4  In Retrospect

One might wonder why we bothered to define a function to draw *Shape* values in the first place, when using the primitive graphics operations directly, as described in the previous chapter, seems almost as good. In particular, it seems that we could easily define new IO functions for each of the shapes that we are interested in drawing, and even have these functions take floating-point values as parameters. In other words, something like this:

$$
\begin{array}{lll}
drawRectangle & :: & Side \rightarrow Side \rightarrow IO\ () \\
drawEllipse & :: & Radius \rightarrow Radius \rightarrow IO\ () \\
drawRtTriangle & :: & Side \rightarrow Side \rightarrow IO\ () \\
drawPolygon & :: & [\,Vertex\,] \rightarrow IO\ ()
\end{array}
$$

$$
\begin{array}{lll}
\textbf{type } Radius & = & Float \\
\textbf{type } Side & = & Float \\
\textbf{type } Vertex & = & (\,Float,\,Float\,)
\end{array}
$$

Indeed, this is possible, and you may wish to define these functions on your own as an exercise.

However, there are a couple of good reasons for doing things "indirectly" using the *Shape* data type as we have in this chapter. First, *Shape* values are "transparent." That is, one can pattern-match against them to learn what their insides look like. For example, we can determine the side lengths of a rectangle, the radii of an ellipse, and so on. In contrast, a value of type *IO* () (i.e., an action) is completely "opaque"; the only thing you can do with it is execute it.

To see the importance of this, suppose I want to do more than one thing with a shape, such as draw it and also compute its area. Then I am better off having a transparent value representing it, to which I can apply a draw function and an area function independently. And if later I decide to define a new operation on *Shapes* – such as a function to compute the perimeter, which we will do in Chapter 6 – then I am in good shape (pardon the pun). Doing all of this with opaque values would be much more cumbersome.

A second (and related) advantage of our indirect approach will become evident in Chapter 8, where we will define a new data type called *Region* that captures ways to *combine* shapes in interesting ways – such as taking their union and intersection – and ways to *transform* them as well – such as scaling and translating them. Having the *Region* data type be transparent will be especially useful, not just because we will want to do more than one thing with them as argued above, but because regions will be able to *share subregions*. This is not as easily done with opaque values.

# CHAPTER FIVE

# Polymorphic and Higher-Order Functions

In this chapter I will introduce two new important ideas. The first is *polymorphism*, the ability to consider entire families of types as one. *Polymorphic data types* are one source of this concept, which is then inherited by functions defined over these data types. The already familiar *list* is the most common example of a polymorphic data type, and it will be discussed at length in this chapter.

The second concept is the *higher-order function*, which is a function that can take one or more functions as arguments or return a function as a result (functions can also be placed in data structures, making the data constructors higher-order too). Together, polymorphic and higher-order functions substantially increase our expressive power and our ability to reuse code. You will see that both of these new ideas naturally follow the foundations that we have already built. (A more detailed discussion of polymorphic functions that operate on lists can be found in Chapter 23.)

## 5.1 Polymorphic Types

In previous chapters we have seen examples of lists of many different kinds of elements – integers, floating-point numbers, points, characters, and even IO actions. You can well imagine situations requiring lists of other element types as well. Sometimes, however, we don't wish to be so particular about the precise type of the elements. For example, suppose we want to define a function *length*, which determines the number of elements in a list. We don't really care whether the list contains integers, characters, or even other lists. We imagine computing the length in exactly the same way in each case. The obvious definition is:

$$
\begin{aligned}
length\ [\ ] \quad &=\ 0 \\
length\ (x : xs) \quad &=\ 1 + length\ xs
\end{aligned}
$$

This definition is self-explanatory. We can read the equations as saying: "The length of the empty list is 0, and the length of a list whose first element is *x* and remainder is *xs*, is 1 plus the length of *xs*."

But what should the type of *length* be? Intuitively, what we'd like to say is that, for *any* type *a*, the type of *length* is $[a] \rightarrow Integer$. In Haskell we write this simply as:

$$length \ :: \ [a] \rightarrow Integer$$

---

**DETAILS**

Generic names for types, such as *a* above, are called *type variables*, and are uncapitalized to distinguish them from specific types such as *Integer*.

---

So *length* can be applied to a list containing elements of *any* type. For example:

$$
\begin{array}{lcl}
length \ [1, 2, 3] & \Rightarrow & 3 \\
length \ ['a', 'b', 'c'] & \Rightarrow & 3 \\
length \ \text{"def"} & \Rightarrow & 3 \\
length \ [[1], [\ ], [2, 3, 4]] & \Rightarrow & 3
\end{array}
$$

Note that the type of the argument to *length* in the last example is $[[Integer]]$; that is, a list of lists of integers.

Here are two other examples of polymorphic list functions, which happen to be predefined in Haskell:

$$
\begin{array}{ll}
head & :: \ [a] \rightarrow a \\
head \ (x : \_) & = \ x \\
\\
tail & :: \ [a] \rightarrow [a] \\
tail \ (\_ : xs) & = \ xs
\end{array}
$$

As discussed briefly in Chapter 1, these two functions take the "head" and "tail," respectively, of any nonempty list:

$$
\begin{array}{lcl}
head \ [1, 2, 3] & \Rightarrow & 1 \\
head \ ['a', 'b', 'c'] & \Rightarrow & 'a' \\
tail \ [1, 2, 3] & \Rightarrow & [2,3] \\
tail \ ['a', 'b', 'c'] & \Rightarrow & ['b', 'c']
\end{array}
$$

Functions such as *length*, *head*, and *tail* are said to be *polymorphic* (*poly* means *many* and *morphic* refers to the structure, or *form*, of objects). Polymorphic functions arise naturally when defining functions on lists and other structured data types. In the remainder of this chapter we will continue studying polymorphic lists, however, in Chapter 7, for example, we will look at another polymorphic data structure, namely a *tree*.

## 5.2 Abstraction Over Recursive Definitions

Recall from Section 4.1, the definition:

$$
\begin{aligned}
transList & :: \; [Vertex] \rightarrow [Point] \\
transList \; [\,] & = \; [\,] \\
transList \; (p : ps) & = \; trans \; p : transList \; ps
\end{aligned}
$$

and from Section 3.1 the definition:

$$
\begin{aligned}
putCharList & :: \; String \rightarrow [IO \; (\,)] \\
putCharList \; [\,] & = \; [\,] \\
putCharList \; (c : cs) & = \; putChar \; c : putCharList \; cs
\end{aligned}
$$

These two functions arose out of completely different contexts: the former in translating between graphics coordinate systems, and the latter in performing text IO. Yet surely these two definitions share something in common; surely there is a repeating pattern of operations here. But it is not quite like any of the examples that we studied in Section 1.4, and therefore, it is unclear how to apply the abstraction principle. What distinguishes this situation is a repeating pattern of *recursion*.

In discerning the nature of a repeating pattern, it's sometimes helpful to identify those things that *aren't* repeating (i.e., those things that are *changing*) because these will be the sources of *parameterization*: those values that must be passed as arguments to the abstracted function. In the case above, these changing values are the functions *trans* and *putChar*; let's consider them instances of a new name, $f$. If we then simply rewrite either of the above functions as a new function – let's call it (*map f*) – which takes an extra argument $f$, we arrive at:

$$
\begin{aligned}
map \; f \; [\,] & = \; [\,] \\
map \; f \; (x : xs) & = \; f \; x : map \; f \; xs
\end{aligned}
$$

With this definition of *map*, we can now redefine *transList* and *putCharList* as:

$$
\begin{aligned}
transList & :: \; [Vertex] \rightarrow [Point] \\
transList \; ps & = \; map \; trans \; ps
\end{aligned}
$$

$$
\begin{aligned}
putCharList & :: \; String \rightarrow [IO \; (\,)] \\
putCharList \; cs & = \; map \; putChar \; cs
\end{aligned}
$$

Note that these definitions are nonrecursive; the common pattern of recursion has been abstracted away and isolated in the definition of *map*. They are also very succinct; so much so, that it is often unnecessary to create new names for these functions at all. For example, in Section 3.1 we used *putCharList* to define *putStr*, whose complete definition was thus:

$$
\begin{array}{lll}
\textit{putStr} & :: & \textit{String} \rightarrow \textit{IO} \ () \\
\textit{putStr s} & = & \textit{sequence}_{-} \ (\textit{putCharList s}) \\[2mm]
\textit{putCharList} & :: & \textit{String} \rightarrow [\textit{IO} \ ()] \\
\textit{putCharList} \ [\,] & = & [\,] \\
\textit{putCharList} \ (c:cs) & = & \textit{putChar} \ c : \textit{putCharList cs}
\end{array}
$$

With *map*, however, we can define this much more directly and succinctly:

$$
\begin{array}{lll}
\textit{putStr} & :: & \textit{String} \rightarrow \textit{IO} \ () \\
\textit{putStr s} & = & \textit{sequence}_{-} \ (\textit{map putChar s})
\end{array}
$$

One of the powers of higher-order functions is that they permit concise yet easy-to-understand definitions such as this. You will see many similar examples throughout the remainder of the text.

To prove that the new versions of these two functions are equivalent to the old ones can be done via calculation, but requires a proof technique called *induction*, because of the recursive nature of the original function definitions. We will discuss inductive proofs in detail, including these two examples, in Chapter 11. In reality, induction is a formalization and generalization of the process above whereby we derived *map* from two of its instances.

### 5.2.1 Map is Polymorphic

What should the type of *map* be? Let's look first at its use in *transList*: it takes the function *trans* :: *Vertex* → *Point* as its first argument, a list of *Vertex*s as its second argument, and it returns a list of *Point*s as its result. So its type must be:

$$
\textit{map} \ :: \ (\textit{Vertex} \rightarrow \textit{Point}) \rightarrow [\textit{Vertex}] \rightarrow [\textit{Point}]
$$

Yet a similar analysis of its use in *putCharList* reveals that *map*'s type should be:

$$
\textit{map} \ :: \ (\textit{Char} \rightarrow \textit{IO} \ ()) \rightarrow [\textit{Char}] \rightarrow [\textit{IO} \ ()]
$$

This apparent anomaly can be resolved by noting that *map*, like *length*, *head*, and *tail*, does not really care what its list element types are, *as long as its functional argument can be applied to them*. Indeed, *map* is *polymorphic*, and its most general type is:

$$map \ :: \ (a \rightarrow b) \rightarrow [a] \rightarrow [b]$$

This can be read: "*map* is a function that takes a function from any type *a* to any type *b*, and a list of *a*'s, and returns a list of *b*'s." The correspondence between the two *a*'s and between the two *b*'s is important: A function that converts *Int*'s to *Char*'s, for example, cannot be mapped over a list of *Char*'s. It is easy to see that in the case of *transList*, *a* is instantiated as *Vertex* and *b* as *Point*, whereas in *putCharList*, *a* and *b* are instantiated as *Char* and *IO* (), respectively.

---

**DETAILS**

It was mentioned in Chapter 1 that every expression in Haskell has an associated type. But with polymorphism, you might wonder if there is just one type for every expression. For example, *map* could have any of these types:

$$(a \rightarrow b) \rightarrow [a] \rightarrow [b]$$
$$(Integer \rightarrow b) \rightarrow [Integer] \rightarrow [b]$$
$$(a \rightarrow Float) \rightarrow [a] \rightarrow [Float]$$
$$(Char \rightarrow Char) \rightarrow [Char] \rightarrow [Char]$$

and so on, depending on how it will be used. However, notice that the first of these types is in some fundamental sense more general than the other three. In fact, every expression in Haskell has a unique type known as its *principal type*: the least general type that captures all valid uses of the expression. The first type above is the principal type of *map*, because it captures all valid uses of *map*, yet is less general than, for example, the type $a \rightarrow b \rightarrow c$. As another example, the principal type of *head* is $[a] \rightarrow a$; the types $[b] \rightarrow a$, $b \rightarrow a$, or even $a$ are too general, whereas something like $[Integer] \rightarrow Integer$ is too specific.[1]

---

### 5.2.2 Using *map*

Now that we can picture *map* as a polymorphic function, it is useful to look back on some of the examples we have worked through to see if

---

[1] The existence of unique principal types is the hallmark feature of the *Hindley-Milner type system* (Hindley, 1969; Milner, 1978), which forms the basis of the type systems of Haskell, ML (Milner et al., 1990), and many other functional languages (Hudak, 1989).

there are any situations where *map* might have been helpful. For starters, recall from Section 1.4.3 the definition of *totalArea*:

*totalArea* = *listSum* [*circleArea* r1, *circleArea* r2, *circleArea* r3]

It should be clear that this can be rewritten as:

*totalArea* = *listSum* (*map circleArea* [r1, r2, r3])

A simple calculation is all that is needed to show that these are the same:

*map circleArea* [r1, r2, r3]
⇒   *circleArea* r1 : *map circleArea* [r2, r3]
⇒   *circleArea* r1 : *circleArea* r2 : *map circleArea* [r3]
⇒   *circleArea* r1 : *circleArea* r2 : *circleArea* r3 : *map circleArea* [ ]
⇒   *circleArea* r1 : *circleArea* r2 : *circleArea* r3 : [ ]
⇒   [*circleArea* r1, *circleArea* r2, *circleArea* r3]

Also recall from Section 4.3 the following function for drawing a list of colored shapes:

**type** *ColoredShapes* = [(*Color, Shape*)]


*drawShapes* :: *Window* → *ColoredShapes* → *IO* ()
*drawShapes* w [ ]
                    = *return* ()
*drawShapes* w ((c, s) : cs)
                    = **do** *draw* w (*withColor* c (*shapeToGraphic* s))
                          *drawShapes* w cs

Using the *sequence_* function introduced in Section 3.1, this can be redefined as:

*drawShapes* w css
    = *sequence_* (*map aux css*)
        **where** *aux* (c, s) = *draw* w (*withColor* c (*shapeToGraphic* s))

This example demonstrates that *map* can be used effectively for IO tasks. I would argue that this definition is clearer than the earlier one, because it abstracts away nicely the repeated IO operation in the function *aux*. A suitable reading of the above code might be: "Sequence together the successive actions of *aux* on each of the colored shapes." That reading is less obvious from the earlier recursive definition.

As a final example of the use of *map*, let's generate a list of eight concentric circles:

*conCircles* = *map circle* [2.4, 2.1..0.3]

---

**DETAILS**

A list [*a, b..c*] is called an *arithmetic sequence,* and is special syntax for the list [*a, a + d, a + 2 * d, ..., c*] where *d = b − a*. Thus, [2.4, 2.1..0.3] is shorthand for the list [2.4, 2.1, 1.8, 1.5, 1.2, 0.9, 0.6, 0.3].

---

We can pair each of these circles with a color:

*coloredCircles* =
    *zip* [*Black, Blue, Green, Cyan, Red, Magenta, Yellow, White*]
        *conCircles*

---

**DETAILS**

The *PreludeList* function *zip* (see Chapter 23) takes two lists and returns a list of the pairwise elements. For example:

*zip* [1, 2, 3] [4, 5, 6]  ⇒  [(1, 4), (2, 5), (3, 6)]

It is defined as:

*zip*                          ::  (*a* → *b* → *c*) → [*a*] → [*b*] → [*c*]
*zip* (*a* : *as*) (*b* : *bs*)  =  (*a, b*) : *zip as bs*
*zip* _ _                      =  [ ]

(Recall that _ is a wildcard pattern, which matches any argument.)

---

This list of color/circle pairs can then be drawn using *drawShapes*:

*main*
    = *runGraphics* (
        **do** *w* ← *openWindow* "Bull's Eye" (*xWin, yWin*)
            *drawShapes w coloredCircles*
            *spaceClose w*
        )

Note that *coloredCircles* is ordered largest circle first; thus *drawShapes* draws them in order of decreasing size (otherwise the larger circles would obscure the smaller ones!). A snapshot of *main* is shown in Fig. 5.1.

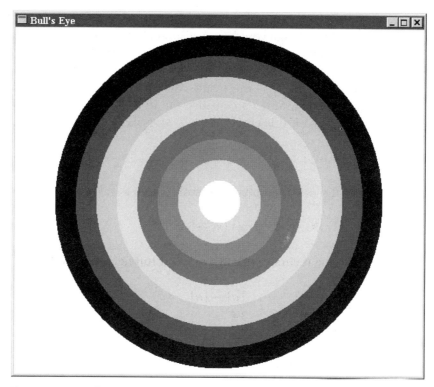

Figure 5.1: A Bull's Eye

In the remainder of the text we will be looking for opportunities to use *map* directly rather than after-the-fact. Indeed, there will be many such opportunities.

## 5.3 Append

Let's now consider the problem of *concatenating* or *appending* two lists together; that is, creating a third list that consists of all the elements from the first list followed by all of the elements of the second. Once again the type of list elements does not matter, so we will define this as polymorphic infix operator (++):

$$(\mathbin{++}) \ :: \ [a] \to [a] \to [a]$$

For example, here are two uses of (++) on different types:

$$[1, 2, 3] \mathbin{++} [4, 5, 6] \ \Longrightarrow \ [1, 2, 3, 4, 5, 6]$$
```
"hello" ++ "world"  ⟹  "hello world"
```

As usual, we can approach this problem by considering the various possibilities that could arise as input. But in the case of $(\!+\!\!+)$ we are given *two* inputs – so which do we consider first? In general, this is not an easy question, but in the case of $(\!+\!\!+)$ we can get a hint about what to do by noting that the result contains firstly all of the elements from the first list. So let's consider the first list first: It could be empty, or nonempty. If it is empty the answer is easy:

$$[\,] +\!\!+ ys \;=\; ys$$

and if it is not empty the answer is also straightforward:

$$(x : xs) +\!\!+ ys \;=\; x : (xs +\!\!+ ys)$$

Note the recursive use of $(\!+\!\!+)$. Our full definition is thus:

$$
\begin{aligned}
&(\!+\!\!+) &&:: \; [a] \rightarrow [a] \rightarrow [a] \\
&[\,] +\!\!+ ys &&= \; ys \\
&(x : xs) +\!\!+ ys &&= \; x : (xs +\!\!+ ys)
\end{aligned}
$$

If we were to have considered instead the second list first, the first equation would still be easy:

$$xs +\!\!+ [\,] \;=\; xs$$

but the second is not so obvious:

$$xs +\!\!+ (y : ys) \;=\; ??$$

So you see, we made the right choice to begin with.

### 5.3.1 The Efficiency and Fixity of Append

In Chapter 11 we will prove the following simple property about $(\!+\!\!+)$:

$$(xs +\!\!+ ys) +\!\!+ zs = xs +\!\!+ (ys +\!\!+ zs)$$

That is, $(\!+\!\!+)$ is *associative*.

But what about the efficiency of the left-hand and right-hand sides of this equation? It is easy to see via calculation that appending two lists together takes a number of steps proportional to the length of the first list (indeed the second list is not evaluated at all). For example:

$$[1, 2, 3] \mathbin{+\!\!+} xs$$
$$\Rightarrow \quad 1 : ([2, 3] \mathbin{+\!\!+} xs)$$
$$\Rightarrow \quad 1 : 2 : ([3] \mathbin{+\!\!+} xs)$$
$$\Rightarrow \quad 1 : 2 : 3 : ([\,] \mathbin{+\!\!+} xs)$$
$$\Rightarrow \quad 1 : 2 : 3 : xs$$

Therefore, the evaluation of $xs \mathbin{+\!\!+} (ys \mathbin{+\!\!+} zs)$ takes a number of steps proportional to the length of $xs$ plus the length of $ys$. But what about $(xs \mathbin{+\!\!+} ys) \mathbin{+\!\!+} zs$? The leftmost append will take a number of steps proportional to the length of $xs$, but then the rightmost append will require a number of steps proportional to the length of $xs$ plus the length of $ys$, for a total cost of:

$$2 * length \; xs + length \; ys$$

Thus, $xs \mathbin{+\!\!+} (ys \mathbin{+\!\!+} zs)$ is more efficient than $(xs \mathbin{+\!\!+} ys) \mathbin{+\!\!+} zs$. This is why the Standard Prelude defines the fixity of $(\mathbin{+\!\!+})$ as:

**infixr** 5 $\mathbin{+\!\!+}$

In other words, if you just write $xs \mathbin{+\!\!+} ys \mathbin{+\!\!+} zs$, you will get the most efficient association, namely the right association $xs \mathbin{+\!\!+} (ys \mathbin{+\!\!+} zs)$. In the next section a more dramatic example of this property will be demonstrated.

## 5.4 Fold

As another example of applying the abstraction principle to a pair of recursive definitions (such as we did for *map*), recall the definition of *listSum* in Section 1.4.3:

```
listSum        ::  [Float] → Float
listSum [ ]     =  0
listSum (x : xs)  =  x + listSum xs
```

Now let's suppose that we need to compute the *product* of the elements of a list. For example, suppose the list contains the number of different colors, sizes, shapes, and so on of boxes that are sold by some company, and we wish to compute exactly the total number of unique boxes. This is simply the product of the numbers in the list. And so we write:

$$
\begin{array}{lcl}
listProd & :: & [Float] \rightarrow Float \\
listProd\ [\,] & = & 1 \\
listProd\ (x:xs) & = & x * listProd\ xs
\end{array}
$$

Surely, these two definitions share something in common, as did *transList* and *putCharList*. Using the process that we used to discover *map*, let's first identify those things that are changing. There are two pairs: the 0 and 1 values (for which we'll use the generic name *init*, for "initial value"), and the (+) and (∗) operators (for which we'll use the generic name *op*, for "operator"). If we now rewrite either of the above functions as a new function – let's call it *fold* – that takes extra arguments *op* and *init*, we arrive at:[2]

$$
\begin{array}{lcl}
fold\ op\ init\ [\,] & = & init \\
fold\ op\ init\ (x:xs) & = & x\ `op`\ fold\ op\ init\ xs
\end{array}
$$

**DETAILS**
I chose infix application for *op* to reflect better the structure of the repeating pattern that we are abstracting.

From this it appears that *fold*'s type should be:

$$
fold\ ::\ (Float \rightarrow Float \rightarrow Float) \rightarrow Float \rightarrow [Float] \rightarrow Float
$$

With this definition of *fold* we can now rewrite the definitions of *listSum* and *listProd* as:

$$
\begin{array}{lcl}
listSum,\ listProd & :: & [Float] \rightarrow Float \\
listSum\ xs & = & fold\ (+)\ 0\ xs \\
listProd\ xs & = & fold\ (*)\ 1\ xs
\end{array}
$$

**DETAILS**
Just as we can turn a function into an operator by enclosing it in backquotes, we can turn an operator into a function by enclosing it in parentheses. This is required in order to pass an operator as a value to another function, as

---

[2] The use of the name "*fold*" for this function is historical, and has little to do with the use of "fold" and "unfold" to describe steps in a calculation.

in the examples above. (If we wrote *fold* + 0 *xs* instead of *fold* (+) 0 *xs* it would look like we were trying to add *fold* to 0 *xs*, which is nonsensical and ill-typed.)

In Chapter 11 we will use induction to prove that these new definitions are equivalent to the old ones.

The function *fold*, like *map*, is a highly useful, and reusable, function, as you will see through many examples in this text. Indeed, it too is polymorphic, for note that it does not depend on the type of the list elements. Its most general type – somewhat trickier than that for *map* – is:

$$fold \;::\; (a \to b \to b) \to b \to [a] \to b$$

This allows us to use *fold* whenever we need to "collapse" a list of elements using a binary (i.e., two-argument) operator.

### 5.4.1 Haskell's Folds

Haskell actually defines two versions of *fold* in the Standard Prelude. The first is called *foldr* ("fold-from-the-right"), which is defined the same as our *fold*:

$$
\begin{aligned}
foldr &\;::\; (a \to b \to b) \to b \to [a] \to b \\
foldr \; op \; init \; [\,] &= init \\
foldr \; op \; init \; (x : xs) &= x \; `op` \; foldr \; op \; init \; xs
\end{aligned}
$$

A good way to think about *foldr* is that it replaces all occurrences of the list operator (:) with its first argument (a function), and replaces [ ] with its second argument. In other words:

$$
\begin{aligned}
&foldr \; op \; init \; (x1 : x2 : \ldots : xn : [\,]) \\
&\Longrightarrow \; x1 \; `op` \; (x2 \; `op` \; (\ldots \; (xn \; `op` \; init) \; \ldots))
\end{aligned}
$$

This might help you to understand the type of *foldr* better, and also explains its name: the list is "folded from the right." Stated another way, for any list *xs*, the following always holds:[3]

$$foldr \; (:) \; [\,] \; xs \;\Longrightarrow\; xs$$

---

[3] We will formally prove this in Chapter 11.

Haskell's second version of *fold* is called *foldl*:

*foldl* :: $(b \rightarrow a \rightarrow b) \rightarrow b \rightarrow [a] \rightarrow b$
*foldl op init* [ ] = *init*
*foldl op init* ($x : xs$) = *foldl op* (*init* 'op' $x$) *xs*

A good way to think about *foldl* is to imagine "folding the list from the left":

*foldl op init* ($x1 : x2 : \ldots : xn : [\,]$)
$\Longrightarrow$ $(\ldots ((init \text{ 'op' } x1) \text{ 'op' } x2) \ldots) \text{ 'op' } xn$

### 5.4.2 Why Two Folds?

Note that if we had used *foldl* instead of *foldr* in the definitions given earlier for *listSum* and *listProd*:

*listSum, listProd* :: [*Integer*] $\rightarrow$ *Integer*
*listSum xs* = *foldl* (+) 0 *xs*
*listProd xs* = *foldl* (∗) 1 *xs*

then nothing would have changed; *foldr* and *foldl* give the same result. Indeed, judging from their types, it looks like the only difference between *foldr* and *foldl* is that each takes its arguments in a different order.

So why does Haskell define two versions of *fold*? It turns out that there are situations where using one is more efficient, and possibly "more defined," than the other. (By more defined, I mean that the function terminates on more values of its input domain.)

Probably the simplest example of this is a generalization of the associativity of (++) discussed in the last section. Suppose that we wish to collapse a list of lists into one list. The Standard Prelude defines the polymorphic function *concat* for this purpose:

*concat* :: [[a]] $\rightarrow$ [a]
*concat xss* = *foldr* (++) [ ] *xss*

For example:

*concat* [[1], [3, 4], [ ], [5, 6]]
$\Rightarrow$ [1, 2, 3, 4, 5, 6]

More importantly, from the earlier discussion it should be clear that this property holds:

*concat* [$xs1, xs2, \ldots, xsn$]
$\Rightarrow$ *foldr* (++) [ ] [$xs1, xs2, \ldots, xsn$]
$\Rightarrow$ $xs1 ++ (xs2 ++ (\ldots (xn ++ [\,])) \ldots)$

The total cost of this computation is proportional to the sum of the lengths of all the lists. If each list has the same length *len*, then this cost is $n * len$.

On the other hand, if we had defined *concat* this way:

$$slowConcat\ xss\ =\ foldl\ (+\!\!+)\ [\ ]\ xss$$

then we have:

$$
\begin{aligned}
&slowConcat\ [xs1,\ xs2,\ \ldots,\ xsn] \\
&\Rightarrow\ foldl\ (+\!\!+)\ [\ ]\ [xs1,\ xs2,\ \ldots,\ xsn] \\
&\Rightarrow\ (\ldots\ (([\ ] +\!\!+ x1) +\!\!+ x2)\ \ldots) +\!\!+ xn
\end{aligned}
$$

If each list has the same length *len*, then the cost of this computation will be:

$$
\begin{aligned}
&len + (len + len) + (len + len + len) + \ldots + (n - 1) * len \\
&\Rightarrow\ n * (n - 1) * len
\end{aligned}
$$

which is considerably worse than $n * len$. Thus, the choice of *foldr* in the definition of *concat* is quite important.

Similar examples can be given to demonstrate that *foldl* is sometimes more efficient than *foldr*. On the other hand, in many cases the choice does not matter at all (consider, for example, (+)). The moral of all this is that care must be taken in the choice between *foldr* and *foldl* if efficiency is a concern.

## 5.5  A Final Example: Reverse

As a final example, consider the problem of creating a list that is the *reverse* of a given list, which I will capture in a function called *reverse*. For example, *reverse* [1, 2, 3] is [3, 2, 1]. Thus, *reverse* takes a single list argument, whose possibilities are the normal ones for a list: It is either empty, or it is not. And so we write:

$$
\begin{aligned}
reverse &\quad ::\quad [a] \to [a] \\
reverse\ [\ ] &\quad =\quad [\ ] \\
reverse\ (x : xs) &\quad =\quad reverse\ xs +\!\!+ [x]
\end{aligned}
$$

This, in fact, is a perfectly good definition for *reverse*. It is certainly clear, except for one small problem: It is terribly inefficient! To see why, first note that the number of steps needed to compute $xs +\!\!+ ys$ is proportional to the length of *xs*. Now suppose that the list argument to *reverse* has length $n$. The recursive call to *reverse* will return a list of length $n - 1$, which is the first argument to $(+\!\!+)$. Thus, the cost to reverse a list of length of $n$ will be proportional to $n - 1$ plus the cost to reverse a list of length $n - 1$. So the total cost is proportional to $(n - 1) + (n - 2) + \cdots + 1 = n(n - 1)/2$, which in turn is proportional to the square of $n$. Can we do better than this? Yes we can.

There is another algorithm for reversing a list, which goes something like this: Take the first element, and put it at the front of an empty auxiliary list; then take the next element and add it to the front of the auxiliary list (thus the auxiliary list now consists of the first two elements in the original list, but in reverse order); then do this again and again until you reach the end of the original list. At that point the auxiliary list will be the reverse of the original one.

This algorithm can be expressed recursively, but the auxiliary list implies that we need a function that takes *two* arguments – the original list and the auxiliary one – yet *reverse* only takes one. So we create an auxiliary function *rev*:

$$
\begin{aligned}
\textit{reverse xs} \ &= \ \textit{rev} \ [ \ ] \ \textit{xs} \\
\textbf{where} \ \textit{rev acc} \ [ \ ] \quad &= \ \textit{acc} \\
\textit{rev acc} \ (x : \textit{xs}) \ &= \ \textit{rev} \ (x : \textit{acc}) \ \textit{xs}
\end{aligned}
$$

The auxiliary list is the first argument to *rev*, and is called *acc* because it behaves as an "accumulator" of the intermediate results. Note how it is returned as the final result once the end of the original list is reached.

A little thought should convince you that this function does not have the quadratic ($n^2$) behavior of the first algorithm, and indeed can be shown to execute a number of steps that is directly proportional to the length of the list, which we can hardly expect to improve upon.

But now, compare the definition of *rev* with the definition of *foldl*:

$$
\begin{aligned}
\textit{foldl op init} \ [ \ ] \quad &= \ \textit{init} \\
\textit{foldl op init} \ (x : \textit{xs}) \ &= \ \textit{foldl op} \ (\textit{init} \ `op` \ x) \ \textit{xs}
\end{aligned}
$$

They are somewhat similar. In fact, suppose we were to slightly rewrite *rev*, yielding:

$$
\begin{aligned}
\textit{rev op acc} \ [ \ ] \quad &= \ \textit{acc} \\
\textit{rev op acc} \ (x : \textit{xs}) \ &= \ \textit{rev op} \ (\textit{acc} \ `op` \ x) \ \textit{xs}
\end{aligned}
$$

Now *rev* looks exactly like *foldl*, and the question becomes whether or not there is a function that can be substituted for *op* that would make the latter definition of *rev* equivalent to the former one. Indeed there is:

$$revOp\ a\ b\ =\ b : a$$

For note that:

$$acc\ `revOp`\ x\ \Rightarrow\ revOp\ acc\ x\ \Rightarrow\ x : acc$$

So *reverse* can be rewritten as:

$$reverse\ xs\ =\ rev\ revOp\ [\ ]\ xs$$
$$\mathbf{where}\ rev\ op\ acc\ [\ ]\qquad=\ acc$$
$$rev\ op\ acc\ (x : xs)\ =\ rev\ op\ (acc\ `op`\ x)\ xs$$

which is the same as:

$$reverse\ xs\ =\ foldl\ revOp\ [\ ]\ xs$$

## 5.6  Errors

Recall the *Shape* data type from Chapter 2. What if negative side lengths are used with the *Rectangle* constructor, or negative radii with the *Ellipse*? This may or may not make sense, depending on the application. In Chapter 8, I will argue that in some cases it does make sense, but careful consideration of these potentially anomalous situations is important. If negative side lengths are used, *area* may compute a negative area. And what will happen when such a figure is drawn?

There are many ways to deal with such situations, again depending on the application, but sometimes we wish to literally stop the program, signaling to the user that some kind of an *error* has occurred. In Haskell this is done with the Standard Prelude function *error* :: *String* → *a*. Note that *error* is polymorphic, meaning that it can be used with any data type. The value of the expression *error s* is ⊥, the completely undefined, or "bottom" value. As an example of its use, suppose that we wish to signal an error when the area of a rectangle with negative side lengths is attempted. We can write:

$$area\ (Rectangle\ s1\ s2)$$
$$|\ s1 >= 0\ \&\&\ s2 >= 0\ =\ s1 * s2$$
$$|\ otherwise\qquad\quad=\ error\ \text{``area: negative side lengths''}$$

The effect of this change is that if the anomalous situation arises, the program will terminate immediately, and the string "area: negative side lengths" will be printed to the standard output area.

**DETAILS**

(&&) and (∥) are Haskell's Boolean "and" and "or" operators, respectively. *b*1 && *b*2 should be read "*b*1 and *b*2"; similarly for (∥). They are defined in the Standard Prelude as:

$$
\begin{aligned}
(\&\&), (\|) \quad &:: \quad Bool \rightarrow Bool \rightarrow Bool \\
True \,\&\&\, x \quad &= \quad x \\
False \,\&\&\, \_ \quad &= \quad False \\
True \parallel \_ \quad &= \quad True \\
False \parallel x \quad &= \quad x
\end{aligned}
$$

Just as we used the constructors in the *Shape* data type for pattern matching in previous chapters, here we are pattern matching against the constructors *True* and *False* of the *Bool* data type.

---

**Exercise 5.1** Rewrite the equation for the area of a polygon given in Section 2.2 in a higher-order, nonrecursive way, using operators such as *map*, *fold*, and so on.

---

**Exercise 5.2** What is the principal type of each of the following expressions:

> *map map*
> *foldl foldl*
> *map foldl*

---

**Exercise 5.3** Rewrite the definition of *length* nonrecursively.

---

**Exercise 5.4** Using higher-order functions that we have now defined, fill in the two missing functions, *f*1 and *f*2, in the evaluation below so that it is valid:

> *f*1 (*f*2 (∗) [1, 2, 3, 4]) 5 ⇒ [5, 10, 15, 20]

---

**Exercise 5.5** Define a function that behaves as each of the following:

1. Doubles each number in a list. For example:

   > *doubleEach* [1, 2, 3] ⇒ [2, 4, 6]

2. Pairs each element in a list with that number and one plus that number. For example:

   > *pairAndOne* [1, 2, 3] ⇒ [(1, 2), (2, 3), (3, 4)]

**3.** Adds together each pair of numbers in a list. For example:

*addEachPair* [(1, 2), (3, 4), (5, 6)] ⟹ [3, 7, 11]

In this exercise and the two that follow, give both recursive and (if possible) nonrecursive definitions, and be sure to include type signatures.

---

**Exercise 5.6** Define a function *maxList* that computes the maximum element of a list. Define *minList* analogously.

---

**Exercise 5.7** Define a function that adds "pointwise" the elements of a list of pairs. For example:

*addPairsPointwise* [(1, 2), (3, 4), (5, 6)] ⟹ (9, 12)

---

**Exercise 5.8** Freddie the Frog wants to communicate privately with his girlfriend Francine by *encrypting* messages sent to her. Frog brains are not large, so they agree on this simple strategy: Each character in the text shall be converted to the character "one greater" than it, based on the representation described below (with wrap-around from 255 to 0). Define functions *encrypt* and *decrypt* that will allow Freddie and Francine to communicate using this strategy.

Hint: Characters are often represented inside a computer as some kind of an integer; in the case of Haskell, a 16-bit unicode representation is used. For this exercise, you will want to use two Haskell functions, *toEnum* and *fromEnum*. The first will convert an integer into a character, the second will convert a character into an integer.

---

**Exercise 5.9** Suppose you are given a nonnegative integer *amt* representing a sum of money, and a list of coin denominations [$v1$, $v2$, ..., $vn$], each being a positive integer. Your job is to make change for *amt* using the coins in the coin supply. Define a function *makeChange* to solve this problem. For example, your function may behave like this:

*makeChange* 99 [5, 1] ⇒ [19, 4]

where 99 is the amount and [5, 1] represents the types of coins (say, nickels and pennies in U.S. currency) that we have. The answer [19, 4] means that we can make the exact change with 19 five-unit coins and 4 single-unit coins; this is the best (in terms of the total number of coins) possible solution.

To make things slightly easier, you may assume that the list representing the coin denominations is given in descending order, and that the single-unit coin is always one of the coin types.

CHAPTER SIX

# Shapes III: Perimeters of Shapes

In this chapter, I will extend the *Shape* module first introduced in Chapter 2 with the ability to compute the *perimeters* of geometric shapes. In the process several techniques involving polymorphic higher-order functions learned in the last chapter will be used. I will also introduce a new idea: the *infinite list*.

Our goal will be to define a new module *Perimeter*, which imports the *Shape* module and exports just one function, *perimeter*, to be defined shortly:

> **module** *Perimeter* (*perimeter*,
>                  **module** *Shape*
>                  ) **where**
> **import** *Shape*

This module also does something new: It exports the entire *Shape* module, as indicated by the phrase "**module** *Shape*" in the export list. The rationale for doing this is that a user of the *Perimeter* module will likely want to use the *Shape* module as well; such a user need only import *Perimeter* now instead of both *Shape* and *Perimeter*.

---

**DETAILS**

To export only a subset of the entities imported from *Shape*, you can omit "**module** *Shape*" from the export list, and simply name explicitly those entities from *Shape* that you want exported.

---

## 6.1 Perimeters of Shapes

Our task is to define a function *perimeter* to compute the perimeters of geometric shapes:

> *perimeter* :: *Shape* → *Float*

Recalling the *Shape* datatype defined in Section 2.1, it is quite straight-forward to compute the perimeters of two of the shapes:

$$perimeter \ (Rectangle \ s1 \ s2) \ \ = \ \ 2 * (s1 + s2)$$
$$perimeter \ (RtTriangle \ s1 \ s2) \ \ = \ \ s1 + s2 + sqrt \ (s1\,\hat{}\,2 + s2\,\hat{}\,2)$$

Next, consider polygons, for which the algorithm, at least, is clear: Simply add together the lengths of each side. But first we have to compute the side lengths. Given the list of vertices of a polygon, we can compute a list of side lengths by:

$$
\begin{aligned}
&sides \qquad\quad :: \ \ [Vertex] \rightarrow [Side] \\
&sides \ [\,] \quad\ \ = \ \ [\,] \\
&sides \ (v : vs) \ = \ \ aux \ v \ vs \\
&\quad \textbf{where} \ aux \ v1 \ (v2 : vs') \ = \ distBetween \ v1 \ v2 : aux \ v2 \ vs' \\
&\qquad\qquad\ aux \ vn \ [\,] \qquad\quad\ \ = \ distBetween \ vn \ v : [\,]
\end{aligned}
$$

The auxiliary function *aux* is defined in a **where** clause nested within *sides* so that it can refer to the first vertex *v* of the original list when it gets to the last vertex *vn*.

This is not the only way to define *sides*. Using polymorphic higher-order functions, it's possible to define it without using recursion.

<hr>

**DETAILS**

I will use the function *zipWith* from the PreludeList module, which takes a function and two lists, and applies the function to successive pairs of elements from the two lists, returning the results in a list. For example:

$$zipWith \ (+) \ [1, 2, 3] \ [4, 5, 6] \ \Rightarrow \ [5, 7, 9]$$

The function *zipWith* can be seen as a generalization of *zip* introduced in the last chapter. Indeed, *zip* is defined in terms of *zipWith* (see Chapter 23).

<hr>

Suppose that the function *distBetween* is used as the first argument to *zipWith*. Then to get a list of side lengths, the two lists that we want are the original list of vertices *vs* and the list (*tail vs* ++ [*head vs*]) (recall that (++) concatenates two lists together). In other words:

$$
\begin{aligned}
&sides \quad\ :: \ \ [Vertex] \rightarrow [Side] \\
&sides \ vs \ = \ zipWith \ distBetween \ vs \ (tail \ vs \mathbin{+\!+} [head \ vs])
\end{aligned}
$$

As a validity check, note that the first element in the result will be *distBetween v1 v2*, and the last element will be *distBetween vn v1*.

Deciding which of these definitions of *sides* is better is a matter of personal taste, although I encourage you to seek out the higher-order, nonrecursive solutions because that style of programming takes more practice than straight recursion, but can lead to very nice results. (Proving these two recursive definitions equivalent again requires *induction*, which we will study in Chapter 11.)

In any case, returning to the problem of computing perimeters, we can write:

$$perimeter\ (Polygon\ vs)\ \ =\ \ foldl\ (+)\ 0\ (sides\ vs)$$

and we are done with polygons!

But what about the perimeter of an ellipse? This will turn out to be our greatest challenge. As discussed in Chapter 1, we should first make sure that we understand the problem well, and so we begin with the mathematics, which tells us that if we define the *eccentricity e* of an ellipse by:

$$e = \frac{\sqrt{r_1^2 - r_2^2}}{r_1}$$

where $r_1$ is the larger of the two radii, then the perimeter is given by the integral:

$$p = 4r_1 \int_{-\pi/2}^{0} \sqrt{1 - e^2 \cos^2 u}\ \ du$$

In the case of a circle, $e = 0$, and the above reduces to the familiar formula $2\pi r$. But for a general ellipse, the above cannot be simplified to any elementary formula. Instead, numerical techniques must be used to approximate it. One might try to directly compute the integral numerically, but, for reasons beyond the scope of this text, a more common approach is to rewrite the integral as a mathematical series of some sort. In the case of the integral above, one such form suitable for numerical evaluation is given as follows. Define the sequence *s* by:

$$
\begin{aligned}
s_1 \ &= \ \tfrac{1}{4}e^2 \\
s_i \ &= \ s_{i-1} \cdot \tfrac{(2i-1)(2i-3)}{4i^2} \cdot e^2, \ \ i \ge 2
\end{aligned}
\tag{1}
$$

The perimeter is then given by:

$$p = 2r_1\pi \left(1 - \sum_{i=1}^{\infty} s_i\right)$$

So much for the mathematics. Now how do we compute this in Haskell? An infinite summation is out of the question, of course, but the thing to note about the sequence $s$ is that each element is smaller than one, and the sequence is monotonically *decreasing* toward zero (i.e., each $s_i$ is slightly smaller than the previous value $s_{i-1}$). On a digital computer we are limited in our ability to compute with real numbers by the accuracy of our choice of number representation, in this case floating-point numbers. At some index $j$ the value of $s_j$ will be smaller than the smallest value $\epsilon$ that we can represent, so there is no use computing elements of the sequence beyond $s_j$.

Therefore, we can test to see if each generated element is smaller than some threshold *epsilon*, whose value in practice should be several times the true $\epsilon$. Of course, we can choose *epsilon* to be even larger; indeed, this choice provides us with a way to control the *accuracy* of the result. Smaller values of *epsilon* yield greater accuracy, but also take longer to compute. (Why?) So, depending on the performance demands and required accuracy of our application, we can adjust *epsilon* accordingly.

For now, let's define *epsilon* as:

*epsilon* = 0.0001 :: *Float*

The eccentricity $e$ is easily defined as:

$e$ = *sqrt* $(r1\hat{}2 - r2\hat{}2)/r1$

Next, how do we compute the summation? It should be clear that we could define a recursive function to accumulate elements of the sequence, returning the sum when the element size becomes less than *epsilon*. But instead, let's try to write a nonrecursive version using higher-order functions. To begin, we define a function *nextEl* that takes a previous sequence element and a current index, and generates from it the current sequence element:

```
nextEl      ::  Float → Float → Float → Float
nextEl e s i  =   s * (2 * i − 1) * (2 * i − 3) * (e^2)/(4 * i^2)
```

This is just the Haskell translation of equation (1).

Using the polymorphic list function *scanl* defined in the Standard Prelude, we will be able to define the sequence *s* easily.

---

**DETAILS**

The function *scanl* behaves just like *foldl* except that it returns a list of intermediate results. For example:

*scanl* $(+)$ 0 [1, 2, 3] $\Rightarrow$ [0, 1, 3, 6]

It is defined in the Standard Prelude (see Chapter 23) as:

| *scanl* | :: | $(a \to b \to a) \to a \to [b] \to [a]$ |
|---|---|---|
| *scanl f q* [ ] | = | $q : [ ]$ |
| *scanl f q* $(x : xs)$ | = | $q : scanl\ f\ (f\ q\ x)\ xs$ |

---

With *scanl* we can express the infinite sequence *s* as:

$s$ = **let** *aux s i* = *nextEl e s i*
    **in** *scanl aux* $(0.25 * e\hat{\ }2)$ [2..]

---

**DETAILS**

A list [a, b..] is special syntax for the infinite list $a : a + d : a + 2 * d : a + 3 * d : \cdots$ where $d = b - a$. Similarly, [a..] is shorthand for the infinite list $a : a + 1 : a + 2 : a + 3 : \cdots$. Thus, [2..] is the infinite list $2 : 3 : 4 : \cdots$. (Expressions such as these are called *arithmetic sequences* and are discussed further in Chapter 24.)

---

If you have some doubts about this, it may help to unfold the first few iterations of the recursive definition of *scanl*. Most importantly, however, do not be alarmed that this list is infinite! If you tried to print *s* on your computer screen, or tried to compute its length, your program would not terminate. However, nothing will go wrong if we are interested only in some *finite part* of the list. Stated another way, Haskell will only generate the part of the list that other parts of your program depend on; this is called *lazy evaluation*. In our case we are interested in all elements of the list up to the one whose value is less than *epsilon*. (Much more will be said about infinite lists in Chapter 14.)

Using one other polymorphic list function from the Standard Prelude, our job will be complete.

**DETAILS**
The function *takeWhile* takes a predicate *p* and a list *xs*, and returns the longest (possibly empty) prefix of *xs*, all of whose elements satisfy the predicate *p*. It is defined in the Standard Prelude (see Chapter 23) as:

$$takeWhile \quad :: \quad (a \to Bool) \to [a] \to [a]$$
$$takeWhile\ p\ [\ ] \quad = \quad [\ ]$$
$$takeWhile\ p\ (x : xs)$$
$$\mid p\ x \qquad = \quad x : takeWhile\ p\ xs$$
$$\mid otherwise \quad = \quad [\ ]$$

The last two lines above use a *guard* to place a qualification on the pattern-matching. Specifically, if the pattern (*x* : *xs*) succeeds, then the guard (*p x*) is evaluated. If it is true, then its right-hand side is the result; otherwise, the next guard is tried, which in this case is the keyword *otherwise*, which always succeeds.

*True* and *False* are called *Boolean values*, and have type *Bool*, which is a data type defined in the Standard Prelude as:

**data** *Bool* = *False* | *True*

Using *takeWhile* we can express the subsequence of *s* that we are interested in as:

**let** *test x* = *x* > *epsilon*
**in** *takeWhile test s*

With this discussion now behind us, let's write out the full definition for the perimeter of an ellipse:

$$perimeter\ (Ellipse\ r1\ r2)$$
$$\mid r1 > r2 \quad = \quad ellipsePerim\ r1\ r2$$
$$\mid otherwise \quad = \quad ellipsePerim\ r2\ r1$$
$$\textbf{where}\ ellipsePerim\ r1\ r2$$
$$= \textbf{let}\ e \qquad = \quad sqrt\ (r1\hat{}2 - r2\hat{}2)/r1$$
$$s \qquad\quad = \quad scanl\ aux\ (0.25 * e\hat{}2)\ [2..]$$
$$aux\ s\ i \ = \quad nextEl\ e\ s\ i$$
$$test\ x \quad = \quad x > epsilon$$
$$sSum \quad = \quad foldl\ (+)\ 0\ (takeWhile\ test\ s)$$
$$\textbf{in}\ 2 * r1 * pi * (1 - sSum)$$

**DETAILS**

The second and third lines above are another example of the use of pattern guards. If the pattern (*Ellipse r1 r2*) succeeds, then the guard $r1 > r2$ is evaluated. If it is true, then its right-hand side is the result; otherwise, the next guard is tried, which in this case is the *otherwise* keyword, which always succeeds.

Remember that our formula for the perimeter only works when $r1$ is greater than $r2$. This condition is checked by the guards, so that the auxiliary function *ellipsePerim* always receives the radii in the correct order. Hopefully, you can relate the rest of the code back to the original formula straightforwardly.

# CHAPTER SEVEN

# Trees

We have so far only scratched the surface of the many kinds of useful data types that can be created in Haskell. In this chapter I will introduce the use of *recursive* and *tree-shaped* data types. In the process we will look at a few motivating examples of trees, but will use them more concretely in the next chapter when we create a data type of *geometric regions*.

## 7.1  A Tree Data Type

In Chapter 2 we defined a data type called *Shape*:

> **data** *Shape*  =  *Rectangle Side Side*
> |  *Ellipse Radius Radius*
> |  *RtTriangle Side Side*
> |  *Polygon* [*Vertex*]
> **deriving** *Show*
>
> **type** *Radius*  =  *Float*
> **type** *Side*  =  *Float*
> **type** *Vertex*  =  (*Float, Float*)

Note that every value created of this type has the same relative size, except that the list of vertices in a polygon can be arbitrarily long. In fact, lists are an example of a data type whose elements can be of any size, from [ ] to a conceptually infinite list. Lists are built-in to the Haskell language, but if they weren't, we could easily define a data type that would behave in the same way:

> **data** *List a*  =  *Nil* | *MkList a* (*List a*)

There are two things different about this data type from ones we've defined earlier. First, it is *polymorphic*. This is indicated by the fact that the name of the type, *List*, takes a type as an argument. In other words, the principal types of the constructors are:

$$Nil \quad :: \; List \; a$$
$$MkList \; :: \; a \rightarrow List \; a \rightarrow List \; a$$

which are in direct correspondence with the types of Haskell's built-in list constructors:

$$[\,] \; :: \; [a]$$
$$(:) \; :: \; a \rightarrow [a] \rightarrow [a]$$

The second important aspect of the *List* data type definition is that it is *recursive*. That is, the type *List a* is defined in terms of *List a*. This recursive structure is what allows lists to be arbitrarily long (or even infinite), just as a recursive function may be called an arbitrary number of times (or even loop forever).

Another thing to note about the recursive structure of *List a* is that it is *linear*, meaning that for each constructor specification there is at most one occurrence of the recursive type.[1] In other words, lists look like linear sequences of elements.

In contrast, suppose we were to define:

**data** *Tree a* = *Leaf a* | *Branch* (*Tree a*) (*Tree a*)

Here *Branch* has *two* references to *Tree a*, and so we say (as implied by the name) that this is a *tree-shaped* data type, because values of this type look like upside-down trees. This is also why we use *Branch* for the name of the constructor that has two branches – also called *subtrees* – and *Leaf* for the name of the constructor at the very end of a branch.

Note also that *Tree a* is polymorphic, but it doesn't have to be; consider these alternatives:

**data** *IntegerTree* = *Leaf Integer* | *Branch IntegerTree IntegerTree*
**data** *SimpleTree* = *Leaf* | *Branch SimpleTree SimpleTree*

*IntegerTree* only allows integers to be stored in the leaves, and *SimpleTree* has no internal values at all (it may thus have limited use, but it is still perfectly valid).

---

[1] For mutually recursive types this definition needs to be generalized somewhat.

Note that the polymorphic *Tree* data type allows us to place elements in the leaves of the tree, just as we place elements in lists. But the choice of where to place the elements isn't fixed either; we could choose instead to place the elements on the internal branches:

**data** *InternalTree a*  =  *ILeaf*
                    |  *IBranch a* (*InternalTree a*) (*InternalTree a*)

Or we could place elements in leaves *and* branches – in fact, the elements do not have to be of the same type:

**data** *FancyTree a b*  =  *FLeaf a*
                    |  *FBranch b* (*FancyTree a b*) (*FancyTree a b*)

Note now that *FancyTree* is polymorphic in *two* types, *a* and *b*. For example, *FBranch* 42 (*FLeaf True*) (*FLeaf False*) is a proper value of type *FancyTree Bool Integer*.

At this point you should realize that almost anything is possible; it just depends on your application. In the next chapter we will design a tree-shaped data type that has more than one branch-like constructor; in fact it has some linear constructors as well.

In any case, it is helpful to consider the "generic" kinds of trees, such as defined above, and the kinds of operations that might be used with them. For the examples in the next section, we will use the *Tree* data type that we first defined.

## 7.2  Operations on Trees

One common operation that we perform on trees is to apply a function to each of its elements, returning a new tree as a result. From our experience with *map* on lists, we can guess that the type that we want is:

$$mapTree \; :: \; (a \rightarrow b) \rightarrow Tree \; a \rightarrow Tree \; b$$

Indeed, the definition of *mapTree* is not unlike that of *map*:

```
mapTree f (Leaf x)     =  Leaf (f x)
mapTree f (Branch t1 t2) =  Branch (mapTree f t1)
                                   (mapTree f t2)
```

Another operation is to gather together the leaves of the tree and return them in a list. We define a function *fringe* to do this:

$$
\begin{array}{lcl}
\textit{fringe} & :: & \textit{Tree } a \rightarrow [a] \\
\textit{fringe } (\textit{Leaf } x) & = & [x] \\
\textit{fringe } (\textit{Branch } t1\ t2) & = & \textit{fringe } t1 \mathbin{+\!\!+} \textit{fringe } t2
\end{array}
$$

We may also wish to define a function that computes the size (i.e., the number of leaves) of a tree:

$$
\begin{array}{lcl}
\textit{treeSize} & :: & \textit{Tree } a \rightarrow \textit{Integer} \\
\textit{treeSize } (\textit{Leaf } x) & = & 1 \\
\textit{treeSize } (\textit{Branch } t1\ t2) & = & \textit{treeSize } t1 + \textit{treeSize } t2
\end{array}
$$

Let's also define a function to measure tree height, where we define a leaf as having a height of 0:

$$
\begin{array}{lcl}
\textit{treeHeight} & :: & \textit{Tree } a \rightarrow \textit{Integer} \\
\textit{treeHeight } (\textit{Leaf } x) & = & 0 \\
\textit{treeHeight } (\textit{Branch } t1\ t2) & = & 1 + \textit{max } (\textit{treeHeight } t1) \\
& & \quad\quad\quad\quad\ (\textit{treeHeight } t2)
\end{array}
$$

## 7.3 Arithmetic Expressions

One common example of a tree-shaped data type is the set of *arithmetic expressions*. For example, the arithmetic expression $(10 + 8/2) * (7 - 4)$ can be seen as the tree shown in Fig. 7.1.

We can capture this idea as a Haskell data type as follows:

$$
\begin{array}{lcl}
\textbf{data } \textit{Expr} & = & \textit{C Float} \mid \textit{Add Expr Expr} \mid \textit{Sub Expr Expr} \\
& \mid & \textit{Mul Expr Expr} \mid \textit{Div Expr Expr}
\end{array}
$$

Alternatively, we can make this look a little more like an actual arithmetic

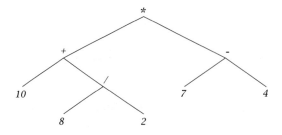

Figure 7.1: Tree-shaped Arithmetic Expression

expression by using infix constructors, as in:

**data** *Expr* = *C Float* | *Expr* :+ *Expr* | *Expr* :− *Expr*
　　　　　| *Expr* :* *Expr* | *Expr* :/ *Expr*

---

**DETAILS**

Infix constructors are just like infix operators in Haskell, but they must begin with a colon. This distinction exists to make it easier to discern pattern matching against infix constructors, and is analogous to the distinction between ordinary names (which must begin with a lower-case character) and constructor names (which must begin with an upper-case character).

---

A floating-point constant such as 42 has the form *C* 42 in this representation, and the remaining constructors perform addition, subtraction, multiplication, and division, respectively. For example, the expression $(10 + 8/2) * (7 − 4)$ given earlier is represented by:

$$(C\ 10\ :+\ (C\ 8\ :/\ C\ 2))\ :*\ (C\ 7\ :−\ C\ 4)$$

An obvious operation that we would like to perform on an *Expr* value is *evaluation*; that is, the computation of its value. For example, the above arithmetic expression has the value 42. We can capture this operation in a function:

*evaluate* :: *Expr* → *Float*

whose definition is quite straightforward:

```
evaluate (C x)      = x
evaluate (e1 :+ e2) = evaluate e1 + evaluate e2
evaluate (e1 :− e2) = evaluate e1 − evaluate e2
evaluate (e1 :* e2) = evaluate e1 * evaluate e2
evaluate (e1 :/ e2) = evaluate e1 / evaluate e2
```

The function *evaluate* is a simple example of an *interpreter* of a language. In this case, the language is very simple, the language of arithmetic expressions. But conceptually, an interprepter for a language such as Haskell works in just the same way: A Haskell program is represented internally as a tree data type, and the Haskell interpreter "walks over the tree" to compute its value. In later chapters we will see other examples of interpreters.

---

**Exercise 7.1**  Look at the definitions of *fringe* and *treeSize*. Recall in Chapter 1 the observation that led to the development of *fold*. Apply that idea here by designing a higher-order function that captures the common pattern of recursion, and then redefine *fringe* and *treeSize* in terms of it. Now do the same for *treeHeight*. Can you think of other useful functions that can be defined in terms of your higher-order function?

---

**Exercise 7.2**  Using this definition of trees:

> **data** *InternalTree a*  =  *ILeaf*
>                        |  *IBranch a* (*InternalTree a*) (*InternalTree a*)

define functions:

> *takeTree*       ::  *Int* → *InternalTree a* → *InternalTree a*
> *takeTreeWhile* ::  (*a* → *Bool*) → *InternalTree a* → *InternalTree a*

The function *takeTree* returns the first *n* levels in a tree. For example, if:

> *t*  =  **let** *t′*  =  *IBranch* 1 *ILeaf* *ILeaf*
>           **in** *Branch* 2 *t′* *t′*

then *takeTree* 0 *t* ⟹ *ILeaf* and *takeTree* 1 *t* ⟹ *IBranch* 2 *ILeaf* *ILeaf*. *takeTreeWhile* should behave analogously.

---

**Exercise 7.3**  Using the *InternalTree* data type from the last exercise, define tree versions of the functions *foldr* and *repeat* (there may be more than one way to define these).

---

**Exercise 7.4**  Using any of the above definitions of trees, define tree versions of the list functions *zip* and *zipWith*.

---

**Exercise 7.5**  Enhance the *Expr* data type with *variables* and *let expressions*, similar in intent to Haskell's variables and let expressions, although you may assume that the let expression does not allow recursive definitions. Also enhance the *evaluate* function to yield the proper value. For example:

> *evaluate* (*Let* "x" (*C* 5) (*V* "x" :+ *V* "x"))
>    ⟹  10

where *Let* and *V* are the new constructors in the *Expr* data type. Unbound variables should be treated as errors.

# CHAPTER EIGHT

# A Module of Regions

In this chapter I will use ideas developed in the last chapter to extend the functionality of geometric shapes defined in Chapter 2. In particular, we will consider the problem of combining shapes into larger, possibly overlapping, *regions*. We will not be interested in computing the area or perimeter of these regions (no easy task, by the way, with the shapes allowed to overlap in arbitrary ways), but rather we will want to know whether a particular point lies within a region. Regions are thus located on a two-dimensional (i.e., *Cartesian*) plane.

The functionality that we develop will be encapsulated in a module called *Region*:

> **module** *Region* (*Region* (*Shape, Translate, Scale, Complement,*
> *Union, Intersect, Empty*),
> *Coordinate,*
> *containsS, containsR,*
> **module** *Shape*
> ) **where**
> **import** *Shape*

Note that this module imports the *Shape* module, and exports a data type called *Region*, functions *containsS* and *containsR*, and the entire *Shape* module.

## 8.1 The Region Data Type

Our first task will be to define a data type that captures the various kinds of regions that interest us:

> $--$ A Region is either:
> **data** *Region* = *Shape Shape*     $--$ primitive shape
> | *Translate Vector Region*     $--$ translated region

■ 87 ■

|   *Scale Vector Region*          $--$ scaled region
|   *Complement Region*            $--$ inverse of region
|   *Region 'Union' Region*        $--$ union of regions
|   *Region 'Intersect' Region*    $--$ intersection of regions
|   *Empty*                        $--$ empty region

   **deriving** *Show*

**type** *Vector* = (*Float*, *Float*)

---

**DETAILS**

The first line here looks odd: The name *Shape* appears twice in *Shape Shape*. The first occurrence, however, is the name of a new *constructor* in the *Region* data type, whereas the second is the name of an existing *data type* defined in Chapter 2. Haskell allows using the same name to define a constructor and a data type because they can never be confused. The context in which they are used will always be sufficient to distinguish them.

This example also demonstrates the use of program *comments*. Any text to the right of "$--$" until the end of the line is considered to be a comment, and is effectively ignored by a Haskell implementation. Haskell also permits *nested* comments, which have the form {- *this is a comment* -} and can appear anywhere in a program.

---

The comments to the right of the code describe each kind of region fairly well. Note the use of infix syntax for *Union* and *Intersect* (recall that *x* '*f*' *y* is equivalent to *f x y*). These two constructors are in fact what make *Region* a tree-shaped data type, as discussed in the previous chapter. Indeed, an important aspect of this data type is that it is *recursive*, just like the *Tree* data types. Thus, regions may be arbitrarily complex, containing an arbitrary (even infinite!) number of components.

The use of infix for union and intersection is handy, but has one problem. Expressions such as:

   *r*1 '*Union*' *r*2 '*Union*' *r*3
   *r*1 '*Intersect*' *r*2 '*Union*' *r*3

are *ambiguous*, the first because *Union* has no associativity, the second because *Union* and *Intersect* have equal precedence. We could add parentheses to disambiguate these expressions, but a better solution is to provide *fixity declarations* at the top of the module for each of the constructors, using mathematical conventions:

   **infixr**  5  '*Union*'
   **infixr**  6  '*Intersect*'

This gives both operators right associativity, and gives *Intersect* higher precedence than *Union*. So the above two expressions would be parsed as:

r1 'Union' (r2 'Union' r3)
(r1 'Intersect' r2) 'Union' r3

---

**DETAILS**

Fixity declarations must appear at the top of a module. The above declarations establish *right* associativity; use **infixl** for left associativity, and **infix** for no associativity. The precedence levels must be in the range 0 to 9, inclusive, with 0 being the weakest, 9 the strongest. If no fixity declaration is given for an operator, it is assumed to have left associativity and highest precedence (in other words, **infixl** 9).

---

Before I present formally what regions really *mean*, I will first try to convey intuitively what they mean through a couple of examples. Here is an example of two squares and a circle:

**let** *circle*  =  *Shape* (*Ellipse* 0.5 0.5)
    *square*  =  *Shape* (*Rectangle* 1 1)
**in** (*Scale* (2, 2) *circle*)
    'Union' (*Translate* (1, 0) *square*)
    'Union' (*Translate* (−1, 0) *square*)

This region is shown graphically in Fig. 8.1, where the shaded areas denote the composite region. Note how the scaling and translation work, and that there are two instances of the rectangle *s*.

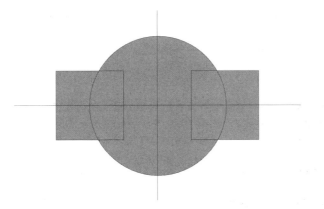

Figure 8.1: A Sample Region

As another example, here is an infinite sequence of circles, each with radius 1, and each placed on the positive x-axis so that the centers are spaced 2 units apart:

$$oneCircle \quad = \quad Shape\ (Ellipse\ 1\ 1)$$
$$manyCircles \quad = \quad [\,Translate\ (x,\,0)\ oneCircle \mid x \leftarrow [0,\,2..]\,]$$

**DETAILS**

The list *manyCircles* demonstrates the use of a *list comprehension*. The expression $[exp \mid x \leftarrow xs]$ is just shorthand for the expression $map\ (\backslash x \rightarrow exp)\ xs$. It is preferable to the latter, however, because it resembles more closely set notation in mathematics, namely:

$$\{\,exp \mid x \in xs\,\}$$

Recall that $[0,\,2..]$ is the infinite list $0:2:4:6:8\ \cdots$. Therefore, *manyCircles* is the infinite list:

$[\,Translate\ (0,\,0)\ oneCircle,$
$\quad Translate\ (2,\,0)\ oneCircle,$
$\quad Translate\ (4,\,0)\ oneCircle,$

$\quad \cdots$

The form $x \leftarrow xs$ is called a *generator,* and in general more than one is allowed, as in:

$$[(x,\,y) \mid x \leftarrow [0,\,1,\,2],\ y \leftarrow [\,'a',\,'b'\,]\,]$$

which evaluates to the list:

$$[(0,\,'a'),\ (0,\,'b'),\ (1,\,'a'),\ (1,\,'b'),\ (2,\,'a'),\ (2,\,'b')]$$

The order here is important; that is, note that the left-most generator changes least quickly.

There are several other useful features of list comprehensions, but they are not used in this text. Consult the Haskell Report for details.

We can construct a finite region from this by taking some portion of it, using the Standard Prelude function *take*, then folding *Union* over the result, as in:

$$fiveCircles \quad = \quad foldr\ Union\ Empty\ (take\ 5\ manyCircles)$$

Note the use of *Empty* as the "init" argument to *foldr*. This region is shown graphically in Fig. 8.2.

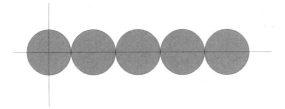

Figure 8.2: Five Unit Circles

**DETAILS**

The function *take* is defined in the Standard Prelude as:

$$
\begin{aligned}
take &\qquad :: \quad Int \rightarrow [a] \rightarrow [a] \\
take\ 0\ \_ &\qquad = \quad [\ ] \\
take\ \_\ [\ ] &\qquad = \quad [\ ] \\
take\ n\ (x:xs)\ |\ n > 0 &\qquad = \quad x : take\ (n-1)\ xs \\
take\ \_\ \_ &\qquad = \quad error \\
&\qquad\qquad\quad \text{``take: negative argument''}
\end{aligned}
$$

Recall that *error* :: *String* → *a* causes the program to immediately terminate, and the string argument is printed to the standard output area.

We can also define more complex operations on regions, given the primitive constructors captured in the *Region* datatype. For example, here is the definition of a function that constructs the difference between two regions:

$$r1\ \text{`difference`}\ r2\ =\ r1\ \text{`Intersect`}\ (Complement\ r2)$$

---

**Exercise 8.1**  Define a function that creates five circles (of the same size and orientation shown in Fig. 8.2) by intersecting a region containing an infinite sequence of circles with a suitably sized and positioned rectangle. What are the trade-offs in using this kind of definition compared to *fiveCircles* defined above?

## 8.2  The Meaning of Shapes and Regions

We've now seen some graphical examples of shapes and regions, but examples do not constitute a concrete definition. What, exactly, *is* a shape or a region? As we have defined them so far, they are nothing more than Haskell datatypes. Their *meaning* relates to what they represent, which in turn relates to how we intend to use them. In the next section, for example, we intend to write a function that determines whether a point lies within a region or not. But what, exactly, does that mean? We might choose to simply write the Haskell program for such a function, and declare *that* to be the meaning, but somehow that is not entirely satisfying.

So let's make an attempt to define the meaning of shapes and regions in some formal sense. This is not too difficult, really, because mathematicians have already done it for us. Shapes and regions are just *sets of points* on some surface, and for our purposes it suffices to consider the surface to be the *Cartesian plane*. Indeed, the shaded areas of Figs. 8.1 and 8.2 are simply a way of visualizing these sets of points.

### 8.2.1 The Meaning of Shapes

To begin, let's consider the meaning of primitive shapes. As an example, we can define a rectangle of length $a$ and width $b$ as the set:

$$\{ (x,y) \mid (-\frac{a}{2} \le x \le \frac{a}{2}) \wedge (-\frac{b}{2} \le y \le \frac{b}{2}) \} \tag{8.1}$$

Note that implicit in this definition is the fact that the rectangle is centered on the origin $(0,0)$.

Similarly, a circle of radius $r$ can be described as the set:

$$\{ (x,y) \mid x^2 + y^2 \le r^2 \}$$

More generally, an ellipse with radii $r_1$ (along the $x$ axis) and $r_2$ (along the $y$ axis), is defined by the set:

$$\{ (x,y) \mid \left(\frac{x}{r_1}\right)^2 + \left(\frac{y}{r_2}\right)^2 \le 1 \} \tag{8.2}$$

Note that the circle and ellipse are also centered over the origin.

What about a polygon? For simplicity we will consider only *convex* polygons (the more general case is left as an exercise). The location of a polygon on the Cartesian plane is obvious from its list of vertices. But to describe the set of points defined by a polygon requires knowing when a point is to the left of or to the right of one of its sides. Specifically, consider a side $z$ (also called a *ray*) from vertex $(x_1, y_1)$ to vertex $(x_2, y_2)$; does a point $(x, y)$ lie to the left or to the right of $z$? A bit of mathematics reveals that it is on or to the left of $z$ just when:

$$s \times v \geq t \times u$$
$$where \quad (s, t) \quad = \quad (x - x_1, y - y_1) \tag{8.3}$$
$$(u, v) \quad = \quad (x - x_2, y - y_2)$$

Now, it should be clear that a point is contained within a convex polygon if it is to the left of *every* side, assuming that the vertices are traversed in counter-clockwise order. If the vertices are traversed clockwise, the point is contained if it is to the *right* of every side.

More formally, the set of points defined by a convex polygon with vertices $V = (x_0, y_0), (x_1, y_1), \ldots, (x_{n-1}, y_{n-1})$ listed in counter-clockwise order, is given by:

$$\{ (x, y) \mid s \times v \geq t \times u \tag{8.4}$$
$$where \quad (s, t) \quad = \quad (x - x_i, y - y_i)$$
$$(u, v) \quad = \quad (x - x_{i \oplus 1}, y - y_{i \oplus 1}), \ 0 \leq i \leq (n - 1) \}$$

where $\oplus$ is addition modulo $n$, whose use here cleverly ensures that the side from vertex $(x_{n-1}, y_{n-1})$ back to $(x_0, y_0)$ is not forgotten.

Finally, what is the meaning of a right triangle? Indeed, where on the Cartesian plane should it be located? It seems difficult to center it over the origin, because the notion of "center" is not clear. So somewhat arbitrarily, let's define the corner opposite the hypotenuse to be located at the origin. Then we can use a definition similar to the one above to describe the set of points defined by a right triangle. Better yet, we can simply say that a right triangle with length $a$ and width $b$ defines the same set of points as a polygon with vertices $\{ (0, 0), (a, 0), (0, b) \}$.

It is interesting to note that with this definition we can give meaning to a right triangle with *negative* side lengths. For example, *RtTriangle* $(-10)$ 5 and *RtTriangle* 10 $(-5)$ define shapes in quadrants 2 and 4, respectively, of the Cartesian plane, as shown in Fig. 8.3. (This will affect, of course, the behavior of our area and perimeter functions from previous chapters. Exercise 8.2 is intended to remedy this.)

## 8.2.2 The Encoding of the Meaning of Shapes

How should we encode the meaning of a shape in Haskell? It would seem foolhardy to try to build the entire set, or list, of all of its points. (Why?) But mathematics tells us that every set can be represented by a *characteristic function*, which is simply a predicate that tests for a value's

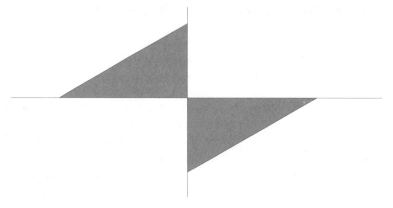

Figure 8.3: The Result of Negative Side Lengths

membership in the set. Therefore, I will define a function:

$$containsS \quad :: \quad Shape \to Coordinate \to Bool$$

$$\textbf{type } Coordinate \;=\; (Float,\ Float)$$

to give meaning to shapes. Thus, the characteristic function, or meaning, of a shape *s* is just *containsS s*, which has the proper type *Coordinate → Bool*. However, we will more often use *containsS* in an infix way: *s* '*containsS*' *p* is *True* just when the point *p* is contained in the shape *s*.

> **DETAILS**
>
> I have chosen the name *Coordinate* instead of *Point* to avoid conflicting with the type *Point* in the SOEGraphics library. You may recall that the type synonym *Vertex* defined in Chapter 2 also refers to (*Float, Float*), but I have chosen a new name to more closely reflect the intended use of the floating-point pairs.

As is usual for the design of a function defined on a data type, we consider each possible shape that *containsS* will be applied to. In doing this, I will use the mathematical meaning of shapes developed in the last section as a guide.

Starting with a rectangle, whose meaning is given as the set expressed in formula (8.1), we write:

$$(Rectangle\ s1\ s2)\ `containsS`\ (x,\ y)$$
$$= \ \textbf{let } t1 \;=\; s1/2$$
$$t2 \;=\; s2/2$$
$$\textbf{in} -t1 <= x\ \&\&\ x <= t1\ \&\&\ -t2 <= y\ \&\&\ y <= t2$$

**DETAILS**
Recall that (&&) and (||) are Haskell's Boolean "and" and "or" operators, respectively. In the above, the precedence of (<=) is higher than the precedence of (&&), and thus, no parentheses are needed.

Note the similarity of this definition to set (8.1). Similarly, we can use the formal meaning of an ellipse, captured in set (8.2), to guide how the Haskell function *containsS* behaves on ellipses:

$$(Ellipse\ r1\ r2)\ \text{`containsS`}\ (x, y)$$
$$= (x/r1)\,\hat{}\,2 + (y/r2)\,\hat{}\,2 <= 1$$

For the remaining two cases – a right triangle and general polygon – we need to first solve the simpler problem of determining whether a point is to the right or left of a directed line, or ray, just as we expressed earlier in property (8.3). In Haskell terms, consider the ray *v* from point *a* to point *b*; we want *p* `isLeftOf` *v* to be *True* just when *p* is on or to the left of *v*:

$$isLeftOf\quad ::\quad Coordinate \rightarrow Ray \rightarrow Bool$$
$$(px, py)\ \text{`isLeftOf`}\ ((ax, ay), (bx, by))$$
$$= \textbf{let}\ (s, t)\quad =\quad (px - ax, py - ay)$$
$$(u, v)\quad =\quad (px - bx, py - by)$$
$$\textbf{in}\ s * v >= t * u$$

**type** *Ray* = (*Coordinate*, *Coordinate*)

This is just a Haskell rendition of property (8.3).

Now recall the meaning of a polygon as captured in set (8.4). We can implement this in Haskell as follows:

$$(Polygon\ pts)\ \text{`containsS`}\ p$$
$$= \textbf{let}\ leftOfList\quad =\quad map\ isLeftOfp$$
$$(zip\ pts\ (tail\ pts + [head\ pts]))$$
$$isLeftOfp\ p'\ =\ isLeftOf\ p\ p'$$
$$\textbf{in}\ and\ leftOfList$$

Note the care taken to ensure that the side from the last vertex back to the first is not forgotten. The last line essentially asks if the point is in fact to the left of each side.

**DETAILS**
*and* and *or* compute the logical "and" and "or," respectively, of all of the elements in a list of Boolean values. They are defined in the Standard Prelude

as:

$$and, or \quad :: \quad [Bool] \rightarrow Bool$$
$$and\ bs \quad = \quad foldr\ (\&\&)\ True\ bs$$
$$or\ bs \quad = \quad foldr\ (||)\ False\ bs$$

For a right triangle, we could take an approach that combined the containment strategies for a rectangle (to handle the two sides) and a polygon (to handle the hypotenuse), but in the presence of possibly negative side lengths, it will turn out to be easier to simply treat the right triangle as a polygon, as was implied in the previous section.

$$(RtTriangle\ s1\ s2)\ `containsS`\ p$$
$$= \quad (Polygon\ [(0, 0), (s1, 0), (0, s2)])\ `containsS`\ p$$

This completes the definition of containment within shapes. Our confidence in its correctness is bolstered by its strong correspondence to the mathematical specifications developed earlier. Let's now continue with this same process as we consider containment within regions.

### 8.2.3 The Meaning of Regions

It is easy to define mathematically the meaning of union and intersection of regions. Because we are defining the meaning of regions as sets, the union of regions $r_1$ and $r_2$ is just $r_1 \cup r_2$, and the intersection is just $r_1 \cap r_2$! Also easy is the complement of $r$, given by:

$$\{ p \mid p \notin r \} \tag{8.5}$$

The effect of translation is to move each point in a set a certain distance along the $x$ and $y$ axes. In particular, given a translation vector $(u, v)$, every point $(x, y)$ in the original region is transformed to a point $(x + u, y + v)$ in the new region. So the meaning of the translation of a region $r$ is given by the set:

$$\{ (x + u, y + v) \mid (x, y) \in r \} \tag{8.6}$$

Similarly, the effect of scaling a region $r$ by a vector $(u, v)$ is to change each point $(x, y)$ to a point $(x * u, y * v)$:

$$\{ (x * u, y * v) \mid (x, y) \in r \} \tag{8.7}$$

Finally, the empty region is just the empty set $\emptyset$.

### 8.2.4  The Encoding of the Meaning of Regions

We will capture the meaning of regions in a function *containsR*:

$$containsR \;\; :: \;\; Region \rightarrow Coordinate \rightarrow Bool$$

Considering each constructor in turn, the first is easy:

$$(Shape\ s)\ `containsR`\ p \;\; = \;\; s\ `containsS`\ p$$

Recall that translation moves a point $(x, y)$ to a point $(x + u, y + v)$, as captured in set (8.6). Thus, to see if a point is in a translated region, all we have to do is translate the point in the opposite direction (an *inverse* translation), and test if the resulting point is in the untranslated region:

$$(Translate\ (u,\ v)\ r)\ `containsR`\ (x,\ y)$$
$$= \;\; r\ `containsR`\ (x - u,\ y - v)$$

Similarly, recall that scaling moves a point $(x, y)$ to a point $(x*u, y*v)$, as captured in set (8.7). Thus, to see if a point is in a scaled region, we apply the inverse scaling to the point and see if it is in the unscaled region:

$$(Scale\ (u,\ v)\ r)\ `containsR`\ (x,\ y)$$
$$= \;\; r\ `containsR`\ (x/u,\ y/v)$$

The definition of containment for the *Complement* and *Empty* constructors is easy:

$$(Complement\ r)\ `containsR`\ p \;\; = \;\; not\ (r\ `containsR`\ p)$$
$$Empty\ `containsR`\ p \qquad\qquad = \;\; False$$

Finally, to see if a point is in the union of two regions, we check to see if it is in either region; and to see if it is in the intersection, we check to see if it is in both:

$$(r1\ `Union`\ r2)\ `containsR`\ p$$
$$= \;\; r1\ `containsR`\ p\ \|\ r2\ `containsR`\ p$$
$$(r1\ `Intersect`\ r2)\ `containsR`\ p$$
$$= \;\; r1\ `containsR`\ p\ \&\&\ r2\ `containsR`\ p$$

The complete definitions of *containsR* and *containsS* are shown in Fig. 8.4.

---

**Exercise 8.2**  Modify the previous definitions of *area* and *perimeter* so that negative arguments work properly (the area and perimeter should always be positive).

```
containsR  ::  Region → Coordinate → Bool

(Shape s) ʻcontainsRʻ p
        =  s ʻcontainsSʻ p
(Translate (u, v) r) ʻcontainsRʻ (x, y)
        =  r ʻcontainsRʻ (x − u, y − v)
(Scale (u, v) r) ʻcontainsRʻ (x, y)
        =  r ʻcontainsRʻ (x/u, y/v)
(Complement r) ʻcontainsRʻ p
        =  not (r ʻcontainsRʻ p)
(r1 ʻUnionʻ r2) ʻcontainsRʻ p
        =  r1 ʻcontainsRʻ p ‖ r2 ʻcontainsRʻ p
(r1 ʻIntersectʻ r2) ʻcontainsRʻ p
        =  r1 ʻcontainsRʻ p && r2 ʻcontainsRʻ p
Empty ʻcontainsRʻ p
        =  False


containsS  ::  Shape → Coordinate → Bool

(Rectangle s1 s2) ʻcontainsSʻ (x, y)
        =  let t1  =  s1/2
               t2  =  s2/2
           in − t1 <= x && x <= t1 && − t2 <= y && y <= t2
(Ellipse r1 r2) ʻcontainsSʻ (x, y)
        =  (x/r1)^2 + (y/r2)^2 <= 1
(Polygon pts) ʻcontainsSʻ p
        =  let leftOfList  =  map (isLeftOf p)
                                 (zip pts
                                      (tail pts ++ [head pts]))
           in and leftOfList
(RtTriangle s1 s2) ʻcontainsSʻ p
        =  (Polygon [(0, 0), (s1, 0), (0, s2)]) ʻcontainsSʻ p
```

Figure 8.4: The Complete Definitions of *containsR* and *containsS*

---

**Exercise 8.3** Define a function *annulus* :: *Radius* → *Radius* → *Region* that creates an annulus, or "donut," whose inner radius is the first argument, and outer is the second.

---

**Exercise 8.4** The definition of *containsS* for polygons requires that the list of vertices be in clockwise order. Redefine it so that the list could be in *either* order.

---

**Exercise 8.5**   Add a constructor *HalfPlane* to the *Region* data type such that *HalfPlane* $p1$ $p2$ denotes the infinite region, or half plane, to the left of the line formed by the two points $p1$ and $p2$. Extend the definition of *containsR* to include this constructor.

---

**Exercise 8.6**   Assume that there is a *HalfPlane* constructor as described in the previous exercise. Assume also that there is no *Polygon* constructor. Instead, define a function *polygon* that realizes convex polygons in terms of *HalfPlane* (and possibly other constructors).

---

**Exercise 8.7**   Define a function *flipX* :: *Region* → *Region* that flips a region about the x-axis. Also define a *flipY* function analogously.

## 8.3   Algebraic Properties of Regions

Consider the two regions:

$$ra = r1\ `Union`\ (r2\ `Union`\ r3)$$
$$rb = (r1\ `Union`\ r2)\ `Union`\ r3$$

As Haskell values, these two regions are not the same. As regions, however, they share the property that a point is contained in *ra* if and only if it is contained in *rb*. Therefore, let's define a notion of *equivalence* of regions:

---

**Definition**   Two regions $r1$ and $r2$ are *equivalent*, written $r1 \equiv r2$, if and only if:[1]

$$(\forall p)\ r1\ `containsR`\ p \ \Rightarrow\ r2\ `containsR`\ p$$

The equivalence of regions such as *ra* and *rb* can be captured by a set of *axioms* that state algebraic properties of regions, such as associativity, distributivity, commutativity, and so on. For example:

---

**Axiom 1**   *Union* and *Intersection* are *associative*. That is, for any $r1$, $r2$, and $r3$:

$$r1\ `Union`\ (r2\ `Union`\ r3)\ \equiv\ (r1\ `Union`\ r2)\ `Union`\ r3$$
$$r1\ `Intersect`\ (r2\ `Intersect`\ r3)\ \equiv\ (r1\ `Intersect`\ r2)\ `Intersect`\ r3$$

---

[1] Recall that, in our notation, the direction of ⇒ only reflects the direction of our calculations; but all calculations are reversible, so the arrow really goes both ways. In particular, do not confuse this symbol with "implication" as used in mathematical logic.

We can prove this axiom easily; here is the case for *Union* (the case for *Intersect* is almost identical):

$(r1\ \text{`Union`}\ (r2\ \text{`Union`}\ r3))\ \text{`containsR`}\ p$
$\Rightarrow\ (r1\ \text{`containsR`}\ p)\ \|\ ((r2\ \text{`Union`}\ r3)\ \text{`containsR`}\ p)$
$\Rightarrow\ (r1\ \text{`containsR`}\ p)\ \|\ ((r2\ \text{`containsR`}\ p)\ \|\ (r3\ \text{`containsR`}\ p))$
$\Rightarrow\ ((r1\ \text{`containsR`}\ p)\ \|\ (r2\ \text{`containsR`}\ p))\ \|\ (r3\ \text{`containsR`}\ p)$
$\Rightarrow\ ((r1\ \text{`Union`}\ r2)\ \text{`containsR`}\ p)\ \|\ (r3\ \text{`containsR`}\ p)$
$\Rightarrow\ ((r1\ \text{`Union`}\ r2)\ \text{`Union`}\ r3)\ \text{`containsR`}\ p$

This axiom relies (in the third step) on the property that (‖) is also associative.

As another example, consider this axiom:

---

**Axiom 2** *Union* and *Intersection* are *commutative*. That is, for any $r1$ and $r2$:

$r1\ \text{`Union`}\ r2\ \equiv\ r2\ \text{`Union`}\ r1$
$r1\ \text{`Intersect`}\ r2\ \equiv\ r2\ \text{`Intersect`}\ r1$

The proof is again simple, shown here for *Union* (and relying on the property that (‖) is commutative):

$(r1\ \text{`Union`}\ r2)\ \text{`containsR`}\ p$
$\Rightarrow\ (r1\ \text{`containsR`}\ p)\ \|\ (r2\ \text{`containsR`}\ p)$
$\Rightarrow\ (r2\ \text{`containsR`}\ p)\ \|\ (r1\ \text{`containsR`}\ p)$
$\Rightarrow\ (r2\ \text{`Union`}\ r1)\ \text{`containsR`}\ p$

As you can see, what we are doing is establishing the validity of the standard algebraic properties of sets, but more importantly, we are doing so for our *implementation* of them. With these properties well established, you can feel confident about performing program transformations involving equivalent regions.

Below are three other axioms whose proofs are left as an exercise. Two of them refer to the value *univ*, or "universe," defined by:

$univ\ =\ Complement\ Empty$

---

**Axiom 3** *Union* and *Intersection* are *distributive*. That is, for any $r1$, $r2$, and $r3$:

$r1\ \text{`Intersect`}\ (r2\ \text{`Union`}\ r3)$
$\equiv\ (r1\ \text{`Intersect`}\ r2)\ \text{`Union`}\ (r1\ \text{`Intersect`}\ r3)$

$r1\ \text{`Union`}\ (r2\ \text{`Intersect`}\ r3)$
$\equiv\ (r1\ \text{`Union`}\ r2)\ \text{`Intersect`}\ (r1\ \text{`Union`}\ r3)$

---

**Axiom 4**  For any *r*:

> *r* 'Union' *Empty*  ≡  *r*
> *r* 'Intersect' *univ*  ≡  *r*

---

**Axiom 5**  For any *r*:

> *r* 'Union' *Complement r*  ≡  *univ*
> *r* 'Intersect' *Complement r*  ≡  *Empty*

Collectively, these five axioms capture the essence of what is known as a *Boolean algebra* (Wiitala, 1987).

---

**Exercise 8.8**  Complete the proofs of the five axioms for regions.

---

**Exercise 8.9**  The axioms for regions provide a basis from which *theorms* can be proved. Prove the following theorems using only the axioms (i.e., do not unfold the definition of *containsR*):

> *r* 'Intersect' *r*  ≡  *r*
> *r* 'Union' *r*  ≡  *r*
>
> *r* 'Union' *univ*  ≡  *univ*
> *r* 'Intersect' *Empty*  ≡  *Empty*
>
> *r*1 'Union' (*r*1 'Intersect' *r*2)  ≡  *r*1
> *r*1 'Intersect' (*r*1 'Union' *r*2)  ≡  *r*1
>
> *Complement* (*Complement r*)  ≡  *r*
>
> *Complement Empty*  ≡  *univ*
> *Complement univ*  ≡  *Empty*
>
> *Complement* (*r*1 'Union' *r*2)
>     ≡   *Complement r*1 'Intersect' *Complement r*2
> *Complement* (*r*1 'Intersect' *r*2)
>     ≡   *Complement r*1 'Union' *Complement r*2

## 8.4  In Retrospect

The habit of taking the time to really understand the meaning of our programs, such as the meaning of the shape and region data types just concluded, is strongly encouraged. This understanding should ideally be done independently of your programming language, yet achieving it will reap great benefits when you actually sit down to write your program.

Before closing this chapter, let's pause for a minute and reflect on a few other things that we have done. The first is the fact that we have mentioned a few constraints on our data types that Haskell's type system is unable to enforce. One is the implicit assumption (made explicit through our discussion of negative side lengths for a right triangle) that some floating-point arguments to constructors are expected to be positive; for example, the radii of an ellipse. What should we do about this? Haskell does not have a "positive floating-point number" data type,[2] so our choices are as follows:

1. We could ignore the problem. Indeed, if all we are concerned about is the proper behavior of *containsR*, then negative side lengths for rectangles don't matter (because rectangles are centered on the origin), negative radii don't matter (the radii are always squared), and we decided that negative side lengths for right triangles are a Good Thing!

2. We could define functions that test for improper values and cause a run-time error. For example, here is a function that invokes an error if either side of a rectangle is negative:

$$
\begin{array}{ll}
rectangle & :: \; Side \rightarrow Side \rightarrow Shape \\
rectangle \; s1 \; s2 & = \\
\quad | \; s1 >= 0 \;\&\&\; s2 >= 0 & = \; Rectangle \; s1 \; s2 \\
\quad | \; otherwise & = \; error \; \texttt{"negative side lengths"}
\end{array}
$$

Of course, this solution causes the program to terminate prematurely.

3. Alternatively, we could try to take corrective action:

$$
\begin{array}{ll}
rectangle & :: \; Side \rightarrow Side \rightarrow Shape \\
rectangle \; s1 \; s2 & = \; Rectangle \; (abs \; s1) \; (abs \; s2)
\end{array}
$$

---

**DETAILS**

*abs* is Haskell's *absolute value* function.

---

4. Sometimes, however, the fix cannot be done at the point the error is detected, but must be reported back by propagating an appropriate error value to some other part of the program. To achieve this, one could use the *Maybe* data type, defined in the Standard Prelude as:

**data** *Maybe a* = *Nothing* | *Just a*

---

[2] Neither does any other mainstream language that I am aware of. Ensuring that such a property is not violated is not possible at compile-time, for any suitably rich set of operations on floating-point numbers.

in which case *rectangle* could be defined as:

$$
\begin{array}{lll}
rectangle & :: & Side \rightarrow Side \rightarrow Maybe\ Shape \\
rectangle\ s1\ s2 & = & \\
\quad |\ s1 >= 0\ \&\&\ s2 >= 0 & = & Just\ (Rectangle\ s1\ s2) \\
\quad |\ otherwise & = & Nothing
\end{array}
$$

Note that this design is reflected by a change in the type signature, but now the results of calls to *rectangle* can be inspected in other parts of the program; indeed, they can be handled differently in each case.

5. We could prove that nowhere in our program do we use improper arguments.

Another constraint that is beyond any conventional type system is the requirement that the list of vertices to the polygon constructor be given in counter-clockwise order, and, even more subtle, that it describes a *convex* polygon! Our choices in dealing with this are similar to those above, although ignoring the problem may not be a good idea, because very wrong behavior of *containsR* may result. But there is another option: We could remove the constraint entirely, thus allowing not only concave polygons, but also ones that have sides that intersect each another (i.e., "self-crossing," as described in Chapter 2). The meaning of such a polygon becomes more sophisticated, but it can be made to work.

While we're at it, let's expand our self-critique to include the entire design of our shape and region data types and the various operators on them. As mentioned in a previous chapter, much of this design was driven by pedagogy: the need to give compelling examples that demonstrated a variety of ideas in problem solving as well as specific Haskell language features. But, in reality, if our goal were just to create regions of various sorts, and to determine point membership within them, there are various things that we might choose to do differently. For example:

1. There is no need for a right triangle constructor; a general polygon will do just fine. The same is true for the rectangle.
2. There is no need for side and radius arguments for rectangles and ellipses, respectively. Instead, we can just have a *unit square* and *unit circle* constructor.
3. In addition to scaling and translating regions, it is also desirable to *rotate* them. In fact, all three of these transformations can be combined into a single one, called an *affine transformation*, which can be represented as a single matrix (Foley et al., 1996).

A design based on these ideas is arguably more elegant, and simplifies the design of functions such as *containsR*.

---

**Exercise 8.10** Prove the following facts:

*Rectangle s*1 *s*2 'containsS' *p* = *Rectangle* (−*s*1) *s*2 'containsS' *p*
*Ellipse r*1 *r*2 'containsS' *p* = *Ellipse* (−*r*1) *r*2 'containsS' *p*

---

**Exercise 8.11** Define a function that checks to see if a list of vertices describes a convex polygon. You may assume that the vertices are in the order that defines its sides. Then rewrite the *area* function so that *error* is called if the *Shape* value is a polygon that is not convex.

---

**Exercise 8.12** Redefine *containsS* so that it accepts any list of vertices as an argument to the polygon constructor, again in an order that defines its sides. (If you wish, you may disallow self-crossing polygons.)

---

**Exercise 8.13** Redefine the *Region* data type to allow only a unit circle, polygon, empty region, and affine transformation. Redefine *containsR* to work properly with this new design. (The book (Foley et al., 1996) is a good reference for the mathematics necessary for this exercise.)

# CHAPTER NINE

# More About Higher-Order Functions

You have now seen several examples where functions are passed as arguments to other functions, such as with *fold* and *map*. In this chapter, I will show several examples where functions are also returned as values. This will lead to several techniques for improving definitions that we have already written – techniques that we will use often in the remainder of the text.

## 9.1 Currying

The first improvement relates to the notation we have used to write function applications, such as *simple x y z*. Although I have noted the similarity of this to the mathematical notation *simple*(*x*, *y*, *z*), in fact, there is an important difference, namely that *simple x y z* is actually equivalent to (((*simple x*) *y*) *z*). In other words, function application is *left associative*, taking one argument at a time.

Let's look at the expression (((*simple x*) *y*) *z*) a bit closer: There is an application of *simple* to *x*, the result of which is applied to *y*; so (*simple x*) must be a function! The result of this application, ((*simple x*) *y*), is then applied to *z*, so ((*simple x*) *y*) must also be a function!

Because each of these intermediate applications yields a function, it seems perfectly reasonable to define a function such as:

$$multSumByFive \;=\; simple\; 5$$

What is *simple* 5? From the above argument, we know that it must be a function. And from the definition of *simple* in Section 1.1, we might guess that this function takes two arguments, and returns 5 times their sum.

Indeed, we can *calculate* this result as follows:

*multSumByFive a b*
$\Rightarrow$ (*simple* 5) *a b*
$\Rightarrow$ *simple* 5 *a b*
$\Rightarrow$ 5 $*$ (*a* + *b*)

The intermediate step with parentheses is included just for clarity. This method of applying functions to one argument at a time, yielding intermediate functions along the way, is called *currying*, after the logician Haskell B. Curry who popularized the idea.[1] It is helpful to look at the types of the intermediate functions as arguments are applied:

*simple* :: *Float* → *Float* → *Float* → *Float*
*simple* 5 :: *Float* → *Float* → *Float*
*simple* 5 *a* :: *Float* → *Float*
*simple* 5 *a b* :: *Float*

How can we use currying to improve any of the previous examples? One place is in these defintions of *listSum* and *listProd* (in which I have changed the type to *Float*'s):

*listSum, listProd* :: [*Float*] → *Float*
*listSum xs*    =  *foldl* (+) 0 *xs*
*listProd xs*   =  *foldl* ($*$) 1 *xs*

which can be slightly simplified to:

*listSum, listProd* :: [*Float*] → *Float*
*listSum*    =  *foldl* (+) 0
*listProd*   =  *foldl* ($*$) 1

Similarly, these definitions:

*and, or* :: [*Bool*] → *Bool*
*and xs*  =  *foldr* (&&) *True xs*
*or xs*   =  *foldr* (||) *False xs*

can be rewritten as:

*and, or* :: [*Bool*] → *Bool*
*and*   =  *foldr* (&&) *True*
*or*    =  *foldr* (||) *False*

---

[1] It was actually Schönfinkel who first called attention to this idea (Schönfinkel, 1924), but the word "schönfinkelling" is rather a mouthful!

I will refer to this kind of simplification as "currying simplification" or just "currying," even though it actually has a more technical name, "eta contraction."

---

**DETAILS**

Some care should be taken when using this simplification idea. In particular, note that the equation $f\ x = g\ x\ y\ x$ cannot be simplified to $f = g\ x\ y$, because then the $x$ would become undefined!

---

Here is a more interesting example, in which I will use currying simplification three times. Recall from Section 5.5 the definition of *reverse* using *foldl*:

$$reverse\ xs\ =\ foldl\ revOp\ [\ ]\ xs$$
$$\textbf{where}\ revOp\ acc\ x\ =\ x : acc$$

Using the polymorphic function *flip*, which is defined in the Standard Prelude as:

$$flip\qquad ::\ (a \to b \to c) \to (b \to a \to c)$$
$$flip\ f\ x\ y\ =\ f\ y\ x$$

it should be clear that *revOp* can be rewritten as:

$$revOp\ acc\ x\ =\ flip\ (:)\ acc\ x$$

But now currying simplification can be used twice to reveal that:

$$revOp\ =\ flip\ (:)$$

This, along with a third use of currying, allows us to rewrite the definition of *reverse* simply as:

$$reverse\ =\ foldl\ (flip\ (:))\ [\ ]$$

This is in fact the way *reverse* is defined in the Standard Prelude.

---

**Exercise 9.1** In the last chapter the following portion of the definition of *containsS* appeared:

$$(Polygon\ pts)\ `containsS`\ p$$
$$= \textbf{let}\ leftOfList\quad =\quad map\ isLeftOfp$$
$$(zip\ pts\ (tail\ pts + [head\ pts]))$$
$$isLeftOfp\ p'\ =\ isLeftOf\ p\ p'$$
$$\textbf{in}\ and\ leftOfList$$

Rewrite this using currying to simplify.

---

**Exercise 9.2**   Show that *flip* (*flip f*) is the same as *f*.

---

**Exercise 9.3**   What is the type of *ys* in:

$$xs\ =\ [1, 2, 3] :: [Float]$$
$$ys\ =\ map\ (+)\ xs$$

---

**Exercise 9.4**   Define a function *applyEach* that, given a list of functions, applies each to some given value. For example:

$$applyEach\ [simple\ 2\ 2, (+3)]\ 5\ \Rightarrow\ [14, 8]$$

where *simple* is as defined in Section 1.1.

---

**Exercise 9.5**   Define a function *applyAll* that, given a list of functions [*f*1, *f*2, ..., *fn*] and a value *v*, returns the result *f*1 (*f*2 (... (*fn v*) ...)). For example:

$$applyAll\ [simple\ 2\ 2, (+3)]\ 5\ \Rightarrow\ 20$$

---

**Exercise 9.6**   Recall the discussion about the efficiency of (+) and *concat* in Chapter 5. Which of the following functions is more efficient, and why?

$$appendr, appendl\ ::\ [a] \rightarrow [a] \rightarrow [a]$$
$$appendr\qquad\ =\ foldr\ (flip\ (+))\ [\,]$$
$$appendl\qquad\ =\ foldl\ (flip\ (+))\ [\,]$$

---

## 9.2   Sections

With a bit more syntax, we can also curry applications of infix operators such as (+). This syntax is called a *section*, and the idea is that, in an expression such as (*x* + *y*), you can omit either the *x* or the *y*, and the result (with the parentheses still intact) is a function of that missing argument. If *both* variables are omitted, it is a function of *two* arguments. In other words, the expressions (*x*+), (+*y*), and (+) are equivalent, respectively, to the functions:

$$
\begin{aligned}
f1\ y &= x + y \\
f2\ x &= x + y \\
f3\ x\ y &= x + y
\end{aligned}
$$

For example, consider this code fragment from Section 6.1:

**let** *test x* = *x > epsilon*
**in** *takeWhile test s*

It can be simplified to:

*takeWhile* (*> epsilon*) *s*

The definition for the perimeter of an ellipse that uses this fragment can likewise be simplified.

For another example, suppose that we need to determine whether each number in a list is positive. Instead of writing:

*posInts* :: [*Integer*] → [*Bool*]
*posInts xs* = *map test xs*
                **where** *test x* = *x > 0*

we can simply write:

*posInts* :: [*Integer*] → [*Bool*]
*posInts xs* = *map* (*> 0*) *xs*

which can be further simplified using currying:

*posInts* :: [*Integer*] → [*Bool*]
*posInts* = *map* (*> 0*)

This is an extremely concise definition.

As you gain experience with higher-order functions, you will not only be able to start writing such definitions directly, but you will also start *thinking* in "higher-order" terms. We will see many examples of this kind of reasoning throughout the text.

---

**Exercise 9.7**   Define a function *twice* that, given a function *f*, returns a function that applies *f* twice to its argument. For example:

(*twice* (+1)) 2 ⇒ 4

What is the principal type of *twice*? Describe what *twice twice* does, and give an example of its use. How about *twice twice twice* and *twice* (*twice twice*)?

**Exercise 9.8** Generalize *twice* defined in the previous exercise by defining a function *power* that takes a function $f$ and an integer $n$, and returns a function that applies the function $f$ to its argument $n$ times. For example:

$power (+2) 5 1 \implies 11$

Use *power* to define something (anything!) useful.

## 9.3 Anonymous Functions

The final way to define a function in Haskell is in some sense the most fundamental: it is called an *anonymous function*.[2] As a simple example, an anonymous function that increments its numeric argument by one can be written $\backslash x \to x + 1$. Anonymous functions are most useful in situations where you don't wish to name them, which is why they are called "anonymous." Anonymity is a property also shared by sections, but sections can only be derived from a single infix function. As an example, to add one and then divide by two every element of a list, we could write:

$map (\backslash x \to (x + 1)/2) \; xs$

An even better example is an anonymous function that pattern-matches its argument, as in:

$map (\backslash(a, b) \to a + b) \; xs$

---

**DETAILS**
Anonymous functions can only perform one match against an argument. That is, you cannot stack together several anonymous functions to define one function, as you can with equations. For example, this is disallowed:

$map (\backslash(Rectangle \; s1 \; s2) \to True$
$\quad (Ellipse \; r1 \; r2) \; \to \; False) \; shapes$

If you have a need to do this, you should instead either define a function using equations, or use a **case** expression, which will be introduced in Chapter 10.

---

[2] Most authors call these *lambda expressions*, because the concept is drawn directly from Church's lambda calculus (Church, 1941). Indeed, the "\" in the Haskell syntax is meant to resemble the lowercase Greek character $\lambda$.

Anonymous functions are considered most fundamental because definitions such as that for *simple* given in Chapter 1:

*simple x y z* $=$ $x * (y + z)$

can be written instead as:

*simple* $=$ $\backslash x\ y\ z \rightarrow x * (y + z)$

---

**DETAILS**

$\backslash x\ y\ z \rightarrow exp$ is shorthand for $\backslash x \rightarrow \backslash y \rightarrow \backslash z \rightarrow exp$.

---

We can also use anonymous functions to explain precisely the behavior of sections. In particular, note that:

$(x+)$ $\Rightarrow$ $\backslash y \rightarrow x + y$
$(+y)$ $\Rightarrow$ $\backslash x \rightarrow x + y$
$(+)$ $\Rightarrow$ $\backslash x\ y \rightarrow x + y$

---

**Exercise 9.9** Suppose we define a function *fix* as:

*fix f* $=$ *f* (*fix f*)

What is the principal type of *fix*? (This is tricky!) Suppose further that we have a recursive function:

*remainder* :: *Integer* $\rightarrow$ *Integer* $\rightarrow$ *Integer*
*remainder a b* = **if** $a < b$ **then** *a*
                 **else** *remainder* $(a - b)$ *b*

Rewrite this function using *fix* so that it is not recursive. (Also tricky!) Do you think that this process can be applied to *any* recursive function?

## 9.4 Function Composition

An example of polymorphism that has nothing to do with data structures arises from the desire to take two functions *f* and *g* and "glue them together," yielding another function *h* that first applies *g* to its argument, and then applies *f* to that result. This is called function *composition*, and Haskell predefines a simple infix operator (.) to achieve it, as follows:

(.)       ::  $(b \rightarrow c) \rightarrow (a \rightarrow b) \rightarrow a \rightarrow c$
$(f . g)\ x$ $=$ $f\ (g\ x)$

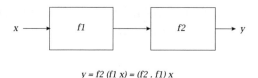

$$y = f2 \ (f1 \ x) = (f2 \ . \ f1) \ x$$

Figure 9.1: Gluing Two Functions Together

Note the type of the operator (.); it is completely polymorphic. Note also that the result of the first function to be applied – some type *b* – must be the same as the type of the argument to the second function to be applied. Pictorially, if you think of a function as a black box that takes input at one end and returns some output at the other, function composition is like connecting two boxes together, end to end, as shown in Fig. 9.1.

The ability to compose functions using (.) is extremely useful. For example, consider this function to compute the sum of the areas of circles with various radii:

> *totalCircleArea*          ::   [*Float*] → *Float*
> *totalCircleArea radii*   =   *listSum* (*map circleArea radii*)

We can first add parentheses to emphasize the application of interest:

> *totalCircleArea*          ::   [*Float*] → *Float*
> *totalCircleArea radii*   =   *listSum* ((*map circleArea*) *radii*)

then rewrite as a function composition:

> *totalCircleArea*          ::   [*Float*] → *Float*
> *totalCircleArea radii*   =   (*listSum* . (*map circleArea*)) *radii*

and finally use currying to simplify:

> *totalCircleArea*   ::   [*Float*] → *Float*
> *totalCircleArea*   =   *listSum* . *map circleArea*

Similarly, this definition:

> *totalSquareArea*        ::   [*Float*] → *Float*
> *totalSquareArea sides*   =   *listSum* (*map squareArea sides*)

can be rewritten as:

> *totalSquareArea*   ::   [*Float*] → *Float*
> *totalSquareArea*   =   *listSum* . *map squareArea*

And from Section 5.2, we wrote this definition for *putStr*:

> *putStr*     ::   *String* → *IO* ()
> *putStr s*   =   *sequence_* (*map putChar s*)

which can be simplified to:

> *putStr* :: *String* → *IO* ()
> *putStr* = *sequence_* . *map putChar*

But let's also create additional compositions. A function that determines whether all of the elements in a list are greater than zero, and one that determines if at least one is greater than zero, can be written:

> *allOverZero, oneOverZero* :: [*Integer*] → *Bool*
> *allOverZero* = *and* . *posInts*
> *oneOverZero* = *or* . *posInts*

Note that the auxiliary function *posInts* is simple enough that we could incorporate its definition directly, as in:

> *allOverZero, oneOverZero* :: [*Integer*] → *Bool*
> *allOverZero* = *and* . *map* (> 0)
> *oneOverZero* = *or* . *map* (> 0)

In the remainder of this text I will not refrain from writing definitions such as this directly, using a small set of rich polymorphic functions, such as *fold* and *map*, plus a few others drawn from the Prelude and Standard Libraries.

---

**Exercise 9.10**   Rewrite this example:

> *map* (\x → (x + 1)/2) *xs*

using a composition of sections.

---

**Exercise 9.11**   Consider the expression:

> *map f* (*map g xs*)

Rewrite this using function composition and a single call to *map*. Then rewrite the earlier example:

> *map* (\x → (x + 1)/2) *xs*

as a "map of a map."

---

**Exercise 9.12**   Go back to any exercises prior to this chapter, and simplify your solutions using ideas learned here.

# CHAPTER TEN

# Drawing Regions

In Chapters 2 and 8 we defined modules for geometric shapes and regions, respectively. We will now build a third layer onto this structure: a module that provides the ability to color regions and to place them on a "virtual desktop" in a graphics window. These colored regions will be called *pictures*. Once placed, you will be able to "click" on a picture using the mouse, which will cause that picture to rise to the surface of the desktop (i.e., any objects partially occluding it will be pushed beneath it). As usual, I will begin the discussion by providing the module interface:

> **module** *Picture* (*Picture* (*Region*, *Over*, *EmptyPic*),
>             *Color* (*Black*, *Blue*, *Green*, *Cyan*,
>                     *Red*, *Magenta*, *Yellow*, *White*),
>             *regionToGRegion*, *shapeToGRegion*,
>             *drawRegionInWindow*, *drawPic*, *draw*, *spaceClose*,
>             **module** *Region*
>             ) **where**
> **import** *Draw*
> **import** *Region*
> **import** *SOEGraphics hiding* (*Region*)
> **import** *qualified SOEGraphics as G* (*Region*)

---

**DETAILS**

The last two lines above look strange, and arise because both the *Region* module and the *SOEGraphics* module define a data type called *Region*, so importing them both into the same module causes a *name clash*, which Haskell (quite sensibly) does not allow. In order to use them both, I first import all of the *SOEGraphics* module except for *Region*; that's what the next to the last line does. Then I import *SOEGraphics* as a *qualified module*, at the same time renaming it to *G*, and furthermore I only import *Region* from it. All of this is achieved by the last line above. The end result is that in the *Picture* module, the *Region* data type defined in *SOEGraphics* has the name *G.Region*, whereas the one from module *Region* is just called *Region*. (If I had omitted *"as G"* from the last line above, then the new *Region* type would be referred to as *SOEGraphics.Region*.)

Note that the *Region* module is imported and exported; and recall that the *Region* module includes the *Shape* module. So by importing the *Picture* module somewhere, we effectively import all three modules; by importing the *Region* module, we effectively import it and the *Shape* module; and by importing *Shape*, we get just that module. This reflects the hierarchical structure of our design.

## 10.1 The Picture Data Type

Let's first define a *Picture* data type:

**data** *Picture* = *Region Color Region*
         | *Picture 'Over' Picture*
         | *EmptyPic*
  **deriving** *Show*

where the *Color* type is defined in module *SOEGraphics* as:

**data** *Color* = *Black* | *Blue* | *Green* | *Cyan*
         | *Red* | *Magenta* | *Yellow* | *White*

So, for example, *Region Red* (*Shape* (*Ellipse* 10 10)) is a picture of a red circle with radius 10. Regions will be centered on the origin, which will be at the center of the graphics window that we will soon create.

## 10.2 Drawing Pictures

Assume for now that we have a function *drawRegionInWindow* that, as the name suggests, draws regions.

    *drawRegionInWindow* :: *Window* → *Color* → *Region* → *IO* ()

We can then define a *drawPic* function for pictures as follows:

$$
\begin{array}{lll}
drawPic & :: & Window \rightarrow Picture \rightarrow IO\ () \\
drawPic\ w\ (Region\ c\ r) & = & drawRegionInWindow\ w\ c\ r \\
drawPic\ w\ (p1\ `Over`\ p2) & = & \textbf{do}\ drawPic\ w\ p2;\ drawPic\ w\ p1 \\
drawPic\ w\ EmptyPic & = & return\ ()
\end{array}
$$

---

**DETAILS**

Although the layout rules are generally used to align commands in a **do** expression, several commands may be placed on the same line if they are separated by a semicolon. This is convenient when the commands are very short, as in the example above. In fact, this same rule may be used to override the layout rules in a **let** or **where** expression, as in:

**let** $x$ = 1; $y$ = 2
**in** $x + y$

---

This is quite straightforward; the only tricky thing is making sure to draw $p2$ before $p1$, because that's what is implied in drawing $p1$ "over" $p2$. Drawing one object on top of another essentially occludes the one on the bottom!

## 10.3 Drawing Regions

To define *drawRegionInWindow* will require a bit more thought. In particular, we need to carefully consider the problem of drawing things such as intersected and unioned regions. For union, the answer seems easy enough: Just draw the two regions in either order, and the result on the screen will appear to be their union. But what about intersection? How do we draw the intersection of arbitrarily scaled and translated ellipses and polygons, for example? And what about complement?

Indeed, these are very hard problems! The best general method is to compute the actual set of pixels to represent each region, and then compute the intersection or complement of these sets. It turns out that the Windows 95/NT graphics libraries have routines that do just that (using arrays to represent the pixel sets for efficiency), and the *SOEGraphics* library provides access to them. Unfortunately, the library uses the name *Region* to refer to these values, which is the same name that we used in Chapter 8. So to distinguish these new regions from ours we will call them *graphics regions*. Furthermore, because graphics regions are defined in

```
createRectangle  ::  Point → Point → G.Region
createEllipse    ::  Point → Point → G.Region
createPolygon    ::  [Point] → G.Region


andRegion        ::  G.Region → G.Region → G.Region
orRegion         ::  G.Region → G.Region → G.Region
xorRegion        ::  G.Region → G.Region → G.Region
diffRegion       ::  G.Region → G.Region → G.Region


drawRegion       ::  G.Region → Graphic
```

Figure 10.1: Interface for Graphics Regions

the Haskell module *SOEGraphics*, which is imported under pseudonym *G*, the type of graphics regions is actually *G.Region* in the module we are currently defining.

Fig. 10.1 summarizes the entities imported from *SOEGraphics* having to do with regions. From this figure the correspondence between graphics regions and our notion of a region should be relatively clear. Indeed, our primary goal in the remainder of this section will be to define a function:

$$regionToGRegion \ :: \ Region → G.Region$$

that converts one of our regions into a graphics region. With this function, the definition of the *drawRegionInWindow* function needed in the last section is straightforward:

```
drawRegionInWindow   ::   Window → Color → Region → IO ()
drawRegionInWindow w c r
                  =   drawInWindow w
                         (withColor c
                            (drawRegion (regionToGRegion r)))
```

The algorithm reflected here is quite simple: Convert a region into a graphics region, and then draw it with a particular color.

### 10.3.1  From Regions to Graphics Regions: First Attempt

The main discrepency between regions and graphics regions is that the latter do not have scale or translation operations. We will have to do this ourselves, but how?

As an experiment, suppose that the only constructors in the *Region* datatype were *Shape* and *Scale*, and the only constructor in the *Shape* datatype was *Rectangle*. Further, suppose that our job is simply to convert this datatype into another one called *NewRegion*:

**data** *NewRegion* = *Rect Side Side*

One way to do this is as follows:

*regToNReg* :: *Region* → *NewRegion*
*regToNReg* (*Shape* (*Rectangle sx sy*))
            = *Rect sx sy*
*regToNReg* (*Scale* (*x, y*) *r*)
            = *regToNReg* (*scaleReg* (*x, y*) *r*)

*scaleReg* (*x, y*) (*Shape* (*Rectangle sx sy*))
            = *Shape* (*Rectangle* (*x* ∗ *sx*) (*y* ∗ *sy*))
*scaleReg* (*x, y*) (*Scale s r*)
            = *Scale s* (*scaleReg* (*x, y*) *r*)

This idea can be easily generalized to the original data types with all of their constructors, and it does, in fact, perform the translation correctly. Unfortunately, it is terribly inefficient, even in this simple form! To see why, suppose we have a region:

(*Scale* (*x1, y1*) (*Scale* (*x2, y2*) (... (*Shape* (*Rectangle sx sy*)))))

where the ... represents an arbitrary number of further scalings. Now consider the following calculation:

*regToNReg* (*Scale* (*x1, y1*) (*Scale* (*x2, y2*)
                            (... (*Shape* (*Rectangle sx sy*)))))
⟹ *regToNReg* (*Scale* (*x2, y2*)
                (... (*Shape* (*Rectangle* (*x1* ∗ *sx*) (*y1* ∗ *sy*)))))
⟹ *regToNReg* (... (*Shape* (*Rectangle* (*x2* ∗ *x1* ∗ *sx*) (*y2* ∗ *y1* ∗ *sy*))))

Note that the original *Region* value is traversed completely (by *scaleReg*) for every occurrence of *Scale*. So if there are $n$ nested occurrences of *Scale*, and it takes on the order of $n$ steps to make a traversal, then the total cost of a call to *regToNReg* is $n + (n - 1) + (n - 2) + \cdots + 2 + 1 = n(n + 1)/2$ steps. This is not satisfactory! Intuitively, at least, it seems as if we should only have to traverse the data structure once.

## 10.3.2 From Regions to Graphics Regions: Second Attempt

So let's try a different approach: Why not *accumulate* the scaling information during a single traversal of the region until we reach the primitive shapes, which then get scaled exactly once? This is in fact quite easy to define:

$$
\begin{array}{lcl}
regToNReg & :: & Region \rightarrow NewRegion \\
regToNReg\ r & = & rToNR\ (1,\ 1)\ r
\end{array}
$$

$$
\begin{array}{lcl}
rToNR & :: & (Float,\ Float) \rightarrow Region \rightarrow NewRegion \\
rToNR\ (x1,\ y1)\ (Shape\ (Rectangle\ sx\ sy)) \\
& = & Rect\ (x1 * sx)\ (y1 * sy) \\
rToNR\ (x1,\ y1)\ (Scale\ (x2,\ y2)\ r) \\
& = & rToNR\ (x1 * x2,\ y1 * y2)\ r
\end{array}
$$

A little thought should (hopefully) convince you that this only traverses the data structure once (i.e., a cost on the order of $n$ steps rather than $n(n+1)/2$. This is quite a bit of savings, and the code is somewhat simpler, too! (It is worth noting the similarity of this situation to that of naively reversing a list in Section 5.5. Both naive algorithms resulted in a cost proportional to the square of the size of the data structure, and both inefficiencies were solved by introducing an "accumulator" argument to keep track of partial results.)

Returning now to our original problem, we can use the same principle above to define a function *RegionToGRegion* that converts a *Region* into a graphics region (of type *G.Region*):

$$
\begin{array}{lcl}
regionToGRegion & :: & Region \rightarrow G.Region \\
regionToGRegion\ r & = & regToGReg\ (0,\ 0)\ (1,\ 1)\ r
\end{array}
$$

Note that the auxilliary function *regToGReg* takes two extra arguments instead of one, because we must keep track of not just scaling, but also translation:

$$
\begin{array}{lcl}
regToGReg & :: & Vector \rightarrow Vector \rightarrow Region \rightarrow G.Region \\
\textbf{type}\ Vector & = & (Float,\ Float)
\end{array}
$$

The first argument is for the accumulated translation, and the second for accumulated scaling.

Assuming a function whose definition we will return to later:

$$
shapeToGRegion\ ::\ Vector \rightarrow Vector \rightarrow Shape \rightarrow G.Region
$$

then the treatment of *Shape* values is easy:

> *regToGReg loc sca* (*Shape s*)
>    = *shapeToGRegion loc sca s*

Given the accumulator arguments, the treatment of scaling is also straightforward:

> *regToGReg loc* (*sx, sy*) (*Scale* (*u, v*) *r*)
>    = *regToGReg loc* (*sx* ∗ *u, sy* ∗ *v*) *r*

Translation is slightly more complex, because we have to scale the translation factors by the accumulated scaling parameters prior to the translation:

> *regToGReg* (*lx, ly*) (*sx, sy*) (*Translate* (*u, v*) *r*)
>    = *regToGReg* (*lx* + *u* ∗ *sx, ly* + *v* ∗ *sy*) (*sx, sy*) *r*

The graphics library does not have an operator to create an empty graphics region, so to represent the *Empty* region, we create a rectangle with side lengths of zero:

> *regToGReg loc sca Empty*
>    = *createRectangle* (0, 0) (0, 0)

Next, let's consider *Union*:

> *regToGReg loc sca* (*r*1 'Union' *r*2)
>    = **let** *gr*1  = *regToGReg loc sca r*1
>          *gr*2  = *regToGReg loc sca r*2
>      **in** *orRegion gr*1 *gr*2

It turns out that we will use this sequence of operations – creating two graphics regions and combining them into a third using some kind of combining function – several times, so let's apply the abstraction principle and rewrite the above treatment of union as follows:

> *regToGReg loc sca* (*r*1 'Union' *r*2)
>    = *primGReg loc sca r*1 *r*2 *orRegion*

> *primGReg loc sca r*1 *r*2 *op*
>    = **let** *gr*1  = *regToGReg loc sca r*1
>          *gr*2  = *regToGReg loc sca r*2
>      **in** *op gr*1 *gr*2

Note the very simple use of the higher-order function *op*. It is a trivial matter to calculate that this definition is equivalent to the original one. With this change, intersection is easily defined:

*regToGReg loc sca* (*r*1 '*Intersect*' *r*2)
    = *primGReg loc sca r*1 *r*2 *andRegion*

To complete the definition of *regToGReg*, there is one other constructor that we need to define the meaning of: *Complement*. Unfortunately, there is no single graphics region function that will do what we want. Instead, we define a function that creates a region consisting of the entire graphics window, and then use *diffRegion* to "subtract out" the argument to *Complement*. More precisely:

*regToGReg loc sca* (*Complement r*)
    = *primGReg loc sca winRect r diffRegion*

*winRect*  ::  *Region*
*winRect*  =  *Shape* (*Rectangle*
                (*pixelToInch xWin*) (*pixelToInch yWin*))

Note that *winRect* is just a *Region* that exactly matches the size and location of the window. *diffRegion* computes a graphics region that is equivalent to its first argument minus its second.

### 10.3.3  Translating Shapes into Graphics Regions

In the last section we assumed the existence of a function:

*shapeToGRegion*  ::  *Vector* → *Vector* → *Shape* → *G.Region*

that translated shapes into graphics regions. Let's now define this function simply by using the primitive operations that create graphics regions for rectangles, ellipses, and polygons. For starters, here is the definition for a rectangle:

*shapeToGRegion* (*lx*, *ly*) (*sx*, *sy*) (*Rectangle s*1 *s*2)
        = *createRectangle* (*trans* ($-s1/2$, $-s2/2$)) (*trans* ($s1/2$, $s2/2$))
          **where** *trans* (*x*, *y*)  =  (*xWin2* + *inchToPixel* (($x + lx$) * *sx*),
                            *yWin2* − *inchToPixel* (($y + ly$) * *sy*))

*xWin2*  =  *xWin* '*div*' 2
*yWin2*  =  *yWin* '*div*' 2

The key idea here is the use of the auxiliary function *trans* to translate between our coordinates and those of the graphics window. This involves three critical computations:

1. The scaling and translation of the rectangle's coordinates.
2. The conversion of those coordinates to pixel coordinates.
3. The translation of those pixel coordinates to the center of the screen.

The treatment of an ellipse is similar:

$$shapeToGRegion\ (lx,\ ly)\ (sx,\ sy)\ (Ellipse\ r1\ r2)$$
$$=\ createEllipse\ (trans\ (-r1,\ -r2))\ (trans\ (r1,\ r2))$$
$$\textbf{where}\ trans\ (x,\ y)\ =\ (xWin2 + inchToPixel\ ((x + lx) * sx),$$
$$yWin2 - inchToPixel\ ((y + ly) * sy))$$

The convenience of having *trans* defined as a separate function becomes especially handy when dealing with a polygon:

$$shapeToGRegion\ (lx,\ ly)\ (sx,\ sy)\ (Polygon\ vs)$$
$$=\ createPolygon\ (map\ trans\ vs)$$
$$\textbf{where}\ trans\ (x,\ y)\ =\ (xWin2 + inchToPixel\ ((x + lx) * sx),$$
$$yWin2 - inchToPixel\ ((y + ly) * sy))$$

**DETAILS**
Recall that *createPolygon* takes a list of points as its argument.

Finally, because there is no graphics operation to directly create a right triangle, we use *createPolygon* to make one for us:

$$shapeToGRegion\ (lx,\ ly)\ (sx,\ sy)\ (RtTriangle\ s1\ s2)$$
$$=\ createPolygon\ (map\ trans\ [(0,\ 0),\ (s1,\ 0),\ (0,\ s2)])$$
$$\textbf{where}\ trans\ (x,\ y)\ =\ (xWin2 + inchToPixel\ ((x + lx) * sx),$$
$$yWin2 - inchToPixel\ ((y + ly) * sy))$$

**DETAILS**
Note that the definition of *trans* is identical in each of the above four equations. It would be better to have just one definition of *trans*. One approach to doing this is to define *trans* at the top level of the module, but doing so requires extra arguments (why?), as in:

$$trans\ sx\ sy\ (x,\ y)\ =\ (xWin2 + inchToPixel\ ((x + lx) * sx),$$
$$yWin2 - inchToPixel\ ((y + ly) * sy))$$

Each call to *trans* would then have to supply these extra arguments. A better solution is to use Haskell's **case** expression, which allows multiple pattern-matches on an expression without using equations. Using a **case** expression, *shapeToGRegion* can be rewritten as:

> *shapeToGRegion* :: *Vector → Vector → Shape → G.Region*

> *shapeToGRegion* (*lx*, *ly*) (*sx*, *sy*) *s*
>     = **case** *s* **of**
>         *Rectangle s1 s2*
>             → *createRectangle* (*trans* (−*s1*/2, −*s2*/2))
>                                 (*trans* (*s1*/2, *s2*/2))
>         *Ellipse r1 r2*
>             → *createEllipse* (*trans* (−*r1*, −*r2*))
>                               (*trans* (*r1*, *r2*))
>         *Polygon vs*
>             → *createPolygon* (*map trans vs*)
>         *RtTriangle s1 s2*
>             → *createPolygon* (*map trans* [(0, 0), (*s1*, 0), (0, *s2*)])
>       **where** *trans*      :: *Vertex → Point*
>               *trans* (*x*, *y*)  =  (*xWin2* + *inchToPixel* (*lx* + *x* ∗ *sx*),
>                                    *yWin2* − *inchToPixel* (*ly* + *y* ∗ *sy*))

Now there is only one equation, so only one definition of *trans* is needed. Furthermore, there is only one set of patterns for *shapeToRegion*'s first two arguments.

Note: The same layout rules apply to the vertical alignment of the patterns in a **case** expression that are used for the vertical alignment of the equations in a **let** or **where** expression. Also note the use of a nested type signature.

### 10.3.4 Examples

A simple function to draw a given picture can be defined as:

> *draw* :: *String → Picture → IO* ()
> *draw s p*
>     = *runGraphics* $
>         **do** *w ← openWindow s* (*xWin*, *yWin*)
>             *drawPic w p*
>             *spaceClose w*

**DETAILS**
The operator ($) is defined in the Standard Prelude as:

$$(\$) \quad :: \quad (a \to b) \to a \to b$$
$$f \ \$ \ x \ = \ f \ x$$

In other words it is the "apply" operator, and off-hand seems rather useless! It is convenient, however, in avoiding the use of parentheses, because $f \ (g \ x)$ can be written $f \ \$ \ g \ x$. That is the sole reason for using it above, which would otherwise have to be written as:

*draw* :: *String → Picture → IO ()*
*draw s p*
     = *runGraphics (*
         **do** *w ← openWindow* "Region Test" *(xWin, yWin)*
            *drawPic w p*
            *spaceClose w*
         *)*

Other logical relations between regions can be defined. For example, here is the *exclusive union* of two regions, analogous to the exclusive or of boolean values:

*xUnion*          ::   *Region → Region → Region*
*p1* 'xUnion' *p2*   =   *(p1* 'Intersect' *Complement p2)* 'Union'
                          *(p2* 'Intersect' *Complement p1)*

Using the same shapes as *sh*1 through *sh*4 from module *Draw*, we can define four regions:

*r*1   =   *Shape (Rectangle* 3 2)
*r*2   =   *Shape (Ellipse* 1 1.5)
*r*3   =   *Shape (RtTriangle* 3 2)
*r*4   =   *Shape (Polygon* [(−2.5, 2.5), (−3.0, 0), (−1.7, −1.0),
                           (−1.1, 0.2), (−1.5, 2.0)])

and then combine them into a picture in interesting ways. For example:

*reg*1   ▬   *r*3 'xUnion' (*r*1 'Intersect' *Complement r*2 'Union' *r*4)
*pic*1   =   *Region Blue reg*1

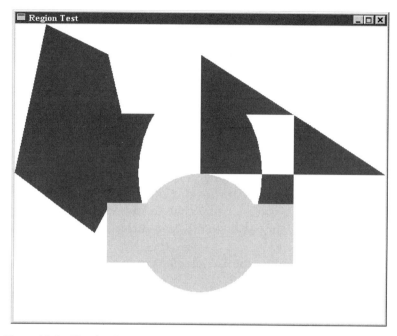

Figure 10.2: Simple Picture Demo

Of course, we can translate and scale things, too. Here is the example given at the very beginning of Chapter 8:

$reg2$ = **let** $circle$ = $Shape$ ($Ellipse$ 0.5 0.5)
        $square$ = $Shape$ ($Rectangle$ 1 1)
    **in** ($Scale$ (2, 2) $circle$)
        '$Union$' ($Translate$ (1, 0) $square$)
        '$Union$' ($Translate$ (−1, 0) $square$)
$pic2$ = $Region$ $Yellow$ ($Translate$ (0, −1) $reg2$)

Finally, we can also combine pictures:

$pic3$ = $pic2$ '$Over$' $pic1$

The pictures $pic1$, $pic2$, and $pic3$ can be drawn by applying the function $draw$ to each of them. Fig. 10.2 is a snapshot of $pic3$.

---

**Exercise 10.1**    Use $draw$ to draw each of the above pictures. Also try drawing the "five circles" example at the beginning of Chapter 8, scaling the region appropriately to make it fit in the graphics window. Make up some of your own examples as well.

## 10.4 User Interaction

Now we can draw pictures in a graphics window. In this section I will show you how user interaction via the mouse can move regions to the surface of the desktop.

Suppose we have a list *regs* of regions in reverse of the order that they should be drawn in the graphics window; that is, in the order that they appear top-to-bottom on the virtual desktop. Then if the mouse is clicked at location *p*, we can use the containment strategy from Section 8.2 to determine which region this point might be contained in. If we search *regs* from the beginning, the first region *r* that contains *p* must be the one we are looking for, because if any other region contains *p* it must be below *r* and thus further down in the list. This region *r* should then be moved to the *front* of the list (i.e., to the top of the virtual desktop).

We can create the list of regions from a *Picture* quite simply as follows:

*pictToList*                 ::   *Picture* → [(*Color*, *Region*)]

*pictToList EmptyPic*      =   []
*pictToList* (*Region c r*)    =   [(*c*, *r*)]
*pictToList* (*p*1 '*Over*' *p*2)   =   *pictToList p*1 ++ *pictToList p*2

Note the similarity of this function to *fringe* defined in Section 7.2.

Next we define a function *adjust* that, given a list of regions *regs* and a point *p* :: *Coordinate*, returns a pair (*hit*, *rs*) where *hit* is the upper-most region containing *p*, and *rs* is the same as *regs* but with *hit* removed. If none of the regions contains *p* we will return *Nothing* as the first element and *regs* as the second (recall from Section 8.4 the discussion about the *Maybe* data type).

*adjust*   ::   [(*Color*, *Region*)] → *Coordinate* →
                    (*Maybe* (*Color*, *Region*), [(*Color*, *Region*)])

*adjust* [] *p*
   =   (*Nothing*, [])
*adjust* ((*c*, *r*) : *regs*) *p*
    = **if** *r* '*containsR*' *p* **then** (*Just* (*c*, *r*), *regs*)
       **else let** (*hit*, *rs*)   =   *adjust regs p*
           **in** (*hit*, (*c*, *r*) : *rs*)

This recursive function looks tricky enough that one might expect difficulty in finding a nonrecursive solution. But using the *break* function from the Standard Prelude, we can define *adjust* as follows:

*adjust regs p*
  = **case** (*break* (\(_, *r*) → *r* 'containsR' *p*) *regs*) **of**
      (*top, hit : rest*)  →  (*Just hit, top* ++ *rest*)
      (_, [ ])      →  (*Nothing, regs*)

---

**DETAILS**

The function *break* takes a list and splits it into two at the first point at which its predicate argument is *True*. For example:

*break* (> 3) [1..6]  ⟹  ([1, 2, 3], [4, 5, 6])

(See Chapter 23.)

This definition also demonstrates that a **case** expression can pattern match against any expression, not just function arguments.

---

Finally, we need a looping function that draws the list of regions (in reverse order!), waits for a mouse click, adjusts the list of regions, and repeats. We will use the simple strategy for now that when the mouse is clicked on a portion of the virtual desktop not covered by a region, the entire process terminates.

*loop*       ::  *Window* → [(*Color, Region*)] → *IO* ()

*loop w regs*  =
  **do** *clearWindow w*
      *sequence_* [*drawRegionInWindow w c r* | (*c, r*) ← *reverse regs*]
      (*x, y*) ← *getLBP w*
      **case** (*adjust regs* (*pixelToInch* (*x* − *xWin2*),
                      *pixelToInch* (*yWin2* − *y*))) **of**
        (*Nothing, _*)        →  *closeWindow w*
        (*Just hit, newRegs*)  →  *loop w* (*hit : newRegs*)

Note how the *regs* argument to *loop* serves as the state of the overall display, and is updated on each recursive call.

## 10.5  Putting it all Together

Combining user interaction with picture drawing is our final task, which at this point is very straightforward, and captured in the function *draw2*:

> *draw2*  ::  *String → Picture → IO* ()
> *draw2 s p*
>    =  *runGraphics* $
>      **do** *w ← openWindow s* (*xWin, yWin*)
>        *loop w* (*pictToList p*)

### 10.5.1  Examples

Using regions *r*1 through *r*4 from Section 10.3.4, we can create four simple pictures:

> *p*1, *p*2, *p*3, *p*4  ::  *Picture*
> *p*1         = *Region Red r*1
> *p*2         = *Region Blue r*2
> *p*3         = *Region Green r*3
> *p*4         = *Region Yellow r*4

then combine them into one, and draw them:

> *pic*   ::  *Picture*
> *pic*   = *foldl Over EmptyPic* [*p*1, *p*2, *p*3, *p*4]
> *main* = *draw2* "Picture Click Test" *pic*

Fig. 10.3 shows the initial orientation of the pictures and the result of clicking on the blue ellipse.

---

**Exercise 10.2**  Run the above program, being sure that clicking on each picture raises it to the top of the graphics window.

---

**Exercise 10.3**  Here is a shorter definition of *loop*, obtained by collapsing *adjust* and the old version of *loop* into a single function:

> *loop w regs*
>   = **do** *clearWindow w*
>       *sequence_*
>         (*map* (*uncurry* (*drawRegionInWindow w*))
>           (*reverse regs*))
>       (*x, y*) ← *getLBP w*
>       **let** *aux* (_, *r*)  =  *r* 'containsR' (*pixelToInch* (*x − xWin2*),
>                              *pixelToInch* (*yWin2 − y*))
>       **case** (*break aux regs*) **of**
>        (_, [ ])           →  *closeWindow w*
>        (*top, hit : bot*)   ·  *loop w* (*hit* : (*top* ⊔ *bot*))

Prove that this version is equivalent to the old.

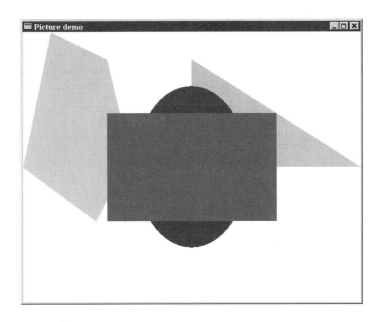

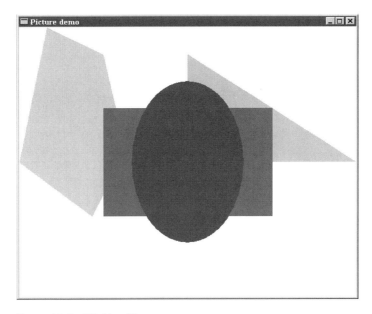

Figure 10.3: Clicking Pictures

**Exercise 10.4** Write a Haskell program that allows you to *drag and drop* pictures: When the left mouse button is pressed, the picture under it should rise to the top, and as long as the left button is held down, the picture should follow the position of the mouse. Once the button is released, the picture should remain fixed at its last position. (You will have to consult Haskell's *SOEGraphics* library to determine the appropriate mouse operations to use.)

# CHAPTER ELEVEN

# Proof by Induction

In this chapter I will introduce a powerful proof technique based on *mathematical induction*. With it we will be able to prove complex and important properties of programs that cannot be accomplished with proof-by-calculation alone. The inductive proof method is one of the most powerful and common methods for proving program properties.

## 11.1  Induction and Recursion

*Induction* is very closely related to *recursion*. In fact, in certain contexts the terms are used interchangeably; in others, one is preferred over the other primarily for historical reasons. I like to think of them as being duals of each other: Induction is used to describe things starting with something very simple, and building up from there, whereas recursion describes the whole thing first, working backward to the simple case.

For example, although I have previously used the phrase *recursive data type*, in fact data types are often described inductively, such as a list:

> A *list* is either empty, or it is a pair consisting of a value and another list.

On the other hand, we usually describe functions that manipulate lists, such as *map* and *foldr*, as being recursive. This is because when you apply a function such as *map*, you apply it initially to the whole list, and work backwards toward [ ]. But these differences between induction and recursion run no deeper: They are really just two sides of the same coin.

This chapter is about *inductive properties* of programs (but based on the above argument could just as rightly be called *recursive properties*) that are not usually proven via calculation alone. Proving inductive properties usually involves the inductive nature of data types and the recursive nature of functions defined on the data types.

As an example, suppose that $P$ is an inductive property of a list. In other words, $P(l)$ for some list $l$ is either true or false (no middle ground here!). To prove this property inductively, we do so based on the length of the list: Starting with length 0, we first prove $P([])$ (using our standard method of proof-by-calculation).

Now for the key step: Assume for the moment that $P(xs)$ is true for any list $xs$ whose length is less than or equal to $n$. Then if we can prove (via calculation) that $P(x : xs)$ is true for any $x$ (i.e., that $P$ is true for lists of length $n + 1$), then the claim is that $P$ is true for lists of *any* (finite) length.

Why is this so? Well, from the first step above we know that $P$ is true for length 0, so the second step tells us that it's also true for length 1. But if it's true for length 1, then it must also be true for length 2; similarly for lengths 3, 4, and so on. So $P$ is true for lists of any length!

It it important to realize, however, that a property being true for every finite list does not necessarily imply that it is true for every infinite list. The property "the list is finite" is a perfect example of this! I will explain how to prove properties of infinite lists in Chapter 14.

To summarize, to prove a property $P$ by induction on the length of a list, we proceed in two steps:

1. Prove $P([])$ (this is called the *base step*).
2. Assume that $P(xs)$ is true (this is called the *induction hypothesis*), and prove that $P(x : xs)$ is true (this is called the *induction step*).

## 11.2 Examples of List Induction

Okay, enough talk. Let's see this idea in action. Recall in Section 5.1 the following property about *foldr*:

$$(\forall xs) \; foldr \; (:) \; [\;] \; xs \;\; \Longrightarrow \;\; xs$$

We will prove this by induction on the length of $xs$. Following the ideas above, we begin with the base step by proving the property for length 0 (i.e., for $xs = [\;]$):

$$foldr \; (:) \; [\;] \; [\;] \;\; \Rightarrow \;\; [\;]$$

This step is immediate from the definition of *foldr*. Now for the induction step: We first *assume* that the property is true for all lists *xs* of length *n*, and then prove the property for list *x* : *xs*. Again, proceeding by calculation:

> *foldr* (:) [ ] (*x* : *xs*)
>   ⇒  *x* : *foldr* (:) [ ] *xs*
>   ⇒  *x* : *xs*

And we are done; the induction hypothesis is what justifies the second step.

Now let's do something a bit harder. Suppose we are interested in proving the following property:

(∀*xs*, *ys*) *length* (*xs* ++ *ys*) = *length xs* + *length ys*

Our first problem is to decide which list to perform the induction over. A little thought (in particular, a look at how the definitions of *length* and (++) are structured) should convince you that *xs* is the right choice. (If you do not see this, you are encouraged to try the proof by induction over the length of *ys*!) Again, following the ideas above, we begin with the base step by proving the property for length 0 (i.e., for *xs* = [ ]):

> *length* ([ ] ++ *ys*)
>   ⇒  *length ys*
>   ⇒  0 + *length ys*
>   ⇒  *length* [ ] + *length ys*

For the induction step, we first assume that the property is true for all lists *xs* of length *n*, and then prove the property for list *x* : *xs*. Again proceeding by calculation:

> *length* ((*x* : *xs*) ++ *ys*)
>   ⇒  *length* (*x* : (*xs* ++ *ys*))
>   ⇒  1 + *length* (*xs* ++ *ys*)
>   ⇒  1 + (*length xs* + *length ys*)
>   ⇒  (1 + *length xs*) + *length ys*
>   ⇒  *length* (*x* : *xs*) + *length ys*

And we are done. The transition from the third to the fourth line is where we used the induction hypothesis.

## 11.2.1  Proving Function Equivalences

At this point it is a simple matter to return to Chapter 5 and supply the proofs that functions defined using *map* and *fold* are equivalent to the recursive versions. In particular, let's prove first that:

*transList ps = map trans ps*

for any finite list *ps*, where:

*transList* [ ] = [ ]
*transList* (*p* : *ps*) = *trans p* : *transList ps*

We proceed by induction, starting with the base case *ps* = [ ]:

*transList* [ ]
⇒  [ ]
⇒  *map trans* [ ]

Next we assume that *transList ps = map trans ps* holds, and try to prove
that *transList* (*p* : *ps*) = *map trans* (*p* : *ps*) (note the use of the induction
hypothesis in the second step):

*transList* (*p* : *ps*)
⇒  *trans p* : *transList ps*
⇒  *trans p* : *map trans ps*
⇒  *map trans* (*p* : *ps*)

The proof that *putCharList cs = map putChar cs* is equally easy, and is
left as an exercise.

Similarly, we can prove that *listSum xs = fold* (+) 0 *xs*, where:

*listSum* [ ]      =  0
*listSum* (*x* : *xs*)  =  *x + listSum xs*

First the base case:

*listSum* [ ]
⇒  0
⇒  *fold* (+) 0 [ ]

Then the induction step:

*listSum* (*x* : *xs*)
⇒  *x + listSum xs*
⇒  *x + fold* (+) 0 *xs*
⇒  *fold* (+) 0 (*x* : *xs*)

These proofs were quite easy.

For something much more challenging, consider the definition of *reverse* given in Chapter 5:

*reverse*1 [ ]       =  [ ]
*reverse*1 (*x* : *xs*)  =  *reverse*1 *xs* ++ [*x*]

and the version defined in Chapter 9:

*reverse*2 *xs*  =  *foldl* (*flip* (:)) [ ] *xs*

We would like to show that these are the same (i.e., that *reverse*1 *xs* = *reverse*2 *xs* for all finite lists *xs*). In carrying out this proof, I will demonstrate two new ideas, the first being that induction can be used to prove the equivalence of two programs. The second is the need for an *auxiliary property*, which is proved independently of the main result.

The base case is easy, as is often the case:

*reverse*1 [ ]
  ⇒  [ ]
  ⇒  *foldl* (*flip* (:)) [ ] [ ]
  ⇒  *reverse*2 [ ]

Assume now that *reverse*1 *xs* = *reverse*2 *xs*. The induction step proceeds as follows:

*reverse*1 (*x* : *xs*)
  ⇒  *reverse*1 *xs* ++ [*x*]
  ⇒  *reverse*2 *xs* ++ [*x*]
  ⇒  *foldl* (*flip* (:)) [ ] *xs* ++ [*x*]
  ⇒  ???

But now what do we do? Intuitively, it seems that the following property, which I will call property (1), should hold:

*foldl* (*flip* (:)) [ ] *xs* ++ [*x*]
  ⇒  *foldl* (*flip* (:)) [ ] (*x* : *xs*)

in which case we could complete the proof as follows:

  . . .
  ⇒  *foldl* (*flip* (:)) [ ] *xs* ++ [*x*]
  ⇒  *foldl* (*flip* (:)) [ ] (*x* : *xs*)
  ⇒  *reverse*2 (*x* : *xs*)

The ability to see that if we could just prove one thing, then perhaps we could prove another, is a useful skill in conducting proofs. In this case we have reduced the overall problem to one of proving property (1), which simplifies the structure of the proof, although not necessarily the difficulty. These auxiliary properties are often called *lemmas* in mathematics, and in many cases their proofs become the most important contributions, because they are often at the essence of a problem.

In fact, if you try to prove property (1) directly, you will run into a problem, namely, that it is not *general* enough. So first I will generalize property (1) (while renaming $x$ to $y$), as follows:

$$foldl \ (flip \ (:)) \ ys \ xs +\!\!+ [y]$$
$$\Rightarrow \ foldl \ (flip \ (:)) \ (ys +\!\!+ [y]) \ xs$$

I will call this property (2). If it is true for any finite $xs$ and $ys$, then property (1) is also true, because:

$$foldl \ (flip \ (:)) \ [\ ] \ xs +\!\!+ [x]$$
$$\Rightarrow \ \{ \ property \ (2) \ \}$$
$$foldl \ (flip \ (:)) \ ([\ ] +\!\!+ [x]) \ xs$$
$$\Rightarrow \ \{ \ unfold \ (+\!\!+) \ \}$$
$$foldl \ (flip \ (:)) \ [x] \ xs$$
$$\Rightarrow \ \{ \ fold \ (flip \ (:)) \ \}$$
$$foldl \ (flip \ (:)) \ (flip \ (:) \ [\ ] \ x) \ xs$$
$$\Rightarrow \ \{ \ fold \ foldl \ \}$$
$$foldl \ (flip \ (:)) \ [\ ] \ (x : xs)$$

You are encouraged to try proving property (1) directly, and hopefully you will come to the same conclusion that I did about the need for generalization. This is not always easy to see, but is sometimes an important step is constructing a proof, because, despite being somewhat counterintuitive, it is often the case that making a property more general (and therefore more powerful) makes it easier to prove.

In any case, how do we prove property (2)? Using induction, of course. Setting $xs$ to [ ], the base case is easy:

$$foldl \ (flip \ (:)) \ ys \ [\ ] +\!\!+ [y]$$
$$\Rightarrow \ \{ \ unfold \ foldl \ \}$$
$$ys +\!\!+ [y]$$
$$\Rightarrow \ \{ \ fold \ foldl \ \}$$
$$foldl \ (flip \ (:)) \ (ys +\!\!+ [y]) \ [\ ]$$

and the induction step proceeds as follows:

$$foldl \; (flip \; (:)) \; ys \; (x : xs) + [y]$$
$$\Rightarrow \; \{ \text{unfold } foldl \; \}$$
$$foldl \; (flip \; (:)) \; (flip \; (:) \; ys \; x) \; xs + [y]$$
$$\Rightarrow \; \{ \text{unfold } flip \; \}$$
$$foldl \; (flip \; (:)) \; (x : ys) \; xs + [y]$$
$$\Rightarrow \; \{ \text{induction hypothesis} \}$$
$$foldl \; (flip \; (:)) \; ((x : ys) + [y]) \; xs$$
$$\Rightarrow \; \{ \text{unfold } (+) \; \}$$
$$foldl \; (flip \; (:)) \; (x : (ys + [y])) \; xs$$
$$\Rightarrow \; \{ \text{fold } foldl \; \}$$
$$foldl \; (flip \; (:)) \; (ys + [y]) \; (x : xs)$$

## 11.3 Useful Properties on Lists

There are many useful properties of functions on lists that require inductive proofs. Tables 11.1 and 11.2 list a number of them involving functions used in this text, but I leave their proofs as an exercise for you (except for one; see below). In any case, you should assume that these properties are true, and use them freely in proving other properties of your programs. In fact, some of these properties can be used to simplify the proof that *reverse1* and *reverse2* are the same; see if you can find them![1]

(Note, by the way, that in the first rule for *map* in Fig. 11.1, the type of $\backslash x \rightarrow x$ on the left-hand side is $a \rightarrow b$, whereas on the right-hand side it is $[a] \rightarrow [b]$; i.e. these are really two different functions.)

### 11.3.1 Function Strictness

Note that the last rule for *map* in Fig. 11.1 is only valid for *strict* functions. A function $f$ is said to be strict if $f \perp = \perp$. For example, the successor function $(+1)$ is strict, because $(+1) \perp = \perp +1 = \perp$. In other words, if you apply $(+1)$ to a nonterminating computation, you end up with a nonterminating computation.

Not all functions in Haskell are strict, and we have to be careful to say on which argument a function is strict. For example, $(+)$ is strict on both of its arguments, which is why the section $(+1)$ is also strict. On the

---

[1] More thorough discussions of these properties and their proofs may be found in (Bird and Wadler, 1988; Bird, 1998).

**Properties of *map*:**

$$map \ (\backslash x \to x) = \backslash x \to x$$
$$map \ (f \cdot g) = map \ f \cdot map \ g$$
$$map \ f \cdot tail = tail \cdot map \ f$$
$$map \ f \cdot reverse = reverse \cdot map \ f$$
$$map \ f \cdot concat = concat \cdot map \ (map \ f)$$
$$map \ f \ (xs +\!\!+ ys) = map \ f \ xs +\!\!+ map \ f \ ys$$

For all strict $f$:

$$f \cdot head = head \cdot map \ f$$

**Properties of the *fold* functions:**

(1) If *op* is associative, and $e \ `op` \ x = x$ and $x \ `op` \ e = x$ for all $x$, then for all finite $xs$:

$$foldr \ op \ e \ xs = foldl \ op \ e \ xs$$

(2) If the following are true:

$$x \ `op1` \ (y \ `op2` \ z) = (x \ `op1` \ y) \ `op2` \ z$$
$$x \ `op1` \ e = e \ `op2` \ x$$

then for all finite $xs$:

$$foldr \ op1 \ e \ xs = foldl \ op2 \ e \ xs$$

(3) For all finite $xs$:

$$foldr \ op \ e \ xs = foldl \ (flip \ op) \ e \ (reverse \ xs)$$

Table 11.1: Some Useful Properties of *map* and *fold*.

other hand, the constant function:

$$const \ x \ y \ = \ x$$

is strict on its first argument (why?), but not its second, because $const \ x \ \bot = x$, for any $x$.

**DETAILS**
Understanding strictness requires a careful understanding of Haskell's pattern-matching rules. For example, consider the definition of (&&) from the Standard Prelude:

```
(&&)        ::  Bool → Bool → Bool
True && x   =   x
False && _  =   False
```

When choosing a pattern to match, Haskell starts with the top, leftmost pattern, and works to the right and downward. So in the above, (**&&**) first evaluates its left argument. If that value is *True*, then the first equation succeeds, and the second argument gets evaluated because that is the value that is returned. But if the first argument is *False*, the second equation succeeds. In particular, *it does not bother to evaluate the second argument at all*, and simply returns *False* as the answer. This means that (**&&**) is strict in its first argument, but not its second.

A more detailed discussion of pattern matching is found in Appendix B.

Let's now look more closely at the last law for *map*, which says that for all strict $f$:

$$f . head = head . map \ f$$

Let's try to prove this property, starting with the base case, but ignoring for now the strictness constraint on $f$:

$$f \ (head \ [ \ ])$$
$$\Rightarrow \ f \ \bot$$

---

**Properties of (++):**
For all *xs*, *ys*, and *zs*:

$$(xs ++ ys) ++ zs = xs ++ (ys ++ zs)$$
$$xs ++ [ \ ] = [ \ ] ++ xs = xs$$

**Properties of *take* and *drop*:**
For all finite nonnegative *m* and *n*, and finite *xs*:

$$take \ n \ xs ++ drop \ n \ xs = xs$$
$$take \ m . take \ n = take \ (min \ m \ n)$$
$$drop \ m . drop \ n = drop \ (m + n)$$
$$take \ m . drop \ n = drop \ n . take \ (m + n)$$

For all finite nonnegative *m* and *n* such that $n \geq m$:

$$drop \ m . take \ n = take \ (n - m) . drop \ m$$

**Properties of reverse:**
For all finite *xs*:

$$reverse \ (reverse \ xs) = xs$$
$$head \ (reverse \ xs) = last \ xs$$
$$last \ (reverse \ xs) = head \ xs$$

Table 11.2: Useful Properties of Other Functions Over Lists

Base case ($n = 0$):

$f\ x\ 0 * f\ x\ 0$
$\Rightarrow\ 1 * 1$
$\Rightarrow\ 1$
$\Rightarrow\ f\ (x * x)\ 0$

Induction step ($n + 1$):

$f\ x\ (n + 1) * f\ x\ (n + 1)$
$\Rightarrow\ (x * f\ x\ n) * (x * f\ x\ n)$
$\Rightarrow\ (x * x) * (f\ x\ n * f\ x\ n)$
$\Rightarrow\ (x * x) * f\ (x * x)\ n$
$\Rightarrow\ f\ (x * x)\ (n + 1)$

Figure 11.1: Proof That $f\ x\ n * f\ x\ n = f\ (x * x)\ n$

The value *head* [ ] is an error, which you will recall has value $\perp$. So you can see immediately that the issue of strictness might play a role in the proof, because without knowing anything about $f$, there is no further calculation to be done here. Similarly, if we start with the right-hand side:

*head* (*map f* [ ])
$\Rightarrow$ *head* [ ]
$\Rightarrow \perp$

It should be clear that for the base case to be true, it must be that $f\ \perp = \perp$ (i.e., $f$ must be strict). Thus, we have essentially "discovered" the constraint on the theorem through the process of trying to prove it! (This is not an uncommon phenomenon.)

The induction step is less problematic:

$f$ (*head* ($x : xs$))
$\Rightarrow$ $f\ x$
$\Rightarrow$ *head* ($f\ x : map\ f\ xs$)
$\Rightarrow$ *head* (*map f* ($x : xs$))

and we are done.

---

**Exercise 11.1** From Chapter 5, prove that *putCharList cs = map putChar cs* and that *listProd xs = fold* ($*$) 1 *xs*, for all finite lists *cs* and *xs*.

---

**Exercise 11.2** Prove as many of the properties in Tables 11.1 and 11.2 as you can.

**Exercise 11.3** Which of the following functions are strict (if the function takes more than one argument, specify on which arguments it is strict): *reverse*, *simple*, *map*, *tail*, *area*, *regionToGRegion*, (&&), (*True* &&), (*False* &&), and the following function:

$$
\begin{aligned}
&ifFun &&:: && Bool \to a \to a \to a \\
&ifFun\ pred\ cons\ alt &&= && \textbf{if}\ pred\ \textbf{then}\ cons\ \textbf{else}\ alt
\end{aligned}
$$

## 11.4 Induction on Other Data Types

Proof by induction is not limited to lists. For example, we can use it to reason about natural numbers.[2] Suppose we define an exponentiation function as follows:

$$
\begin{aligned}
&(\hat{}) &&:: && Integer \to Integer \to Integer \\
&x\hat{}0 &&= && 1 \\
&x\hat{}n &&= && x * x\hat{}(n-1)
\end{aligned}
$$

> **DETAILS**
> ($*$) is defined in the Standard Prelude to have precedence level 7, and recall that if no **infix** declaration is given for an operator it defaults to precedence level 9, which means that ($\hat{}$) has precedence level 9, which is higher than that for ($*$). Therefore, no parentheses are needed to disambiguate the last line in the definition above, which corresponds nicely to mathematical convention.

Now suppose that we want to prove that:

$$
(\forall x, n \geq 0, m \geq 0)\ x\hat{}(n+m) = x\hat{}n * x\hat{}m
$$

We proceed by induction on $n$, beginning with $n = 0$:

$$
\begin{aligned}
&x\hat{}(0+m) \\
\Rightarrow\ &x\hat{}m \\
\Rightarrow\ &1 * (x\hat{}m) \\
\Rightarrow\ &x\hat{}0 * x\hat{}m
\end{aligned}
$$

---

[2] Indeed, one could argue that a proof by induction over finite lists is really an induction over natural numbers, because it is an induction over the *length* of the list, which is a natural number.

Next we assume that the property is true for numbers less than or equal to $n$, and prove it for $n + 1$:

$$x\char`^((n + 1) + m)$$
$$\Rightarrow \ x * x\char`^(n + m)$$
$$\Rightarrow \ x * (x\char`^n * x\char`^m)$$
$$\Rightarrow \ (x * x\char`^n) * x\char`^m$$
$$\Rightarrow \ x\char`^(n + 1) * x\char`^m$$

and we are done.

Or are we? What if, in the definition of (^), $x$ or $n$ is *negative*? Because a negative integer is not a natural number, we could dispense with the problem by saying that these situations fall beyond the bounds of the property we are trying to prove. But let's look a little closer. If $x$ is negative, the property we are trying to prove still holds (why?). But if $n$ is negative, $x\char`^n$ will not terminate (why?). As diligent programmers we may wish to defend against the latter situation by writing:

```
(^)                :: Integer → Integer → Integer
x^0                = 1
x^n | n < 0        = error "negative exponent"
    | otherwise    = x * x^(n - 1)
```

If we consider nonterminating computations and ones that produce an error to both have the same value, namely *bottom*, then these two versions of (^) are equivalent. Pragmatically, however, the latter is clearly superior.

Note that the above definition will test for $n < 0$ on every recursive call, when actually the only call in which it could happen is the first. Therefore, a slightly more efficient version of this program would be:

```
(^)                :: Integer → Integer → Integer
x^n | n < 0        = error "negative exponent"
    | otherwise    = f x n
  where f x 0  = 1
        f x n  = x * f x (n - 1)
```

Proving the property stated earlier for this version of the program is straightforward, with one minor distinction: What we really need to prove is that the property is true for $f$; that is:

$$(\forall x, n \geq 0, m \geq 0) \;\; f\, x\, (n + m) = f\, x\, n * f\, x\, m$$

from which the proof for the whole function follows trivially.

### 11.4.1  A More Efficient Exponentiation Function

However, in fact there is a more serious inefficiency in our exponentiation function: We are not taking advantage of the fact that, for any even number $n$, $x^n = (x * x)^{n/2}$. Using this fact, here is a more clever way to accomplish the exponentiation task, using the names (^!) and *ff* for our functions to distinguish them from the previous versions:

```
(^!)                :: Integer → Integer → Integer
x^!n |  n < 0       =  error "negative exponent"
     | otherwise    =  ff x n
  where ff x n |  n == 0      =  1
              |  even n      =  ff (x * x) (n 'quot' 2)
              | otherwise    =  x * ff x (n − 1)
```

---

**DETAILS**

*quot* is Haskell's *quotient* operator, which returns the integer quotient of the first argument divided by the second, rounded toward zero.

---

You should convince yourself that, intuitively at least, this version of exponentiation is not only correct, but also more efficient. More precisely, (^) executes a number of steps proportional to $n$, whereas (^!) executes a number of steps proportional to the $\log_2$ of $n$. The Standard Prelude defines (^) similarly to the way I have defined (^!) here.

Because intuition is not always reliable, let's *prove* that this version is equivalent to the old. That is, we wish to prove that $x^\wedge n = x^\wedge !n$ for all $x$ and $n$.

A quick look at the two definitions reveals that what we really need to prove is that $f\, x\, n = ff\, x\, n$, from which it follows immediately that $x^\wedge n = x^\wedge !n$. We do this by induction on $n$, beginning with the base case $n = 0$:

$$f\, x\, 0 \;\; \Rightarrow \;\; 1 \;\; \Rightarrow \;\; ff\, x\, 0$$

so the base step holds trivially. The induction step, however, is considerably more complicated. We must consider two cases: $n + 1$ is either even, or it is odd. If it is odd, we can show that:

$$f\ x\ (n + 1)$$
$$\Rightarrow\ x * f\ x\ n$$
$$\Rightarrow\ x * ff\ x\ n$$
$$\Rightarrow\ ff\ x\ (n + 1)$$

and we are done (note the use of the induction hypothesis in the second step).

If $n + 1$ is even, we might try proceeding in a similar way:

$$f\ x\ (n + 1)$$
$$\Rightarrow\ x * f\ x\ n$$
$$\Rightarrow\ x * ff\ x\ n$$

But now what shall we do? Because $n$ is odd, we might try unfolding the call to $ff$:

$$x * ff\ x\ n$$
$$\Rightarrow\ x * (x * ff\ x\ (n - 1))$$

but this doesn't seem to be getting us anywhere. Furthermore, *folding* the call to $ff$ (as we did in the odd case) would involve *doubling n* and taking the square root of $x$, neither of which seems like a good idea!

We could also try going in the other direction:

$$ff\ x\ (n + 1)$$
$$\Rightarrow\ ff\ (x * x)\ ((n + 1)\ \text{‘quot‘}\ 2)$$
$$\Rightarrow\ f\ (x * x)\ ((n + 1)\ \text{‘quot‘}\ 2)$$

The use of the induction hypothesis in the second step needs to be justified, because the first argument to $f$ has changed from $x$ to $x * x$. But recall that the induction hypothesis states that for *all* values $x$, and all natural numbers up to $n$, $f\ x\ n$ is the same as $ff\ x\ n$. So this is okay.

But even allowing this, we seem to be stuck again! Instead of pushing this line of reasoning further, let's pursue a different tact based on the (valid) assumption that if $m$ is even, then:

$$m = m\ \text{‘quot‘}\ 2 + m\ \text{‘quot‘}\ 2$$

Let's use this fact together with the property that we proved in the last section:

$f\ x\ (n+1)$
$\Rightarrow\ f\ x\ ((n+1)\ 'quot'\ 2 + (n+1)\ 'quot'\ 2)$
$\Rightarrow\ f\ x\ ((n+1)\ 'quot'\ 2) * f\ x\ ((n+1)\ 'quot'\ 2)$

Next, as with the proof in the last section involving *reverse*, let's make an assumption about a property that will help us along. Specifically, what if we could prove that $f\ x\ n * f\ x\ n$ is equal to $f\ (x * x)\ n$? If so, we could proceed as follows:

$f\ x\ ((n+1)\ 'quot'\ 2) * f\ x\ ((n+1)\ 'quot'\ 2)$
$\Rightarrow\ f\ (x * x)\ ((n+1)\ 'quot'\ 2)$
$\Rightarrow\ ff\ (x * x)\ ((n+1)\ 'quot'\ 2)$
$\Rightarrow\ ff\ x\ (n+1)$

and we are finally done. Note the use of the induction hypothesis in the second step, as justified earlier. The proof of the auxiliary property is not difficult, but also requires induction (see Fig. 11.1).

Aside from improving efficiency, one of the pleasant outcomes of proving that (^) and (^!) are equivalent is that *anything that we prove about one function will be true for the other.* For example, the validity of the property that we proved earlier:

$x\hat{\ }(n+m) = x\hat{\ }n * x\hat{\ }m$

immediately implies the validity of:

$x\hat{\ }!(n+m) = x\hat{\ }!n * x\hat{\ }!m$

Although (^!) is more efficient than (^), it is also more complicated, so it makes sense to try proving new properties for (^), because the proofs will likely be easier.

The moral of this story is that you shouldn't throw away old code that is simpler but less efficient than a newer version. That old code can serve at least two good purposes. First, if it is simpler, it is likely to be easier to understand, and thus serves a useful role in documenting your effort. Second, as we have just discussed, if it is provably equivalent to the new code, then it can be used to simplify the task of proving properties about the new code.

**Exercise 11.4**  The function (^!) can be made more efficient by noting that in the last line of the definition of *ff*, *n* is odd, and therefore $n - 1$ must be even, so the test for *n* being even on the next recursive call could be avoided. Redefine (^!) so that it avoids this (minor) inefficiency.

---

**Exercise 11.5**  Consider this definition of the *factorial* function:[3]

$$fac1 \quad :: \quad Integer \rightarrow Integer$$
$$fac1 \; 0 \; = \; 1$$
$$fac1 \; n \; = \; n * fac1 \; (n - 1)$$

and this alternative definition:

$$fac2 \quad :: \quad Integer \rightarrow Integer$$
$$fac2 \; n \; = \; fac' \; n \; 1$$
$$\textbf{where } fac' \; 0 \; x \; = \; x$$
$$\qquad\qquad fac' \; n \; x \; = \; fac' \; (n - 1) \; (n * x)$$

Prove that *fac1* $n$ = *fac2* $n$ for all nonnegative integers $n$.

---

[3] The factorial function is defined mathematically as:

$$factorial \; n = \begin{cases} 1 & \text{if } n = 0 \\ n * factorial(n - 1) & \text{otherwise} \end{cases}$$

# CHAPTER TWELVE

# Qualified Types

Recall that a polymorphic type such as $(a \rightarrow a)$ is really shorthand for $\forall(a)a \rightarrow a$, which can be read "*for all* types $a$, functions mapping elements of type $a$ to elements of type $a$." Note the emphasis on *for all*.

In practice, however, there are times when we would prefer to limit a polymorphic type to a smaller number of possibilities. A good example is a function such as $(+)$. It's probably not a good idea to limit $(+)$ to a *single* (that is, *mono*morphic) type such as *Integer* $\rightarrow$ *Integer* $\rightarrow$ *Integer*, because there are other kinds of numbers – such as floating-point and complex numbers – that we would like to perform addition on. Nor is it a very good idea to have a different addition function for each type of number we wish to add, because that would require giving each a different name, such as *addInteger*, *addFloat*, *addComplex*, and so on. And, unfortunately, we can't give $(+)$ a type such as $a \rightarrow a \rightarrow a$, because this would imply that we could add things other than numbers, such as characters, lists, tuples, and any type that you might define on your own!

Haskell provides a solution to this problem through the use of *qualified types*. Conceptually, you can think of a qualified type just as a polymorphic type, except that in place of "*for all* types $a$" we will be able to say "for all types *a that are members of class C*," where the class $C$ can be thought of as a set of types. For example, suppose there is a class *Num* with members *Integer*, *Float*, and *Complex*. Then we could give an accurate type for $(+)$, namely: $\forall(a \in Num)a \rightarrow a \rightarrow a$. But in Haskell, instead of writing $\forall(a \in Num) \cdots$ we will write *Num* $a \Rightarrow \cdots$. So the proper type signature for $(+)$ is:

$(+) \ :: \ Num \ a \Rightarrow a \rightarrow a \rightarrow a$

which should be read: "for all types $a$ that are members of the class *Num*, $(+)$ has type $a \rightarrow a \rightarrow a$." Members of a class are also called *instances* of the class, and I will use these two terms interchangeably in the remainder of the text.

> **DETAILS**
> It is important not to confuse *Num* with a data type or a constructor within a data type, even though the same syntax ("*Num a*") is used. *Num* is a *type class*, and the context of its use (namely, to the left of a ⇒) is always sufficient to determine this fact.

The ability to qualify polymorphic types is a unique feature of Haskell, and, as you will soon see, provides great expressiveness. In particular, you will see that it is possible to define your own type class and its members. But first, let's look at another example of a predefined qualified type in Haskell.

## 12.1 Equality

*Equality* between two expressions *e*1 and *e*2 in Haskell means that the value of *e*1 is the same as the value of *e*2. Another way to view equality is that you should be able to substitute *e*1 for *e*2 wherever they appear in a program, without affecting the result of that program.

In general, however, it is not possible for a program to determine the equality of two expressions; consider, for example, determining the equality of two infinite lists, or the equality of two functions of type *Integer* → *Integer*. The ability to compute the equality of two values is called *computational equality*. Even though by the above simple examples it is clear that computational equality is strictly weaker than full equality, it is still an operation that we would like to use in many ordinary programs.

Haskell's operator for computational equality is (==). Partly because of the problem mentioned above, there are many types for which we would like equality defined, but some for which we might not. For example, we often want to compare two characters, two integers, two floating-point numbers, and so forth. On the other hand, comparing the equality of functions is difficult, and in general not possible. Thus, Haskell has a type class called *Eq*, so that the equality operator (==) can be given the qualified type:

$$(==) \ :: \ Eq \ a \Rightarrow a \rightarrow a \rightarrow Bool$$

In other words, (==) is a function that, for any type *a* in the class *Eq*, tests two values of type *a* for equality, returning a Boolean (*Bool*) value as a result. Among *Eq*'s instances are the types *Char* and *Integer*, so that the following calculations hold:

$$42 == 42 \;\;\Rightarrow\;\; True$$
$$42 == 43 \;\;\Rightarrow\;\; False$$
$$'a' ==' a' \;\;\Rightarrow\;\; True$$
$$'a' ==' b' \;\;\Rightarrow\;\; False$$

Furthermore, the expression $42 == \; 'a'$ is *ill-typed*; Haskell is clever enough to know when qualified types are ill-formed.

One of the nice things about qualified types is that they work in the presence of ordinary polymorphism. In particular, the type constraints can be made to propagate through polymorphic data types. For example, because *Integer* and *Float* are members of *Eq*, so are the types (*Integer*, *Char*), [*Integer*], [*Float*], and so on. Thus:

$$[42, 43] == [42, 43] \;\;\Rightarrow\;\; True$$
$$[4.2, 4.3] == [4.3, 4.2] \;\;\Rightarrow\;\; False$$
$$(42, 'a') == (42, 'a') \;\;\Rightarrow\;\; True$$

We will see how this is done is a later section.

Type constraints also propagate through function definitions. For example, consider this definition of the function *elem*, which tests for membership in a list:

```
x 'elem' [ ]      =  False
x 'elem' (y : ys)  =  x == y || x 'elem' ys
```

Note the use of (==) on the right-hand side of the second equation. The principal type for *elem* is thus:

$$elem \;::\; Eq\ a \Rightarrow a \rightarrow [a] \rightarrow Bool$$

This should be read, "For every type *a* that is an instance of the class *Eq*, *elem* has type $a \rightarrow [a] \rightarrow Bool$." This is just what we want. It expresses the fact that *elem* is not defined on all types, just those for which computational equality is defined.

The above type for *elem* is also its principal type, and Haskell will infer this type if no signature is given. Indeed, if you were to write the type signature:

$$elem \;::\; a \rightarrow [a] \rightarrow Bool$$

you would encounter a type error, because this type is fundamentally *too general*, and the Haskell type system will complain.

> **DETAILS**
> On the other hand, you could write:
>
> $elem \ :: \ Integer \rightarrow [Integer] \rightarrow Bool$
>
> if you expect to use *elem* only on lists of integers. In other words, using a type signature to constrain a value to be less general than its principal type is okay.

As another example of this idea, a function that squares its argument:

$square \ x \ = \ x * x$

has principal type $Num \ a \Rightarrow a \rightarrow a$, because $(*)$, like $(+)$, has type $Num \ a \Rightarrow a \rightarrow a \rightarrow a$. Thus:

$square \ 42 \ \Rightarrow \ 1764$
$square \ 4.2 \ \Rightarrow \ 17.64$

I will have much more to say about the *Num* class shortly.

## 12.2  Defining Your Own Type Classes

Haskell provides a mechanism whereby you can create your own qualified types, by defining a new type class and specifying which types are members, or "instances" of it. Indeed, the type classes *Num* and *Eq* are not built-in as primitives in Haskell, but rather are simply predefined in the Standard Prelude.

To see how this is done, let's take the *Eq* class as an example. It is created by the following *type class declaration*:

**class** *Eq a* **where**
    $(==) \ :: \ a \rightarrow a \rightarrow Bool$

The connection between $(==)$ and *Eq* is important: The above declaration should be read "a type *a* is an instance of the class *Eq* only if there is an operation $(==) :: a \rightarrow a \rightarrow Bool$ defined on it."

> **DETAILS**
> $(==)$ is called an *operation* in the class *Eq*, and in general more than one operation is allowed in a class. We will see examples of this shortly.

So far so good. But how do we specify which types are instances of the class *Eq*, and the actual behavior of (==) on each of those types? This is done with an *instance declaration*. For example:

**instance** *Eq Integer* **where**
   *x* == *y*  =  *IntegerEq x y*

The definition of (==) is called a *method*. The function *IntegerEq* happens to be the primitive function that compares integers for equality, but in general any valid expression is allowed on the right-hand side, just as for any other function definition. The overall instance declaration is essentially saying: "The type *Integer* is an instance of the class *Eq*, and here is the method corresponding to the operation (==)." Given this declaration, we can now compare fixed-precision integers for equality using (==). Similarly:

**instance** *Eq Float* **where**
   *x* == *y*  =  *floatEq x y*

allows us to compare floating-point numbers using (==).

More importantly, data types that you have defined on your own can also be made instances of the class *Eq*. Consider, for example, the recursive *Tree* data type defined in Chapter 7, repeated here for convenience:

**data** *Tree a*  =  *Leaf a | Branch* (*Tree a*) (*Tree a*)

Before writing the instance declaration for the *Tree* data type, let's ask ourselves a few questions. First, how do we test two branches for equality? The obvious answer is that we recursively compare for equality the corresponding pairs of subtrees, and if both pairs are equal, then the branches that we started with must be equal. Second, how do we test for the equality of two leaves? The obvious answer here is that we compare the values stored in the two leaves for equality. But, how do we know that we are even able to compare these values for equality? That should only be possible if the type of the values in the leaves is itself an instance of the class *Eq*. We need to state this constraint on the values in the leaves, and so we write:

**instance** *Eq a* ⇒ *Eq* (*Tree a*) **where**
   *Leaf a* == *Leaf b*          =  *a* == *b*
   *Branch l1 r1* == *Branch l2 r2*  =  *l1* == *l2* && *r1* == *r2*
   _ == _                     =  *False*

Note the constraint *Eq a* in the first line. This declaration thus says that we can compare trees of *a*'s for equality as long as we know how to compare *a*'s for equality. If the constraint were omitted from the instance declaration, a static type error would result.

In reality, the class *Eq* as defined in Haskell's Standard Prelude is slightly richer than what we have defined above. Here is its exact form:

**class** *Eq a* **where**
   (==), (/=) :: $a \rightarrow a \rightarrow Bool$
   $x$ /= $y$     = *not* ($x$ == $y$)
   $x$ == $y$    = *not* ($x$ /= $y$)

This is an example of a class with two operations: one for equality, the other for inequality. It also demonstrates the use of a *default method*, one for each operator. If a method for a particular operation is omitted in an instance declaration, then the default one defined in the class declaration, if it exists, is used instead. For example, the three instances of *Eq* defined earlier will work perfectly well with the above class declaration, yielding just the right definition of inequality that we want: the logical negation of equality.

A useful slogan that helps to distinguish type classes from ordinary polymorphism is as follows: "Polymorphism captures similar structure over different values, while type classes capture similar operations over different structures." For example, a sequence of integers, sequence of characters, and so on, can be captured as a polymorphic *List*, whereas equality of integers, equality of trees, and so on, can be captured by a class such as *Eq*.

As a final example of this idea, recall in Chapter 8 that we defined two functions:

   *containsS* :: *Shape* $\rightarrow$ *Point* $\rightarrow$ *Bool*
   *containsR* :: *Region* $\rightarrow$ *Point* $\rightarrow$ *Bool*

These functions capture a common operation (point containment) defined over different structures (shapes and regions). Thus, we could define a type class to capture this idea; let's call it *PC* for "point containment:"

**class** *PC t* **where**
   *contains* :: $t \rightarrow Point \rightarrow Bool$

The following two rather trivial instance declarations are all that is needed to allow us to use the same function, *contains*, to test for point membership in either a *Shape* or *Region*.

> **instance** *PC Shape* **where**
>   *contains* = *containsS*

> **instance** *PC Region* **where**
>   *contains* = *containsR*

For example, both *Rectangle* 2 3 'contains' *p* and (*r*1 'Union' *r*2) 'contains' *p* are well-typed Boolean expressions.

## 12.3 Inheritance

Haskell also supports a notion called *inheritance*. For example, we may wish to define a class *Ord*, which "inherits" all of the operations in *Eq*, but in addition has a set of comparison operations and minimum and maximum functions (a fuller definition of *Ord*, as taken from the Standard Prelude, is given in Chapter 24):

> **class** *Eq a* ⇒ *Ord a* **where**
>   (<), (<=), (>=), (>) :: $a \rightarrow a \rightarrow Bool$
>   *max*, *min*           :: $a \rightarrow a \rightarrow a$

Note the constraint *Eq a* ⇒ in the **class** declaration. We say that *Eq* is a *superclass* of *Ord* (conversely, *Ord* is a *subclass* of *Eq*), and any type that is an instance of *Ord* must also be an instance of *Eq*. The reason that this extra constraint makes sense is that to perform comparisons such as $a <= b$ and $a >= b$ implies that we know how to compute $a == b$.

As an example, we could make *Tree* an instance of *Ord* as follows (note the constraint *Ord a* ⇒ …):

> **instance** *Ord a* ⇒ *Ord* (*Tree a*) **where**
>   *Leaf* _ < *Branch* _ _          =   *True*
>   *Leaf a* < *Leaf b*              =   $a < b$
>   *Branch* _ _ < *Leaf* _          =   *False*
>   *Branch l*1 *r*1 < *Branch l*2 *r*2  =   $l1 < l2$ **&&** $r1 < r2$
>
>   *t*1 <= *t*2                     =   $t1 < t2$ **||** $t1 == t2$
>                                    …

By itself, this instance declaration would cause a type error. But because we have already made *Tree* an instance of *Eq*, everything is fine.

Another benefit of inheritance is shorter constraints. For example, the type of a function that uses operations from both the *Eq* and *Ord* classes can use the constraint (*Ord a*) rather than (*Eq a, Ord a*), because *Ord* "implies" *Eq*.

As an example of the use of *Ord*, a generic *sort* function (such as the *quicksort* example from Exercise 12.3) should be able to sort lists of any type that is an instance of *Ord*, and thus its most general type should be:

$$quicksort \ :: \ (Ord \ a) \Rightarrow [a] \rightarrow [a]$$

This typing for *quicksort* arises because of the use of the comparison operators such as < and > = in its definition.

---

**DETAILS**

Haskell also permits *multiple inheritance*, because classes may have more than one superclass. Name conflicts are avoided by the constraint that a particular operation can be a member of at most one class in any given scope. For example, the declaration

**class** (*Eq a, Show a*) $\Rightarrow$ *C a* **where**    ...

creates a class *C* which inherits operations from both *Eq* and *Show*.

Finally, class methods may have additional class constraints on any type variable except the one defining the current class. For example, in this class:

**class** *C a* **where**
    $m \ :: \ Eq \ b \Rightarrow a \rightarrow b$

the method *m* requires that type *b* is in class *Eq*. However, additional class constraints on type *a* are not allowed in the method *m*; these would instead have to be part of the context in the class declaration.

---

## 12.4  Haskell's Standard Type Classes

The Standard Prelude defines many useful type classes, including *Eq* and *Ord*. They are described in detail in Chapter 24. In addition, the Haskell Report and the Library Report contain useful examples and discussions of type classes; you should feel encouraged to read through them.

Here I will briefly describe the *Num* class, which we have been using implicitly throughout much of the text. With this explanation a few more of Haskell's secrets will be revealed.

As you know, Haskell provides several kinds of numbers, some of which we have used already: *Int*, *Integer*, and *Float*. What you probably don't know yet is that these numbers are instances of various type classes arranged in a rather complicated hierarchy. The reason for this is that there are many operations, such as (+), *abs*, and *sin*, that are common among some of these number types. For example, we would expect (+) to be defined on every kind of number, whereas *sin* might only be applicable to either single precision (*Float*) or double-precision (*Double*) floating-point numbers.

Control over what is allowed and what isn't is the purpose of the type class hierarchy. At the top of the hierarchy, and therefore containing operations that are valid for all numbers, is the class *Num*. It is defined as:

```
class (Eq a, Show a) ⇒ Num a where
    (+), (−), (∗)  ::  a → a → a
    negate         ::  a → a
    abs, signum    ::  a → a
    fromInteger    ::  Integer → a
```

Note that (/) is *not* an operation in this class. The operation *negate* is the negation function; *abs* is the absolute value function; and *signum* is the sign function, which returns −1 if its argument is negative, 0 if it is 0, and 1 if it is positive. The operation *fromInteger* converts an *Integer* into a value of type $Num\ a \Rightarrow a$, which is useful for certain coercion tasks.

---

**DETAILS**

Haskell also has a negation operator, which is Haskell's only prefix operator. However, it is just shorthand for *negate*. That is, −*e* in Haskell is shorthand for *negate e*.

The operation *fromInteger* also has a special purpose. You might have wondered how it is that we can write the number 42, say, both in a context requiring an *Int* and in one requiring a *Float*. Somehow Haskell "knows" that the 42 is the one that is required in a given context. But, what is the type of 42 itself? The answer is that it has type $Num\ a \Rightarrow a$, for some $a$ to be determined by its context. (If this seems strange, remember that [ ] by itself is also somewhat ambiguous; it is a list, but a list of what? The best we can say about its type is that it is [*a*] for some *a* yet to be determined.)

The way this is achieved in Haskell is that 42 is actually shorthand for *fromInteger* 42. Because *fromInteger* has type $Num\ a \Rightarrow Integer \to a$, then *fromInteger* 42 has type $Num\ a \Rightarrow a$.

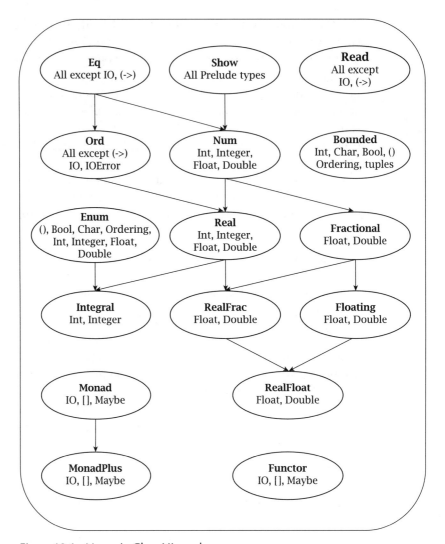

Figure 12.1: Numeric Class Hierarchy

The complete hierarchy of numeric classes is shown in Fig. 12.1. Note that some of the classes are subclasses of certain non-numeric classes, such as *Eq* and *Show*. The comments below each class name refer to the Standard Prelude types that are instances of that class. See Chapter 24 for more detail.

The Standard Prelude actually defines only the most basic numeric types: *Int*, *Integer*, *Float*, and *Double.* Other numeric types, such as rational numbers (*Ratio a*) and complex numbers (*Complex a*), are defined in libraries. The connection between these types and the numeric classes

| Numeric Type | Type Class | Description |
|---|---|---|
| *Int* | *Integral* | Fixed-precision integers |
| *Integer* | *Integral* | Arbitrary-precision integers |
| *Integral a ⇒ Ratio a* | *RealFrac* | Rational numbers |
| *Float* | *RealFloat* | Real floating-point, single precision |
| *Double* | *RealFloat* | Real floating-point, double precision |
| *RealFloat a ⇒ Complex a* | *Floating* | Complex floating-point |

Figure 12.2: Standard Numeric Types

is given in Fig. 12.2. The instance declarations implied by this table can be found in the Haskell Report.

At this point a function that we have used often in this text can finally be explained. Recall the definition of *intToFloat*:

$$
\begin{array}{lll}
intToFloat & :: & Int \to Float \\
intToFloat\ n & = & fromInteger\ (toInteger\ n)
\end{array}
$$

The operation *fromInteger* was explained above, and the class *Integral* has an operation *toInteger* :: *Integral a ⇒ a → Integer* that, as the name implies, converts a type that is a member of class *Integral* into an *Integer*. So, to convert an *Int* into a *Float*, we first convert it into an *Integer* using *toInteger*, then into a value of type *Num a ⇒ a* using *fromInteger*. Then by giving a type signature that essentially declares *a* to be *Float*, we are done!

This may seem like a lot of trickery in order to achieve this simple task, but the point of it all is *generality*. Note that there are $n(n-1)$ different coercions between pairs of $n$ numeric types. Haskell's numeric class hierarchy permits us to define these coercion functions as we need them, using a fixed set of operations such as *fromInteger* and *toInteger*.

## 12.5 Derived Instances

Recall the *Eq* instance for trees in Section 12.1. Such a declaration is simple – and boring – to produce. We require that the element type in the leaves be an equality type; then, two leaves are equal if and only if they contain equal elements, and two branches are equal if and only if their left and right subtrees are equal, respectively. Any other two trees are unequal.

In fact, for any data type that we define, the above description can be adapted quite readily. Because of this, Haskell provides a mechanism whereby instance declarations for types in the class *Eq* can be created *automatically.* This is done by including a **deriving** clause in the data type declaration:

> **data** *Tree a* = *Leaf a* | *Branch* (*Tree a*) (*Tree a*)
> **deriving** *Eq*

Adding the **deriving** clause implicitly produces an *Eq* instance declaration exactly like the one in Section 12.1.

The *Ord* instance for *Tree* is slightly more complicated than the *Eq* instance, but it too can be derived. The strategy for determining ordering on the constructors in a data type is to use the same order that they appear in the data declaration, and the arguments of a constructor are compared from left to right. With this strategy, we can write:

> **data** *Tree a* = *Leaf a* | *Branch* (*Tree a*) (*Tree a*)
> **deriving** (*Eq, Ord*)

to derive an instance of *Tree* for \\*Eq* and *Ord*.

---

**DETAILS**

When instances of more than one class are derived for the same data type, they appear grouped in parentheses as above. In this case *Eq must* appear if *Ord* does (unless an explicit instance for *Eq* is given), because *Eq* is a superclass of *Ord*.

---

In addition, instances of *Enum, Bounded, Ix, Read,* and *Show* (see Chapter 24) can also be generated by the **deriving** clause. These type classes are widely used in Haskell programming, making the deriving mechanism very useful.

Many of the predefined data types in Haskell have **deriving** clauses, even ones with special syntax. For example, if we could write a data type declaration for lists it would look something like this:

> **data** [*a*] = [ ]
> | *a* : [*a*]
> **deriving** (*Eq, Ord*)

The derived *Eq* and *Ord* instances for lists are the usual ones; in particular, character strings, as lists of characters, are ordered as determined by the underlying *Char* type, with an initial substring being less than a longer string; for example, "cat" < "catalog" is *True.*

In practice, *Eq* and *Ord* instances are almost always derived, rather than user-defined. In fact, you should provide your own definitions of equality and ordering predicates only with some trepidation, being careful to maintain the expected algebraic properties of equivalence relations and total orders (more on this later). An intransitive (==) predicate, for example, could be disastrous, confusing readers of the program who may expect (==) to be transitive. Nevertheless, it is sometimes necessary to provide *Eq* or *Ord* instances different from those that would be derived.

Lists also have a *Show* instance, but it is not derived, because, after all, it has special syntax. Also, when *show* is applied to a string such as "Hello", it should generate a string that, when printed, will look like "Hello". This means that it must include characters for the quotation marks themselves, which in Haskell is achieved by prefixing the quotation mark with the "escape" character \. Given the following data declaration:

> **data** *Hello* = *Hello*
>   **deriving** *Show*

it is then instructive to ponder over the following calculations:

> *show Hello* ⟹ "Hello"
> *show* (*show Hello*) ⟹ *show* "Hello" ⟹ "\"Hello\""
> *show* (*show* (*show Hello*)) ⟹ "\"\\\"Hello\\\"\""

---

**DETAILS**

To refer to the escape character itself, it must also be escaped; thus "\\" prints as \.

---

For further pondering, consider the following program. See if you can figure out what it does, and why:[1]

> *main*   = *putStr* (*quine q*)
> *quine s* = *s* ++ *show s*
> *q*      = "main = putStr (quine q)\nquine s = s ++ show s\nq = "

Derived *Read* (*Show*) instances are possible for all types whose component types also have *Read* (*Show*) instances. *Read* and *Show* instances for most of the standard types are provided in the Standard Prelude. Some types, such as the function type (→), have a *Show* instance that simply

---

[1] The essence of this idea is due to Willard Van Orman Quine (Quine, 1966), and its use in a computer program is discussed by Hofstadter (Hofstadter, 1979). It was adapted to Haskell by Jón Fairbairn.

generates the string "<<function>>", but not a corresponding *Read* instance.

The textual representation defined by a derived *Show* instance is consistent with the appearance of constant Haskell expressions of the type in question. For example, from:

> **data** *Color* = *Red* | *Orange* | *Yellow* | *Green* | *Blue* | *Indigo* | *Violet*
> **deriving** (*Eq*, *Enum*, *Show*)

we can expect that:

> *show* [*Red*..]
> ⟹ "[Red,Orange,Yellow,Green,Blue,Indigo,Violet]"

Further details about derived instances can be found in the Haskell Report.

## 12.6 Reasoning With Type Classes

Type classes often imply a set of *laws* that govern the use of the operators in the class. For example, for the *Eq* class, we can expect the following laws to apply for every instance of the class:

> $(x \mathrel{/{=}} y) = not \ (x == y)$
> $(x == y) \ \& \& \ (y == z) \ \supseteq \ (x == z)$

where ⊇ should be read "implies that."

However, there is no way to guarantee these laws. A user may create an instance of *Eq* that violates them, and, in general, Haskell has no way to enforce them. Nevertheless, it is useful to state the laws that interest us for a certain class, and to state the expectation that all instances of the class be "law-abiding." Then as diligent functional programmers, we should ensure that every instance that we write, whether for our own class or someone else's, is in fact law-abiding.

As another example, consider the *Ord* class, whose instances are intended to be *totally ordered*, which means that the following laws should hold, for all *a*, *b*, and *c*:

> $a <= a$
> $(a <= b) \ \& \& \ (b <= c) \ \supseteq \ (a <= c)$
> $(a <= b) \ \& \& \ (b <= a) \ \supseteq \ (a == b)$
> $(a \mathrel{/{=}} b) \ \supseteq \ (a < b) \ \| \ (b < a)$

Similar laws should hold for (>).

But alas, our instance of *Tree* in the class *Ord* does not satisfy all of these laws! To see why, consider these two trees:

$$t1 \;=\; Branch\;(Leaf\;1)\;(Leaf\;3)$$
$$t2 \;=\; Branch\;(Leaf\;2)\;(Leaf\;2)$$

Clearly $t1 == t2$ is false, but the problem is, so are $t1 < t2$ and $t2 < t1$, thus violating the last law above.

To fix the problem, we need to use a *lexicographic ordering* on trees, such as used in a dictionary. For example, "polygon" comes before "polymorphic," using a left-to-right comparison of the letters. The new instance declaration looks like this:

```
instance Ord a ⇒ Ord (Tree a) where
    Leaf _ < Branch _ _                        =  True
    Leaf a < Leaf b                            =  a < b
    Branch _ _ < Leaf _                        =  False
    Branch l1 r1 < Branch l2 r2 | l1 < l2      =  True
                                | l1 == l2 && r1 < r2  =  True
                                | otherwise    =  False
    ...
```

In the equation comparing two branches, the first line is analogous to saying that "apple" comes before "banana" because 'a' comes before 'b,' and the second line is analogous to saying that "polygon" comes before "polymorphic" because "poly" is equal to "poly" and "gon" comes before "morphic."

This example shows the value of checking to ensure that each instance obeys the laws of its class. Of course, that check should come in the way of a proof. This example also highlights the utility of derived instances, because the derived instance of *Tree* for the class *Ord* is equivalent to that above, yet is done automatically.

---

**Exercise 12.1** Prove that the instance of *Tree* in the class *Eq* satisfies the laws of its class. Also prove that the modified instance of *Tree* in the class *Ord* satisfies the laws of its class.

---

**Exercise 12.2** Write out appropriate instance declarations for the *Color* type in the classes *Eq*, *Ord*, and *Enum*.

---

**Exercise 12.3** The problem of *sorting* a list from lowest value to highest is one of the most-studied problems in computer science; there are literally dozens of algorithms for doing it. Here is an example of a "divide-and-conquer" algorithm known as *Quicksort*. To sort a list of ordered values, do the following:

1. If the list is empty, it's already sorted.
2. Otherwise, take the first element of the list; call it $x$.
3. From the rest of the list, create two lists, one containing all of the elements less than $x$, the other containing all of the elements greater than or equal to $x$.
4. Then sort (using this strategy recursively) the two new lists.
5. Finally, concatenate them together, sticking $x$ in the middle.

Write a polymorphic function *quicksort* to perform Quicksort on a list of ordered values (the type signature of this function was given in Section 12.3).

---

**Exercise 12.4** Shapes and regions were defined in previous chapters as data types, and operations such as area, perimeter, draw, and others, were later defined on them. Consider now a completely different approach based on type classes. The idea is to define separate type classes for "things that have an area," "things that have a perimeter," "things that can be drawn," and so forth. Then each kind of "thing," such as a rectangle, an ellipse, a union, and so on is defined as a separate data type that is made an instance of these classes. Implement and explore the consequences of this orthogonal design.

# CHAPTER THIRTEEN

# A Module of Simple Animations

In previous chapters you learned how to draw simple geometric shapes in a graphics window. Although you also learned how to manipulate these pictures somewhat using the mouse, they were otherwise *static*. In this chapter I will explain how to make these pictures *dynamic*; that is, how to program *animations*. In doing so you will learn several new ideas, such as how to use timers and how to use polymorphism and type classes in unique ways.

**module** *Animation* **where**

**import** *Shape*
**import** *Draw*
**import** *Picture*
**import** *SOEGraphics hiding* (*Region*)
**import** *qualified SOEGraphics as G* (*Region*)
**import** *Win32Misc* (*timeGetTime*)
**import** *Word* (*word32ToInt*)

## 13.1 What is an Animation?

An *animation* is a continuous, time-varying image. However, the animations that you see in the movies, on TV, or on your computer screen only *seem* to be moving continuously. In reality they are created by a sequence of static images – called *frames* – that are displayed in such rapid succession that they appear to be continuous to the human eye. The rate at which this phenomenon occurs is somewhere between 20 and 30 times per second, depending on lighting conditions and other factors. I will use the rate of 30 times per second, or 30 *Hertz*, abbreviated 30 Hz. Televisions, computers, and motion pictures all use this fundamental physiological phenomenon to give the illusion of continuous movement.

So the question is, how do we program an animation? The only graphics IO operation that we have discussed so far is *drawInWindow*, but note that drawing things using this operation is *accumulative*. That is, we never erase anything, nor even do so much as clear the screen. Even the user interaction given in Chapter 10 does not clear the screen; each successive rendition of the stack of regions is drawn right over the previous rendition. This works because each new picture completely hides the old one.

This will *not* work, however, if we are drawing a person walking across the screen, or a ball bouncing in a box. (Unless you like the psychedelic effect that the resulting "blurred image" will induce!) There are several standard ways of dealing with this problem:

1. Some graphics systems support a mode of drawing called "XOR mode," in which a pixel color is computed as the exclusive-or (XOR) of the desired color and the background color. The nice thing about this is that if you draw the same thing twice in exactly the same place, then the screen reverts to the background color, effectively "erasing" what was just drawn.[1]

   The advantage of this approach is that you don't have to redraw an entire frame at each time-step; it is only necessary to redraw the moving part of the scene. However, it is limited in applicability, because the animation must be drawn over a homogeneous background, otherwise the image being drawn will change colors at the boundaries of the underlying colors, according to the algorithm above.

2. Alternatively, we could take a more direct approach, as implied earlier: Simply clear the screen before drawing each frame. The advantage of this is generality; it will work regardless of the nature of the animation. But it has the disadvantage that the entire frame must be redrawn, and thus if it takes longer than about 33 milliseconds (the period of one cycle at 30 Hz) to draw a frame, then the animation will begin to "flicker" somewhat as observed by humans.

3. As a refinement on the more direct approach, many graphics systems support *buffered* graphics, which results in smoother animations, for the following reason.

   Every graphics window has its own memory – basically a two-dimensional array – into which an image is drawn. If one image is drawn over another, this memory is simply overwritten with the

---

[1] This is because, mathematically, $a \oplus a = 0$, and $a \oplus 0 = a$, where $\oplus$ is the exclusive-or operation on binary numbers. Thus $b \oplus a \oplus a = b$.

representation of the new image. The graphics hardware then reads from this memory and displays on the screen what is there, but there is no synchronization between this reading and the above writing. Thus, there will typically be some overlap between these processes, which often results in a certain degree of flicker.

To prevent this problem, many graphics systems have a secondary memory – called a *buffer* – into which a new frame is drawn. Once this memory is completely written with the new image, the graphics hardware is told to use this new memory instead of the old. Thus, the graphics hardware never "sees" the process of writing into the memory, and the flicker is thus eliminated. The old memory is then available as the buffer for the next frame.

In this chapter I will explain how to achieve the third approach, using the *SOEGraphics* library. First, however, let us consider the issue of how to *represent* an animation in Haskell.

## 13.2 Representing an Animation

Based on the previous discussion, the most obvious way to represent an animation in Haskell would seem to be a list of frames. We could then define various operations on animations, such as one to combine animations similar to the *Over* constructor in the *Picture* data type defined in Chapter 10.

However, animations are not just static pictures, and thus, there may be other things that we will want to do with/to them. For example, we may wish to speed them up, or slow them down. Although doubling the speed of an animation represented as a list is no problem (simply delete every other frame), changing the speed by a nonintegral factor (such as 2.5), or slowing an animation down, is problematical. It seems that we would have to somehow *interpolate* between images. In general, such an interpolation will be difficult if not impossible given the primitive operations at our disposal.

Therefore, I will use a different, more abstract, and ultimately more accurate, approach: An animation will be represented as a *function* from time to an image. And because there may be different kinds of "images" that are time-varying, we will define a *polymorphic* animation as follows:

**type** *Animation a* = *Time → a*
**type** *Time* = *Float*

So, *Animation Shape*, *Animation Region*, and *Animation Picture* are the types of animations of shapes, regions, and pictures, respectively, defined in previous chapters. But in addition, we can even have *Animation Int* and *Animation Float*, which, although are not typically things that we draw, will nevertheless be useful to us.

This representation of an animation has another important property: The animation will run at the right speed, regardless of how long it takes to compute each frame. If computing a frame takes longer than about 33 ms, then the resulting animation may not be as smooth as we would like, but it will still run at exactly the right speed, and will run at that speed regardless of how fast the underlying CPU is.

For some examples, here is an animated "pulsating" ball:

> *rubberBall* :: *Animation Shape*
> *rubberBall t* = *Ellipse* (*sin t*) (*cos t*)

---

**DETAILS**
The functions *sin* and *cos* are Haskell's sine and cosine functions, respectively.

---

By defining one radius as the sine of *t*, and the other as the cosine of *t*, the ball will get very skinny first in one direction, then the other, with a total cycle time of $\pi$ seconds (assuming that *t* is a measure of seconds).

For a slight contrast, here is a fixed-size ball that moves in a revolving, circular motion (like a planet or moon):

> *revolvingBall* :: *Animation Region*
> *revolvingBall t*
>          = **let** *ball* = *Shape* (*Ellipse* 0.2 0.2)
>            **in** *Translate* (*sin t*, *cos t*) *ball*

Note that this is an animated *Region*, because we want to use the *Translate* constructor. By defining the translation in the *x* direction as the sine of *t*, and in the *y* direction as the cosine of *t*, we get a circular motion about the origin.

We can also create a *Picture* animation that combines the above two animations, yielding a yellow ball revolving around a red pulsating ball:

> *planets* :: *Animation Picture*
> *planets t*
>          = **let** *p*1 = *Region Red* (*Shape* (*rubberBall t*))
>              *p*2 = *Region Yellow* (*revolvingBall t*)
>          **in** *p*1 'Over' *p*2

Finally, here's a simple animation of a *String*:

*tellTime* :: *Animation String*
*tellTime t* = "The time is: " ++ *show t*

## 13.3 An Animator

The above animations are all well and good, but as usual we now have to figure out how to draw them! Our goal will be to define a function:

*animate* :: *String → Animation Graphic → IO* ()

such that *animate title anim* will open a window with title *title* and display the animation *anim*, which generates *Graphic* values that are drawn in the graphics window.

For example, to animate the *rubberBall* in blue, we would write:

*main*1 :: *IO* ()
*main*1 = *animate* "Animated Shape"
        (*withColor Blue . shapeToGraphic . rubberBall*)

> **DETAILS**
> Recall that *rubberBall* has type *Animation Shape* (i.e., *Time → Shape*), *shapeToGraphic* has type *Shape → Graphic*, and *withColor Blue* has type *Graphic → Graphic*; thus the composition of the three has type *Time → Graphic* (i.e. *Animation Graphic*).

Or to animate the *tellTime* text, we just write:

*main*2 :: *IO* ()
*main*2 = *animate* "Animated Text" (*text* (100, 200) . *tellTime*)

> **DETAILS**
> Recall that *text* has type *Point → String → Graphic*.

We will return to similar examples that animate *revolvingBall* (a *Region* animation) and *planets* (a *Picture* animation) later.

In order to define *animate* there are a few new graphics operations that you must learn:

1. *openWindowEx* is a version of *openWindow*, "extended" with additional functionality. Its type is:

$$openWindowEx \;\; :: \;\; String \rightarrow Maybe\ Point \rightarrow Maybe\ Point \rightarrow$$
$$(Graphic \rightarrow DrawFun) \rightarrow Maybe\ Word32 \rightarrow$$
$$IO\ Window$$

> **DETAILS**
>
> *Word*32 is the type of binary 32-bit words. A value of this type can be converted into an *Int* using *word32ToInt* :: *Word32* → *Int*.

Executing the command:

$$w \leftarrow openWindowEx\ title\ (Just\ (x,\ y))\ (Just\ (w,\ h))$$
$$drawFun\ (Just\ 30)$$

will create a graphics window *w* with title *title*, width *w*, height *h*, and upper left-hand corner at location (*x*, *y*). In addition, it will have a *timer* (see below) that "ticks" every 30 ms, and the graphics will be generated using the drawing function *drawFun*. (Choosing *Nothing* for the position or size results in default position or size, and choosing *Nothing* for the timer argument results in no timer at all.)

2. The detailed use of the *drawFun* function above is beyond the scope of this text, but normally one of two predefined functions are chosen: *drawGraphic*, for nonbuffered graphics, and *drawBufferedGraphic*, for buffered graphics. Because we want buffered graphics, we will use the latter function in this chapter.

3. *getWindowTick* :: *Window* → *IO* () gets the next tick of the timer. More precisely, it will not "return" until the next timer tick either occurs, or has already occurred since the last *getWindowTick* operation.

4. *timeGetTime* :: *IO Word32* returns the current time as a 32-bit binary word in milliseconds. This time may not have any bearing on the current time of day, or the time since the program was started, or anything else very predictable. It is just a large, positive number that increments once every millisecond.

5. *setGraphic* :: *Window* → *Graphic* → *IO* () sets the graphic image to be drawn in a window. It is different from the *drawInWindow* function introduced in Chapter 3 in that it is *not accumulative*. The graphic argument replaces what was already there, rather than adding to it.

**DETAILS**
An alternative way to achieve this is to first clear the graphic window using *clearWindow*, then use *drawInWindow* to draw the new one; *setGraphic* essentially accomplishes this in one step rather than two.

The definition of the *animate* function is shown in Fig. 13.1. It is fairly straightforward, except for two things: First, because *timeGetTime* is initially a fairly unpredictable number, I have taken the approach of capturing in *t*0 the time at which the program begins, and subtracting this from each subsequent time. This has the effect of starting all animations at time 0.

Second, note the use of the timer, which is set to 30 milliseconds. You may wonder why I didn't just keep a counter for the current time, to which 30 is added on each iteration through the loop! The answer is that, if an animation frame takes longer than 30 ms to generate, I may miss a timer tick, in which case the current time would become inaccurate.

Of course, you may then wonder why I have a timer at all. Why not simply run the animation as fast as I can? The answer to this is two-fold:

```
animate :: String → Animation Graphic → IO ()

animate title anim
        = runGraphics (
          do w ← openWindowEx title (Just (0, 0)) (Just (xWin, yWin))
                     drawBufferedGraphic (Just 30)
             t0 ← timeGetTime
             let loop =
                   do t ← timeGetTime
                      let ft = intToFloat (word32ToInt (t − t0))/1000
                      setGraphic w (anim ft)
                      getWindowTick w
                      loop
             loop
          )
```

**DETAILS**
Note the two uses of a **let** within the **do** notation. These are different from the normal **let** expression, in that there is no body, as in **let** *x* = 1 **in** *body*. It is simply a convenient way to give names to values while continuing the flow of control within the **do** notation.

Figure 13.1: The *animate* Function

1. There is no sense drawing images faster than every 30 ms, because the human eye will not be able to tell the difference. Furthermore, there may be other applications running on your computer that could be productively using the extra cycles.
2. The *setGraphic* command does not actually perform any graphics IO; all it does is set the graphics routine to be used when the graphics IO is performed by the operating system. Because most implementations of Haskell are not truly multithreaded, *getWindowTick* implicitly relinquishes control back to the operating system, which initiates the graphics IO.

At the beginning of this section, I showed examples of using *animate* for a *Shape* animation (*rubberBall*) and a *String* animation (*tellTime*):

$$main1 = animate \text{``Animated Shape''}$$
$$(withColor\ Blue\ .\ shapeToGraphic\ .\ rubberBall)$$

$$main2 = animate \text{``Animated Text''}\ (text\ (100,\ 200)\ .\ tellTime)$$

To animate a *Region* it is convenient to first define a function to convert *Region*s to graphic values:

$$regionToGraphic\ ::\ Region \rightarrow Graphic$$
$$regionToGraphic\ =\ drawRegion\ .\ regionToGRegion$$

Using this function we can now animate the revolving ball (painting it yellow for aesthetics) given in the previous section:

$$main3\ ::\ IO\ ()$$
$$main3\ =\ animate \text{``Animated Region''}$$
$$(withColor\ Yellow\ .\ regionToGraphic\ .\ revolvingBall)$$

To animate *Picture*s we have to work a bit harder to come up with a function to convert *Picture*s to *Graphic* values. In particular, we will have to consider the structure of the *Picture* data type itself:

$$picToGraphic\ ::\ Picture \rightarrow Graphic$$
$$picToGraphic\ (Region\ c\ r)$$
$$\qquad\qquad =\ withColor\ c\ (regionToGraphic\ r)$$
$$picToGraphic\ (p1\ \text{`Over`}\ p2)$$
$$\qquad\qquad =\ picToGraphic\ p1\ \text{`overGraphic`}\ picToGraphic\ p2$$
$$picToGraphic\ EmptyPic$$
$$\qquad\qquad =\ emptyGraphic$$

Using *picToGraphic* we can now easily animate the *planets* example from the previous section:

*main4* :: *IO* ()
*main4* = *animate* "Animated Picture" (*picToGraphic* . *planets*)

Nine successive snapshots of this animation, spaced $\pi/8$ seconds apart and thus completing one cycle of the pulsating ball and one-half cycle of the revolving ball, are shown in Fig. 13.2 (ordered left-to-right and top-to-bottom).

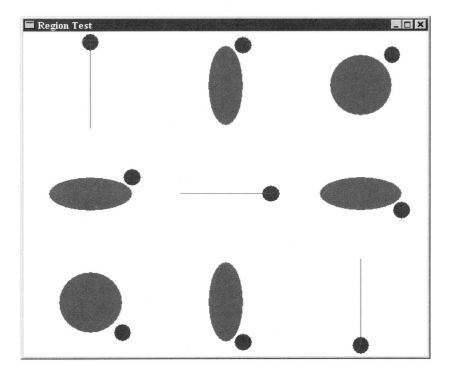

Figure 13.2: The Planets Animation

## 13.4 Fun With Type Classes

### 13.4.1 Rising to the Level of Animations

For every operation on the underlying static images, it is convenient to have an analogous operation that works at the level of animations. For example, concentrating on *Picture* animations for the moment, we can first define an empty *Picture* animation:

> *emptyA*   ::  *Animation Picture*
> *emptyA t* = *EmptyPic*

and a function *overA* that combines two *Picture* animations into one:

> *overA*        ::  *Animation Picture* → *Animation Picture* →
>                       *Animation Picture*
> *overA a*1 *a*2 *t* =  *a*1 *t* 'Over' *a*2 *t*

With these we can also define a function that collapses a list of animations into one:

> *overManyA* ::  [*Animation Picture*] → *Animation Picture*
> *overManyA* =  *foldr overA emptyA*

This general process is often described as "lifting" values from a domain *a*, say, to a domain *T a*. In the examples above, we are lifting from type *Picture* to type *Animation Picture*.

The only problem with this idea is that different names are used for the analogous operations at each level. In what follows I will show how lifting can be generalized and combined with type classes to avoid this problem.

### 13.4.2 Type Classes to the Rescue

Remember the slogan: "Polymorphism captures similar structure over different values, while type classes capture similar operations over different structures." For example, a sequence of integers, sequence of characters, and so on, can be captured as a polymorphic *List*, whereas equality of integers, equality of trees, and so on, can be captured by a class such as *Eq*. We have used polymorphism in a number of ways already in programming graphics and animations; can we also use type classes?

There are in fact two (related) ways that type classes can help us in organizing our animation operations:

1. We can make *pre-existing* operations work on animations by making the *Animation* type an instance of the appropriate class. For example,

we can use the arithmetic operators $(+)$, $(*)$, and others, on animations by making *Animation* an instance of *Num*.

2. We can capture *new* operations that are generic to both animations and the underlying static values by creating a new type class. For example, as shown earlier, the functions *emptyA* and *overA* work for *Animation*s, and the similar functions (actually constructors) *EmptyPic* and *Over* work for *Picture*s.

The only real difference between these two approaches is that in one case there is an existing type class, and in the other case there is not. But in both cases, the first thing that we need to do is make an animation a true data type, with its own constructor, rather than a type synonym.

> **DETAILS**
> Remember that a type synonym simply renames an existing type. For example, *Animation a* is just a shorthand for *Time → a*. However, type synonyms are not allowed in instance declarations, so we cannot write, for example:
>
> **instance** *Eq* (*Animation a*) **where** ...
>
> nor can we write:
>
> **instance** *Eq* (*Time → a*) **where** ...
>
> because each argument to the constructor (→) is required to be a simple variable. The reasons for these constraints are too technical to discuss here, but the strategy below is adequate in avoiding them.

I will in fact use a more general name than *Animation* for this type, to emphasize that the underlying datatype is not always an image of some sort:

**newtype** *Behavior a* $=$ *Beh* (*Time → a*)

> **DETAILS**
> A **newtype** declaration is just like a **data** declaration, except that it can only be used to define data types with a *single* constructor (such as *Beh* above). The new data type is different from the analogous one created by a **data** declaration, in that there is *no* computational overhead in having the constructor; it is as if the data type were defined as a **type** synonym. You can think of a **newtype** declaration as defining a "new type" with exactly the same structure, behavior, and performance as the underlying type.

A simple interface to *animate* yields an animator for picture behaviors:

$$animateB \qquad\qquad :: \quad String \rightarrow Behavior\ Picture \rightarrow IO\ ()$$
$$animateB\ s\ (Beh\ pf) \quad = \quad animate\ s\ (picToGraphic\ .\ pf)$$

Fig. 13.3 shows all of the instance declarations required to make *Behavior* an instance of the class *Floating*, which, in turn, requires instances of *Fractional*, *Num*, *Show*, and *Eq*, because of the subclass constraints.

```
instance Eq (Behavior a) where
  a1 == a2  =  error "Can't compare behaviors."

instance Show (Behavior a) where
  showsPrec n a1  =  error "<< Behavior >>"

instance Num a ⇒ Num (Behavior a) where
  (+)          =  lift2 (+)
  (*)          =  lift2 (*)
  negate       =  lift1 negate
  abs          =  lift1 abs
  signum       =  lift1 signum
  fromInteger  =  lift0 . fromInteger

instance Fractional a ⇒ Fractional (Behavior a) where
  (/)          =  lift2 (/)
  fromRational  =  lift0 . fromRational

instance Floating a ⇒ Floating (Behavior a) where
  pi     =  lift0 pi
  sqrt   =  lift1 sqrt
  exp    =  lift1 exp
  log    =  lift1 log
  sin    =  lift1 sin
  cos    =  lift1 cos
  tan    =  lift1 tan
  asin   =  lift1 asin
  acos   =  lift1 acos
  atan   =  lift1 atan
  sinh   =  lift1 sinh
  cosh   =  lift1 cosh
  tanh   =  lift1 tanh
  asinh  =  lift1 asinh
  acosh  =  lift1 acosh
  atanh  =  lift1 atanh
```

Figure 13.3: *Behavior* Instances

These classes contain all of the standard arithmetic operations, such as (+), (*), (/), and *negate*, as well as transcendental functions such as *sin*, *cos*, *tan*, and many others.

Note in these definitions the use of the following handy polymorphic functions that lift operations on the static values to operations on *Behavior*s:

$$lift0 \quad :: \quad a \to Behavior\ a$$
$$lift0\ x \ = \ Beh\ (\backslash t \to x)$$

$$lift1 \quad :: \quad (a \to b) \to (Behavior\ a \to Behavior\ b)$$
$$lift1\ f\ (Beh\ a)$$
$$\qquad = \ Beh\ (\backslash t \to f\ (a\ t))$$

$$lift2 \quad :: \quad (a \to b \to c) \to (Behavior\ a \to Behavior\ b \to Behavior\ c)$$
$$lift2\ g\ (Beh\ a)\ (Beh\ b)$$
$$\qquad = \ Beh\ (\backslash t \to g\ (a\ t)\ (b\ t))$$

$$lift3 \quad :: \quad (a \to b \to c \to d) \to$$
$$\qquad\qquad (Behavior\ a \to Behavior\ b \to Behavior\ c \to Behavior\ d)$$
$$lift3\ g\ (Beh\ a)\ (Beh\ b)\ (Beh\ c)$$
$$\qquad = \ Beh\ (\backslash t \to g\ (a\ t)\ (b\ t)\ (c\ t))$$

The end result of all this is that operations that we normally perform on floating-point numbers, say, can now be done on animated (i.e., time-varying) floating-point numbers. This idea becomes especially useful if we define a function:

$$time \ :: \ Behavior\ Time$$
$$time \ = \ Beh\ (\backslash t \to t)$$

because now, something like *time* + 5 is really a time-varying function (i.e., it is equivalent to $Beh\ (\backslash t \to t + 5)$). To see this, we can reason via calculation:

$$time + 5$$
$$\Rightarrow \ \{ \text{ unfold overloadings for } time,\ (+),\ \text{and } 5 \ \}$$
$$(lift2\ (+))\ (Beh\ (\backslash t \to t))\ (Beh\ (\backslash t \to 5))$$
$$\Rightarrow \ \{ \text{ unfold } lift2 \ \}$$
$$(\backslash (Beh\ a)\ (Beh\ b) \to Beh\ (\backslash t \to a\ t + b\ t))\ (Beh\ (\backslash t \to t))\ (Beh\ (\backslash t \to 5))$$
$$\Rightarrow \ \{ \text{ unfold anonymous function } \}$$
$$Beh\ (\backslash t \to (\backslash t \to t)\ t + (\backslash t \to 5)\ t)$$
$$\Rightarrow \ \{ \text{ unfold two anonymous functions } \}$$
$$Beh\ (\backslash t \to t + 5)$$

Although you might expect a potentially large overhead in high degrees of overloading such as this, a good compiler will be able to remove it almost entirely for many applications.

### 13.4.3  Defining New Type Classes for Behaviors

The second way that we can use qualified types is to define a new type class that captures "similar operations over different structures." For example, as discussed earlier, it is desirable to have operations, such as *empty* and *over*, for both *Picture*s and *Animation*s. So we can define a type class:

> **class** *Combine a* **where**
>     *empty* :: *a*
>     *over*  :: *a → a → a*

Class *Combine* should perhaps more rightly be called *Monoid*, because it captures the signature of a monoid in abstract algebra. Other examples of monoids useful to programming are lists:

> **instance** *Combine* [*a*] **where**
>     *empty* = [ ]
>     *over*  = (++)

and functions with a common domain and range:

> **instance** *Combine* (*Fun a*) **where**
>     *empty*                = *Fun id*
>     *Fun a* 'over' *Fun b* = *Fun* (*a.b*)

> **newtype** *Fun a* = *Fun* (*a → a*)

(Can you think of others?)

Here are instances of *Combine* for the data types *Picture* and *Behavior*; note the context constraining the latter:

> **instance** *Combine Picture* **where**
>     *empty* = *EmptyPic*
>     *over*  = *Over*

> **instance** *Combine a* ⇒ *Combine* (*Behavior a*) **where**
>     *empty* = *lift0 empty*
>     *over*  = *lift2 over*

**DETAILS**
Although these last two equations look recursive, it is important to realize that, for example, *over* on the the left-hand side of the last equation has type:

*Combine a ⇒ Behavior a → Behavior a → Behavior a*

whereas the occurrence on the right-hand side has type:

*Combine a ⇒ a → a → a*

That is, they are really two different functions, just overloaded with the same name.

These instance declarations allow us to write things such as the following (rather contrived) example:

*m* :: *Behavior Picture*
*m* = **let** *a* = *lift0* (*empty* '*over*' *p*)
      **in** *a* '*over*' *empty*

*p* :: *Picture*
*p* – *empty*

**DETAILS**
It is interesting to note that if the two type signatures above are removed, then the types of the resulting equations are *ambiguous*; there is not enough information to determine the types uniquely! To see this, note that *p* could be either a *Picture* or a *Behavior Picture*, in which case *m* would either have type *Behavior Picture* or *Behavior* (*Behavior Picture*), respectively. But in both cases, the typing makes sense.

With *empty* and *over* thus suitably defined, we can also define other overloaded operations without requiring them to be operations in the type class itself. The function *overMany* is a good example of this:

*overMany* :: *Combine a ⇒ [a] → a*
*overMany* = *foldr over empty*

## 13.5 Lifting to the Limit

It is not unreasonable to lift as many values as possible to the level of behaviors, and in doing so gain some degree of abstraction over the unlifted variants. For example, if we lift these values:

$$
\begin{array}{lll}
reg & = & lift2\ Region \\
shape & = & lift1\ Shape \\
ell & = & lift2\ Ellipse \\
red & = & lift0\ Red \\
yellow & = & lift0\ Yellow \\
translate\ (Beh\ a1,\ Beh\ a2)\ (Beh\ r) \\
\quad\quad = & Beh\ (\backslash t \rightarrow Translate\ (a1\ t,\ a2\ t)\ (r\ t))
\end{array}
$$

then we can redefine the red revolving ball example as follows:

$$
\begin{array}{lll}
revolvingBallB & :: & Behavior\ Picture \\
revolvingBallB
\end{array}
$$
$$
\begin{array}{l}
= \textbf{let}\ ball\ =\ shape\ (ell\ 0.2\ 0.2) \\
\quad\ \textbf{in}\ reg\ red\ (translate\ (sin\ time,\ cos\ time)\ ball)
\end{array}
$$

$$
\begin{array}{lll}
main5 & :: & IO\ () \\
main5 & = & animateB\ \text{“Revolving Ball Behavior”}\ revolvingBallB
\end{array}
$$

Perhaps a more useful form of lifting involves predicates and conditionals. For example, we can lift comparison operators such as:

$$
\begin{array}{lll}
(>*) & :: & Ord\ a \Rightarrow Behavior\ a \rightarrow Behavior\ a \rightarrow Behavior\ Bool \\
(>*) & = & lift2\ (>)
\end{array}
$$

Lifting the conditional operator is slightly problematical, because of its special syntax. But if we define:

$$iffun \quad :: \quad Bool \to a \to a \to a$$
$$iffun\ p\ c\ a \ = \ \textbf{if}\ p\ \textbf{then}\ c\ \textbf{else}\ a$$

then it is easy:

$$cond \ :: \ Behavior\ Bool \to Behavior\ a \to Behavior\ a \to Behavior\ a$$
$$cond \ = \ lift3\ iffun$$

Combining the above two liftings allows us to write things such as:

$$flash \ :: \ Behavior\ Color$$
$$flash \ = \ cond\ (sin\ time >\!* 0)\ red\ yellow$$

This time-varying color can be used, for example, in place of *red* in *revolvingBallB* to yield a ball that flashes between the colors red and yellow every $\pi$ seconds.

## 13.6 Time Transformation

Now for something completely different, suppose we want to do *time transformations* on behaviors; for example, we may wish to speed up or slow down an animation. It is straightforward to define a polymorphic function *timeTrans* of type:

$$timeTrans \ :: \ Behavior\ Time \to Behavior\ a \to Behavior\ a$$

Its definition is:

$$timeTrans\ (Beh\ f)\ (Beh\ a) \ = \ Beh\ (\backslash t \to a\ (f\ t))$$

or in other words:

$$timeTrans\ (Beh\ f)\ (Beh\ a) \ = \ Beh\ (a\,.\,f)$$

So, for example, to double the speed of an animation *anim*, we simply do:

$$timeTrans\ (2 * time)\ anim$$

Or to display two versions of an animation, one five seconds behind the other, we can do:

*timeTrans* (5 + *time*) *anim* '*over*' *anim*

We can even make an animation go backwards in time, using:

*timeTrans* (*negate time*) *anim*

Any kind of animation can be time transformed. For example, we can speed up the rate at which *flash* (defined in the previous section) changes color, and use it to control the color of a revolving ball:

*flashingBall*  ::  *Behavior Picture*
*flashingBall*
           = **let** *ball*  =  *shape* (*ell* 0.2 0.2)
              **in** *reg* (*timeTrans* (8 ∗ *time*) *flash*)
                    (*translate* (*sin time*, *cos time*) *ball*)

*main6*  ::  *IO* ()
*main6*  =  *animateB* "Flashing Ball" *flashingBall*

Note that the time transformation is applied to just *flash*, which increases the rate of flashing without increasing the speed of the ball.

As a final example, let's define a rotating ring of flashing balls. I will do this by creating a sequence of eight *flashingBall* values, each time-transformed evenly-spaced over $2\pi$ seconds:

*revolvingBalls*  ::  *Behavior Picture*
*revolvingBalls*
           =  *overMany* [*timeTrans* (*lift0* (*t* ∗ *pi*/4)
               + *time*) *flashingBall* | *t* ← [0..7]]

*main7*  ::  *IO* ()
*main7*  =  *animateB* "Lots of Flashing Balls"
               *revolvingBalls*

## 13.7   A Final Example: A Kaleidoscope Program

Besides translation and scaling, it is sometimes useful to *rotate* images. Because it is conceivable to rotate shapes, regions, pictures, and animations, we can define a type class to capture the idea of "turnable" data types:

**class** *Turnable a* **where**
   *turn*  ::  *Float* → *a* → *a*

Here are the instance declarations for *Behavior* and *Picture*:

**instance** *Turnable Picture* **where**
    *turn theta* (*Region c r*)    =  *Region c* (*turn theta r*)
    *turn theta* (*p1* '*Over*' *p2*)  =  *turn theta p1* '*Over*' *turn theta p2*
    *turn theta EmptyPic*      =  *EmptyPic*

**instance** *Turnable a* ⇒ *Turnable* (*Behavior a*) **where**
    *turn theta* (*Beh b*)  =  *Beh* (*turn theta . b*)

Unfortunately, there is no easy way to rotate an ellipse, except for certain special cases (such as when the ellipse is a circle, in which case rotation is trivial). Rotating scaled regions is also problematic. In what follows I will define rotation just for polygons, leaving other cases as an exercise.

Rotating polygons requires first defining the rotation of a coordinate about the origin:

*rotate*  ::  *Float* → *Coordinate* → *Coordinate*
*rotate theta* (*x*, *y*)
      = (*x* ∗ *c* + *y* ∗ *s*, *y* ∗ *c* − *x* ∗ *s*)
          **where** (*s*, *c*)  =  (*sin theta*, *cos theta*)

Here *theta* is assumed to be the turning angle measured in radians. Given this function, it is straightforward to define rotation for polygons:

**instance** *Turnable Shape* **where**
    *turn theta* (*Polygon ps*)  =  *Polygon* (*map* (*rotate theta*) *ps*)

**instance** *Turnable Region* **where**
    *turn theta* (*Shape sh*)  =  *Shape* (*turn theta sh*)

Fig. 13.4 shows an interesting use of *turn* in defining a *kaleidoscope*, similar to some screen savers that you have probably seen.[2] The function *kaleido* is a kaleidoscope generator, and *kaleido1* and *kaleido2* demonstrate two uses of it. The best way to understand the effect of these programs is to just run them:

*main8*  ::  *IO* ()
*main8*
        = **do** *animateB* "`kaleido1 (close window for next demo)`"
                *kaleido1*
            *animateB* "`kaleido2`" *kaleido2*

---

[2] This program was originally written by Sigbjorn Finne, and later adapted to this textbook by Valery Trifonov.

```
slowTime  =  0.1 * time

kaleido      ::  Integer → (Float → Behavior Coordinate)
                      → Behavior Picture

kaleido n f  =
  lift2 turn (pi * sin slowTime) $
  overMany (zipWith reg (map lift0 (cycle spectrum))
                        (map (flip turn poly) rads))
  where
    rads  =  map (((2 * pi/fromInteger n)*) . fromInteger) [0..n − 1]
    poly  =  polyShapeAnim (map f rads)

kaleido1  =  kaleido 6 star
  where star x  =  syncPair (2 * cos (v * c + l),
                            2 * abs (sin (slowTime * s − l)))
          where v      =  lift0 x
                l      =  v * (slowTime + 1)
                (s, c) =  (sin l, cos l)

kaleido2  =  kaleido 9 star
  where star x  =  syncPair (2 * abs (sin (v * a + slowTime)),
                            2 * abs (cos (a + slowTime)))
          where v  =  lift0 x
                a  =  v + slowTime * sin (v * slowTime)

syncList    ::  [Behavior a] → Behavior [a]
syncList l  =  Beh (\t → map (\(Beh f) → f t) l)

syncPair                  ::  (Behavior a, Behavior b) → Behavior (a, b)
syncPair (Beh x, Beh y)  =  Beh (\t → (x t, y t))

    − − Create an animated polygon from a list of point behaviors
polyShapeAnim  ::  [Behavior Coordinate] → Behavior Region
polyShapeAnim  =  lift1 (Shape . Polygon) . syncList

    −− The interesting colors (assuming Black background)
spectrum  ::  [Color]
spectrum  =  [c | c ← [minBound..], c /= Black]
```

Figure 13.4: A Kaleidoscope Program

Note the technique here of running two sequential graphics programs; when the first graphics window is closed, the other one is opened. Fig. 13.5 shows two snapshots of the first kaleidoscope in action. I will say no more about the operation of these programs, because it is mostly a matter of aesthetics. As an exercise, see if you can define your own version of a kaleidoscope.

---

**DETAILS**

Note in Fig. 13.4 the definition of *spectrum*:

$$spectrum = [c \mid c \leftarrow [minBound..], c \mathrel{/=} Black]$$

The *Color* data type is defined in the *SOEGraphics* library as:

**data** *Color*
   = *Black | Blue | Green | Cyan | Red | Magenta | Yellow | White*
      **deriving** (*Eq, Ord, Bounded, Enum, Ix, Show, Read*)

Therefore, *Color* is an instance of the class *Bounded*, which captures data types that are linearly bounded (i.e., ones that have both a minimum value called *minBound*, and a maximum value called *maxBound*). See Chapter 24. In the case of *Color*, the deriving mechanism assigns *Black* as the *minBound*, and *White* as the *maxBound*, as you might expect. Thus, *spectrum* above is equivalent to:

$$spectrum = [c \mid c \leftarrow [Black..], c \mathrel{/=} Black]$$

Why not define it this way in the first place? Or even better:

$$spectrum = [c \mid c \leftarrow [Blue..]]$$

The reason is that if the *Color* data type later changes – for example, the colors are reordered, or some new color is added that is "less than" *Black* – then the version using *minBound* will still be correct, whereas the versions using *Black* or *Blue* may not be.

---

**Exercise 13.1** Create instances for *Region*s and *Shape*s in the class *Combine*. Can you think of a reasonable instance for strings? How about floating-point numbers?

---

**Exercise 13.2** Make the *planets* example more realistic by doing the following:

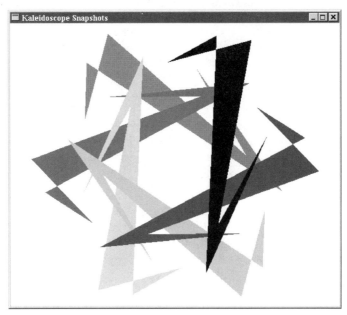

Figure 13.5: Two Snapshots of Kaleidoscope Program

1. Create two orbiting systems: one of a moon around a planet, the other of the planet-moon system itself revolving around a sun.
2. Make the orbits elliptical.
3. Have the orbiting body move *behind* the other body during one-half of the cycle, and *in front* during the other half (this is the trickiest part).
4. Finally, have the orbiting body get larger as it approaches the observer, and smaller as it gets farther away.

---

**Exercise 13.3** Build a clock, complete with a face, second hand, minute hand, and hour hand. Implement the hands as animations.

---

**Exercise 13.4** Using the animation principles developed in this chapter, design your own variation of a kaleidoscope or other "screen-saver" program.

---

**Exercise 13.5** In Section 13.7 these instances of the class *Turnable* were defined:

> **instance** *Turnable Shape* **where**
>    *turn theta* (*Polygon ps*) = *Polygon* (*map* (*rotate theta*) *ps*)

> **instance** *Turnable Region* **where**
>    *turn theta* (*Shape sh*) = *Shape* (*turn theta sh*)

Complete these as much as possible for the remaining constructors in the *Shape* and *Region* data types. You will find that most of them are straightforward. The exceptions are listed below along with suggestions on how to treat them:

1. Treat rectangles and right triangles as polygons.
2. For an ellipse, test for special cases such as a circle, a radius of zero, or angles that are multiples of $\pi/2$ (you may wish to test for *sin theta* equal to 0 or 1), and give the correct result; signal an error otherwise.
3. For a scaled region, test for special cases such as unit or zero scaling, or angles that are multiples $\pi/2$, and give the correct result; signal an error otherwise.

---

**Exercise 13.6** Haskell B. Curry, after whom the language Haskell was named, was best known for his work on *combinatory logic*, which was based on primitive functions called *combinators*. The three most basic of these were called *S*, *K*, and *I*, and had the following meanings, expressed in Haskell:

$$
\begin{aligned}
i\,x &= x \\
k\,x\,y &= x \\
s\,f\,g\,x &= f\,x\,(g\,x)
\end{aligned}
$$

It is interesting to then note the following relationships between these values and the lifting functions defined in Section 13.4:

$$
\begin{aligned}
time &= Beh\ i \\
lift0\ x &= Beh\ (K\ x) \\
lifti\ f\ (Beh\ b1)\ &\dots\ (Beh\ bi) \\
&= Beh\ (s\ h\ bi)\ \textbf{where}\ Beh\ h\ =\ liftj\ f\ b1\ \dots\ bj
\end{aligned}
$$

where $i >= 1$ and $j = i - 1$.

Prove the last relationship above.

# CHAPTER FOURTEEN

# Programming With Streams

Recall that in Chapter 6 we used an infinite list to simulate a mathematical sequence used in the calculation of the perimeter of an ellipse. When a list is used in a context where it will always be infinite, it is commonly called a *stream*. Many problems can be elegantly, concisely, and efficiently expressed using streams, which we will explore in this chapter. With the power of streams there are also inherent dangers, which we will also explore. In the next chapter we will use streams in a central way in the implementation of a language for expressing reactive animations.

## 14.1 Lazy Evaluation

Because streams are never finite, it would seem natural to define a special polymorphic data type for them, such as:

> **data** *Stream a* = *a* :ˆ *Stream a*

Although we could certainly do this, it is more convenient to use Haskell lists to "simulate" streams by just never using the empty list constructor [ ]. The main advantage of this approach is that we can then reuse many polymorphic functions already defined on lists rather than redefining them on a new data type.

In Chapter 6 we used list comprehensions to create the infinite list [2..], but is there a more fundamental way to create this list? Here is one way:

> *twos* = 2 : *twos*

Let's compute this value by calculation:

*twos*

$\Rightarrow$ 2 : *twos*

$\Rightarrow$ 2 : 2 : *twos*

$\Rightarrow$ 2 : 2 : 2 : *twos*

...

There is, of course, no end to this calculation. An important distinction exists, however, between this calculation and ones that we have labeled as "infinite loops" and given the value $\perp$ in previous chapters: this calculation is producing useful information, namely the successive elements of a list. Its value is an *infinite list*, or stream. A stream contains an infinte amount of information, whereas $\perp$ contains no information whatsoever.

**DETAILS**

Try running this example; in Hugs, if you type *twos* to the evaluation prompt, it will go into an infinite loop printing 2's.[1]

Now consider the expression *head twos*. Recalling the definition of *head* in Section 5.1:

*head*       :: $[a] \rightarrow a$
*head* $(x : \_)$ = $x$

one way to compute its value is like this:

*head twos*

$\Rightarrow$  *head* $(2 : twos)$

$\Rightarrow$  2

However, what is to prevent us, or an implementation of Haskell, from performing the following calculation instead:

*head twos*
*head* $(2 : twos)$
*head* $(2 : 2 : twos)$
*head* $(2 : 2 : 2 : twos)$
...

This calculation is also nonterminating! Of course, if at any time in this sequence we decide to apply the rule for *head*, the calculation will immediately terminate with the same value as above, namely 2. So it seems

---

[1] In the rest of this chapter I will describe the behavior of Hugs on several different programs. In each case Hugs was running with its standard heap size on a Windows NT machine with a 400 MHz processor and 256 MB of RAM.

that although, as pointed out in Chapter 1, every expression in Haskell will yield the same value no matter what calculation order is chosen, there are some calculation orders that might not terminate.

Fortunately, there is a particular calculation order, known as *normal order*, that is guaranteed to yield a value if in fact one exists. Normal-order calculation is more commonly referred to as *lazy evaluation*, and the strategy behind it is very simple: If a rule or rules can be applied to more than one position in an expression, use the rule corresponding to the *outermost* position in the expression. For example, starting with the expression:

*head twos*

we cannot yet apply the rule for *head*, so there is only one applicable rule, the one for *twos*, yielding:

*head* (2 : *twos*)

Now there are two applicable rules, the one for *head* (...) and the one for *twos*. However, *twos* is contained within *head* (...), and thus the latter is outermost. So we apply the rule for *head*, yielding:

2

Haskell effectively uses normal-order calculation when executing a program, although it also shares expressions in some ways to be described shortly. The only subtlety in using normal-order calculation is the notion of "outermost." For example, consider this function:

*ignore*    ::  $a \rightarrow b \rightarrow b$
*ignore a b*  =  *b*

If we evaluate *ignore twos* 42 using normal-order calculation we immediately arrive at 42. However, if we write it as *twos* '*ignore*' 42, then we may be tempted to evaluate *twos* first. Just remember that in any function application (whether infix or otherwise), the arguments are "within" the function application, and thus the application itself is outermost.

In a **let** expression the body is outermost, not any of the bindings. This is because the bindings just introduce names that are used *within* the body. A similar argument holds with respect to a **where** clause.

Finally, the sole purpose of a **case** expression is to specify one of the rules to apply. Its calculation order is driven by the need to match an expression against a value, moving top-to-bottom and left-to-right, as discussed in Chapter 1 and detailed in Appendix B.

## 14.2 Recursive Streams

Many problems are most easily solved using *recursive* streams. The use of recursive streams, a very powerful programming idiom, will be explored in detail in this section. Consider, for example, the *Fibonacci sequence*:

1, 1, 2, 3, 5, 8, 13, 21, 34, 55, ...

in which the first two numbers are 1, and each subsequent number is the sum of its two predecessors. The value of the *n*th Fibonacci number is defined mathematically as:

$$fib(n) = \begin{cases} 1 & \text{if } n = 0 \lor n = 1 \\ fib(n-1) + fib(n-2) & \text{if } n \geq 2 \end{cases}$$

From this definition, a Haskell function can be defined straightforwardly to compute the *n*th Fibonacci number:

```
fib   :: Integer → Integer
fib 0  =  1
fib 1  =  1
fib n  =  fib (n − 1) + fib (n − 2)
```

There is only one problem: This function is horribly inefficient!

---

**DETAILS**

Try running this program on successively larger values of *n*; in Hugs, values larger than only 20 or so cause a noticeable delay.

---

To understand the cause of this inefficiency, let's begin the calculation of, say, *fib* 8:

*fib* 8
⟹  *fib* 7 + *fib* 6
⟹  (*fib* 6 + *fib* 5) + (*fib* 5 + *fib* 4)
⟹  ((*fib* 5 + *fib* 4) + (*fib* 4 + *fib* 3))
   +((*fib* 4 + *fib* 3) + (*fib* 3 + *fib* 2))
⟹  (((*fib* 4 + *fib* 3) + (*fib* 3 + *fib* 2))
   +((*fib* 3 + *fib* 2) + (*fib* 2 + *fib* 1)))
   +(((*fib* 3 + *fib* 2) + (*fib* 2 + *fib* 1))
   +((*fib* 2 + *fib* 1) + (*fib* 1 + *fib* 0)))
...

It is easy to see that this calculation is blowing up exponentially. That is, to compute the *n*th Fibonacci number will require a number of steps proportional to $2^n$. Sadly, many of the computations are being repeated, but in general we cannot expect a Haskell implementation to realize this and take advantage of it. So what do we do?

One solution is to construct the Fibonacci sequence directly as an infinite stream. The key to this construction is noticing that if we add pointwise the Fibonacci sequence to the tail of the Fibonacci sequence, we get the tail of the tail of the Fibonacci sequence:

| 1 | 1 | 2 | 3 | 5 | 8  | 13 | 21 | Fibonacci sequence         |
|---|---|---|---|---|----|----|----|----------------------------|
| 1 | 2 | 3 | 5 | 8 | 13 | 21 | 34 | tail of Fibonacci sequence |
|   | 2 | 3 | 5 | 8 | 13 | 21 | 34 | 55 | tail of tail of Fibonacci sequence |

This leads naturally to the following definition of the Fibonacci sequence:

> *fibs* :: [*Integer*]
> *fibs* = 1 : 1 : *zipWith* (+) *fibs* (*tail fibs*)

Note the concise and naturally recursive nature of this definition. Evaluating *take* 10 *fibs* yields:

> [1, 1, 2, 3, 5, 8, 13, 21, 34, 55]

as expected.

---

**DETAILS**
Try running *take n fibs* with successively larger values of *n*; you will find that it runs very fast, even though the Fibonacci numbers start getting quite large. In fact, in Hugs the time is dominated by how long it takes to print the numbers; try running *fibs* !! 1000 to see how quickly a single value can be computed and printed.

---

This program is very efficient. To see why, we can proceed by calculation. The first step is easy:

> *fibs*
> ⇒  1 : 1 : *add fibs* (*tail fibs*)

where, for succinctness, I have written *add* for *zipWith* (+).

However, if we now simply substitute the definition of *fibs* for both of its occurrences, we find ourselves heading toward the same exponential blow-up that we saw earlier:

> ⇒  1 : 1 : *add* (1 : 1 : *add fibs* (*tail fibs*))
>              (1 : *add fibs* (*tail fibs*))

Fortunately, a Haskell implementation will be cleverer than this by sharing *fibs* as well as its tail. Starting from the beginning again, this sharing is noticeable immediately after the first step:

> *fibs*
> ⇒ 1 : 1 : *add fibs* (*tail fibs*)

at which point we can express the sharing of the tail using a **where** clause:

> ⇒ 1 : *tf*
> **where** *tf* = 1 : *add fibs* (*tail fibs*)
> ⇒ 1 : *tf*
> **where** *tf* = 1 : *add fibs tf*

We can also express the sharing of the tail of the tail in preparation for unfolding *add* (I will use *tf*2, *tf*3, and so forth, for the names of the successive tails):

> ⇒ 1 : *tf*
> **where** *tf* = 1 : *tf*2
> **where** *tf*2 = *add fibs tf*

Finally, we can unfold *add* to yield:

> ⇒ 1 : *tf*
> **where** *tf* = 1 : *tf*2
> **where** *tf*2 = 2 : *add tf tf*2

Repeating this process, we introduce even more sharing, and unfold *add* again:

> ⇒ 1 : *tf*
> **where** *tf* = 1 : *tf*2
> **where** *tf*2 = 2 : *tf*3
> **where** *tf*3 = *add tf tf*2
> ⇒ 1 : *tf*
> **where** *tf* = 1 : *tf*2
> **where** *tf*2 = 2 : *tf*3
> **where** *tf*3 = 3 : *add tf*2 *tf*3

But now note that *tf* is only used in one place, and thus might as well be eliminated, yielding:

> ⇒ 1 : 1 : *tf*2
> **where** *tf*2 = 2 : *tf*3
> **where** *tf*3 = 3 : *add tf*2 *tf*3

At this point we can begin to repeat the sequence of introducing a new **where** clause to capture sharing, *unfold*ing *add*, and then eliminating the outermost **where** binding. This will yield successively longer versions of the result. Here is one more application of that sequence:

$\Rightarrow$  $1 : 1 : tf2$
    **where** $tf2$ $=$ $2 : tf3$
                **where** $tf3$ $=$ $3 : tf4$
                        **where** $tf4$ $=$ $add\ tf2\ tf3$
$\Rightarrow$  $1 : 1 : tf2$
    **where** $tf2$ $=$ $2 : tf3$
                **where** $tf3$ $=$ $3 : tf4$
                        **where** $tf4$ $=$ $5 : add\ tf3\ tf4$
$\Rightarrow$  $1 : 1 : 2 : tf3$
            **where** $tf3$ $=$ $3 : tf4$
                    **where** $tf4$ $=$ $5 : add\ tf3\ tf4$

The reason that there are always at least two **where** clauses is that *fibs* recurses on itself as well as its tail. The elimination of the **where** clause corresponds to the garbage collection of unused memory by an implementation.

Although this process may seem a bit tedious, it is important only when wanting to reason about the efficiency (in time and space) of the calculation. If you are just interested in the resulting values, you can, of course, use the exponentially expanding calculation, with no fear that you might get a different answer.

## 14.3 Stream Diagrams

Another way to reason about both the value and efficiency of *fibs* involves thinking of streams as little "wires" along which values flow, and functions like *add* as little black boxes that take as input two of these wires and output a third. With this viewpoint we can *draw* the equation describing *fibs* as shown in Fig. 14.1. Here the constructor (:) is represented as a circle whose meaning is this: The first value on its output wire is the single value on its left input wire, and the remaining values are whatever appears on the right input wire. Finally, any wire that "forks" sends its values to both destinations.

With this framework in mind, let's now reason about the output wire of *fibs* in Fig. 14.1. The first two values are clearly 1. The third value is the first value on the output wire of *add*, which is surely 2. This value is also the second value on the tail of *fibs*, so now we know that the second value out of *add* is 3, which becomes the fourth value of *fibs*. Continuing

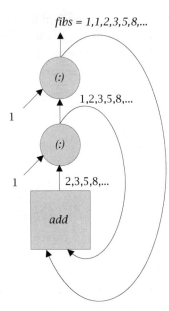

Figure 14.1: Stream Diagram for the Fibonacci Sequence

in this way it is easy to compute as many of the values on the wires as we want.

Let's try another example. In networking and distributed computing there is a notion of *client-server interactions*, where a program known as a *server* handles requests from a *client* program. For example, a web server might receive requests from a user's web browser; the former is the server, the latter is the client. The communication is two-way – the server will typically send data back to the client in response to a request – and continuous – many requests may be serviced even over a relatively short period of time.

We can model this using streams as follows. Suppose there is a type *Request* of requests, and a type *Response* of responses. The client and server types are thus:

$$client \quad :: \quad [Response] \rightarrow [Request]$$
$$server \quad :: \quad [Request] \rightarrow [Response]$$

Their interaction is then neatly captured by these mutually recursive equations:

$$reqs \quad = \quad client\ resps$$
$$resps \quad = \quad server\ reqs$$

To make this more concrete, let's do something really simple: The server will receive integers as requests, and will return as responses the successor to each integer. The client will issue a single integer as the first request, and then pass on each integer it receives from the server as subsequent requests. In Haskell:

**type** *Request* = *Integer*
**type** *Response* = *Integer*

*client ys* = 1 : *ys*
*server xs* = *map* (+1) *xs*

Let's compute the value of *reqs* by calculation, being careful to perform outermost calculations first:

*reqs*
  ⇒ *client resps*
  ⇒ 1 : *resps*
  ⇒ 1 : *server reqs*

Note now that *reqs* is "chasing its tail," and thus we introduce sharing and then unfold *server*:

  ⇒ 1 : *tr*
    **where** *tr* = *server reqs*
  ⇒ 1 : *tr*
    **where** *tr* = 2 : *server tr*
  ⇒ 1 : *tr*
    **where** *tr* = 2 : *tr2*
        **where** *tr2* = *server tr*
  ⇒ 1 : *tr*
    **where** *tr* = 2 : *tr2*
        **where** *tr2* = 3 : *server tr2*
  ⇒ 1 : 2 : *tr2*
    **where** *tr2* = 3 : *server tr2*

and so on, just as we did for *fibs*.

We can also draw the equations as a stream diagram, as shown in Fig. 14.2. Note the values on the wires. Indeed, if we evaluate *take* 10 *reqs* we get the expected result:

[1, 2, 3, 4, 5, 6, 7, 8, 9, 10]

## 14.4  Lazy Patterns

Suppose now that the client program wishes to test the first (and only the first) response coming back from the server, to be sure that it satisfies

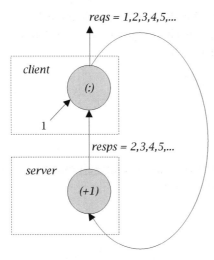

Figure 14.2: Stream Diagram for Client-Server Interactions

some predicate *ok*. That is:

$$client\ (y:ys)\ =\ \textbf{if}\ ok\ y\ \textbf{then}\ 1:(y:ys)$$
$$\textbf{else}\ error\ \text{``faulty server''}$$

The nature of *ok* is unimportant, and so I will make it completely trivial:

$$ok\ y\ =\ True$$

Now let's see what this seemingly harmless change does to our calculation:

*reqs*
  ⇒  *client resps*
  ⇒  *client* (*server reqs*)
  ⇒  *client* (*server* (*client resps*))
  ⇒  *client* (*server* (*client* (*server reqs*)))
  . . .

This does not terminate! The problem is that *client* cannot be unfolded until *resps* shows its head and tail; but *server* likewise cannot be unfolded until *reqs* shows its head and tail. Deadlock!

**DETAILS**
Try running this code; in Hugs the error message "ERROR: control stack overflow" occurs, which is usually indicative of an infinitely deep nesting of function calls, such as the calculation above is unfolding into.

This problem highlights a subtle aspect of pattern-matching, namely that it sometimes causes evaluation to be too eager. The problem can be circumvented in two ways. The most obvious is to rewrite *client* like this:

> *client ys* = 1 : **if** *ok* (*head ys*) **then** *ys*
> **else** *error* "faulty server"

Two changes were made here: The pattern-matching was eliminated by using the explicit selector function *head*, and the conditional was pushed inside of the list. You should verify that in fact this allows the calculation to proceed properly as before. (Of course you will also find that running the code will no longer cause an error.)

An alternative solution is to use a special kind of pattern in Haskell, called a *lazy pattern*, which defers the pattern-matching in a way that is effectively the same as using explicit selector functions. Any pattern *p* can be made lazy by preceding it with a tilde, as in ˜*p*. Although we still need to push the conditional inside of the list, we can use a lazy pattern to rewrite *client* like this:

> *client* ˜(*y* : *ys*) = 1 : **if** *ok y* **then** *y* : *ys*
> **else** *error* "faulty server"

Although this doesn't seem like much of a difference, there are situations where large numbers of explicit selector functions can be avoided by using a lazy pattern, and the result is often arguably more declarative.

Perhaps the easiest way to calculate using lazy patterns is to use **where** clauses (once again!) to express the delayed pattern match. For example, let's calculate *reqs* with the latest version of *client*:

> *reqs*
> ⇒  *client resps*
> ⇒  1 : **if** *ok y* **then** *y* : *ys*
>         **else** *error* "faulty server"
>     **where** *y* : *ys* = *resps*
> ⇒  1 : (*y* : *ys*)
>     **where** *y* : *ys* = *resps*
> ⇒  1 : *resps*

At this point we are back at the third step in the original calculation, and the rest of the calculation proceeds as before.

**DETAILS**

As another example of the use of lazy patterns, consider this alternative definition of the Fibonacci sequence:

$$fibs' \qquad :: \quad [Integer]$$
$$fibs'@(1:tfibs) \;=\; 1:1:zipWith\;(+)\;fibs'\;tfibs$$

which has the (small) advantage of not using *tail* on the right-hand side, because it is available in "destructured" form on the left-hand side as *tfib*. This kind of equation is called a *pattern binding* because it is a top-level equation in which the entire left-hand side is a pattern (i.e., both *fibs'* and *tfibs* are bound within the scope of the declaration).

Using reasoning similar to that used earlier, you might conclude that this program will not generate any output. But it does, because in Haskell, pattern bindings have an implicit ˜ in front of them, reflecting the most common behavior expected of pattern bindings. Thus, lazy patterns play an important role in Haskell, if only implicitly.

---

**Exercise 14.1** Given a list of primes *ps*, write a recursive stream representing the infinite sequence of numbers that are divisible by no primes other than 1 or an element of *ps*.[2] Or, stated inductively:

■ 1 is in the sequence.
■ if *n* is in the sequence, so is $n * p$ for each *p* in *ps*.

## 14.5 Memoization

I will now do something rather odd, but otherwise seemingly harmless, to the program for *fibs*. I will turn it into a function:

$$fibsFn \quad :: \quad () \rightarrow [Integer]$$
$$fibsFn\;x \;=\; 1:1:zipWith\;(+)\;(fibsFn\;())\;(tail\;(fibsFn\;()))$$

**DETAILS**

Recall that () is the *unit* data type in Haskell, and it has exactly one value: (). Thus, () denotes both the name of the data type and its value. Although

---

[2] This problem is discussed in (Dijkstra, 1976) where it is attributed to R.W. Hamming.

the following is not valid Haskell syntax, it captures the intended meaning of the unit data type:

**data** () = ()

See Appendix A for further details.

This program unfortunately reverts to the exponential behavior of our original *fib* function, and to make matters worse has a huge (exponential) *space leak*. A program (whether written in Haskell or some other language) with a space leak is one that uses memory space so quickly that it detrimentally affects performance. The leak can be so bad that the program runs out of memory before computing the desired result. Such is the case for *fibsFn* above.

**DETAILS**
Evaluating *take n* (*fibsFn* ()) works using Hugs for values of *n* up to about 20, but for any larger number the program runs out of memory and halts with the error message: "ERROR: Garbage collection fails to reclaim sufficient space."

To understand the source of the space leak, we can again proceed by calculation. The first two steps are the same as before:

*fibsFn* ()
  ⇒  1 : 1 : *add* (*fibsFn* ()) (*tail* (*fibsFn* ()))
  ⇒  1 : *tf*
      **where** *tf*  =  1 : *add* (*fibsFn* ()) (*tail* (*fibsFn* ()))

But here is where the problem begins. We cannot expect an implementation to perform the following step:

  ⇒  1 : *tf*
      **where** *tf*  =  1 : *add* (*fibs* ()) *tf*

because there is no way to know, in general, whether the expression *fibsFn* () on the right-hand side is the same as the *fibsFn* () that we started with. Therefore, an implementation cannot conclude that *tail* (*fibsFn* ()) is the same as *tf*. You might argue that, because the () data type has only one value, surely an implementation can deduce that these applications of *fibsFn* are the same. But even simple generalizations of this task become unreasonable. For example, suppose that we use the *Integer* data type instead of (), and apply *fibsFn* in each case to expressions that compute the same value, but not obviously so.

The point is that, in general, an implementation cannot be expected to detect this kind of sharing involving function applications, and thus the best that we can do for the next step in the calculation above is:

$$\Rightarrow \quad 1 : tf$$
$$\textbf{where } tf \;=\; 1 : add\,(fibsFn\,())$$
$$(tail\,(1:1:add\,(fibsFn\,())\,(tail\,(fibsFn\,()))))$$

Unfortunately, this is clearly headed toward an exponential blowup in both time and space, as claimed earlier.

Of course, the fix to this particular problem is quite easy: just use *fibs* instead of *fibsFn*! But there are times when such a change is not possible, or at least not desirable. Indeed, we will run into such a situation in Chapter 15. What can we do in such circumstances?

One solution is to use a technique called *memoization*, in which a primitive function called *memo* with type:

$$memo \;::\; (a \rightarrow b) \rightarrow (a \rightarrow b)$$

is used such that the following relationship holds:

$$memo\ f\ x \;=\; f\ x$$

In fact this would be a suitable definition of *memo* (which is really just the identity function over functions), if *memo* did not have one other very important property: A function *memo f* keeps track of what values it is applied to, and what the result is in each case. If the function is ever applied to the same value more than once, it will simply look up the answer associated with that value rather than recompute it each time.

Memo functions are not part of the Haskell standard, and their design is beyond the scope of this textbook. One design issue, for example, is how many previous values a memo function should keep track of. Sometimes just one value is needed, as will be the case when we use this technique in Chapter 15. There we will use the function *memo*1 imported from a nonstandard library called *Memo*1. This memo function saves just one previous argument and its value. If the function is applied to an argument other than the saved one, the new result is computed, and the new argument/value pair replaces the previous one.

The expression *fibsFn* can also be memoized using *memo*1, because *fibsFn* is applied to exactly one value, (), ever. The memoization is achieved as follows:

$$mfibsFn \quad :: \quad () \rightarrow [Integer]$$
$$mfibsFn\ x \ = \ \textbf{let}\ mfibs \ = \ memo1\ mfibsFn$$
$$\textbf{in}\ 1:1: zipWith\ (+)\ (mfibs\ ())\ (tail\ (mfibs\ ()))$$

This is somewhat contrived, of course, because as mentioned above the more obvious solution is to use *fibs*. But hopefully the example illustrates well enough the technique; if not, its use in Chapter 15 should be much more convincing.

## 14.6  Inductive Properties of Infinite Lists

For something completely different, let's now turn to the problem of proving inductive properties of streams. In Chapter 11 you learned how to prove inductive properties over lists. Tables 11.1 and 11.2 provide a summary of many such properties. The question is, how many of these properties hold for infinite lists as well as finite lists?

For example, this relationship between *take*, *drop*, and (++):

$$take\ n\ xs ++ drop\ n\ xs = xs$$

is true even if *xs* is infinite (you should convince yourself intuitively of this fact). On the other hand, this property of *reverse*:

$$reverse\ (reverse\ xs) = xs$$

is clearly *not* true if *xs* is infinite, because in that case the left-hand side will not terminate (i.e., its value is ⊥).

How can we formally prove such results? Recall that the special value ⊥ denotes both nonterminating and error-producing computations. Another way to view this value when reasoning about infinite lists is to think of ⊥ as an *approximation* to an answer. More specifically, it is the *least* approximation (thus the name "bottom") that has absolutely no content whatsoever.

In Haskell, every data type, whether built-in or user-defined, has a ⊥ value. For example, every *Integer* value can be approximated by $\perp_{Integer}$, although the subscript is usually omitted if it is obvious from the context in which the bottom value is being used. We can construct a polymorphic version of this value as follows:

$$bot \quad :: \quad a$$
$$bot \ = \ bot$$

In the case of lists, the situation is more interesting, because every tail of a list is also a list, and so could also be approximated by ⊥. For example, the following are increasingly more accurate approximations to the list [1, 2, 3, 4], culminating in the complete list itself:

```
⊥
1 :⊥
1 : 2 :⊥
1 : 2 : 3 :⊥
1 : 2 : 3 : 4 :⊥
1 : 2 : 3 : 4 : [ ]
```

Most interesting is the case of *infinite* lists, which are mathematically the *limit* of an infinite sequence of increasing approximations. For example, the limit of this infinite sequence:

```
⊥
1 :⊥
1 : 2 :⊥
1 : 2 : 3 :⊥
1 : 2 : 3 : 4 :⊥
1 : 2 : 3 : 4 : 5 :⊥
1 : 2 : 3 : 4 : 5 : 6 :⊥
1 : 2 : 3 : 4 : 5 : 6 : 7 :⊥
...
```

is the infinite list of natural numbers [1, 2..]. $\perp_{List}$ and any list whose tail is $\perp_{List}$ is called a *partial list*. Every infinite list can be described as the limit of an increasing sequence of partial lists.

Keep in mind that although ⊥ is conceptually a member of every data type in Haskell, and we can generate that value using something like *bot* defined earlier, any attempt to *test* for *bot*, either through pattern-matching or an explicit equality test, will lead to nontermination (i.e., it will lead to ⊥ itself). Pragmatically, you can think of this task as checking for an error condition or nontermination, which in general is provably not possible.

Now, the point of all of this is the following. Suppose that we have a property involving lists, call it *P*, expressed as an equation in Haskell. If we can prove that this property is true for every partial list in a sequence whose limit is the infinite list *xs*, then the property *P* is also true of *xs*.

How do we prove that the property is true of every partial list? By induction, of course! But now the base case is different from that used with finite lists: Instead of the empty list [ ], simply use the least defined list ⊥ instead.

More precisely, to prove that a property *P*, expressed as an equation in Haskell, is true of all infinite lists, we proceed in two steps:

1. Prove $P(\bot)$ (the base case).
2. Assume that $P(xs)$ is true (the induction hypothesis), and prove that $P(x : xs)$ is true (the induction step).

You are probably wondering why the phrase "expressed as an equation in Haskell" is used to constrain the property of interest. The problem is that the leap from a property being true for every partial list in an approximating sequence to the property being true for the infinite list itself is not justified for all properties. The simplest counterexample is the property that states "the list is partial." This is trivially satisfied by every partial list, but is clearly not true of the limit, an infinite list. Fortunately, there is no way to write this property as an equation in Haskell, and for reasons that are beyond the scope of this text, that constraint is enough to guarantee that our proof technique is sound.

Consider the first example given earlier:

*take n xs* ++ *drop n xs* = *xs*

and recall the definitions of *take* and (++):

```
take              :: Int → [a] → [a]
take 0 _          = [ ]
take _ [ ]        = [ ]
take n (x : xs) | n > 0 = x : take (n − 1) xs

(++)              :: [a] → [a] → [a]
[ ] ++ ys         = ys
(x : xs) ++ ys    = x : (xs ++ ys)
```

From this we can easily prove the base case as follows:

$$take \; n \; \perp \; \mathbin{+\!\!+} \; drop \; n \; \perp$$
$$\Rightarrow \; \perp \; \mathbin{+\!\!+} \; drop \; n \; \perp$$
$$\Rightarrow \; \perp$$

As mentioned earlier, any attempt to pattern-match against $\perp$ will lead to nontermination, or $\perp$. Because *take* pattern-matches on its second argument, and $(\mathbin{+\!\!+})$ on its first, the above two steps are thereby justified. The proof of the induction step is straightforward (and thus omitted). This then establishes by induction that the property is true of every partial list, and therefore of every infinite list as well.

Now consider the second example given earlier:

$$reverse \; (reverse \; xs) = xs$$

which I claimed was not valid for infinite lists. Undaunted, however, let's try to prove its correctness, starting with the base case $xs = \perp$:

$$reverse \; (reverse \; \perp)$$
$$\Rightarrow \;\; reverse \; \perp$$
$$\Rightarrow \; \perp$$

So the property in fact holds for the base case. Moving on to the induction step:

$$reverse \; (reverse \; (x : xs))$$
$$\Rightarrow \;\; \{ \; unfold \; reverse \; \}$$
$$reverse \; (reverse \; xs \mathbin{+\!\!+} [x])$$
$$\Rightarrow \;\; \{ \; lemma \; (see \; below) \; \}$$
$$reverse \; [x] \mathbin{+\!\!+} reverse \; (reverse \; xs)$$
$$\Rightarrow \;\; \{ \; unfold \; reverse \; \}$$
$$[x] \mathbin{+\!\!+} reverse \; (reverse \; xs)$$
$$\Rightarrow \;\; \{ \; induction \; hypothesis \; \}$$
$$[x] \mathbin{+\!\!+} xs$$
$$\Rightarrow \;\; \{ \; unfold \; (\mathbin{+\!\!+}) \; \}$$
$$x : ([\,] \mathbin{+\!\!+} xs)$$
$$\Rightarrow \;\; \{ \; unfold \; (\mathbin{+\!\!+}) \; \}$$
$$x : xs$$

So the induction step works as well, implying that the property *does* in fact hold for infinite lists! This contradicts our intuition, so what went wrong?

The problem is in the implied lemma in the second step of the proof above, which, generally stated, is:

*reverse* (*xs* ++ *ys*) = *reverse ys* ++ *reverse xs*

In order to use this lemma in the proof above, it must be true of partial lists. But it isn't, a fact easily discovered when we try to prove just the base case. Starting with the left-hand side, we have:

*reverse* (⊥ ++ *ys*)
  ⇒  *reverse* ⊥
  ⇒  ⊥

whereas the right-hand side yields:

*reverse ys* ++ *reverse* ⊥
  ⇒  *reverse ys* ++ ⊥

These are clearly not equal (unless *ys* is also partial, but that is a special case, and is certainly not true in the context where the lemma was used in the proof above). On the other hand, the lemma and the original property both hold for finite lists, which can be proved using the techniques from Chapter 11.

This example highlights the care that needs to be taken in conducting formal proofs of program properties. In particular, conditions associated with the validity of a property need to be observed.

Returning to Tables 11.1 and 11.2, it turns out that every property listed there that is not qualified with the statement "for all finite lists..." is valid for infinite lists. The proofs of each of these are left as an exercise.

---

**Exercise 14.2** Prove as many of the properties in Tables 11.1 and 11.2 as you can, for infinite lists.

---

**Exercise 14.3** Prove that *fib n* = *fibs* !! *n* for all $n \geq 0$.

---

**Exercise 14.4** Describe each of the following infinite lists, and use *take* to evaluate the first 10 elements of each.

*xs*  =  1 : *map* (∗2) *xs*
*ys*  =  [1] : [*zipWith* (+) (0 : *q*) (*q* ++ [0]) | *q* ← *ys*]

---

**Exercise 14.5** Show that *cycle* is the identity function on infinite lists. In other words, show that for any infinite list *lst*, *cycle lst* == *lst*.

**Exercise 14.6** Consider the problem of symbolically manipulating polynomials in a single variable, such as:

$$1 + 2x^2 - 4x^3 + 3x^5$$

with the assumption that *all* polynomials contain an *infinite* number of terms (ones we normally think of as finite simply have zeros for the higher-order coefficients). So let's represent such polynomials by an infinite list of floating-point coefficients:

**type** *Poly* = [*Float*]

For example, the above polynomial can be represented by:

*pn* :: *Poly*
*pn* = 1 : 0 : 2 : (−4) : 0 : 3 : *repeat* 0

---

**DETAILS**

The function *repeat* is defined in the Standard Prelude (see Chapter 23) as:

*repeat* :: *a* → [*a*]
*repeat x* = *xs* **where** *xs* = *x* : *xs*

---

There are several things we might wish to do with polynomials. One is to multiply them by a constant. Here's a function *scale* that will do just that:

*scale* :: *Float* → *Poly* → *Poly*
*scale a* = *map* (∗*a*)

Your job is to provide the following additional functions over polynomials:

1. *addPoly* :: *Poly* → *Poly* → *Poly* is a function that takes two polynomials and returns their sum.
2. *subPoly* :: *Poly* → *Poly* → *Poly* is a function that takes two polynomials and returns their difference.
3. *mulPoly* :: *Poly* → *Poly* → *Poly* is a function that takes two polynomials and returns their product.
4. *divPoly* :: *Poly* → *Poly* → *Poly* is a function that takes two polynomials and returns their quotient.

The first two of these – *addPoly* and *subPoly* – are easy to define. For the other two, it might be helpful to review some basic algebra. Consider first multiplying two polynomials:

$$\sum_{i=0}^{\infty} a_i x^i \sum_{i=0}^{\infty} b_i x^i \;=\; \left( a_0 + x \sum_{i=0}^{\infty} a_{i+1} x^i \right) \sum_{i=0}^{\infty} b_i x^i$$

$$=\; a_0 \sum_{i=0}^{\infty} b_i x^i + x \sum_{i=0}^{\infty} a_{i+1} x^i \sum_{i=0}^{\infty} b_i x^i$$

This derivation should serve as a strong hint for developing a definition of *mulPoly*. Similarly, by a derivation similar to the above, we can show that:

$$\frac{\displaystyle\sum_{i=0}^{\infty} a_i x^i}{\displaystyle\sum_{i=0}^{\infty} b_i x^i} \;=\; \frac{a_0}{b_0} + x \frac{\displaystyle\sum_{i=0}^{\infty} \left( a_{i+1} - \frac{a_0}{b_0} b_{i+1} \right) x^i}{\displaystyle\sum_{i=0}^{\infty} b_i x^i}$$

which should help you to define *divPoly*.

---

**Exercise 14.7**   Recall from first grade math that:

$$\frac{1}{1 - x - x^2} = 1 + x + 2x^2 + 3x^3 + 5x^4 + 8x^5 + \dots$$

Use this result to write the world's most convoluted Fibonacci sequence generator, and check its correctness by *take*ing the first 10 elements.

---

**Exercise 14.8**   Instead of using special names, such as *addPoly*, *mulPoly*, and so on, for polynomials, create instances of existing type classes to use names such as $(+)$, $(*)$, and others.

# CHAPTER FIFTEEN

# A Module of Reactive Animations

In Chapter 13 you learned how to progam dynamic, graphical animations in a highly abstract, declarative manner. But there is one thing missing: *reactivity*. That is, the ability of our animations to react to user input or other external stimuli. In Chapter 10 you learned how user input could alter a graphics image, so at first blush, doing so for animations would seem to be just as easy. The problem is, we have lifted our thought processes and programming style to a level where we are manipulating continuous, never-ending animations, and the notion of a discrete event, such as a mouse press, does not fit in so well. For example, try to write a program, at the level of *Behavior*s, for a simple ball that changes color from red to blue when the mouse is pressed. I think that you will find this to be quite difficult.

In solving this problem I will borrow some ideas from a (nonstandard) Haskell library called *Fran*, which is short for *functional reactive animation*. Fran, and the version of it that we will develop in this chapter, are examples of *domain specific languages*, or DSLs. A DSL is a language that is designed for a specific application domain, in this case reactive animations. Haskell is an excellent vehicle for directly implementing DSLs without having to create a new language from scratch. In this way we say that the DSL is *embedded* in Haskell, or that Haskell is the *host language* for the DSL. To distinguish our language from Fran, I will call it FAL, for *functional animation language*.[1]

I will begin by describing FAL by example. I will then describe a partial implementation of FAL based on streams which, because of its simplicity,

---

[1] Fran is described in (Elliott, Hudak, 1997; Elliott, 1997); see also the Haskell home page for information on the latest release. Related approaches to graphics and animation programming in functional languages include (Arya, 1986, 1989; Zilles et al., 1988; Finne, Peyton Jones, 1995; Lucas, Zilles, 1987; Schechter et al., 1994; Henderson, 1982).

can also serve as its specification. Once this foundation is established, I will describe various extensions to FAL, culminating in a final example, a twenty-line program to play the game of *paddleball*. Although the actual rendering of FAL animations is deferred until Chapter 17, you can run any of the examples in this chapter by using the function:

*reactimate* :: *String* → *Behavior Graphic* → *IO* ()

which is similar to the *animate* function from Chapter 13.

## 15.1 FAL by Example

As with animations in Chapter 13, the key data type in FAL is the polymorphic *Behavior* of continuous, time-varying values. Constant behaviors include numbers (such as 1 :: *Behavior Float*) and colors (such as *red* :: *Behavior Color*). Also as in Chapter 13, time is represented by the behavior *time* :: *Behavior Float*, and most of our animations will have type *Behavior Picture*.

On the other hand, in our approach to user interaction in Chapter 10, pictures were static, and once drawn there was a natural "pause" in the computation when we could check for and respond to user input events, such as mouse and key presses. In FAL, however, user input events are more declarative, much in the way that the animations themselves are declarative. For example, left button presses are represented by the value *lbp* :: *Event* () (in constrast to the command *getLBP* :: *Window* → *IO* ()), and key presses by *key* :: *Event Char* (instead of *getKey* :: *Window* → *IO Char*). Furthermore, the declarative reading of *lbp* (and *key*) is that it is an event *stream* containing all of the left button presses (and key presses), not just one.

### 15.1.1 Basic Reactivity

More concretely, suppose that we wish to generate a color behavior that starts out as red, and changes to blue when the left mouse button is pressed. In FAL we would write:

*color1* :: *Behavior Color*
*color1* = *red* 'untilB' (*lbp* −>> *blue*)

> **DETAILS**
> The name *untilB* is used to avoid conflict with the function *until* defined in the Standard Prelude.

This can be read "behave as red until the left button is pressed, then change to blue." I can then use *color*1 to color (or *paint*) an animation, as follows:

*ball*1   ::   *Behavior Picture*
*ball*1   =   *paint color*1 *circ*

*circ*   ::   *Behavior Region*
*circ*   =   *translate* (*cos time, sin time*) (*ell* 0.2 0.2)

Here *ell* 0.2 0.2 creates a circle with radius 0.2, and the translation causes it to revolve about the center of the screen with period $2\pi$ seconds. Thus, *ball*1 is a revolving circle that changes from red to blue when the left mouse button in pressed.

As a simple variation of this, suppose that we want the color of the ball to change from red to blue on the first left button press, back to red on the second, blue on the third, and so on. This idea is easily captured through recursion (all of the *color* examples in this section have type *Behavior Color*, and thus the type signatures will be omitted):

*color*1*r*   =   *red* '*untilB*' *lbp* −>>
                *blue* '*untilB*' *lbp* −>>
                *color*1*r*

Using *color*1*r* instead of *color*1 to paint the ball defined above gives the desired result.

### 15.1.2 Event Choice

This is all fine for one kind of event, but sometimes it is desirable to choose between two different behaviors based on different user inputs. For example, this version of *color*:

*color*2   =   *red* '*untilB*' ((*lbp* −>> *blue*) .|. (*key* −>> *yellow*)) will start off as red and change to blue if the left mouse button is pressed, or to yellow if a key is pressed. The (.|.) operator can be read as the "or" of its event arguments.

As in the previous example, we may also wish for this behavior to repeat itself; that is, for subsequent mouse and key presses to create a never-ending choice between blue and yellow. Using recursion, we can express this desired behavior as:

$$color2r = red \text{ `untilB` } colorEvent \textbf{ where}$$
$$colorEvent = (lbp ->> blue \text{ `untilB` } colorEvent) .|.$$
$$(key ->> yellow \text{ `untilB` } colorEvent)$$

### 15.1.3 Recursive Event Processing

As you might imagine, the recursive definition of behaviors and events, such as found in *color1r* and *color2r*, arises rather often. It turns out that, just as we defined higher-order functions like *map* and *fold* to capture common patterns of recursion on lists, it is also useful to define operators that capture common patterns of recursion on behaviors and event streams. The most important of these is an operator called *switch*, which is just like *untilB* except that it repeatedly processes its second argument, the event stream (i.e., it responds to each successive event). For example, this version of the last example:

$$color2h = red \text{ `switch` } ((lbp ->> blue) .|. (key ->> yellow))$$

looks a lot like *color2*, but because *switch* is used instead of *untilB*, it behaves precisely like *color2r*, yet is considerably more concise. The key insight to understanding the difference between *switch* and *untilB* is that events in FAL are really event *streams*, and *untilB* responds only to the first event, whereas *switch* responds to all of them.

When using *switch* it also becomes convenient to define other operators that deal with entire event streams, as demonstrated by this version of *color1*:

$$color1h = red \text{ `switch` } (lbp \text{ `withElem_` } cycle [blue, red])$$

which behaves just like *color1r*. Here *withElem_* essentially converts a stream of left button press events into a stream of color events. Because *switch* processes each of them, the resulting color behavior will switch to each new color event as it occurs.

### 15.1.4 Events with Data

It is also possible to receive *data* from certain events, such as the character from a key press. For example, this version of color:

$$color3 \ = \ white \ `switch` \ (key \ =>> \ \backslash c \ \rightarrow$$
$$\mathbf{case} \ c \ \mathbf{of} \ 'R' \ \rightarrow \ red$$
$$'B' \ \rightarrow \ blue$$
$$'Y' \ \rightarrow \ yellow$$
$$\_ \ \rightarrow \ white)$$

will begin as white, then provide a continuous choice (because of the use of *switch*) between three colors depending on what key is pressed, or back to white if none of the three colors is selected. Note the use of $(=>>)$ instead of $(->>)$ used previously; the former receives data from the event, the latter does not.

### 15.1.5 Snapshot

Suppose now in *color3* above that the color should remain the same if a key other than one of the special three is pressed. To do this we need to somehow take a "snapshot" of the color just before the event, and use that color instead of white in the last line above. That is:

$$color4 \ = \ white \ `switch` \ ((key \ `snapshot` \ color4) \ =>> \ \backslash (c, old) \ \rightarrow$$
$$\mathbf{case} \ c \ \mathbf{of} \ 'R' \ \rightarrow \ red$$
$$'B' \ \rightarrow \ blue$$
$$'Y' \ \rightarrow \ yellow$$
$$\_ \ \rightarrow \ lift0 \ old)$$

The function *snapshot* combines an event (in this case *key*) with a behavior (in this case *color4*), returning an event whose value is that of the original event paired with a "snapshot" of the behavior at the time the event occurs (in this case the pair $(c, old)$). Here the effect is that a key-press event returns not just the character $c$, but the current value of *color4* as well. This color, *old*, is a static color value, not a color behavior, so to turn it back into a behavior, the constant-lifting function *lift0* is applied to it, as we did in Chapter 13.

### 15.1.6 Boolean Events

Sometimes it is desirable to convert a Boolean behavior $b$ into an event that occurs as long as $b$ is *True*. The function *while* does this. For example, *while* ($time \ >* \ 5$) is an event that does not occur until time has exceeded five seconds, and then starts to occur "infinitely often."

Perhaps more natural than this is the function *when* that transforms a Boolean behavior into an event that occurs exactly "when" the Boolean behavior becomes *True* (instead of occurring infinitely often "while" it is true). For example:

$$color5 \ = \ red \ `untilB` \ (when \ (time \ >* \ 5) \ ->> \ blue)$$

defines a color that starts off as red and becomes blue after five seconds. A nice application of *when* appears in the bouncing ball example below.

### 15.1.7 Integration

One of the most useful operations we can add to FAL is *integration* of numeric behaviors over time. For example, the physical equations that describe the position of a mass under the influence of an accelerating force $f$ can be written as:

$$
\begin{aligned}
s, v \ &:: \ Behavior \ Float \\
s \ &= \ s0 + integral \ v \\
v \ &= \ v0 + integral \ f
\end{aligned}
$$

where $s0$ and $v0$ are the initial position and velocity, respectively. Note the similarity of these equations to the mathematical equations describing the physical system:

$$
\begin{aligned}
s(t) &= s_0 + \int_0^t v(t)\,dt \\
v(t) &= v_0 + \int_0^t f(t)\,dt
\end{aligned}
$$

Combining this idea with *when* we can define a bouncing ball with a constant horizontal velocity:

$$
\begin{aligned}
ball2 \ = \ &paint \ red \ (translate \ (x, y) \ (ell \ 0.2 \ 0.2)) \\
\textbf{where} \ g \ &= \ -4 \\
x \ &= \ -3 + integral \ 0.5 \\
y \ &= \ 1.5 + integral \ v \\
v \ &= \ integral \ g \ `switch` \ (hit \ `snapshot\_` \ v => > \backslash v' \ \rightarrow \\
&\quad \ lift0 \ (-v') + integral \ g) \\
hit \ &= \ when \ (y \ <* \ -1.5)
\end{aligned}
$$

The parameter $g$ simulates gravity (i.e., the negative accelerating force exerted on the ball). The detection of a bounce is captured in *hit*, and occurs when the ball's $y$ coordinate drops below $-1.5$. Note how a snapshot of the velocity is taken, and negated every time a "hit" occurs. One subtlety is that the second computation of *integral g* starts from zero after the hit occurs.

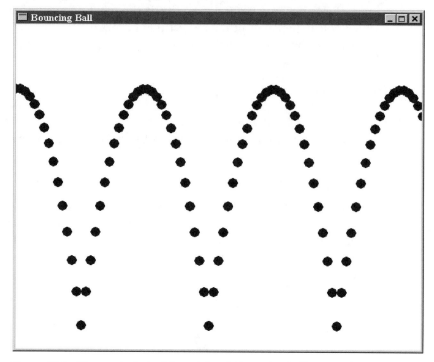

Figure 15.1:  Demonstration of Reactivity: A Bouncing Ball

This is a very declarative description of a bouncing ball, and similar techniques will be used at the end of this chapter to define a simple game of *paddleball*. Fig. 15.1 shows a visual trace of the ball as it bounces across the screen.

In this section I have tried to give a representative sample of the many interesting operators that one might imagine on behaviors and events. We will return later to several variations and enhancements of these basic ideas. However, before getting carried away, let's see if we can specify, via an implementation, the behavior of this new language FAL.

## 15.2  Implementing FAL

**module** *Fal* **where**

**import** *SOEGraphics hiding* (*Region, Event*)
**import** *qualified SOEGraphics as G* (*Region, Event*)
**import** *Animation* (*picToGraphic*)
**import** *Shape*
**import** *Picture*
**import** *Memo*

Note that there is only one entity imported from the *Animation* module. This is because the design of FAL will require completely new representations for the underlying behaviors; we are essentially starting from scratch.

The following fixity declarations will make the writing of FAL programs less awkward by eliminating the need for many parentheses:

**infixr** 1  =>>, ->>
**infixr** 1  'untilB', 'switch', 'stepAccum', 'step'
**infixl** 0  .|.
**infixr** 4  <*, >*
**infixr** 3  &&*
**infixr** 2  ||*

### 15.2.1  An Implementation Strategy

I will first describe an implementation strategy informally, with emphasis on the *types* of behaviors and events. As with nonreactive animations, there is a base domain *Time*, which abstractly should be thought of as real numbers, but in practice is approximated by floating-point numbers:

**type** *Time*  =  *Float*

What differentiates FAL from the nonreactive animations in Chapter 13 is the notion of an *event* such as a mouse or key press. The SOEGraphics Library defines a data type *G.Event* as follows:

**data** *G.Event*
       =  *Key* {*char* :: *Char*, *isDown* :: *Bool*}
       |  *Button* {*pt* :: *Point*, *isLeft*, *isDown* :: *Bool*}
       |  *MouseMove* {*pt* :: *Point*}
       |  *Resize*
       |  *Closed*
     **deriving** *Show*

where I have used the name *G.Event* (recall that the SOEGraphics Library was imported using pseudonym *G*), to distinguish it from the *Event* data type that I will define later in this chapter. (Of course *G.Event* is not legal Haskell syntax in this context.) The field labels give some strong hints about what the various fields are for, although that does not concern us at the moment.

Unfortunately, this notion of an event is different from the one that we want for FAL, and thus I choose to rename *G.Event* as *UserAction*:

**type** *UserAction*  =  *G.Event*

**DETAILS**

The above data declaration for *G.Event* uses Haskell's *field label* syntax, and is equivalent to:

> **data** *G.Event*
> = *Key Char Bool*
> | *Button Point Bool Bool*
> | *MouseMove Point*
> | *Resize*
> | *Closed*
> **deriving** *Show*

except that the former also defines the field labels *char*, *isDown*, *pt*, and *isLeft*, which can be used both to create and select from *G.Event* values. For example, these two equations:

> $k$ = *Key 'a' True*
> $b$ = *Button* (0, 0) *True False*

are equivalent to these:

> $k$ = *Key* {*char* = *'a'*, *isDown* = *True*}
> $b$ = *Button* {*pt* = (0, 0), *isLeft* = *True*, *isDown* = *False*}

The latter are more descriptive, however, and the order of the fields doesn't matter; these equations would do just as well:

> $k$ = *Key* {*isDown* = *True*, *char* = *'a'*}
> $b$ = *Button* {*isLeft* = *True*, *isDown* = *False*, *pt* = (0, 0)}

Field labels can also be used to select from *G.Event* values:

> *char k* ⇒ *'a'*
> *char b* ⇒ *error ...*
> *isDown k* ⇒ *True*
> *isDown b* ⇒ *False*

They can also be used to selectively update a subset of the fields of an existing *G.Event* value:

> $k$ {*char* = *'b'*} ⇒ *Key 'b' True*

and can be used selectively in pattern matching:

> *incr* (*Button* {*pt* = (*x*, *y*)}) = (*x* + 1, *y* + 1)

> Field labels do not change the basic nature of a data type; they are simply
> a convenient syntax for referring to the components of a data structure by
> name rather than by position.

Recall that the value of a nonreactive behavior as described in Chapter 13 is determined solely by a time $t :: Time$. Now, however, its value is determined not only by time, but also by a sequence of user actions. A reasonable representation for behaviors would therefore seem to be:

```
newtype Behavior1 a
    = Behavior1 ([(UserAction, Time)] → Time → a)
```

in which the user actions are time-stamped to indicate when they occur (in Chapter 17 I will explain how this is done). In other words, given a list of time-stamped user actions *uas*, the value of a behavior *Behavior1 bf* at time *t* is just *bf uas t*.

## 15.2.2  Incremental Sampling

Unfortunately, there is a serious drawback with representing behaviors in this way. In order to draw an animation in a graphics window we will have to sample a FAL program at many time values, as we did for nonreactive animations in Chapter 13. But if *Behavior1* is used, we will have to start at the very beginning of the stream of user actions each time, working our way down to the point in time that we are interested in. This is computationally expensive not only in time, but also in space. We will have to hold onto the entire event stream for the duration of the program, and this event stream keeps growing as more and more user actions are received (i.e., a space leak). Our FAL program will eventually either run out of memory, or become so sluggish in response time that it will be unusable.

Before describing a solution to this problem, I will describe a solution to a similar but simpler problem. Suppose that we have a function:

```
inList  ::  [Int] → Int → Bool
```

which determines the membership of an integer in a list whose elements are ordered from lowest to highest. That is, *inList xs x* returns *True* if *x* is in the list *xs*, and false otherwise.

The function *inList* can be defined to take advantage of the fact that its list argument is ordered, by ceasing the search once it reaches a greater value than the one being searched for. If the value is not in the list, and the length of the list is $n$, then this function will only have to perform $n/2$ comparisons on average, instead of the $n$ required if the list were not ordered. However, this is not much of a savings, and is only realized when the element is not in the list.

Now suppose that we have an ordered list of integers, say $ys :: [Int]$, each of which we want to test for membership in a list $xs$. We could compute the list of Boolean results by:

$$result1 \ :: \ [Bool]$$
$$result1 \ = \ map \ (inList \ xs) \ ys$$

For example, given $xs = [2, 4, 6, 8, 10]$ and $ys = [3, 6, 9]$, we would expect $result1 = [False, True, False]$. Because *inList xs* is computed for each element in $ys$, the result will take about $m * n/2$ comparisons on average, where $m$ and $n$ are the lengths of $ys$ and $xs$, respectively.

But surely we can do better. Because both lists are ordered, we could search for the first element, and once its presence is known, begin the search for the second element at the point where the search for the first ended, and so on. This will only require $m + n$ steps in the worst case, which is considerably better than $m * n/2$. We can define a function to do this as follows:

$$result2 \qquad\qquad\qquad :: \ [Bool]$$
$$result2 \qquad\qquad\qquad = \ manyInList \ xs \ ys$$

$$manyInList \qquad\qquad :: \ [Int] \rightarrow [Int] \rightarrow [Bool]$$
$$manyInList \ [\ ] \ \_ \qquad\quad = \ [\ ]$$
$$manyInList \ \_ \ [\ ] \qquad\quad = \ [\ ]$$
$$manyInList \ (x : xs) \ (y : ys) \ =$$
$$\quad \textbf{if} \ x < y \ \textbf{then} \ manyInList \ xs \ (y : ys)$$
$$\qquad\qquad \textbf{else} \ (x == y) : manyInList \ (x : xs) \ ys$$

There is another important advantage of this approach: There is no space leak. Suppose that $xs$ is very long, perhaps hundreds of thousands of elements. With the first approach above, $xs$ will grow in size as it is demanded, until the *result1* list is completely released by whatever parts of the program are using it. In contrast, using *manyInList*, if the *result2* list is consumed one element at a time, the portions of the $xs$ list that have already been searched will be released for reuse by the garbage collector. The space leak has gone away.

In the case of FAL, the situation is surprisingly similar to this. Given behavior *Behavior1 bf*, *bf* has type:

$bf$ :: [(*UserAction*, *Time*)] → *Time* → *a*

which is analogous to *inList*:

*inList* :: [*Int*] → *Int* → *Bool*

What we now want to do is sample these behaviors not just at one time, but at many monotonically increasing values of time. If we take the approach used in *result*1 above, we will experience the inefficiency alluded to at the start of this section. Instead, let's choose to represent behaviors with the type:

**newtype** *Behavior2 a*
    = *Behavior2* ([(*UserAction*, *Time*)] → [*Time*] → [*a*])

which is analogous to *manyInList*:

*manyInList* :: [*Int*] → [*Int*] → [*Bool*]

This choice avoids the computational expense in both time and space of the more naive approach implied by *Behavior1*.

### 15.2.3  Final Refinements

There are three other refinements to be made to our representation of behaviors:

1.  Note in *Behavior2* that *Time* appears twice. If we could conveniently only ask for a behavior's value at the user action times, then we could eliminate one of the *Time* representations. This yields:

    **newtype** *Behavior3 a*
        = *Behavior3* ([*UserAction*] → [*Time*] → [*a*])

2.  To allow sampling a behavior at times other than user action times, we could lift *UserAction* into a *Maybe* type, using *Nothing* to represent a "nonoccurrence:"

    **newtype** *Behavior4 a*
        = *Behavior4* ([*Maybe UserAction*] → [*Time*] → [*a*])

3.  Finally, because we will eventually want to memoize (as we did in Chapter 14) certain functions of this type, it is necessary to uncurry

the two arguments in this functional form, yielding the following as our final representation for behaviors:

**newtype** *Behavior a*
   =  *Behavior* ((([*Maybe UserAction*], [*Time*]) → [*a*])

I should also point out that in this representation, if two events have the same timestamp, one will have to appear before the other in the linear stream. Thus, our implicit approach to dealing with nondeterminism is to eliminate it by forcing an order between simultaneous events.

### 15.2.4  Representing Events

By concentrating on the type representation of behaviors, we were able to do a surprising amount of design without committing to an implementation, which is not uncommon when programming in Haskell, and is a process that is encouraged. It is also not uncommon for this design process to be iterative: A commitment to a particular representation type turns out to be problematical later, and thus, redesign is called for. Indeed, in the case of events, my choice of representation type will perhaps not be as obvious until the implementation of specific events is revealed. Nevertheless, a nice relationship exists between the event and behavior types, as described below.

As mentioned earlier, events in FAL are a bit more abstract than the events imported from the SOEGraphics Library. To motivate the design, think of an event as just a behavior where, at each time *t*, the event either occurs (indicated as *Just x* for some *x*), or does not occur (indicated as *Nothing*). In other words:

**type** *Event a*  =  *Behavior* (*Maybe a*)

However, for type safety, I prefer to represent events using a new data type:

**newtype** *Event a*
   =  *Event* ((([*Maybe UserAction*], [*Time*]) → [*Maybe a*])

## 15.3  The Implementation

Now that we have suitable types for behaviors and events, we can give meaning to the various FAL operators. I will begin with the meaning of some of the behaviors introduced earlier, and return to the meaning of events shortly.

### 15.3.1 Behaviors

#### Time

Consider the simple behavior *time*. Because *time* does not depend on user actions, it ignores that argument. Its sequence of values at time samples *ts* is just *ts*, as you would expect.

```
time  ::  Behavior Time
time  =  Behavior (\(_, ts) → ts)
```

#### Lifting Constants

For another simple case, let's define the meaning of constant behaviors, such as *red* and *blue*, used in the earlier examples. To facilitate this we can first define a function to lift constants to the level of behaviors as we did in Chapter 13.

```
constB    ::  a → Behavior a
constB x  =  Behavior (\_ → repeat x)
```

It is then easy to define particular constant behaviors:

```
red, blue ::  Behavior Color
red       =  constB Red
blue      =  constB Blue
```

So, for example, the constant behavior *red* is represented as an infinite stream of *Red* values.

#### Lifting Functions

I will define a general strategy for lifting functions similar to the concept introduced in Exercise 13.6. The basic idea is that from the generalized lifting operator:

```
($*)  ::  Behavior (a → b) → Behavior a → Behavior b
Behavior ff $* Behavior fb
      =  Behavior (\uts → zipWith ($) (ff uts) (fb uts))
```

and the constant lifting operator:

```
lift0  ::  a → Behavior a
lift0  =  constB
```

all other lifting operators can be defined:

$$lift1 \;::\; (a \to b) \to (Behavior\ a \to Behavior\ b)$$
$$lift1\ f\ b1$$
$$= \; lift0\ f\ \$\!*\ b1$$

$$lift2 \;::\; (a \to b \to c) \to (Behavior\ a \to Behavior\ b \to Behavior\ c)$$
$$lift2\ f\ b1\ b2$$
$$= \; lift1\ f\ b1\ \$\!*\ b2$$

$$lift3 \;::\; (a \to b \to c \to d) \to$$
$$(Behavior\ a \to Behavior\ b \to Behavior\ c \to Behavior\ d)$$
$$lift3\ f\ b1\ b2\ b3$$
$$= \; lift2\ f\ b1\ b2\ \$\!*\ b3$$

and so on.

Fig. 15.2 shows specific liftings used in this chapter, but of course, there may be many others of interest to you. In addition, there are those that arise when *Behavior* is made an instance of the various numeric classes. However, these liftings turn out to be exactly the same as those used in Chapter 13, as shown in Fig. 13.3, and thus, are not repeated here.

## Reactivity

The operators *untilB* and *switch* represent the juncture of behaviors and events in FAL, and in that sense are crucial to the semantics of FAL. Their definitions are relatively concise, but have a couple of subtle aspects that require some explanation. Let's look first at their types, which are identical:

$$untilB,\ switch \;::\; Behavior\ a \to Event\ (Behavior\ a) \to Behavior\ a$$

Note that the second argument is an event that yields behaviors as its values. These are the new behaviors that the overall behavior will switch to as the events occur. Intuitively speaking, we can describe the semantics of the two operators as follows:

1. *b* 'untilB' *es* initially behaves as *b*, then switches to the first behavior in the event stream *es* when it occurs.
2. *b* 'switch' *es* initially behaves as *b*, then switches to the first behavior in the event stream *es* when it occurs, then to the next one, and so on.

```
pairB  ::  Behavior a → Behavior b → Behavior (a, b)
pairB  =  lift2 (,)


fstB   ::  Behavior (a, b) → Behavior a
fstB   =  lift1 fst
sndB   ::  Behavior (a, b) → Behavior b
sndB   =  lift1 snd


paint  ::  Behavior Color → Behavior Region → Behavior Picture
paint  =  lift2 Region


red, blue, yellow, green, white, black  ::  Behavior Color
red                                     =  lift0 Red
blue                                    =  lift0 Blue
yellow                                  =  lift0 Yellow
green                                   =  lift0 Green
white                                   =  lift0 White
black                                   =  lift0 Black


shape  ::  Behavior Shape → Behavior Region
shape  =  lift1 Shape


ell, rec  ::  Behavior Float → Behavior Float → Behavior Region
ell x y   =  shape (lift2 Ellipse x y)
rec x y   =  shape (lift2 Rectangle x y)


translate  ::  (Behavior Float, Behavior Float)
                → Behavior Region → Behavior Region
translate (Behavior fx, Behavior fy) (Behavior fp)
        =  Behavior (\uts → zipWith3 aux (fx uts) (fy uts) (fp uts))
           where aux x y p  =  Translate (x, y) p


(>∗), (<∗)  ::  Ord a ⇒ Behavior a → Behavior a → Behavior Bool
(>∗)        =  lift2 (>)
(<∗)        =  lift2 (<)


(&&∗), (||∗)  ::  Behavior Bool → Behavior Bool → Behavior Bool
(&&∗)         =  lift2 (&&)
(||∗)         =  lift2 (||)


over  ::  Behavior Picture → Behavior Picture → Behavior Picture
over  =  lift2 Over
```

Figure 15.2: Standard Liftings for Reactive Behaviors

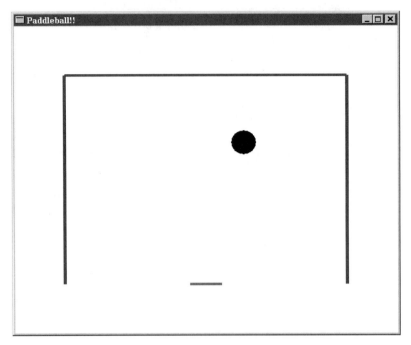

Figure 15.3: Paddleball

We can capture this semantics formally, starting with *untilB*, as follows

> *Behavior fb 'untilB' Event fe  =*
> *memoB $ Behavior (\uts@(us, ts) → loop us ts (fe uts) (fb uts))*
> **where** *loop (_ : us) (_ : ts) ~(e : es) (b : bs)  =*
> *b :* **case** *e* **of**
> *Nothing            → loop us ts es bs*
> *Just (Behavior fb') → fb' (us, ts)*
>
> *memoB              :: Behavior a → Behavior a*
> *memoB (Behavior fb) = Behavior (memo1 fb)*

**DETAILS**
The second line of this definition contains what is called an *"as" pattern.*
$p@(x, y)$ matches exactly the same values that $(x, y)$ matches, except that
in addition to providing names ($x$ and $y$) for the first and second elements
of the pair, it also assigns the name $p$ to the pair itself. This is convenient
whenever there is a need to refer to pieces of a pattern and the whole pattern
itself on the right-hand side of an equation. The idea can be used with any
pattern, even nested ones.

Note that as long as the event stream yields *Nothing*, the values of the original behavior *fb* are placed in the output stream. But once the event occurs, its associated behavior *fb'* takes over.

One subtle aspect of this definition is that the change to the new behavior does not happen until one step *after* the event occurs (as indicated by the fact that *b* is always the first value in the result stream). This is necessary to ensure that recursive behaviors are well defined, as we shall see later. A related subtlety is the lazy pattern-match on events: Evaluating them too eagerly can cause recursive behaviors to become "deadlocked." Finally, note the use of memoization to avoid a potentially exponential blowup in space, similar to that discussed in Chapter 14.

The definition of *switch* is quite similar:

> *Behavior fb* `switch` *Event fe* =
>   *memoB* $ *Behavior* (\*uts*@(*us*, *ts*) → *loop us ts* (*fe uts*) (*fb uts*))
>     **where** *loop* (_ : *us*) (_ : *ts*) ˜(*e* : *es*) (*b* : *bs*) =
>         *b* : **case** *e* **of**
>             *Nothing*                → *loop us ts es bs*
>             *Just* (*Behavior fb'*)  → *loop us ts es* (*fb'* (*us*, *ts*))

The last line is the only one that differs, causing the original event stream to be further processed via the recursive loop.

### 15.3.2  Events

Let us turn now to the implementation of events.

### Mouse Button Presses

For a simple example of an event, consider *lbp*. It must filter through the user actions, returning a true event only when a left button press occurs. A user action *Button p True True* means that the left button was pressed while at point *p*, so we have:

> *lbp*  ::  *Event* ()
> *lbp*  =  *Event* (\(*uas*, _) → *map getlbp uas*)
>         **where** *getlbp* (*Just* (*Button* _ *True True*))  =  *Just* ()
>             *getlbp* _                        =  *Nothing*

### Event Map

*lbp*, of course, returns unit () values, not behaviors. To use it with *untilB* and *switch* there must be a way of turning these values into behaviors.

A number of operators could be defined in FAL for doing this, but let's start with the simplest, $(->>)$, as used in the very first example given earlier:

$$color1 \quad :: \quad Behavior \ Color$$
$$color1 \quad = \quad red \ `untilB` \ lbp \ ->> \ blue$$

> **DETAILS**
> Taking advantage of the **infix** declarations given at the start of this section, I have dropped the parentheses around $lbp\ ->>\ blue$. I will do similar simplifications to each of the examples as they are reintroduced in what follows.

From what has been described thus far, it is clear that in this example $(->>)$ should have type:

$$(->>) \quad :: \quad Event \ () \rightarrow Behavior \ Color \rightarrow Event \ (Behavior \ Color)$$

But to increase its utility I will give it the polymorphic type:

$$(->>) \quad :: \quad Event \ a \rightarrow b \rightarrow Event \ b$$

In fact, $(->>)$ is actually a specialized version of a more general operator $(=>>)$ whose type is:

$$(=>>) \quad :: \quad Event \ a \rightarrow (a \rightarrow b) \rightarrow Event \ b$$

If you reverse the order of the two arguments to $(=>>)$ in this signature, you will see a strong similarity to the type of *fmap*. Indeed, we could make *Event* an instance of the class *Functor*, although I prefer using the infix operator $(=>>)$ instead. In any case, its meaning is straightforward:

$$Event \ fe =>> f \quad = \quad Event \ (\backslash uts \rightarrow map \ aux \ (fe \ uts))$$
$$\textbf{where} \ aux \ (Just \ a) \quad = \quad Just \ (f \ a)$$
$$aux \ Nothing \quad = \quad Nothing$$

However, even though I chose not to make *Event* an instance of *Functor*, I can still take advantage of the fact that *Maybe* is an instance of *Functor*, and rewrite the above definition very compactly as:

$$Event \ fe =>> f \quad = \quad Event \ (map \ (fmap \ f) . fe)$$

Finally, $(->>)$ can now be defined in terms of $(=>>)$:

$$e ->> v \quad = \quad e =>> \backslash\_ \rightarrow v$$

## Predicate Events

The function *while* turns a Boolean behavior into an event, and thus has type:

> *while* :: *Behavior Bool → Event* ()

It is defined by:

> *while* (*Behavior fb*)
>     = *Event* (\\*uts → map aux* (*fb uts*))
>        **where** *aux True* = *Just* ()
>                *aux False* = *Nothing*

In order to define *when* I will first define a function that removes duplicate succesive events in an event stream:

> *unique*                :: *Eq a ⇒ Event a → Event a*
> *unique* (*Event fe*) =
>    *Event* (\\*uts → aux* (*fe uts*))
>    **where** *aux xs*                   = *zipWith remdup* (*Nothing* : *xs*) *xs*
>           *remdup x y* | *x* == *y*     = *Nothing*
>                  | *otherwise* = *y*

The function *when* is then easily defincd:

> *when* :: *Behavior Bool → Event* ()
> *when* = *unique . while*

## Integration

The function *integral* is defined by:

> *integral* :: *Behavior Float → Behavior Float*
> *integral* (*Behavior fb*)
>     = *Behavior* (\\*uts*@(*us*, *t* : *ts*) → 0 : *loop t* 0 *ts* (*fb uts*))
>        **where** *loop t0 acc* (*t1* : *ts*) (*a* : *as*)
>             = **let** *acc′* = *acc* + (*t1* − *t0*) ∗ *a*
>                **in** *acc′* : *loop t1 acc′ ts as*

This function simulates the definition of the integral of a function in calculus (if it exists):

$$\int_{t=0}^{T} f(t)\,dt = \lim_{\Delta t \to 0} \sum_{n=0}^{T/\Delta t} f(\Delta t \cdot n) \cdot \Delta t$$

except that the $\Delta t$ in our case is variable, depending on when a user action occurs (which, if you will recall from an earlier discussion and will be elaborated on in Chapter 17, includes events corresponding to when we wish to sample the behavior).

### 15.3.3 An Example

Before populating FAL with more operators, let's pause briefly and run a test program. Because behaviors are polymorphic, we don't have to worry about how to display an animation, and can instead just look at, for example, the result of a *Color* behavior such as the one given earlier:

$$color1 \;\; :: \;\; Behavior\ Color$$
$$color1 \;\; = \;\; red\ `untilB`\ lbp\ ->>\ blue$$

Suppose that the user actions and time stamps are:

$$uas \;\; = \;\; cycle\ [Nothing,\ Just\ (Button\ (0,\ 0)\ True\ True),\ Nothing]$$
$$ts \;\; = \;\; [1,\ 2..]\ ::\ [Time]$$

where I have used *cycle* to ensure that the user action list is infinite, as is required by *switch*. We can compute the resulting value stream as follows:

$$stream1 \;\; = \;\; \textbf{let}\ Behavior\ fb \;\; = \;\; color1$$
$$\textbf{in}\ take\ 3\ (fb\ (uas,\ ts))$$

The result is [*Red*, *Red*, *Blue*], which hopefully corresponds to your understanding of FAL, but if not, it is worthwhile to compute this result by calculation (despite the tedium!). To simplify matters, I will take the liberty of omitting the *Event* and *Behavior* data constructors, thus writing things like:

$$lbp\ (uas,\ ts)$$

instead of

$$\textbf{let}\ Event\ fe \;\; = \;\; lbp$$
$$\textbf{in}\ fe\ (uas,\ ts)$$

First I will compute the value of the nested event:

$$(lbp\ ->>\ blue)\ (uas,\ ts)$$
$$\implies\ (lbp\ =>>\ \backslash_-\ \rightarrow\ blue)\ (uas,\ ts)$$
$$\implies\ (map\ (fmap\ (\backslash_-\ \rightarrow\ blue))\ .\ fe)\ (uas,\ ts)$$
$$\qquad \textbf{where}\ fe\ (uas,\ _-)\ =\ map\ getlbp\ uas$$
$$\implies\ map\ (fmap\ (\backslash_-\ \rightarrow\ blue))\ (fe\ (uas,\ ts))$$
$$\qquad \textbf{where}\ fe\ (uas,\ _-)\ =\ map\ getlbp\ uas$$
$$\implies\ map\ (fmap\ (\backslash_- \cdot\ blue))\ (Nothing : Just\ () : Nothing : \ldots)$$
$$\implies\ Nothing : Just\ blue : Nothing : \ldots$$

Using the names:

$$tuas \;\; = \;\; tail \; uas$$
$$ttuas \;\; = \;\; tail \; (tail \; uas)$$
$$tts \;\; = \;\; tail \; ts$$
$$ttts \;\; = \;\; tail \; (tail \; ts)$$

the overall result is then:

$(red\ `switch`\ (lbp \; ->> \; blue))\ (uas,\ ts)$
$\Longrightarrow \;\; loop\ uas\ ts\ ((lbp \; ->> \; blue)\ (uas,\ ts))\ (red\ (uas,\ ts))$
$\Longrightarrow \;\; loop\ uas\ ts\ (Nothing : Just\ blue : Nothing : \ldots)\ (red\ (uas,\ ts))$
$\Longrightarrow \;\; loop\ uas\ ts\ (Nothing : Just\ blue : Nothing : \ldots)\ (repeat\ Red)$
$\Longrightarrow \;\; loop\ uas\ ts\ (Nothing : Just\ blue : Nothing : \ldots)\ [Red..]$
$\Longrightarrow \;\; Red : loop\ tuas\ tts\ (Just\ blue : Nothing : \ldots)\ [Red..]$
$\Longrightarrow \;\; Red : Red : loop\ ttuas\ ttts\ (Nothing : \ldots)\ (blue\ (ttuas,\ ttts))$
$\Longrightarrow \;\; Red : Red : loop\ ttuas\ ttts\ (Nothing : \ldots)\ [Blue..]$
$\Longrightarrow \;\; Red : Red : Blue : \ldots$

as expected.

## 15.4  Extensions

In this section various other FAL operators will be defined, starting with the remainder of the ones used in the examples given earlier. Be sure that you understand how and why each of them works the way it does.

The operator *withElem_* was used in this example given earlier:

$$color1h \;\; = \;\; red\ `switch`\ (lbp\ `withElem\_`\ cycle\ [blue,\ red])$$

It is actually an instance of a more general operator, *withElem*, whose definition is:

$withElem \qquad\qquad :: \;\; Event\ a \rightarrow [b] \rightarrow Event\ (a,\ b)$
$withElem\ (Event\ fe)\ bs \;\; = \;\; Event\ (\backslash uts \rightarrow loop\ (fe\ uts)\ bs)$
$\quad\textbf{where}\ loop\ (Just\ a : evs)\ (b : bs) \;\; = \;\; Just\ (a,\ b) : loop\ evs\ bs$
$\qquad\qquad loop\ (Nothing : evs)\ bs \qquad = \;\; Nothing : loop\ evs\ bs$

The definition of *withElem_* is then easy:

$withElem\_ \qquad :: \;\; Event\ a \rightarrow [b] \rightarrow Event\ b$
$withElem\_\ e\ bs \;\; = \;\; e\ `withElem`\ bs \;=>>\; snd$

---

**DETAILS**

The use of _ as a suffix to a function is a *convention* for indicating that the version of the function with the underbar is the same as the one without, except that some argument or result is purposely omitted. For example, looking at the type signatures in this case, the first element in the result pair of *withElem* is omitted in *withElem_*.

---

The *color2* program is an example of the use of an "or" operator (.|.) on events:

$$color2 \;\; = \;\; red \text{ 'untilB' } (lbp \; ->> \; blue \; .|. \; key \; ->> \; yellow)$$

which is defined as:

$$(.|.) \;\; :: \;\; Event\ a \to Event\ a \to Event\ a$$
$$Event\ fe1 \; .|. \; Event\ fe2$$
$$\qquad = \;\; Event\ (\backslash uts \to zipWith\ aux\ (fe1\ uts)\ (fe2\ uts))$$
$$\qquad\qquad \textbf{where } aux\ Nothing\ Nothing \;\; = \;\; Nothing$$
$$\qquad\qquad\qquad aux\ (Just\ x)\ \_ \qquad\quad = \;\; Just\ x$$
$$\qquad\qquad\qquad aux\ \_\ (Just\ y) \qquad\quad = \;\; Just\ y$$

Note that this function "favors" the left event when two events occur simultaneously.[2]

The *color2* example also uses a primitive event *key*, which is defined by:

$$key \;\; :: \;\; Event\ Char$$
$$key \;\; = \;\; Event\ (\backslash(uas,\ \_) \to map\ getkey\ uas)$$
$$\qquad\qquad \textbf{where } getkey\ (Just\ (Key\ ch\ True)) \;\; = \;\; Just\ ch$$
$$\qquad\qquad\qquad getkey\ \_ \qquad\qquad\qquad\qquad = \;\; Nothing$$

The definition of *color3* demonstrates the use of (=>>), which I have already defined. The definition of *color4*, however, also uses the *snapshot* operator:

$$color4 \;\; = \;\; white \text{ 'switch' } (key \text{ 'snapshot' } color4 \; =>> \; \backslash(c,\ old) \to$$
$$\qquad\qquad\qquad \textbf{case } c \textbf{ of } 'R' \;\; \to \;\; red$$
$$\qquad\qquad\qquad\qquad\qquad 'B' \;\; \to \;\; blue$$
$$\qquad\qquad\qquad\qquad\qquad 'Y' \;\; \to \;\; yellow$$
$$\qquad\qquad\qquad\qquad\qquad \_ \;\; \to \;\; lift0\ old)$$

---

[2] Ideally, we would like for this choice to be made nondeterministically, but to do so in a deterministic language such as Haskell requires more sophistication than what I have shown here. (One possibility is to use Haskell's *Random* Library, but that requires going through the IO system.)

whose definition is given by:

$$snapshot \quad :: \quad Event\ a \to Behavior\ b \to Event\ (a,\ b)$$
$$Event\ fe\ `snapshot`\ Behavior\ fb$$
$$= \quad Event\ (\backslash uts \to zipWith\ aux\ (fe\ uts)\ (fb\ uts))$$
$$\textbf{where}\ aux\ (Just\ x)\ y \quad = \quad Just\ (x,\ y)$$
$$aux\ Nothing\ \_ \quad = \quad Nothing$$

As was the case with *withElem*, we can define a version of *snapshot* called *snapshot*_ that throws away the first component of the result:

$$snapshot\_ \quad :: \quad Event\ a \to Behavior\ b \to Event\ b$$
$$snapshot\_\ e\ b \quad = \quad e\ `snapshot`\ b =>> snd$$

By the way, note that *color*4 is recursive, through the use of *snapshot*. This common situation is what motivates the need for *switch* to switch to its new behavior just *after* an event occurrence. Consider for a moment a simplified form of this situation:

$$b1 \quad = \quad b0\ `switch`\ (e\ `snapshot`\ b1 =>> b2)$$

Recalling the definition of *switch*, the first sample in $b1$ is the first sample from $b0$, regardless of *switch*'s second argument. In particular, the lazy pattern-match on *switch*'s second argument ensures that the first value does not depend on the event stream at all. If there *were* such a dependency, then we would have an infinite loop, because that event stream depends on $b1$ (i.e., the stream is chasing its tail!).

### 15.4.1 Variations on *switch*

It is convenient to define a couple of variations to the *switch* operator; in fact, the two described here are defined in terms of *switch*. The first is called *step*, and has type:

$$step \quad :: \quad a \to Event\ a \to Behavior\ a$$

The idea is that $a$ `step` $e$ starts off as $a$ and switches to the successive values associated with the events in $e$. For example, $'A'$ `step` *key* starts off as the character $'A'$ and switches to whatever key is last pressed. That is, it is equivalent to *constB* $'A'$ `step` *key* =>> *constB*. Indeed, *step* can be defined in terms of *switch* as:

$$a\ `step`\ e \quad = \quad constB\ a\ `switch`\ e =>> constB$$

Another useful operation is the function:

$$stepAccum \ :: \ a \to Event \ (a \to a) \to Behavior \ a$$

Here the function associated with each event is applied to the last value of the behavior, to yield a new behavior. The operator *stepAccum* can be defined in terms of *switch* and *snapshot*:

$$a \ `stepAccum` \ e \ = \ b$$
$$\textbf{where} \ b \ = \ a \ `step` \ (e \ `snapshot` \ b => > \ uncurry \ (\$))$$

For example, this behavior:

$$counter \ = \ 0 \ `stepAccum` \ lbp \ -> > \ (+1)$$

is, as the name implies, a counter: Each time the left button is pressed, the value of *counter* increases by one.

As a test of this new operator, note that the value of:

$$stream2 \ = \ \textbf{let} \ Behavior \ fb \ = \ counter$$
$$\textbf{in} \ take \ 20 \ (fb \ (uas, \ ts))$$

is [0, 0, 1, 1, 1, 2, 2, 2, 3, 3, 3, 4, 4, 4, 5, 5, 5, 6, 6, 6].

### 15.4.2 Mouse Motion

As the mouse is moved across a mouse pad, it generates mouse motion events that we would also like to incorporate into FAL, as follows:

$$mm \ :: \ Event \ Coordinate$$
$$mm \ = \ Event \ (\backslash(uas, \_) \to map \ getmm \ uas)$$
$$\qquad \textbf{where} \ getmm \ (Just \ (MouseMove \ pt)) \ = \ Just \ (gPtToPt \ pt)$$
$$\qquad \qquad getmm \ \_ \qquad \qquad \qquad \qquad = \ Nothing$$

The function *gPtToPt* converts a graphics point into a point in our preferred coordinate system:

$$gPtToPt \qquad \qquad :: \ G.Point \to Coordinate$$
$$gPtToPt \ (x, y) \ = \ (pixelToInch \ (x - 300)$$
$$\qquad \qquad \qquad , pixelToInch \ (250 - y))$$

$$pixelToInch \qquad :: \ Int \to Float$$
$$pixelToInch \ n \ = \ intToFloat \ n/100$$

Although *mm* may seem useful, a far more pleasing design is to treat the mouse position as a value *mouse* with type:

    *mouse*  ::  (*Behavior Float*, *Behavior Float*)

That is, *mouse* is a pair of behaviors representing the *x* and *y* positions of the mouse. Given *mm* and *step*, *mouse* is very easy to define:

    *mouse* = (*fstB m*, *sndB m*)
              **where** *m* = (0, 0) '*step*' *mm*

For example, recalling that *translate* has type:

    *translate*  ::  (*Behavior Float*, *Behavior Float*)
              → *Behavior Region* → *Behavior Region*

we can use *mouse* to conveniently control the position of a ball, and at the same time change color based on keyboard input:

    *ball*3  =  *paint color*4 *circ*3
    *circ*3  =  *translate mouse* (*ell* 0.2 0.2)

Try running this example using the *test* function mentioned earlier. The interesting thing about it is that the same source of user actions are used to create both the *color*4 behavior and the *mouse* behavior. This kind of detail is of course hidden at the level of FAL.

## 15.5  Paddleball in Twenty Lines

In this section I will describe a very compact program (actually only 17 lines) that implements a simple version of *paddleball*, where the user has a single paddle with which to whack a ball bouncing off of three walls (i.e., the user acts as the fourth wall). If the user misses, the ball simply drifts off the screen. The program is an excellent example of the clarity and brevity afforded by programming at the level of FAL.

Beginning at the top-most level, I will define a function *paddleball* that takes a velocity argument representing the approximate speed of the ball in inches per second.

    *paddleball vel*  =  *walls* '*over*' *paddle* '*over*' *pball vel*

A good speed to run the animation is 2, so you can run this program by typing *test* (*paddleball* 2).

The walls are represented as long and narrow blue rectangles:

*walls* = **let** *upper* = *paint blue* (*translate* (0, 1.7) (*rec* 4.4 0.05))
*left* = *paint blue* (*translate* (−2.2, 0) (*rec* 0.05 3.4))
*right* = *paint blue* (*translate* (2.2, 0) (*rec* 0.05 3.4))
**in** *upper* 'over' *left* 'over' *right*

The paddle is represented as a short and narrow red rectangle:

*paddle* = *paint red* (*translate* (*fst mouse*, −1.7) (*rec* 0.5 0.05))

Finally, of most interest, the ball is represented as a yellow circle whose position is determined by two sets of recursive, reactive behaviors. These behaviors simulate movement by integrating a velocity that alternates between positive and negative values, depending on which wall the ball last bounced off of.

*pball vel* =
**let** *xvel* = *vel* 'stepAccum' *xbounce* −>> *negate*
*xpos* = *integral xvel*
*xbounce* = *when* (*xpos* >∗ 2 || ∗ *xpos* <∗ − 2)
*yvel* = *vel* 'stepAccum' *ybounce* −>> *negate*
*ypos* = *integral yvel*
*ybounce* = *when* (*ypos* >∗ 1.5
|| ∗ *ypos* 'between' (−2.0, −1.5) &&∗
*fst mouse* 'between' (*xpos* − 0.25, *xpos* + 0.25))
**in** *paint yellow* (*translate* (*xpos*, *ypos*) (*ell* 0.2 0.2))

*x* 'between' (*a*, *b*) = *x* >∗ *a* &&∗ *x* <∗ *b*

Note that if the ball position is within the horizontal boundaries of the paddle as computed from the *x* coordinate of the mouse, and is within 0.5 of the bottom of the paddle, then it is considered as a "hit." Fig. 15.3 shows the game in action.

---

**Exercise 15.1** Implement some or all of the following extensions to the paddleball program:

1. Keep score of how many times the user successfully hits the ball. Display this score dynamically just above or to one side of the game.
2. Reset the game after the ball drifts off the bottom of the screen. Better yet, have the game stop at that moment, and require the user to press a key to restart it.

3. Add a way to suspend, or pause, the game, such as by pressing a certain key.

4. Have the ball begin at some fixed, relatively slow rate, and gradually increase it over time, thus making the game harder the longer it is played.

5. Change the game into a two-player game, and go through five rounds of play, with each player's score being accumulative, and with the winner being declared at the end of the five rounds.

---

**Exercise 15.2**  Simulate a bouncing ball under the influence of gravity within a four-sided box, and add *reciprocity* to the ball. That is, when the ball hits a wall it should lose a bit of its energy, and thus should gradually slow down until it is sitting at the bottom of the box.

---

**Exercise 15.3**  Create a simple arcade game. For example: create a variety of shapes that drift across the screen from both the right and left, and use the mouse to "kill" them. Alternatively, create some kind of weapon at the bottom that shoots missles upwards at the targets.

---

**Exercise 15.4**  Write a program that simulates the game of *Tetris* as closely as possible. You will want to carefully choose data representations for the pieces, and devise ways to rotate them under user control. The speed at which the pieces drift to the bottom should gradually increase over time, and you may want to include a way for the user to to drop a piece directly into place.

---

**Exercise 15.5**  Time transformation in the presence of reactivity is somewhat problematical, in that it is not clear what it means to transform user actions through time. For example, what does it mean to transform user actions into the future, or to run user actions backward? So let's ignore the issue of time transformation of user actions, and simply concentrate on transformation of the dependency on the behavior *time*. Your job is to define a function:

$$timeTrans \;::\; Behavior\ Time \rightarrow Behavior\ a \rightarrow Behavior\ a$$

such that *timeTrans tt b* causes *b* to undergo time transformation *tt*, while responding to user actions in the current timeframe.

Construct an animation that uses *timeTrans* in some interesting way.

# CHAPTER SIXTEEN

# Communicating With the Outside World

In Chapter 3 you learned enough about IO programming in Haskell to handle the graphics tasks encountered in Chapters 4, 10, and 13. In this chapter we will take a closer look at IO programming in Haskell, including more examples of file operations, and several new ideas: file handles, exceptions, channels, and concurrency. Then in the next chapter I will show how these ideas can be put to use in defining the *reactimate* function introduced in Chapter 15 for rendering reactive animations.

The Standard Prelude contains the most basic IO commands, with more advanced ones found in the IO Library, the SOEGraphics Library that we have already seen, and several others. The IO Library contains quite a few useful operations for file manipulation. Rather than trying to remember which is in the Standard Prelude and which is in the IO Library, it's easier to always import the library if you are doing anything beyond the most basic IO tasks.

## 16.1  Files, Channels, and Handles

The first new idea is the concept of a *handle* to a file. A file handle is not unlike the *Window* value returned from the *openWindow* command, where several windows may be opened simultaneously, using the *Window* value to specify in which window subsequent actions are to take place. File handles work the same way. There may be more than one file that is open at the same time, and thus we need a way to distinguish among them.

To obtain a handle (of type *Handle*) to a file there is an operation for *opening* the file for use in subsequent IO operations. There is also an operation for closing a file via reference to its handle.

```
openFile  ::  FilePath → IOMode → IO Handle
hClose    ::  Handle → IO ()
```

**data** *IOMode*  =  *ReadMode* | *WriteMode*
            |  *AppendMode* | *ReadWriteMode*

---

**DETAILS**

By convention, all IO commands that take a handle argument begin with the letter *h*.

---

The *IOMode* specifies whether the file is only to be read (*ReadMode*), only to be written (*WriteMode*), only to be appended to (*AppendMode*), or to be both read and written (*ReadWriteMode*).

While a file is open, characters or strings may be written to, read from, or appended to the file, depending on the mode. For example, operations such as:

$$hPutChar \quad :: \quad Handle \rightarrow Char \rightarrow IO\ ()$$
$$hPutStr \quad\ :: \quad Handle \rightarrow String \rightarrow IO\ ()$$
$$hPutStrLn \ :: \quad Handle \rightarrow String \rightarrow IO\ ()$$
$$hPrint \quad\ \ :: \quad Show\ a \Rightarrow Handle \rightarrow a \rightarrow IO\ ()$$

can be used in write mode, and:

$$hGetChar \ :: \quad Handle \rightarrow IO\ Char$$
$$hGetLine \ :: \quad Handle \rightarrow IO\ String$$

when in read mode.

---

**DETAILS**

*hPutStrLn* and *hPrint* include a "new line" character at the end of the string being written.

---

Haskell also allows the entire contents of a file to be returned as a single string:

$$hGetContents \ :: \quad Handle \rightarrow String$$

Pragmatically, it may seem that *hGetContents* must immediately read an entire file, resulting in poor space and time performance under certain conditions. However, this is not the case. The key point is that *hGetContents* returns a "lazy" list of characters, whose elements are read "by demand" (via normal-order calculation) just like any other list. An implementation can be expected to implement this demand-driven behavior by reading one character at a time from the file as they are required by the computation.

### 16.1.1  Why Use Handles?

Recall that to write to a file without using handles, the IO command:

$$writeFile \quad :: \quad FilePath \rightarrow String \rightarrow IO\ ()$$
$$\textbf{type}\ FilePath \quad = \quad String$$

can be used. There is also a similar command for appending to a file:

$$appendFile \quad :: \quad FilePath \rightarrow String \rightarrow IO\ ()$$

You might wonder then why we don't just use these two commands instead of opening a file and then executing, say, several *hPutStr* commands. The reason is efficiency: Everytime a *writeFile* or *appendFile* command is executed, the file is opened, the string is written, and the file is closed. With one *openFile*, many *hPutStr*'s, and one *hClose*, the file is only opened and closed once.

### 16.1.2  Channels

Handles are also associated with *channels*, which are communication ports not directly attached to files. The most common channels are the standard input area (*stdin*), standard output area (*stdout*), and standard error area (*stderr*).[1] Character and string level IO operations for channels include the same ones listed above for files. Indeed, the *getChar* and *putChar* commands used previously are in fact defined as:

$$getChar \quad = \quad hGetChar\ stdin$$
$$putChar \quad = \quad hPutChar\ stdout$$

Even *hGetContents* can be used with channels, in which case, the end of the channel contents is signaled by an "end-of-channel" character, which on most systems is Ctrl-d ("d" typed while holding down the "Control" key).

---

[1] In principle, these three "areas" are separate, independent areas of the computer screen. In practice, they are all the same.

## 16.2  Exception Handling

So far, we have avoided the issue of errors during IO operations. What would happen, for example, if *hGetChar* encountered the end of a file? We certainly don't want the whole program to terminate when this happens, such as with run-time errors in Haskell. In other words, we would like a way to recover from such anomalous conditions, which we prefer to call *exceptions* rather than errors. Recovering from an exception is called *exception handling*. In Haskell no special syntax or semantics is needed to achieve this; all we need is a few more IO commands.

Exceptions themselves have type *IOError*. Among the operations allowed on this type, there are first of all a collection of predicates that can be used to test for a particular kind of exception. For example, this predicate:

> *isEOFError*  ::  *IOError* → *Bool*

determines whether an end-of-file exception has occurred.[2]

More importantly, there is a function *catch*, which does the actual exception handling. The first argument to *catch* is an IO action that we are attempting to execute. The second argument is an *exception handler* of type *IOError* → *IO a*.

> *catch*  ::  *IO a* → (*IOError* → *IO a*) → *IO a*

The metaphor to grasp here is this: In the command *catch command handler*, any exception that occurs in *command* (which may generate a long sequence of actions, perhaps even infinite) gets "thrown" outward, to be "caught" by the exception handler *handler*. Control is effectively transferred to the handler by applying it to the *IOError* that occurred. If *command* succeeds, the handler is ignored.

For example, this version of *getChar* returns a newline character if any kind of exception is encountered:

> *getChar'*  ::  *IO Char*
> *getChar'*  =  *catch getChar* (\\*e* → *return* '\n')

---

[2] You might wonder why the Haskell designers did not just define *IOError* as a data type that enumerated all possible IO errors. The main reason is that some implementations may support different kinds of such errors, and data types in Haskell are not extensible. Although the predicate approach is more cumbersome to use, it is easy to add support for a new IO error by simply including an additional predicate.

However, this is rather crude because it treats all exceptions in the same manner. If only the end-of-file exception is to be recognized, the *IOError* value must be queried:

```
getChar'  ::  IO Char
getChar'  =  catch getChar (\e → if isEOFError e then return '\n'
                                                  else ioError e)
```

The *ioError* function used here "throws" the exception upward to the next exception handler. In other words, nested calls to *catch* are permitted, and produce nested exception handlers. The function *ioError* may be called from within a normal action sequence or from within an exception handler as in the *getChar'* example above.

Using *getChar'* we can redefine *getLine* to demonstrate the use of nested handlers:

```
getLine'  ::  IO String
getLine'  =  catch getLine'' (\err → "Error: " ++ show err)
             where getLine''  =  do c ← getChar'
                                    if c == '\n' then return ""
                                    else do l ← getLine'
                                            return (c : l)
```

Note how "looping" is achieved simply by a recursive call to *getLine'*. Nested exception handlers allow *getChar'* to catch an end-of-file exception while any other exception results in a string starting with "Error: " to be returned from *getLine'*.

If you do not provide an exception handler for your program, or fail to catch a particular exception that occurs, Haskell invokes a default exception handler that prints out the exception and terminates your program.

Here is a larger example: Suppose that we wish to copy one file to another, with the file names provided by the user in response to a prompt from our program. The process of prompting the user, getting the filename, and opening the file is done twice, so let's first define a function to capture this process:

```
module Main where
import IO

getAndOpenFile  ::  String → IOMode → IO Handle
```

*getAndOpenFile prompt mode*
   = **do** *putStr prompt*
         *name ← getLine*
         *catch* (**do** *handle ← openFile name mode*
                  *return handle*)
             (\\*error →* **do** *putStrLn* (`"Cannot open "` ++ *name*)
                       *print error*
                       *getAndOpenFile prompt mode*)

Note that the error itself is printed to give the user some notion of the source of the problem (this is possible because *IOError* is an instance of the class *Show*). Once the error is printed, the process is tried again through the recursive call to *getAndOpenFile*.

With this task behind us, the rest is relatively simple:

*main* = **do** *fromHandle ← getAndOpenFile* `"Copy from: "` *ReadMode*
         *toHandle ← getAndOpenFile* `"Copy to: "` *WriteMode*
         *contents ← hGetContents fromHandle*
         *hPutStr toHandle contents*
         *hClose fromHandle*
         *hClose toHandle*
         *putStrLn* `"Done."`

By using the lazy *hGetContents* function, the entire contents of the file need not be read into memory all at once. If *hPutStr* chooses to buffer the output by writing the string in fixed sized blocks of characters, say, only one block of the input file needs to be in memory at once.

---

**Exercise 16.1**   Write a Haskell program that:

1. Prompts the user for the name of a file by printing something like "`Please type the name of your file:`".
2. Prompts the user for a line of input in a similar way.
3. Prints a Haskell list of all of the words in the line of input that was typed by the user.
4. Writes the line of input to the file.
5. Repeats until the user types the end-of-channel character to end the session. Remember that the end-of-channel will terminate the input stream (i.e., you are looking for the end of the stream, not the end-of-channel character!).

Feel free to add other frills like the printing of a greeting and/or farewell message.

## 16.3  First-Class Channels and Concurrency

There are a number of nonstandard Haskell libraries that define various kinds of useful communication and concurrency mechanisms. Unfortunately, they are too numerous to discuss in this text, and their nonstandard nature means that they are more likely to change compared to the standard libraries. Nevertheless, I will discuss in this section one such library, and will use it in the next chapter when building the infrastruture to render FAL programs in a graphics window.

The module *Channel* defines a notion of *first-class channels* through which Haskell "processes" can communicate asynchronously. These channels are completely different from the ones just discussed – none of the operations in the last section apply to them – so I will use the phrase "first-class channel" to distinguish them.

A first-class channel containing values of type *a* has type *Chan a*. The most important operations defined on this abstract type are:

$$
\begin{array}{ll}
newChan & :: \ IO\ (Chan\ a) \\
writeChan & :: \ Chan\ a \to a \to IO\ () \\
readChan & :: \ Chan\ a \to IO\ a \\
getChanContents & :: \ Chan\ a \to IO\ [a] \\
isEmptyChan & :: \ Chan\ a \to IO\ Bool
\end{array}
$$

A first-class channel implements an *unbounded queue*, which can be written to and read from asynchronously through IO. A queue is a data structure such that the first value written to it is the first value read from it; for this reason it is also known as a FIFO (first-in-first-out) data structure.

For example, to create a channel and write the characters '*a*' and '*b*' to it, simply do:

```
do c ← newChan
   writeChan c 'a'
   writeChan c 'b'
   ...
```

At any later time the channel can be read, which causes the first element in it to be removed and returned. For example, continuing from the above, the code:

**do** ...
    *a ← readChan c*
    *b ← readChan c*
    *return* [*a, b*]

returns the string "ab".

Here now is an extended example: The real power of first-class channels comes when they are combined with *concurrency*; that is, the concurrent execution of more than one part of a Haskell program. The concurrent parts are called *processes*, which are simply values of type *IO* (). The command:

*forkIO* :: *IO* () → *IO* ()

```
module ChannelTest where

import Channel
import ConcBase

main    ::  IO ()
main    =  do c1 ← newChan :: IO (Chan Int)
              c2 ← newChan :: IO (Chan Int)
              forkIO (client c1 c2)
              forkIO (server c2 c1)

client  ::  Chan Int → Chan Int → IO ()
client cin cout
        =  do writeChan cout 1
              loop
           where loop  =  do c ← readChan cin
                             print c
                             writeChan cout c
                             loop

server  ::  Chan Int → Chan Int → IO ()
server cin cout
        =  do loop
           where loop  =  do c ← readChan cin
                             writeChan cout (c + 1)
                             loop
```

Figure 16.1: A Client-Server Program Using First-Class Channels

is used to "fork off" a concurrent process. This function and related concurrency primitives are found in the nonstandard library *ConcBase*.

---

**DETAILS**

The modules *ConcBase*, *Channel*, and several other modules involving concurrency can all be imported together by importing just *Concurrent*, whose sole purpose is to collect these related modules under one name.

---

To see how *forkIO* can be used with first-class channels, let's reimplement the client-server program discussed in Chapter 14. The idea is to:

1. Create two channels – one connecting the output of the client to the input of the server, the other connecting the output of the server to the input of the client.
2. Define the client and server as processes with type *IO* ().
3. Use *forkIO* to spawn off the client and server concurrently.

Fig. 16.1 shows the complete program, which when executed will print the numbers 1, 2, 3, ... (i.e., the infinite sequence of natural numbers).

Although this program is much more "heavy-weight" than the elegant recursive-stream version in Chapter 14, there are situations where the explicit concurrency is important; in particular, when IO is involved. An example of this arises in the next chapter.

# CHAPTER SEVENTEEN

# Rendering Reactive Animations

The functional animation language FAL was defined in Chapter 15. In this chapter we will explore a method to render FAL programs in a graphics window. The fundamental challenge will be interfacing FAL, arguably the most abstract programming style introduced in this textbook, to the relatively low-level interface to graphics windows provided by the Graphics Library.

```
module Reactimate where
import Fal
import SOEGraphics hiding (Region, Event)
import qualified SOEGraphics as G (Region, Event)
import Draw (xWin, yWin, intToFloat)
import Win32Misc (timeGetTime)
import Word (word32ToInt)
import Channel
```

## 17.1 Preliminaries

Analogous to the function *animate* in Chapter 13, our goal is to define a function, which I will call *reactimate*, having type:

$$reactimate \ :: \ String \rightarrow Behavior \ a \rightarrow (a \rightarrow IO \ Graphic) \rightarrow IO \ ()$$

Before doing this, however, there is an important secondary task to be carried out. We need a mechanism to extract a stream of time-stamped user actions (lifted into the *Maybe* data type) from the operating system. We want the stream of user actions to be infinite, and return *Just ua* if there is a user action *ua* present *at the time we ask for it*, and *Nothing* if there is not. The problem is the phrase "at the time we ask for it." How can we make a stream dependent on the execution time of a program? Surely we will need to go through the IO monad to achieve this dependency, and, in fact, I will use the *Channel* abstraction discussed in Chapter 16 to do so. For now, however, let's assume that we have a function:

$$windowUser \ :: \ Window \to IO \ (([Maybe \ UserAction], \ [Time]), \ IO \ ())$$

which behaves as follows. Executing the command:

$$((us, \ ts), \ addEvents) \leftarrow windowUser \ w$$

in a particular window environment yields a user action stream *us* and time stream *ts*. In addition, it yields an IO action *addEvents* that causes the operating system to update *us* with whatever user actions happen to be pending *at that time*, followed by a *Nothing* to indicate that there are no more user actions pending. We can then write our program to process all user actions in *us* until we see a *Nothing*, then execute *addEvents*, and repeat.

Indeed, recall from Chapter 15 that these *Nothing* values, or event "nonoccurrences," are the ones that we are interested in for the purpose of sampling the picture values to be drawn in the graphics window. We can define an *Event* that captures these sample events as follows:

$$sample \ :: \ Event \ ()$$
$$sample \ = \ Event \ (\backslash(us, \ \_) \to map \ aux \ us)$$
$$\textbf{where} \ aux \ Nothing \ = \ Just \ ()$$
$$aux \ (Just \ \_) \ = \ Nothing$$

Curiously, but correctly, *sample* turns *Just* into *Nothing* and *Nothing* into *Just*; this is because the *Nothing*'s in the user action stream are *Just* what we want for the sample events.

Finally, for a given FAL program *franProg* we can describe the picture values that we want by:

$$sample \ `snapshot\_` \ franProg$$

which has type *Event Picture*.

## 17.2 Reactimate

We are finally in a position to define the function *reactimate*, which is shown complete in Fig. 17.1. Note the initial call to *addEvents* to ensure that the user action stream has something in it the first time we look at it.

At the core of *reactimate* is the function *drawPic*, which is applied to each of the picture samples in the event stream generated from the

```
reactimate
   ::  String → Behavior a → (a → IO Graphic) → IO ()
reactimate title franProg toGraphic
   =  runGraphics $
      do w ← openWindowEx title (Just (0, 0)) (Just (xWin, yWin))
              drawBufferedGraphic (Just 30)
         (user, addEvents) ← windowUser w
         addEvents
         let drawPic (Just p)  =
                do g ← toGraphic p
                   setGraphic w g
                   addEvents
                   getWindowTick w
             drawPic Nothing  =  return ()
         mapM_ drawPic
                  (runEvent (sample 'snapshot_' franProg) user)

   runEvent (Event fe) u  =  fe u
```

Figure 17.1: The *reactimate* Function

sampled FAL program. This function converts each picture to a *Graphic*, sets the graphic window to that graphic, calls *addEvents*, and then, as we did in the function *animate* in Chapter 13, calls *getWindowTick* to synchronize control with the operating system.

## 17.3  Window User

All that remains is the definition of *windowUser*. Recall from Chapter 16 the notion of a *channel*. I will use it to implement a user action stream by defining a function:

   *makeStream*  ::  *IO* ([a], a → *IO* ())

as follows:

```
makeStream
   =  do ch ← newChan
         contents ← getChanContents ch
         return (contents, writeChan ch)
```

The meaning of this should be clear: A new channel is created, its contents are converted into a stream using *getChannelContents*, and that stream is returned along with a function to write into the channel.

```
windowUser
   ::  Window → IO (([Maybe UserAction], [Time]), IO ())
windowUser w
   =  do (evs, addEv) ← makeStream
         t0 ← timeGetTime
         let loop rt  =
               do mev ← maybeGetWindowEvent w
                  case mev of
                     Nothing  →  return ()
                     Just e    →  do addEv (Just e, rt)
                                     loop rt
         let addEvents  =
               do t ← timeGetTime
                  let rt  =  w32ToTime (t − t0)
                  loop rt
                  addEv (Nothing, rt)
         return ((map fst evs, map snd evs), addEvents)

w32ToTime t  =  intToFloat (word32ToInt t)/1000
```

Figure 17.2:  The *windowUser* Function

With *makeStream*, the definition of *windowUser* is straightforward, if a bit tedious (see Fig. 17.2). The time *t0* is used to capture the start time of the program, as we did with the *animate* function in Chapter 13. Note that *makeStreams* is used to generate a stream of user-action/time-stamp pairs, which is then "unzipped" to return separate user action and time streams from *windowUser*.

At the core of *windowUser* is the function *addEvents*, which uses a function *maybeGetWindowEvent* from the Graphics Library. This function does what the name implies. If a graphics event *e* is pending, it will return *Just e*; otherwise, it will return *Nothing*. The *loop* in *addEvents* will add each pending event, with a time stamp, to the user-action stream. Finally, the last line in *addEvents* adds a (time-stamped) *Nothing* event to signal that no more events are pending, as discussed earlier.

# CHAPTER EIGHTEEN

# Higher-Order Types

All of the types considered thus far have been *first order*. For example, the type constructor *Tree* has always been paired with an argument, as in *Tree Int* (a tree containing *Int* values) or *Tree a* (representing the family of trees containing *a* values). But *Tree* by itself is a type constructor: something that takes a type as an argument and returns a type as a result. There are no *values* in Haskell that have this type, but such "higher-order" types can be used in **class** declarations in useful ways, as we shall see in this chapter.

## 18.1  The Functor Class

To begin, consider the following *Functor* class defined in the Standard Prelude:[1]

> **class** *Functor f* **where**
>    *fmap*  $::$  $(a \rightarrow b) \rightarrow f\ a \rightarrow f\ b$

> **DETAILS**
> Type applications are written in the same manner as function applications, and are also left associative: The type $T\ a\ b$ is equivalent to $((T\ a)\ b)$.

There is something new here. The type variable $f$ is applied to other types, as in $f\ a$ and $f\ b$. Thus, we would expect $f$ to be a type such as

---

[1] The term *functor* (as well as the term *monad* to be introduced shortly) comes from a branch of abstract mathematics known as *category theory* (Pierce, 1991). This reflects the strong mathematical principles that underly Haskell, but otherwise does not concern us here (i.e., you do not need to know anything about category theory to understand Haskell's functors and monads).

*Tree*, which can be applied to an argument. Indeed, a suitable instance of *Functor* for type *Tree* would be:

```
instance Functor Tree where
    fmap f (Leaf x)        =  Leaf (f x)
    fmap f (Branch t1 t2)  =  Branch (fmap f t1) (fmap f t2)
```

Recall that in Section 7.2 we defined a function *mapTree* that behaved just as the above *fmap* method, so we could have instead written:

```
instance Functor Tree where
    fmap  =  mapTree
```

Such an instance declaration declares that *Tree*, rather than *Tree a*, is an instance of *Functor*.

Note that in Haskell we write *Tree Int* for trees of integers, and we say that *Tree* is a type constructor. And we write [*Int*] for lists of integers. However, what is the type constructor for lists? Because of Haskell's special syntax for the list data type, there is also a special syntax for its type constructor, namely [].

---

**DETAILS**

Similarly, for tuples the type constructors are (,), (,,), (,,,), and so on, and the type constructor for the function type is ($\rightarrow$). This means that the following pairs of types are equivalent: [*a*] and [] *a*, *f* $\rightarrow$ *g* and ($\rightarrow$) *f g*, (*a, b*) and (,) *a b*, and so on.

---

This allows us to create an instance of *Functor* for lists, as follows:

```
instance Functor [ ] where
    fmap f [ ]       =  [ ]
    fmap f (x : xs)  =  f x : fmap f xs
```

Note the use of [] here in two ways: as a value in the list data type, and as a type constructor as described above.

Of course, the above declaration is equivalent to:

```
instance Functor [ ] where
    fmap  =  map
```

where *map* is the familiar function that we have been using since Chapter 5. This instance is in fact predefined in the Standard Prelude.

The nice thing about the *Functor* class, of course, is that we can now use the same name, *fmap*, for both lists and trees (and any other data type for which an instance of *Functor* is declared). This could not have been done without higher-order type constructors, and here demonstrates the ability to handle generic "container" types, allowing functions such as *fmap* to work uniformly over them.

As I mentioned in Section 12.6, type classes often imply a set of *laws* that govern the use of the operators in the class. In the case of the *Functor* class, the following laws are expected to hold:

$$fmap\ id = id$$
$$fmap\ (f \cdot g) = fmap\ f \cdot fmap\ g$$

> **DETAILS**
> The function *id* is the *identity function*, $\x \rightarrow x$. Although *id* is polymorphic, note that if its type on the left-hand side of the equation above is $a \rightarrow a$, then its type on the right must be $t\ a \rightarrow t\ a$, for some type constructor $t$ that is an instance of *Functor*.

These laws ensure that the shape of the "container type" is unchanged by *fmap*, and that the contents of the container are not rearranged by the mapping function. In the sections that follow, additional laws will be stated for each new type class as it is introduced.

---

**Exercise 18.1** Verify that the instances of *Functor* for lists and trees are law-abiding.

## 18.2 The Monad Class

There are several classes in Haskell that are related to the notion of a *monad*, which can be viewed as a generalization of the principles that underlie IO. Because of this, although the names of the classes and methods may seem unusual, these "monadic" operations are rather intuitive and useful for general programming.[2]

---

[2] Moggi (Moggi, 1989) was one of the first to point out the value of monads in describing the semantics of programming languages, and Wadler first popularized their use in functional programming (Wadler, 1992; Peyton Jones and Wadler, 1993).

There are three classes associated with monads: *Functor* (which we've discussed already), *Monad* (also defined in the Standard Prelude), and *MonadPlus* (defined in the Standard Library *Monad*).

The *Monad* class defines four basic operators: (>>=) (often pronounced "bind"), (>>) (often pronounced "sequence"), *return*, and *fail*:

**class** *Monad m* **where**
   (>>=)  ::  *m a* → (*a* → *m b*) → *m b*
   (>>)   ::  *m a* → *m b* → *m b*
   *return*  ::  *a* → *m a*
   *fail*    ::  *String* → *m a*

   *m* >> *k*  =  *m* >>= \\_ → *k*
   *fail s*    =  *error s*

The default methods for (>>) and *fail* define behaviors that are almost always just what is needed. Therefore, most instances of *Monad* need only define (>>=) and *return*.

Before giving examples of particular instances of *Monad*, I will first reveal another secret in Haskell, namely that the **do** syntax is actually shorthand for use of the monadic operators! The rules for this are a bit more involved than those for other syntax we've seen, but are still straightforward. The first rule is this:

**do** *e* ⇒ *e*

So something like **do** *putStr* "Hello World" is equivalent to just *putStr* "Hello World".

The next rule is:

**do** *e1*; *e2*; ...; *en*
  ⇒ *e1* >> **do** *e2*; ...; *en*

For example, combining this rule with the previous one means that:

**do** *writeFile* "testFile.txt" "Hello File System"
    *putStr* "Hello World"

is equivalent to:

*writeFile* "testFile.txt" "Hello File System" >>
*putStr* "Hello World"

Note now that the sequencing of two commands is just the application of the function (>>) to two values of type *IO* (). There is no magic here – it is all just functional programming!

**DETAILS**
What is the type of (>>) above? From the type class declaration we know that its most general type is:

(>>) :: *Monad m ⇒ m a → m b → m b*

However, in the case above, its two arguments both have type *IO* (), so the type of (>>) must be:

(>>) :: *IO* () → *IO* () → *IO* ()

That is, *m* = *IO*, *a* = (), and *b* = (). Thus, the type of the result is *IO* (), as expected.

The rule for pattern matching is the most complex, because we must deal with the situation where the pattern match fails:

**do** *pat* ← *e*1; *e*2; . . .; *en*
    ⇒   **let** *ok pat*  =  **do** *e*2; . . .; *en*
            *ok* \_    =   *fail* " . . . "
        **in** *e*1 >>= *ok*

The right way to think of (>>=) above is simply this: It "executes" *e*1, and then applies *ok* to the result. What happens after that is defined by *ok*. If the match succeeds, the rest of the commands are executed, otherwise the operation *fail* in the monad class is called, which in most cases (because of the default method) results in an *error*.

**DETAILS**
The string argument to *error* is a compiler-generated error message, preferably giving some indication of the location of the pattern-match failure.

A special case of the above rule is the case where the pattern *pat* is just a name, in which case the match cannot fail, so the rule simplifies to:

**do** *x* ← *e*1; *e*2; . . .; *en*
    ⇒   *e*1 >>= \*x* → **do** *e*2; . . .; *en*

The final rule deals with the **let** notation within a **do** expression:

**do let** *decllist*; *e*2; . . .; *en*
    ⇒   **let** *decllist* **in do** *e*2; . . .; *en*

> **DETAILS**
> Although we have not used this feature, note that a **let** inside of a **do** can take multiple definitions, as implied by the name *decllist*.

As mentioned earlier, because you already understand Haskell IO, you should have a fair amount of intuition about what the monadic operators do. Unfortuantely, we can't look very closely at the instance of *Monad* for the type *IO*, because it ultimately relies on the state of the underlying operating system, which we don't have direct access to other than through primitive operations that communicate with it. Even then, these operations vary from system to system.

Nevertheless, a proper implementation of IO in Haskell is obliged to obey the following *monad laws*:

$$return\ a >>= k \qquad = \quad k\ a$$
$$m >>= return \qquad\quad = \quad m$$
$$m >>= (\backslash x \rightarrow k\ x >>= h) \ = \ (m >>= k) >>= h$$

The first of these laws expresses the fact that *return* simply "sends" its value to the next action. Likewise, the second law says that if we immediately return the result of an action, we might as well just let the action return the value itself. The third law is the most complex, and essentially expresses an *associativity* property for the bind operator ($>>=$). A special case of this law applies to the sequence operator ($>>$):

$$m1 >> (m2 >> m3) \ = \ (m1 >> m2) >> m3$$

in which case the associativity is more obvious.

There is one other monad law, whose purpose is to connect the *Monad* class to the *Functor* class, and therefore only applies to types that are instances of both:

$$fmap\ f\ xs \ = \ xs >>= return.f$$

We will see an example of this shortly.

Of course, this law can also be expressed in **do** notation:

$$fmap\ f\ xs \ = \ \textbf{do}\ x \leftarrow xs;\ return\ (f\ x)$$

as can the previous ones for **do**:

$$\textbf{do}\ x \leftarrow return\ a;\ k\ x = k\ a$$
$$\textbf{do}\ x \leftarrow m;\ return\ x = m$$
$$\textbf{do}\ x \leftarrow m;\ y \leftarrow k\ x;\ h\ y = \textbf{do}\ y \leftarrow (\textbf{do}\ x \leftarrow m;\ k\ x);\ h\ y$$
$$\textbf{do}\ m1;\ m2;\ m3 = \textbf{do}\ (\textbf{do}\ m1;\ m2);\ m3$$

So something like this:

**do** *k* ← *getKey w*
  *return k*

is just equivalent to *getKey w*, according to the second law above. As a
final example, the third law above allows us to transform this:

**do** *k* ← *getKey w*
  *n* ← *changeKey k*
  *respond n*

into this:

**let** *keyStuff*  =  **do** *k* ← *getKey w*
                 *changeKey k*
**in do** *n* ← *keyStuff*
    *respond n*

---

**Exercise 18.2**  Verify the associativity law for (>>), starting with the
associativity law for (>>=).

### 18.2.1  Other Instances of Monad

In addition to *IO*, the Standard Prelude's *Maybe* data type is a predefined
instance of *Monad*:

**instance** *Monad Maybe* **where**
  *Just x* >>= *k*    =  *k x*
  *Nothing* >>= *k*  =  *Nothing*
  *return*       =  *Just*
  *fail s*       =  *Nothing*

> **DETAILS**
> *Maybe* is also a predefined instance of *Functor*:
>
> **instance** *Functor Maybe* **where**
>  *fmap f Nothing*  =  *Nothing*
>  *fmap f (Just x)*  =  *Just (f x)*

When used with this instance, the types of the monad operators are:

(>>=) :: *Maybe a* → (*a* → *Maybe b*) → *Maybe b*
*return* :: *a* → *Maybe a*

I will leave as an exercise the task of proving that this instance is law-abiding.

To see how this might be used, consider a computation involving functions $f :: Int \to Int$, $g :: Int \to Int$, and $x :: Int$:

$g (f\ x)$

Now suppose that each of the calculations using $f$ and $g$ could in fact be erroneous, and thus the results are encoded using the *Maybe* data type. Unfortunately, this can become rather tedious to program, because each result that might be an error must be checked manually, as in:

**case** $(f\ x)$ **of**
   *Nothing*  →  *Nothing*
   *Just y*   →  **case** $(g\ y)$ **of**
                *Nothing*  →  *Nothing*
                *Just z*   →  $z$

Alternatively, you could take advantage of *Maybe*'s membership in the *Monad* class, and convert this into monadic form:

$f\ x >>= \backslash y \to$
$g\ y >>= \backslash z \to$
*return z*

Or, using the more familiar **do** notation:

**do** $y \leftarrow f\ x$
    $z \leftarrow g\ y$
    *return z*

Thus, the tedium of the error check is "hidden" within the monad. In this sense, monads are a good example of the abstraction principle in action (pardon the pun)!

It is also worth noting the following simplification:

$f\ x >>= \backslash y \to$
$g\ y >>= \backslash z \to$
*return z*
   $\Rightarrow$   { currying simplification }
$f\ x >>= \backslash y \to$
$g\ y >>= return$
   $\Rightarrow$   { monad law for *return* }

$$f \; x >>= \setminus y \rightarrow$$
$$g \; y$$
$$\Rightarrow \;\; \{ \text{ currying simplification } \}$$
$$f \; x >>= g$$

So we started with $g \; (f \; x)$ and ended with $f \; x >>= g$; this is not too bad considering the alternative that we started with!

For an even more pleasing result, we can define a monadic composition operator:

$$composeM \qquad :: \; Monad \; m \Rightarrow (b \rightarrow m\,c) \rightarrow (a \rightarrow m\,b) \rightarrow (a \rightarrow m\,c)$$
$$(g \; `composeM` \; f) \; x \; = \; f \; x >>= g$$

in which case we started with $(g \,.\, f) \; x$ and ended with $(g \; `composeM` \; f) \; x$.

---

**DETAILS**

Note the type of *composeM*. It demonstrates that higher-order type constructors are also useful in type signatures.

---

**Exercise 18.3** Recall in Section 10.4 the use of the *Maybe* data type in the function *adjust*. Rewrite this function using monadic operations.

The list data type in Haskell is also a predefined instance of class *Monad*:

```
instance Monad [ ] where
    m >>= k  =  concat (map k m)
    return x  =  [x]
    fail x    =  []
```

---

**DETAILS**

Recall that *concat* takes a list of lists and concatenates them all together. It is defined in the Standard Prelude as:

```
concat    ::  [[a]] → [a]
concat xss  =  foldr (++) [ ] xss
```

---

The types of the monadic operators in this case are:

$$(>>=) :: [a] \rightarrow (b \rightarrow [b]) \rightarrow [b]$$
$$return :: a \rightarrow [a]$$

The monadic functions in this context can be thought of as dealing with "multiple values." Monadic binding takes a set (list) of values and applies a function to each of them, collecting all generated values together. The *return* function creates a singleton list, and *fail* an empty one. For example,

> **do** $x \leftarrow [1, 2, 3]$
> $y \leftarrow [4, 5, 6]$
> *return* $(x, y)$

returns the list:

> $[(1, 4), (1, 5), (1, 6), (2, 4), (2, 5), (2, 6), (3, 4), (3, 5), (3, 6)]$

which happens to be the same list generated by:

> $[(x, y) \mid x \leftarrow [1, 2, 3], y \leftarrow [4, 5, 6]]$

So list comprehension syntax is in essence another kind of monad syntax; indeed, they are not very different! (However, list comprehensions can only be used with lists.)

Note that if:

> **do** $x \leftarrow xs$; *return* $(f\ x)$

is equivalent to:

> $[f\ x \mid x \leftarrow xs]$

(which is clearly just *map f xs*), then at least for the instance of lists in *Monad*, the last monad law makes perfect sense:

> *fmap f xs* $=$ **do** $x \leftarrow xs$; *return* $(f\ x)$

Also note that the *Maybe* data type in monadic form behaves as a sort of truncated list in monadic form: *Nothing* is the same as [ ] and *Just x* is the same as [$x$].)

---

**Exercise 18.4** Verify that all of the instance declarations in this section are law-abiding.

---

**Exercise 18.5** Consider the *identity data type* defined by:

> **data** *Id a* $=$ *Id a*

Create an instance of *Monad* for *Id*, and prove that it is law-abiding.

$$
\begin{array}{ll}
sequence & :: \ Monad \ m \Rightarrow [m \ a] \to m \ [a] \\
sequence & = \ foldr \ mcons \ (return \ [\,]) \\
& \quad\quad\quad \textbf{where} \ mcons \ p \ q \ = \ \textbf{do} \ x \leftarrow p \\
& \quad\quad\quad\quad\quad\quad\quad\quad\quad\quad\quad\quad xs \leftarrow q \\
& \quad\quad\quad\quad\quad\quad\quad\quad\quad\quad\quad\quad return \ (x : xs)
\end{array}
$$

$$
\begin{array}{ll}
sequence\_ & :: \ Monad \ m \Rightarrow [m \ a] \to m \ () \\
sequence\_ & = \ foldr \ (>>) \ (return \ ())
\end{array}
$$

$$
\begin{array}{ll}
mapM & :: \ Monad \ m \Rightarrow (a \to m \ b) \to [a] \to m \ [b] \\
mapM \ f \ as & = \ sequence \ (map \ f \ as)
\end{array}
$$

$$
\begin{array}{ll}
mapM\_ & :: \ Monad \ m \Rightarrow (a \to m \ b) \to [a] \to m \ () \\
mapM\_ \ f \ as & = \ sequence\_ \ (map \ f \ as)
\end{array}
$$

$$
\begin{array}{ll}
(=<<) & :: \ Monad \ m \Rightarrow (a \to m \ b) \to m \ a \to m \ b \\
f =<< x & = \ x >>= f
\end{array}
$$

Figure 18.1: Monadic Utility Functions

## 18.2.2 Other Monadic Operations

The Standard Prelude has several functions specifically designed for use with monads; they are shown in Fig. 18.1. Indeed, one of these we have already used: *sequence_*. Any mystery about how it works should be gone now; it is a very simple fold of the sequencing operator $(>>)$, with *return* () at the end. Note also the definition of *sequence*, a generalization of *sequence_* that returns a list of values of the intermediate results.

Finally, recall from Section 5.2 that we redefined *putStr* as:

$$
\begin{array}{ll}
putStr & :: \ String \to IO \ () \\
putStr \ s & = \ sequence\_ \ (map \ putChar \ s)
\end{array}
$$

Using *mapM_* from Fig. 18.1, this can be rewritten as:

$$
\begin{array}{ll}
putStr & :: \ String \to IO \ () \\
putStr \ s & = \ mapM\_ \ putChar \ s
\end{array}
$$

## 18.3 The MonadPlus Class

The class *MonadPlus*, defined in the Standard Library *Monad*, is used for monads that have a *zero element* and a *plus operator*:

**class** *Monad m* ⇒ *MonadPlus m* **where**
  *mzero* :: *m a*
  *mplus* :: *m a → m a → m a*

The zero element should obey the following laws:

*m* >>= (\*x* → *mzero*)  =  *mzero*
*mzero* >>= *m*       =  *mzero*

and the plus operator should obey these:

*m* 'mplus' *mzero*  =  *m*
*mzero* 'mplus' *m*  =  *m*

By analogy to arithmetic, think of *mzero* as 0, *mplus* as addition, and (>>=) as multiplication. The above laws should then make more sense. For the *Maybe* data type, the zero and plus values are:

**instance** *MonadPlus Maybe* **where**
  *mzero*          =  *Nothing*
  *Nothing* 'mplus' *ys*  =  *ys*
  *xs* 'mplus' *ys*     =  *xs*

and for lists they are:

**instance** *MonadPlus* [ ] **where**
  *mzero*  =  [ ]
  *mplus*  =  (++)

So you can see now that the familiar concatentation operation (++) that we have been using all along for lists is just a special case of the *mplus* operator.

It is worth pointing out that the IO monad is not an instance of the *MonadPlus* class, because it has no zero element. For if it did have a zero element, then the IO action *putStr* "Hello" >> *zero* should *not* print the string "Hello", according to the first zero law above. But this is counterintuitive, or at least is certainly not what the designers of Haskell had in mind for IO.

The *Monad* module in the Standard Library also includes several other useful functions defined in terms of the monadic primitives. You are encouraged to read these for possible use in your own programs.

---

**Exercise 18.6**  Verify that the instances of *MonadPlus* for the *Maybe* and list data types are law-abiding.

## 18.4 State Monads

Monads are commonly used to simulate stateful, or imperative, computations, in which the details of updating and passing around the state are hidden within the mechanics of the monad. Generally speaking, a *state monad* has a type of the form:

**data** *SM a* = *SM* $(S \rightarrow (S, a))$

where $S$ is some fixed state type, and $a$ is the (possibly polymorphic) value type. The instance of this type in *Monad* is given by:

```
instance Monad SM where
    return a
       =  SM (\s → (s, a))
    SM sm0 >>= fsm1
       =  SM $ \ s0 →
             let (s1, a1)  =  sm0 s0
                 SM sm1    =  fsm1 a1
                 (s2, a2)  =  sm1 s1
             in (s2, a2)
```

The last equation in the **let** expression could obviously be eliminated, but I want to stress the symmetry in the treatment of the two commands.

A good example of a state monad, at least abstractly speaking, is Haskell's *IO* type, where the state $S$ is the "state of the world," such as the contents of the file system, the image on a display, and the output of a printer.

But what about creating our own state monad? In the next chapter, a state monad will be used to implement an imperative language for controlling a simulated robot, but before tackling such a big task let's look at a much smaller one: updating the leaves of a tree with successive integers. Given the *Tree* data type from Chapter 7:

```
data Tree a  =  Leaf a | Branch (Tree a) (Tree a)
    deriving Show
```

I will define a function *label* :: *Tree a* → *Tree Integer* such that, for example, the value *test*:

```
test  =  let t  =  Branch (Leaf 'a') (Leaf 'b')
         in label (Branch t t)
```

evaluates to:

> *Branch* (*Branch* (*Leaf* 0) (*Leaf* 1))
>     (*Branch* (*Leaf* 2) (*Leaf* 3))

Without knowing anything about monads, this job is relatively easy:

```
label  ::  Tree a → Tree Integer
label t  =  snd (lab t 0)
```

```
lab  ::  Tree a → Integer → (Integer, Tree Integer)
lab (Leaf a) n
    =  (n + 1, Leaf n)
lab (Branch t1 t2) n
    =  let (n1, t1')  =  lab t1 n
           (n2, t2')  =  lab t2 n1
       in (n2, Branch t1' t2')
```

Although simple, there is an undeniable tedium in "threading" the value of *n* from one call to *lab* to the next. To solve this problem, note that *lab t* has type *Integer* → (*Integer*, *Tree Integer*), which is in the right form for a state monad. Of course, we need a true data type, and so we write:

> **newtype** *Label a* = *Label* (*Integer* → (*Integer*, *a*))

for which the *Monad* instance is just like that for *SM* above:

```
instance Monad Label where
  return a
      =  Label (\s → (s, a))
  Label lt0 >>= flt1
      =  Label $ \ s0 →
            let (s1, a1)  =  lt0 s0
                Label lt1  =  flt1 a1
            in lt1 s1
```

Now I can write the following monadic version of the labeling function:

```
mlabel  ::  Tree a → Tree Integer
mlabel t  =  let Label lt  =  mlab t
                in snd (lt 0)
```

$$mlab \quad :: \quad Tree \; a \rightarrow Label \; (Tree \; Integer)$$
$$mlab \; (Leaf \; a)$$
$$= \quad \textbf{do} \; n \leftarrow getLabel$$
$$return \; (Leaf \; n)$$
$$mlab \; (Branch \; t1 \; t2)$$
$$= \quad \textbf{do} \; t1' \leftarrow mlab \; t1$$
$$t2' \leftarrow mlab \; t2$$
$$return \; (Branch \; t1' \; t2')$$

$$getLabel \quad :: \quad Label \; Integer$$
$$getLabel \quad = \quad Label \; (\backslash n \rightarrow (n + 1, \; n))$$

Note that the threading of the state has been eliminated from *mlab*, as has the incrementing of the state, which has been isolated in the function *getLabel*.

For example, this test case:

$$mtest \quad = \quad \textbf{let} \; t \quad = \quad Branch \; (Leaf \; 'a') \; (Leaf \; 'b')$$
$$\textbf{in} \; mlabel \; (Branch \; t \; t)$$

generates the same result as the nonmonadic version above.

For this simple example, you may decide that eliminating the threading of state is not worth it. Indeed, in reality it has just been moved from the definition of *lab* to the method declaration for (>>=), and the new version of the program is certainly longer than the old! But the capture of repetitious code into one function is the whole point of the abstraction principle. Hopefully, you can imagine a context where threading of state happens more than twice, perhaps hundreds of times, in which case the abstraction will surely pay off. IO is one example of this (imagine threading the state of the world on every IO command). An example involving robots will arise in the next chapter.

## 18.5 Type Class Type Errors

As you know, Haskell's type system detects ill-typed expressions. But what about errors resulting from malformed types? The value (+) 1 2 3 results in a type error because (+) takes only two arguments. Similarly, the type *Tree Int Int* should result in some sort of an error because the *Tree* type constructor takes only a single argument. So, how does Haskell detect malformed types? The answer is a second type system that ensures the correctness of types! That is, each type is assigned its own type –

which is called its *kind* – and these kinds are used to ensure that the type is used correctly.

There are only two kinds that we need to consider:

1. The symbol $*$ represents the kind of type associated with concrete data objects. That is, if the value $v$ has type $t$, then the kind of $t$ must be $*$.
2. If $\kappa_1$ and $\kappa_2$ are kinds, then $\kappa_1 \to \kappa_2$ is the kind of type that takes a type of kind $\kappa_1$ and returns a type of kind $\kappa_2$.

The details of how kinds are used to detect malformed types are beyond the scope of this text, but it is helpful to walk through a familiar example: *Int* has kind $*$, as does the type *Tree Int*. The type constructor *Tree*, however, has kind $* \to *$. Instances of the *Functor* class must all have the kind $* \to *$. Thus, a kind error would result from a declaration such as:

**instance** *Functor Int* **where**   . . .

or

**instance** *Functor* (*Tree Int*) **where**   . . .

Kinds do not appear directly in Haskell programs; the Haskell system infers them without any need for "kind declarations." Kinds stay in the background of a Haskell program except when a kind error occurs, in which case an error message may refer to the kind conflict. Fortunately, kinds are simple enough that your Haskell system should be able to provide descriptive error messages in most cases.

# CHAPTER NINETEEN

# An Imperative Robot Language

It is possible to use a language such as FAL to control things other than graphics images and animations. In particular, one could use FAL to control *robots*, not only in terms of their dynamic movement, but also their interaction with the real world. This is an interesting *declarative* approach to robot control that some researchers have in fact pursued. However, I will not do so here, for two reasons: First, there are no inexpensive, standard robots that I could use to make this effort truly worthwhile (although this may change over the next few years). Second, to demonstrate this idea using a graphically simulated robot would not make it significantly different from what I have already done with FAL.

Therefore, in this chapter I will describe a simple *imperative* language for robot control, using a simple graphics image to simulate the robot motion. My purpose is primarily to demonstrate the use of *monads* to implement stateful (i.e., imperative) computations. The language, which I will call IRL (for "imperative robot language"), is much less sophisticated than FAL, although it still qualifies as an embedded DSL.[1]

The implementation also uses a new data structure, an *array*, as part of the representation of the state of the robot's world. An array is functionally no different from an indexed list, but is more efficient in access time.

**module** *Robot* **where**

**import** *Array*
**import** *List*
**import** *Monad*

---

[1] IRL borrows ideas from *Logo* (Pappert, 1980) and *Karel the Robot* (Pattis, 1981). An approach to using FAL-like ideas to control robots is described in (Peterson, Hudak and Elliott, 1999; Peterson, Hager and Hudak, 1999).

**import** *SOEGraphics*
**import** *Win32Misc* (*timeGetTime*)
**import** *qualified GraphicsWindows as GW* (*getEvent*)

## 19.1 IRL by Example

As I did with FAL, I will begin with a brief description of how to program in IRL, and return to its implementation in the next section. Being an imperative language, the essence of IRL is a set of *commands*. These operations must be sequenced properly to achieve some desired behavior. Not surprisingly, it is most convenient to use the **do** syntax to achieve this, implying that the underlying structure is a monad. All commands in IRL will have type *Robot a* for some suitable type *a*. For example, *move* :: *Robot* () is the command to move one space forward, and *turnRight* :: *Robot* () is the command to turn 90° to the right (and analogously for *turnLeft*). A robot can also draw lines as it moves, and for this purpose, there are commands *penDown* :: *Robot* () and *penUp* :: *Robot* (), which lower and raise the pen (i.e., turn on and off the line drawing, respectively). For example, this sequence:

*drawSquare*
    = **do** *penDown*
        *move*
        *turnRight*
        *move*
        *turnRight*
        *move*
        *turnRight*
        *move*

draws a small square.

It is also possible to tell the robot to face directly in one of four directions – *North*, *South*, *East*, or *West* – with the command *turnTo* :: *Direction* → *Robot* (), as in *turnTo East*. As another example of a command that takes an argument, *setPenColor* :: *Color* → *Robot* () takes a *Color* argument and is used to change the color of the robot's pen, as in *setPenColor Red*.

The robot that is controlled by an IRL program lives in a square world laid out on a grid of fixed size (i.e., it is confined by four walls). There may be other walls as well (even rooms with small openings for doors), depending on how we construct the initial grid (more on this later). The command *blocked* :: *IO Bool* tests to see whether a wall is directly in front of the robot, which would prohibit forward motion. To make it easy to use commands like *blocked*, there is a conditional command *cond* that takes three arguments:

$$cond \ :: \ Robot \ Bool \rightarrow Robot \ a \rightarrow Robot \ a \rightarrow Robot \ a$$

For example, this use of *cond*:

```
evade  ::  Robot ()
evade  =  cond blocked
              (do turnRight
                  move)
              move
```

will move the robot one square forward if it isn't blocked, and one square to the right if it is.

The command *cond*1 is similar to *cond* except that it only takes two arguments; if the predicate is false, no action is taken. So this version of *evade* is equivalent to the one above:

```
evade  ::  Robot ()
evade  =  do cond1 blocked turnRight
             move
```

IRL has one other control operator, *while* :: *Robot Bool* → *Robot* () → *Robot* (), which executes a command (its second argument) repetitively as long as some predicate (its first argument) is true. For example:

```
moveToWall  ::  Robot ()
moveToWall  =  while (isnt blocked)
                   move
```

will move the robot forward until it encounters a wall. Note the use of the logical operator *isnt* :: *Robot Bool* → *Robot Bool*, which is a lifted version of Haskell's Boolean *not* operator. IRL also has lifted binary Boolean operators, such as (&&∗) and (||∗), each of type *Robot Bool* → *Robot Bool* → *Robot Bool*.

Now, moving around in a world of walls may be fun, but it isn't productive until we add *treasure*! Specifically, there may be small *gold coins* lying around that the robot may pick up and put in its pocket, carry around, and possibly drop somewhere else. The command *onCoin* :: *Robot Bool* determines if there is a coin on the current square, *pickCoin* :: *Robot* () picks up a coin if one is there, and *dropCoin* :: *Robot* () drops a coin on the current square if the robot has at least one in its pocket. It is a simple matter to change the *moveToWall* program to accumulate wealth as it moves to the wall:

*getCoinsToWall*  ::  *Robot* ()
*getCoinsToWall*  =  *while* (*isnt blocked*) $
                          **do** *move*
                                *pickCoin*

As a final example, I will define a function that, assuming the robot is initially at the center of the grid, will cause the robot to spiral outwards in such a way as to cover every square of a wall-less world. The algorithm to do this is based on the idea that a square spiral can be formed by turning right, moving $n$ steps in one direction, turning right again, moving $n$ steps again, and then repeating that process for $n + 1$. If the robot repeats this process starting with $n = 1$ and stopping when it is blocked, it will almost have completed a spiral. The full program is as follows:

*spiral*    ::  *Robot* ()
*spiral*    =  *penDown* >> *loop* 1
  **where** *loop n*  =
              **let** *twice*  =  **do** *turnRight*
                              *moven n*
                              *turnRight*
                              *moven n*
          **in** *cond blocked*
                (*twice* >> *turnRight* >> *moven n*)
                (*twice* >> *loop* (*n* + 1))

*moven*    ::  *Int* → *Robot* ()
*moven n*  =  *mapM_* (*const move*) [1..*n*]

This example also demonstrates that we can use existing Haskell functions, such as *mapM_* and *const*, to aid in IRL programming.

There are a couple of other operations in IRL that will be explained later, but the ones described here should be sufficient to motivate the implementation described in the next section. To get a feel for IRL in action, Fig. 19.1 shows an initial robot world with a single room containing lots of gold coins. Fig. 19.2 shows the result of executing a program that is a variation of the *spiral* program above. It starts the robot in the middle of the screen, spirals outward searching for a room, finds the room, searches for the door, enters the room, and then does an exhaustive

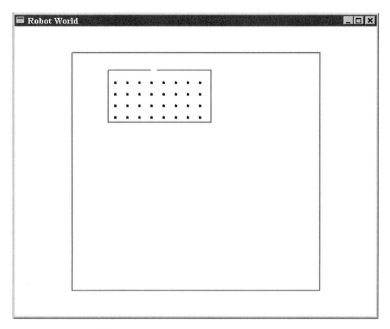

Figure 19.1: Initial Robot World

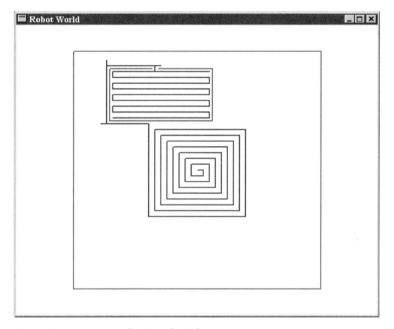

Figure 19.2: Actions of a Greedy Robot

sweep to find all the money. Rather than show you the program for solving this problem, I have left it as Exercise 19.4. Other exercises at the end of the chapter will allow you to extend IRL in interesting and imaginative ways.

## 19.2 *Robot* is a State Monad

Clearly, from the examples in the last section, an implementation of IRL must remember many things as it executes a program. Specifically, it must keep track of:

1. Robot position.
2. Robot orientation.
3. Pen status (up or down).
4. Pen color.
5. Placement of gold coins on the grid.
6. Number of coins in the robot's pocket.

We can capture these six pieces of "robot state" in a data type:

```
data RobotState
    = RobotState
         {position :: Position
         , facing :: Direction
         , pen :: Bool
         , color :: Color
         , treasure :: [Position]
         , pocket :: Int
         }
      deriving Show

type Position  =  (Int, Int)

data Direction  =  North | East | South | West
      deriving (Eq, Show, Enum)
```

The *Color* type is imported from the Graphics Library.

Note that a *Position* is a pair of integers, which represent the $x$ and $y$ coordinates on the grid representing the world. The treasure is a list of coin positions (more than one occurrence of a particular position means that more than one coin is at that position), and the pocket is simply a count of the number of coins in the robot's pocket.

The grid itself does not change, which is why it is not part of the *RobotState*. The only operation that we need to worry about for now involving the grid is *at* :: *Grid* → *Position* → [*Direction*]. Given a grid *g* and a position *p*, *g* '*at*' *p* is the list of directions in which the robot may move from that position. The absence of *East*, for example, means that there is a wall directly to the east.

We are now ready to talk about the nature of the monad type *Robot*. The key insight is the imperative nature of IRL commands: State is taken in as input, possibly queried in some ways, and possibly modified. Its potential for modification means that it must be returned as a result, to be "fed" into the next command. A suitable design would thus seem to be:

**type** *Robot*1 *a* = *RobotState* → *Grid* → (*RobotState*, *a*)

---

**DETAILS**
Recall that a monad of type $S → (S, a)$ is commonly called a *state monad*. Although *Robot*1 is not exactly of this form, it should still be thought of as a state monad, with *Grid* being part of the state that doesn't change (i.e., it is "read-only").

---

The only problem with this design is that we also want to model the robot actions in a graphics window as the program executes. Perhaps the most obvious solution to this problem is:

**type** *Robot*2 *a* = *RobotState* → *Grid* → *Window* →
                     (*RobotState*, *a*, *IO* ())

where I have also added a *Window* argument to specify in which window the graphics will appear.

However, this turns out to be an awkward solution in that IO actions from nested parts of the program need to be accumulated and then assembled using monadic sequencing before being returned as part of the result. A better approach is to include the robot state in the IO state itself (recall that IO is also a state monad), leading to:

**type** *Robot*3 *a* = *RobotState* → *Grid* → *Window* → *IO* (*RobotState*, *a*)

This basic design is good, except that I will use a true data type instead of a type synonym, leading to the final design:

**newtype** *Robot a*
     = *Robot* (*RobotState* → *Grid* → *Window* → *IO* (*RobotState*, *a*))

The only remaining task is to create an instance of *Monad* for the type *Robot*:

```
instance Monad Robot where
    return a
        = Robot (\s _ _ → return (s, a))
    Robot sf0 >>= f
        = Robot $ \ s0 g w → do
                        (s1, a1) ← sf0 s0 g w
                        let Robot sf1  =  f a1
                        (s2, a2) ← sf1 s1 g w
                        return (s2, a2)
```

> **DETAILS**
>
> Note the similarity of this to the instance declaration for the generic state monad *SM* given in Section 18.4.

Be sure that you understand every line of this code; it is the essence of the imperative nature of IRL! In particular, note in the method for ( >>= ) how the initial state *s*0 is modified by the first command to yield a new state *s*1, which in turn is modifed by the second command to yield the final state *s*2.

## 19.3   The Implementation of IRL Commands

Now that the monadic structure is set up, the implementations of the individual commands are relatively straightforward, the most complex task being that of getting the graphics right. For this reason, I will start with commands that do not involve graphics. To make the job easier, it is convenient to first define a few auxiliary functions (none of which are intended for use by the IRL programmer), starting with:

```
right, left  ::  Direction → Direction

right d    =  toEnum (succ (fromEnum d) 'mod' 4)
left d     =  toEnum (pred (fromEnum d) 'mod' 4)
```

> **DETAILS**
>
> Recall that *fromEnum, toEnum, succ,* and *pred* are operations in the class *Enum,* of which *Direction* is a derived instance. The operations *succ* and *pred* here are being applied to the *Int* value returned by *fromEnum,* and

the result is then converted back into a *Direction*. We can't apply *succ* and *pred* directly to the *Direction* value because we need to account for the "wrap-around" from the last constructor in the data type (*West*) to the first (*North*). This is what the modulo arithmetic accomplishes (*succ West* and *pred North* generate errors).

It is also convenient to define two auxiliary functions for updating and querying the state:

$$updateState \quad :: \quad (RobotState \rightarrow RobotState) \rightarrow Robot\ ()$$
$$updateState\ u \quad = \quad Robot\ (\backslash s\ \_\ \_ \rightarrow return\ (u\ s,\ ()))$$

$$queryState \quad :: \quad (RobotState \rightarrow a) \rightarrow Robot\ a$$
$$queryState\ q \quad = \quad Robot\ (\backslash s\ \_\ \_ \rightarrow return\ (s,\ q\ s))$$

### 19.3.1 Robot Orientation

With these functions, the implementations of the IRL commands *turnLeft* and *turnRight* are easy; all that we need to do is update the robot state:

$$turnLeft \quad :: \quad Robot\ ()$$
$$turnLeft \quad = \quad updateState\ (\backslash s \rightarrow s\ \{facing = left\ (facing\ s)\})$$

$$turnRight \quad :: \quad Robot\ ()$$
$$turnRight \quad = \quad updateState\ (\backslash s \rightarrow s\ \{facing = right\ (facing\ s)\})$$

The command *turnTo* is even easier:

$$turnTo \quad :: \quad Direction \rightarrow Robot\ ()$$
$$turnTo\ d \quad = \quad updateState\ (\backslash s \rightarrow s\ \{facing = d\})$$

IRL also has a command for determining the robot direction:

$$direction \quad :: \quad Robot\ Direction$$
$$direction \quad = \quad queryState\ facing$$

Determining if the robot is blocked amounts to checking to see if the direction it is facing is missing from the list of valid directions at the robot's grid position. That is:

$$blocked \quad :: \quad Robot\ Bool$$
$$blocked \quad = \quad Robot\ \$ \ \backslash s\ g\ \_ \rightarrow$$
$$\qquad return\ (s,\ facing\ s\ `notElem`\ (g\ `at`\ position\ s))$$

Finally, let's consider what a move entails. If we assume for now the existence of a command *graphicsMove* (to be defined in Section 19.5) that performs the graphics operations associated with a robot move, the task is fairly straightforward:

```
move  ::  Robot ()
move  =   cond1 (isnt blocked)
              (Robot $ \ s _ w → do
                  let newPos  =  movePos (position s) (facing s)
                  graphicsMove w s newPos
                  return (s {position = newPos}, ())
              )


movePos  ::  Position → Direction → Position
movePos (x, y) d
        =  case d of
               North  →  (x, y + 1)
               South  →  (x, y − 1)
               East   →  (x + 1, y)
               West   →  (x − 1, y)
```

The *graphicsMove* command is defined in Section 19.5.

### 19.3.2  Using the Pen

Implementing the commands for controlling the robot's pen is very easy (shown at the top of Fig. 19.3).

### 19.3.3  Playing With Coins

Fig. 19.3 also shows the implementations for the commands that play with coins. The commands *onCoin* and *coins* are very easy, and the only complication with *pickCoin* and *dropCoin* is once again the graphics. The graphics functions *drawCoin* and *eraseCoin* are defined in Section 19.5.

### 19.3.4  Logic and Control

Fig. 19.4 shows a number of logical operators and control commands. Note that *while* is defined in terms of existing commands, and in that sense is not "primitive." Also note the use of the Monad Library functions *liftM* and *liftM2* to define *isnt*, (>*), and (<*); thus, no special lifting functions need to be defined, as we did for the various kinds of *Behaviors* in previous chapters. However, I did not use *liftM2* to define (||*) and

Using the pen:

```
penUp     ::  Robot ()
penUp     =   updateState (\s → s {pen = False})

penDown   ::  Robot ()
penDown   =   updateState (\s → s {pen = True})

setPenColor     ::  Color → Robot ()
setPenColor c   =   updateState (\s → s {color = c})
```

Playing with coins:

```
onCoin  ::  Robot Bool
onCoin  =   queryState (\s → position s 'elem' treasure s)

coins  ::  Robot Int
coins  =   queryState pocket

pickCoin  ::  Robot ()
pickCoin  =   cond1 onCoin
                  (Robot $ \ s _ w →
                      do eraseCoin w (position s)
                         return (s {treasure = position s 'delete' treasure s,
                                    pocket = pocket s + 1}, ())
                  )

dropCoin  ::  Robot ()
dropCoin  =   cond1 (coins >* return 0)
                  (Robot $ \ s _ w →
                      do drawCoin w (position s)
                         return (s {treasure = position s : treasure s,
                                    pocket = pocket s − 1}, ())
                  )
```

Figure 19.3: Pens and Coins

(&&*), because to do so would make them unnecessarily strict in their second arguments.

**DETAILS**
The functions *liftM* and *liftM*2 are defined in the Monad Library as:

```
liftM    ::  (Monad m) ⇒ (a → b) → (m a → m b)
liftM f  =   \a → do a' ← a
                     return (f a')
```

```
cond       ::  Robot Bool → Robot a → Robot a → Robot a
cond p c a  =  do pred ← p
                 if pred then c else a


cond1 p c  =  cond p c (return ())


while      ::  Robot Bool → Robot () → Robot ()
while p b   =  cond1 p (b >> while p b)


(||*)      ::  Robot Bool → Robot Bool → Robot Bool
b1 ||* b2   =  do p ← b1
                 if p then return True
                      else b2


(&&*)      ::  Robot Bool → Robot Bool → Robot Bool
b1 &&* b2   =  do p ← b1
                 if p then b2
                      else return False


isnt  ::  Robot Bool → Robot Bool
isnt  =  liftM not


(>*), (<*)  ::  Robot Int → Robot Int → Robot Bool
(>*)        =  liftM2 (>)
(<*)        =  liftM2 (<)
```

Figure 19.4: Robot Logic and Control Functions

```
liftM2     ::  (Monad m) ⇒ (a → b → c) → (m a → m b → m c)
liftM2 f   =  \a b → do a' ← a
                        b' ← b
                        return (f a' b')
```

The library also defines functions *liftM3*, *liftM4*, and *liftM5*.

## 19.4  All the World is a Grid

A value of type *Ix a ⇒ Array a b* in Haskell is an *array* containing elements of type *b* that are accessed using values of type *a* as indices and the access function (!) :: *Ix a ⇒ Array a b → a → b*. For example, an array *arr* :: *Array Int Color* is an array of colors; the color at position *i* :: *Int* is just *arr* ! *i*. (Arrays are defined in the *Array* Library.)

> **DETAILS**
> Note the constraint on the index type: It must be an instance of the class *Ix*, which contains operations specifically needed for index calculations. Class *Ix* is a subclass of *Ord* and is defined in detail in Chapter 24. The only thing that you need to know here is that *Int* as well as pairs of *Int* are derived instances of *Ix*.

Functionally, arrays are very similar to lists that are accessed using the (!!) operator, defined in the Standard Prelude such that *xs* !! *n* returns the $(n + 1)$th element of the list. However, using (!!) to access the *i*th element of a list takes a number of steps proportional to *i*, whereas using (!) to access the *i*th element of an array takes a constant number of steps, regardless of *i*. However, this efficiency comes at a cost. Lists can be arbitrarily long, even infinite, whereas arrays are of fixed size, which must be defined at the time the array is first created.

Speaking of which, arrays are created using the function:

$$array \ :: \ Ix \ a \Rightarrow (a, a) \rightarrow [(a, b)] \rightarrow Array \ a \ b$$

The first argument to *array* is a pair of index *bounds*, a low bound and a high bound. The second argument is a list of index/value pairs (which I will call *array entries*); these are the initial values that are stored in the array. For example:

```
colors :: Array Int Color
colors = array (0, 7) [(0, Black), (1, Blue), (2, Green), (3, Cyan),
                       (4, Red), (5, Magenta), (6, Yellow), (7, White)]
```

is an array of eight colors. The value *colors* ! 3 is *Cyan*, and so forth.

> **DETAILS**
> If *Color* is as defined in the Graphics Library:
>
> ```
> data Color = Black | Blue | Green | Cyan
>            | Red | Magenta | Yellow | White
> deriving (Eq, Ord, Bounded, Enum, Ix, Show, Read)
> ```

then *colors* can be defined more succinctly as:

*colors* :: *Array Int Color*
*colors* = *array* (0, 7) (*zip* [0..7] [*Black..White*])

Arrays can also have more than one dimension; for example, an array of type *Array* (*Int, Int*) *Color* is a two-dimensional array (i.e., a *matrix*) of *Color* values. This makes arrays ideal for representing the robot grid, and thus we define:

**type** *Grid* = *Array Position* [*Direction*]

The access operator *at* used in the last section is just the indexing operator (!):

*at* :: *Grid* → *Position* → [*Direction*]
*at* = (!)

In constructing the robot grid I will use a coordinate system similar to that used in the graphics and animation chapters: (0, 0) represents the center of the grid, (−*size*, −*size*) is the lower left-hand corner, and (*size, size*) is the upper right-hand corner, where *size* is whatever we define it to be:

*size* :: *Int*
*size* = 20

The initial grid, which I will name *g*0, should have no walls other than the four surrounding ones. Thus, every interior grid point is represented by the list:

*interior* = [*North, South, East, West*]

whereas the grid points on the "east border," "west border," "northeast corner," and so forth are represented using the lists *eb*, *wb*, *nec*, and so forth defined by:

*nb* = [*South, East, West*]
*sb* = [*North, East, West*]
*eb* = [*North, South, West*]
*wb* = [*North, South, East*]
*nwc* = [*South, East*]
*nec* = [*South, West*]
*swc* = [*North, East*]
*sec* = [*North, West*]

Using list comprehensions to enumerate the proper interior and border points, here then is the definition of $g0$:

$g0$ :: *Grid*
$g0$ = *array* $((-size, -size), (size, size))$
$\quad\quad ([[((i, size), nb) \mid i \leftarrow r] +\!\!+$
$\quad\quad\quad [((i, -size), sb) \mid i \leftarrow r] +\!\!+$
$\quad\quad\quad [((size, i), eb) \mid i \leftarrow r] +\!\!+$
$\quad\quad\quad [((-size, i), wb) \mid i \leftarrow r] +\!\!+$
$\quad\quad\quad [((i, j), interior) \mid i \leftarrow r, j \leftarrow r] +\!\!+$
$\quad\quad\quad [((size, size), nec), ((size, -size), sec),$
$\quad\quad\quad\quad ((-size, size), nwc), ((-size, -size), swc)])$
$\quad\quad$ **where** $r = [1 - size..size - 1]$

To add walls to $g0$, we can use the Array Library function:

$(//)$ :: $Ix\ a \Rightarrow Array\ a\ b \to [(a, b)] \to Array\ a\ b$

which derives a new array from an existing one, differing only in the array entries provided as its second argument. For example:

$colors //[(0, White)\ (7, Black)]$

reverses the positions of *Black* and *White* in *colors* defined earlier.
To help make more walls, I will define functions:

*mkHorWall*, *mkVerWall* :: $Int \to Int \to Int \to [(Position, [Direction])]$

such that *mkHorWall* $x1\ x2\ y$ creates a horizontal wall starting just above grid point $(x1, y)$ and ending just above $(x2, y)$. This implies that all of the grid points just below the line become "north border points," and all points just above become "south border points." The function *mkVerWall* behaves analogously, except that the wall is just to the right of the specified coordinates.

*mkHorWall* $x1\ x2\ y$
$\quad = [((x, y), nb) \mid x \leftarrow [x1..x2]] +\!\!+$
$\quad\quad [((x, y + 1), sb) \mid x \leftarrow [x1..x2]]$

*mkVerWall* $y1\ y2\ x$
$\quad = [((x, y), eb) \mid y \leftarrow [y1..y2]] +\!\!+$
$\quad\quad [((x + 1, y), wb) \mid y \leftarrow [y1..y2]]$

So, to add a horizontal wall to *g*0 from (−5, 10) to (5, 10), we can define:

> *g*1 :: *Grid*
> *g*1 = *g*0//*mkHorWall* (−5) 5 10

Using *mkHorWall* and *mkVerWall* I can also define a function to create the array entries for a box:

> *mkBox* :: *Position* → *Position* → [(*Position*, [*Direction*])]
> *mkBox* (*x*1, *y*1) (*x*2, *y*2)
>      = *mkHorWall* (*x*1 + 1) *x*2 *y*1 ++
>         *mkHorWall* (*x*1 + 1) *x*2 *y*2 ++
>         *mkVerWall* (*y*1 + 1) *y*2 *x*1 ++
>         *mkVerWall* (*y*1 + 1) *y*2 *x*2

However, you will notice that this will create two array entries for each of the four interior corners. For example, the northeast interior corner will have one entry as a north border point and one entry as an east border point. Haskell arrays are designed such that duplicate entries like this cause the value at that point to be undefined (i.e., ⊥).

Although I am sure that you can imagine ways to fix this problem involving a more careful generation of the array entries, there is a much easier fix to this problem. The Array Library function:

> *accum* :: (*Ix a*) ⇒ (*b* → *c* → *b*) → *Array a b* → [(*a*, *c*)] → *Array a b*

is just like (//), except that if it finds duplicate entries, it uses its first argument (a function) to combine them into one. What function can we use for this purpose in the case of *mkBox*? The answer is *intersect*, a List Library function that computes the intersection of two lists. For example, in the northeast corner, we will have:

> [*South*, *East*, *West*] ‘*intersect*‘ [*North*, *South*, *West*]
> ⟹ [*South*, *West*]

which is the representation for a northeast corner, as desired.

Thus, to add a box with lower left-hand corner at (−10, 5) and upper right-hand corner at (−5, 10), we can define:

> *g*2 :: *Grid*
> *g*2 = *accum intersect g*0 (*mkBox* (−15, 8) (2, 17))

If we wish to add a "door" to the box, we can use *union* rather than *intersection* to add unconstrained interior points at the appropriate places. For example, to add a door to the middle of the top wall of the box in *g*2, we can define:

*g*3  ::  *Grid*
*g*3  =  *accum union g*2 [((−7, 17), *interior*), ((−7, 18), *interior*)]

## 19.5  Robot Graphics

You should know enough about graphics programming in Haskell by now that I don't have to explain every line of the code that simulates the robot. Indeed, there is only one new idea introduced in this section, which is the following.

In all the previous uses of graphics in this text, the goal has been to draw a particular picture, then change it to something completely different and draw it again. It was partially for this reason that we used the *drawBufferedGraphics* mode when doing animations.

For the robot simulation, however, I want the graphics to be "incremental." Specifically, I would like to draw all of the walls and coins on the initial grid, and then show the robot running around (at some predetermined rate) doing its thing: drawing lines if the pen is down, picking up coins and thereby making them disappear, and dropping coins and thereby having them reappear in possibly other locations.

Now, I *could* do this by redrawing the entire picture after each robot action, but it turns out to be noticeably inefficient to do this for long robot runs. Therefore, I will choose a different approach. Instead of using the command *drawInWindow*, I will use a new command from the Graphics Library, *drawInWindowNow*. The difference between these is that the former updates the drawing function, but does not do any actual drawing until a screen refresh occurs (such as is initiated by *getWindowTick* and other IO commands). The command *drawInWindowNow*, however, in addition to updating the drawing function for future refreshes, also draws the new graphics immediately. This will give the incremental effect that we want. For example, the *drawLine* function is defined as:

*drawLine*  ::  *Window* → *Color* → *Point* → *Point* → *IO* ()
*drawLine w c p*1 *p*2
        =  *drawInWindowNow w* (*withColor c* (*line p*1 *p*2))

The only problem with this approach is that we must carefully ensure that the graphics actions do not interfere with each other. My approach to ensuring this is the following:

1. Grid points are 10 pixels apart.
2. Walls are drawn halfway between grid points.
3. The robot pen draws lines directly from one grid point to the next.
4. Coins are drawn as yellow circles just above and to the left of each grid point.
5. Coins are erased by drawing black circles over the yellow circles that are already there.

Using this strategy, I first define some top-level constants:

$$
\begin{array}{lll}
d & :: & Int \\
d & = 5 & -\!- \text{ half the distance between grid points}
\end{array}
$$

$$
\begin{array}{lll}
wc, cc & :: & Color \\
wc & = Green & -\!- \text{ color of walls} \\
cc & = Yellow & -\!- \text{ color of coins}
\end{array}
$$

$$
\begin{array}{lll}
xWin, yWin & :: & Int \\
xWin & = 600 \\
yWin & = 500
\end{array}
$$

The remainder of the code is shown in Fig. 19.5. Note the use of *getWindowTick* to cause a short delay after each robot move (this is for aesthetic purposes only, and you may wish to change the tick duration in the following section to suit your personal taste).

> **DETAILS**
> The function *bounds* :: $Ix\ a \Rightarrow Array\ a\ b \rightarrow (a, a)$ is from the Array Library, and does what you might expect: It returns the bounds of its array argument.

## 19.6  Putting it all Together

Using a simple command to wait until the user presses the spacebar:

$$
\begin{array}{l}
spaceWait \ :: \ Window \rightarrow IO\ () \\
spaceWait\ w \\
\qquad = \textbf{do }k \leftarrow getKey\ w \\
\qquad\qquad \textbf{if } k ==' \ ' \textbf{ then } return\ () \\
\qquad\qquad\qquad\qquad \textbf{else } spaceWait\ w
\end{array}
$$

```
drawGrid  ::  Window → Grid → IO ()
drawGrid w wld
       = let (low@(xMin, yMin), hi@(xMax, yMax))   =   bounds wld
             (x1, y1)                              =   trans low
             (x2, y2)                              =   trans hi
         in do drawLine w wc (x1 − d, y1 + d) (x1 − d, y2 − d)
               drawLine w wc (x1 − d, y1 + d) (x2 + d, y1 + d)
               sequence_ [drawPos w (trans (x, y)) (wld 'at' (x, y))
                           | x ← [xMin..xMax], y ← [yMin..yMax]]


drawPos  ::  Window → Point → [Direction] → IO ()
drawPos w (x, y) ds
        = do if North 'notElem' ds
                then drawLine w wc (x − d, y − d) (x + d, y − d)
                else return ()
             if East 'notElem' ds
                then drawLine w wc (x + d, y − d) (x + d, y + d)
                else return ()


drawCoins     ::  Window → RobotState → IO ()
drawCoins w s  =  mapM_ (drawCoin w) (treasure s)


drawCoin      ::  Window → Position → IO ()
drawCoin w p  =  let (x, y)  =  trans p
                 in drawInWindowNow w
                    (withColor cc (ellipse (x − 5, y − 1) (x − 1, y − 5)))


eraseCoin      ::  Window → Position → IO ()
eraseCoin w p  =  let (x, y)  =  trans p
                  in drawInWindowNow w
                     (withColor Black (ellipse (x − 5, y − 1) (x − 1, y − 5)))


graphicsMove  ::  Window → RobotState → Position → IO ()
graphicsMove w s newPos
        = do if pen s then drawLine w (color s) (trans (position s))
                                                (trans newPos)
                      else return ()
             getWindowTick w


trans        ::  Position → Point
trans (x, y)  =  (div xWin 2 + 2 ∗ d ∗ x, div yWin 2 − 2 ∗ d ∗ y)
```

Figure 19.5: Robot Graphics

we can now write a top level function that "runs" an IRL program:

$$
\begin{array}{l}
runRobot \ :: \ Robot \ () \to RobotState \to Grid \to IO \ () \\
runRobot \ (Robot \ sf) \ s \ g \\
\qquad = \ runGraphics \ \$ \\
\qquad\qquad \textbf{do} \ w \leftarrow openWindowEx \ \text{``Robot World''} \ (Just \ (0, 0)) \\
\qquad\qquad\qquad\qquad (Just \ (xWin, \ yWin)) \ drawGraphic \ (Just \ 10) \\
\qquad\qquad\quad drawGrid \ w \ g \\
\qquad\qquad\quad drawCoins \ w \ s \\
\qquad\qquad\quad spaceWait \ w \\
\qquad\qquad\quad sf \ s \ g \ w \\
\qquad\qquad\quad spaceClose \ w
\end{array}
$$

This function opens a window, draws the grid, draws the coins, and then waits for the user to hit the spacebar. It then runs the robot program with starting state *s* and grid *g*. When execution is complete, it waits for the user to again hit the spacebar before closing the window.

The grids *g*0 through *g*3 defined earlier are suitable grids to run programs with. Here is a suitable starting state:

$$
\begin{array}{l}
s0 \ :: \ RobotState \\
s0 \ = \ RobotState \ \{position = (0, 0) \\
\qquad\qquad\qquad\quad , \ pen = False \\
\qquad\qquad\qquad\quad , \ color = Blue \\
\qquad\qquad\qquad\quad , \ facing = North \\
\qquad\qquad\qquad\quad , \ treasure = tr \\
\qquad\qquad\qquad\quad , \ pocket = 0 \\
\qquad\qquad\qquad\quad \}
\end{array}
$$

$$
\begin{array}{l}
tr \ :: \ [Position] \\
tr \ = \ [(x, y) \mid x \leftarrow [-13, -11..1], \ y \leftarrow [9, 11..15]]
\end{array}
$$

The treasure here was designed to place all the coins inside the room in grid *g*3. For example, to run the *spiral* example using *s*0 and *g*0, simply do:

$$
main \ = \ runRobot \ spiral \ s0 \ g0
$$

You should try running some of the other examples given in Section 19.1, as well as some of the ones asked for in the following exercises.

---

**Exercise 19.1** Prove that the instance of *Monad* for type *Robot* given in Section 19.2 obeys the monad laws given in Chapter 18.

---

**Exercise 19.2** Define the following useful commands, not as extensions to the underlying implementation, but in terms of exsiting IRL commands:

1. *repeat :: Robot Bool → Robot () → Robot ()* is just like *while*, except that it executes its second argument at least once before checking the conditional.
2. *blockedLeft*, *blockedRight*, and *blockedBehind*, each of type *Robot Bool*, that determine if the robot is blocked to the left, to the right, and behind, respectively.
3. *wallFollowLeft* and *wallFollowRight* of type *Robot ()* that cause the robot to follow a wall that is immediately to the left or right, respectively. If the robot becomes blocked or the wall disappears, it should stop at that point.

---

**Exercise 19.3** Implement the following commands as primitives:

1. *getPosition :: Robot Point* returns the current position of the robot.
2. *goToPosition :: Point → Robot ()* causes the robot to be "teleported" immediately to the given position.
3. *blockedLeft*, *blockedRight*, and *blockedBehind*, as described in the previous exercise.

---

**Exercise 19.4** Write IRL programs for the following tasks:

1. Modify the *spiral* program given at the beginning of this chapter so that it picks up coins as it finds them, and then distributes them evenly along the top of the grid once the spiral is complete. Create a grid with a number of gold coins scattered about, and test your program on it.
2. Start the robot at the center of the grid again. But now the grid should have a single rectangular room containing some number of gold coins and having exactly one door (one square wide). The room should be situated such that the robot is not initially in it. Have the robot spiral outward again, searching for the room. Once found, it should follow

the walls of the room, looking for the door. It should then enter the room and search for and find all gold coins. Figs. 19.1 and 19.2 show the effect of one solution to this problem.

3. Design a grid with a maze on it, with the starting point at the southwestern-most corner, and the ending point at the northeastern-most corner. Write a program to guide the robot through the maze.

4. Write a program to draw interesting and colorful line drawings of your choosing.

---

**Exercise 19.5** Design and implement some nontrivial extension to the basic robot world or IRL implementation. For example:

■ Allow there to be more than one robot, and allow them to detect each others' presence, cooperate with each other, or blow each other up if you prefer.

■ Observe that our representation of the grid allows for the design of one-way walls or doors (e.g., a horizontal one-way wall is one that can be passed through from the south (say), but not from the north). Add one-way walls to the implementation, and modify the graphics to adequately differentiate them.

■ Add exceptions and exception handlers to IRL, to allow nonlocal exits from loops, etc.

■ Improve the graphics. For example, show the position of the robot regardless of whether the pen is down, and somehow indicate its orientation.

■ Create an instance of *Show* for *RobotState* that formats the state in a nicer way than that given by the derived instance. Use this to print the initial robot state to standard output when the program begins, and to print the final state when the program ends.

---

**Exercise 19.6** Prove the following equivalences:

$$cond\ p\ (c1 >> c)\ (c2 >> c) \implies cond\ p\ c1\ c2 >> c$$
$$repeat\ p\ c \implies c >> while\ p\ c$$
$$turnTo\ d >> direction \implies return\ d$$

Then use the first of these to prove the equivalence of the two versions of *evade* described in Section 19.1.

# Functional Music Composition

In this chapter I will describe a module for expressing *musical structures* in the same high-level, declarative style of functional programming that we have been using for graphics, animation, and other applications. These musical structures consist of primitive entities (such as notes and rests), operations to transform musical structures (such as transpose and tempo-scaling), and operations to combine musical structures to form more complex ones (such as concurrent and sequential composition). From these simple roots, much richer musical ideas can be easily developed.

For convenience, and in the style of Chapters 15 and 19 (where I defined the languages FAL and IRL, respectively), I will refer to the ideas described in this chapter as MDL, for *music description language*. MDL is a simplified version of a more complete computer music library called *Haskore*. In Chapter 21 a module will be developed for interpreting an MDL program as an abstract *performance*, and in Chapter 22 these performances will be converted into *MIDI files*, which are a standard way of interchanging electronic music and can be played on any PC with a standard sound card.[1]

**DETAILS**
If you load the Haskell code for Chapter 22 into Hugs you will be able to play any of the examples presented in this chapter by typing either:

*testWin95 m*
*testNT m*
*testLinux m*

---

[1] Haskore is described in (Hudak et al., 1996, Hudak, 1996); see also the Haskell Home Page for information on the latest release. Other approaches to computer music from a functional programming perspective include (Orlarey et al., 1994, Dannenberg, Fraley, and Velikanja, 1992).

depending on what kind of computer you are using. This command will convert *m* (of type *Music*, to be defined shortly) into a MIDI file, and then automatically invoke the default MIDI file player on your PC so that you can hear the result.

**module** *Music* **where**

## 20.1 The Music Data Type

I will assume that you are familiar with very basic musical concepts such as notes, rests, scales, and chords. Nothing more will be needed to understand what is going on, but of course the richer your musical background, the more applications of the ideas will be apparent to you.

Perhaps the most basic musical concept in MDL is that of a *pitch*, which consists of a *pitch class* (i.e., one of 12 semitones) and an *octave*:

```
type Pitch       = (PitchClass, Octave)
data PitchClass  = Cf | C | Cs | Df | D | Ds | Ef | E | Es | Ff | F
                 |  Fs | Gf | G | Gs | Af | A | As | Bf | B | Bs
     deriving (Eq, Show)
type Octave      = Int
```

*Cf* is read as "C-flat" and normally written as C♭, *Cs* is read "C-sharp" and normally written as C♯; and so on. A *Pitch* is a pair consisting of a pitch class and an octave. Octaves are just integers, but I have defined a separate data type for pitch classes, because distinguishing enharmonics (that is, pitches that sound the same, such as G♯ and A♭) may be important in certain contexts. When tuning instruments or entire orchestras, there is a notion of "A440", which is the note A at 440 Hz; by convention, I will designate that pitch as (*A*, 4) in the above design.

Musical structures are captured in MDL by the *Music* data type:

```
data Music  =  Note Pitch Dur
            |  Rest Dur
            |  Music :+: Music
            |  Music :=: Music
            |  Tempo (Ratio Int) Music
            |  Trans Int Music
            |  Instr IName Music
     deriving (Show, Eq)

type Dur    = Ratio Int
```

A *Note* is its pitch paired with its duration (in number of whole notes). A *Rest* also has a duration, but of course no pitch. From these two atomic constructors, we can build more complex musical structures as follows:

- *m*1 :+: *m*2 is the "sequential composition" of *m*1 and *m*2 (i.e., *m*1 and *m*2 are played in sequence).
- *m*1 :=: *m*2 is the "parallel composition" of *m*1 and *m*2 (i.e., *m*1 and *m*2 are played simultaneously).
- *Tempo a m* scales the rate at which *m* is played (i.e., its tempo) by a factor of *a*.
- *Trans i m* transposes *m* by interval *i* (in semitones).
- *Instr iname m* declares that *m* is to be performed using instrument *iname*, which is one of 129 names shown in Fig. 20.1. (These odd names are from the *General MIDI Standard*, which is explained in more detail in Chapter 21.)

It is convenient to represent these ideas in Haskell as a recursive data type because we may wish to not only build musical structures, but also take them apart, analyze their structure, print them, transform them, interpret them for performance purposes, and so on. This is the same kind of argument used to justify *Shape*, *Region*, and other data types in this text.

Note that durations and tempo scalings are represented using *rational numbers*; specifically, as ratios of two Haskell *Int* values. This is more accurate than using floating-point numbers, as long as overflow does not occur, and for musical structures it is often just the right representation, where many concepts are often expressed as ratios ("quarter-notes," "triplets," "dotted-notes," etc.). An alternative to this design is to make *Music* polymorphic in the numeric type, but the extra complexity does not seem to be worth the trouble.

Treating pitches simply as integers is useful in many settings, so let's also define a notion of *absolute pitch*:

**type** *AbsPitch* = *Int*

along with some functions for converting between *Pitch* values and *AbsPitch* values:

```
absPitch         :: Pitch → AbsPitch
absPitch (pc, oct) = 12 * oct + pcToInt pc

pitch     :: AbsPitch → Pitch
pitch ap  = ([C, Cs, D, Ds, E, F, Fs, G, Gs, A, As, B] !! mod ap 12,
             quot ap 12)
```

```
data IName
    = AcousticGrandPiano | BrightAcousticPiano | ElectricGrandPiano
    | HonkyTonkPiano | RhodesPiano | ChorusedPiano
    | Harpsichord | Clavinet | Celesta | Glockenspiel | MusicBox
    | Vibraphone | Marimba | Xylophone | TubularBells
    | Dulcimer | HammondOrgan | PercussiveOrgan
    | RockOrgan | ChurchOrgan | ReedOrgan
    | Accordion | Harmonica | TangoAccordion
    | AcousticGuitarNylon | AcousticGuitarSteel | ElectricGuitarJazz
    | ElectricGuitarClean | ElectricGuitarMuted | OverdrivenGuitar
    | DistortionGuitar | GuitarHarmonics | AcousticBass
    | ElectricBassFingered | ElectricBassPicked | FretlessBass
    | SlapBass1 | SlapBass2 | SynthBass1 | SynthBass2
    | Violin | Viola | Cello | Contrabass | TremoloStrings
    | PizzicatoStrings | OrchestralHarp | Timpani
    | StringEnsemble1 | StringEnsemble2 | SynthStrings1
    | SynthStrings2 | ChoirAahs | VoiceOohs | SynthVoice
    | OrchestraHit | Trumpet | Trombone | Tuba
    | MutedTrumpet | FrenchHorn | BrassSection | SynthBrass1
    | SynthBrass2 | SopranoSax | AltoSax | TenorSax
    | BaritoneSax | Oboe | Bassoon | EnglishHorn | Clarinet
    | Piccolo | Flute | Recorder | PanFlute | BlownBottle
    | Shakuhachi | Whistle | Ocarina | Lead1Square
    | Lead2Sawtooth | Lead3Calliope | Lead4Chiff
    | Lead5Charang | Lead6Voice | Lead7Fifths
    | Lead8BassLead | Pad1NewAge | Pad2Warm
    | Pad3Polysynth | Pad4Choir | Pad5Bowed
    | Pad6Metallic | Pad7Halo | Pad8Sweep
    | FX1Train | FX2Soundtrack | FX3Crystal
    | FX4Atmosphere | FX5Brightness | FX6Goblins
    | FX7Echoes | FX8SciFi | Sitar | Banjo | Shamisen
    | Koto | Kalimba | Bagpipe | Fiddle | Shanai
    | TinkleBell | Agogo | SteelDrums | Woodblock | TaikoDrum
    | MelodicDrum | SynthDrum | ReverseCymbal
    | GuitarFretNoise | BreathNoise | Seashore
    | BirdTweet | TelephoneRing | Helicopter
    | Applause | Gunshot | Percussion
    deriving (Show, Eq, Ord, Enum)
```

Figure 20.1: General MIDI Instrument Names

$$pcToInt \quad :: \quad PitchClass \rightarrow Int$$
$$pcToInt \; pc \; = \; \textbf{case} \; pc \; \textbf{of}$$

| | | |
|---|---|---|
| $Cf$ | $\rightarrow$ $-1$ | $--$ should Cf be 11? |
| $C$ | $\rightarrow$ $0$ | |
| $Cs$ | $\rightarrow$ $1$ | |
| $Df$ | $\rightarrow$ $1$ | |
| $D$ | $\rightarrow$ $2$ | |
| $Ds$ | $\rightarrow$ $3$ | |
| $Ef$ | $\rightarrow$ $3$ | |
| $E$ | $\rightarrow$ $4$ | |
| $Es$ | $\rightarrow$ $5$ | |
| $Ff$ | $\rightarrow$ $4$ | |
| $F$ | $\rightarrow$ $5$ | |
| $Fs$ | $\rightarrow$ $6$ | |
| $Gf$ | $\rightarrow$ $6$ | |
| $G$ | $\rightarrow$ $7$ | |
| $Gs$ | $\rightarrow$ $8$ | |
| $Af$ | $\rightarrow$ $8$ | |
| $A$ | $\rightarrow$ $9$ | |
| $As$ | $\rightarrow$ $10$ | |
| $Bf$ | $\rightarrow$ $10$ | |
| $B$ | $\rightarrow$ $11$ | |
| $Bs$ | $\rightarrow$ $12$ | $--$ should Bs be 0? |

Should *Cf* be interpreted as 11 instead of -1, and *Bs* as 0 instead of 12? I don't know. In most cases it will not matter, but it is an interesting concern.

---

**DETAILS**

(!!) is Haskell's zero-based list-indexing function; *list* !! *n* returns the $(n+1)$th element in *list*. It is defined in the Prelude as:

```
infixl            9 !!
(!!)              :: [a] → Int → a
(x : _) !! 0      = x
(_ : xs) !! n | n > 0  = xs !! (n − 1)
(_ : _) !! _      = error "PreludeList.!!: negative index"
[ ] !! _          = error "PreludeList.!!: index too large"
```

*mod* and *quot* are methods in the *Integral* class. *mod x n* computes the value of *x* modulo n; *quot x n* computes the integer quotient of *x* divided by *n*.

We can also define a function *trans*, which transposes pitches (analogous to *Trans*, which transposes values of type *Music*):

$$trans \quad :: \quad Int \rightarrow Pitch \rightarrow Pitch$$
$$trans\ i\ p \ = \ pitch\ (absPitch\ p + i)$$

Finally, for convenience, let's create simple names for familiar notes, durations, and rests, as shown in Fig. 20.2. Despite the large number of them, these names are sufficiently arcane that name clashes are unlikely.

---

**Exercise 20.1** Prove that *abspitch . pitch = id*, and, up to enharmonic equivalences, *pitch . abspitch = id*.

---

> $cf, c, cs, df, d, ds, ef, e, es, ff, f, fs, gf, g, gs, af, a, as, bf, b, bs$
> $\quad :: \quad Octave \rightarrow Dur \rightarrow Music$
>
> $cf\ o \ = \ Note\ (Cf, o);\ c\ o = Note\ (C, o);\ cs\ o = Note\ (Cs, o)$
> $df\ o \ = \ Note\ (Df, o);\ d\ o = Note\ (D, o);\ ds\ o = Note\ (Ds, o)$
> $ef\ o \ = \ Note\ (Ef, o);\ e\ o = Note\ (E, o);\ es\ o = Note\ (Es, o)$
> $ff\ o \ = \ Note\ (Ff, o);\ f\ o = Note\ (F, o);\ fs\ o = Note\ (Fs, o)$
> $gf\ o \ = \ Note\ (Gf, o);\ g\ o = Note\ (G, o);\ gs\ o = Note\ (Gs, o)$
> $af\ o \ = \ Note\ (Af, o);\ a\ o = Note\ (A, o);\ as\ o = Note\ (As, o)$
> $bf\ o \ = \ Note\ (Bf, o);\ b\ o = Note\ (B, o);\ bs\ o = Note\ (Bs, o)$
>
> $wn,\ hn,\ qn,\ en,\ sn,\ tn \qquad\qquad :: \quad Dur$
> $dhn,\ dqn,\ den,\ dsn \qquad\qquad\ :: \quad Dur$
>
> $wnr,\ hnr,\ qnr,\ enr,\ snr,\ tnr\ \ :: \quad Music$
> $dhnr,\ dqnr,\ denr,\ dsnr \qquad :: \quad Music$
>
> $wn \ = \ 1;\ wnr = Rest\ wn \qquad -\!-$ whole
> $hn \ = \ 1\%2;\ hnr = Rest\ hn \qquad -\!-$ half
> $qn \ = \ 1\%4;\ qnr = Rest\ qn \qquad -\!-$ quarter
> $en \ = \ 1\%8;\ enr = Rest\ en \qquad -\!-$ eight
> $sn \ = \ 1\%16;\ snr = Rest\ sn \qquad -\!-$ sixteenth
> $tn \ = \ 1\%32;\ tnr = Rest\ tn \qquad -\!-$ thirty-second
>
> $dhn \ = \ 3\%4;\ dhnr = Rest\ dhn \qquad -\!-$ dotted half
> $dqn \ = \ 3\%8;\ dqnr = Rest\ dqn \qquad -\!-$ dotted quarter
> $den \ = \ 3\%16;\ denr = Rest\ den \qquad -\!-$ dotted eighth
> $dsn \ = \ 3\%32;\ dsnr = Rest\ dsn \qquad -\!-$ dotted sixteenth

Figure 20.2: Convenient Note Names and Pitch Conversion Functions

---

**Exercise 20.2**    Prove that *trans i* (*trans j p*) = *trans* (*i* + *j*) *p*.

## 20.2 Higher-Level Constructions

With this modest beginning, we can already express quite a few musical relationships in MDL simply and effectively.

### 20.2.1 Lines and Chords

Two common ideas in music are the construction of notes in a horizontal fashion (a *line* or *melody*), and in a vertical fashion (a *chord*):

> *line, chord*  ::  [*Music*] → *Music*
> *line*      =  *foldr* (:+:) (*Rest* 0)
> *chord*     =  *foldr* (:=:) (*Rest* 0)

For example, from the notes in the C major triad in register 4, I can construct a C major arpeggio and chord as well:

> *cMaj*     =  [*n* 4 *qn* | *n* ← [*c*, *e*, *g*]]
>
> *cMajArp*  =  *line cMaj*
> *cMajChd*  =  *chord cMaj*

### 20.2.2 Delay and Repeat

Suppose that we wish to describe a melody *m* accompanied by an identical voice a perfect 5th higher. We can write this very simply as "*m* :=: *Trans* 7 *m*" (seven semitones is a perfect fifth). Similarly, a canon-like structure involving *m* can be expressed as
"*m* :=: *delay d m*," where:

> *delay*      ::  *Dur* → *Music* → *Music*
> *delay d m*  =  *Rest d* :+: *m*

Of course, Haskell's nonstrict semantics also allows us to define infinite musical structures. For example, a musical structure may be repeated *ad nauseum* using this simple function:

> *repeatM*     ::  *Music* → *Music*
> *repeatM m*   =  *m* :+: *repeatM m*

Thus, an infinite ostinato can be expressed in this way, and then used in different contexts that extract only the portion that's actually needed. This will be explained in more detail later.

### 20.2.3 Polyrhythms

For some rhythmical ideas, consider first a simple *triplet* of eighth notes; it can be expressed as "*Tempo* (3%2) *m*," where *m* is a line of three eighth notes. In fact *Tempo* can be used to create quite complex rhythmical patterns. For example, consider the "nested polyrhythms" shown in Fig. 20.3. They can be expressed quite naturally as follows (note the use of the *where* clause in *pr*2 to capture recurring phrases):

$$
\begin{aligned}
&pr1,\ pr2 \ ::\ Pitch \to Music\\
&pr1\ p \quad = \quad Tempo\ (5\%6)\\
&\qquad\qquad\qquad (Tempo\ (4\%3)\ (mkLn\ 1\ p\ qn :\!+\!:\\
&\qquad\qquad\qquad\qquad\qquad Tempo\ (3\%2)\ (mkLn\ 3\ p\ en :\!+\!:\\
&\qquad\qquad\qquad\qquad\qquad\qquad\qquad mkLn\ 2\ p\ sn :\!+\!:\\
&\qquad\qquad\qquad\qquad\qquad\qquad\qquad mkLn\ 1\ p\ qn) :\!+\!:\\
&\qquad\qquad\qquad\qquad mkLn\ 1\ p\ qn) :\!+\!:\\
&\qquad\qquad\qquad Tempo\ (3\%2)\ (mkLn\ 6\ p\ en))\\
\\
&pr2\ p \quad = \quad Tempo\ (7\%6)\\
&\qquad\qquad\qquad (m1 :\!+\!:\\
&\qquad\qquad\qquad Tempo\ (5\%4)\ (mkLn\ 5\ p\ en) :\!+\!:\\
&\qquad\qquad\qquad m1 :\!+\!:\\
&\qquad\qquad\qquad Tempo\ (3\%2)\ m2)\\
&\mathbf{where}\ m1\ =\ Tempo\ (5\%4)\ (Tempo\ (3\%2)\ m2 :\!+\!:\ m2)\\
&\qquad\quad\ m2\ =\ mkLn\ 3\ p\ en\\
\\
&mkLn\ n\ p\ d\ =\ line\ (take\ n\ (repeat\ (Note\ p\ d)))
\end{aligned}
$$

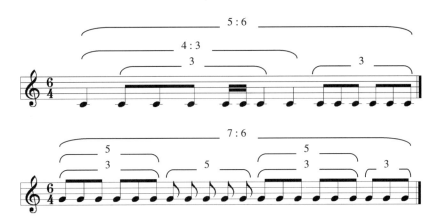

Figure 20.3: Nested Polyrhythms (top: *pr*1; bottom: *pr*2)

Note that *pr*1 and *pr*2 have the same duration: one and one-half beats. (If this is not very obvious, then wait till the function *dur*, which computes the duration of *Music* values, is defined below.) To play these polyrhythms in parallel using middle C and middle G, respectively, we could do the following (middle C is in the 5th octave):

> *pr*12 :: *Music*
> *pr*12 = *pr*1 (*C*, 5) :=: *pr*2 (*G*, 5)

### 20.2.4 Determining Duration

It is sometimes desirable to compute the duration in beats of a musical structure; we can do so as follows:

> *dur* :: *Music* → *Dur*
>
> *dur* (*Note* _ *d*) = *d*
> *dur* (*Rest d*) = *d*
> *dur* (*m*1 :+: *m*2) = *dur m*1 + *dur m*2
> *dur* (*m*1 :=: *m*2) = *dur m*1 'max' *dur m*2
> *dur* (*Tempo a m*) = *dur m*/*a*
> *dur* (*Trans* _ *m*) = *dur m*
> *dur* (*Instr* _ *m*) = *dur m*

For example, *dur pr*12 is 3%2 (i.e., one and one-half beats).

### 20.2.5 Reversing Musical Structure

Using *dur* we can define a function *revM* that reverses any *Music* value. This is straightforward for most *Music* values:

> *revM* :: *Music* → *Music*
>
> *revM n*@(*Note* _ _) = *n*
> *revM r*@(*Rest* _) = *r*
> *revM* (*Tempo a m*) = *Tempo a* (*revM m*)
> *revM* (*Trans i m*) = *Trans i* (*revM m*)
> *revM* (*Instr i m*) = *Instr i* (*revM m*)
> *revM* (*m*1 :+: *m*2) = *revM m*2 :+: *revM m*1

but the treatment of (:=:) is tricky. The problem is that it is not symmetrical with respect to time. Even if *m*1 and *m*2 are *single notes*, if they have different durations, then the reverse of *m*1 :=: *m*2 is not *m*1 :=: *m*2; rather, assuming that *dur m*1 = *d*1 >= *d*2 = *dur m*2, it is

$m1 :=: (Rest\ (d1 - d2) :+: m2)$. With this observation, you can see that the general case is:

$$revM\ (m1 :=: m2)$$
$$= \textbf{let}\ d1\ =\ dur\ m1$$
$$d2\ =\ dur\ m2$$
$$\textbf{in if}\ d1 > d2\ \textbf{then}\ revM\ m1 :=: (Rest\ (d1 - d2) :+: revM\ m2)$$
$$\textbf{else}\ (Rest\ (d2 - d1) :+: revM\ m1) :=: revM\ m2$$

### 20.2.6 Truncating Parallel Composition

Note that the duration of $m1 :=: m2$ is the maximum of the durations of $m1$ and $m2$, and thus if one is infinite, so is the result. Sometimes we would rather have the result be of duration equal to the shorter of the two. This is not as easy as it sounds, because it may require interrupting the longer one in the middle of a note (or notes).

I will define a "truncating parallel composition" operator ($/=$), but first I will define an auxiliary function *cut* such that *cut d m* is the musical structure *m* "cut short" to have at most duration *d*:

```
cut                  ::  Dur → Music → Music
cut d m | d <= 0     =  Rest 0
cut d (Note x d0)    =  Note x (min d0 d)
cut d (Rest d0)      =  Rest (min d0 d)
cut d (m1 :=: m2)    =  cut d m1 :=: cut d m2
cut d (Tempo a m)    =  Tempo a (cut (d * a) m)
cut d (Trans a m)    =  Trans a (cut d m)
cut d (Instr a m)    =  Instr a (cut d m)
cut d (m1 :+: m2)    =  let m1'  =  cut d m1
                            m2'  =  cut (d - dur m1') m2
                        in m1' :+: m2'
```

Note that *cut* is equipped to handle a *Music* value of infinite length. With *cut*, the definition of ($/=:$) is now straightforward:

```
(/=:)        ::  Music → Music → Music
m1 /=: m2    =  cut (min (dur m1) (dur m2)) (m1 :=: m2)
```

Unfortunately, whereas *cut* can handle infinite-duration music values, ($/=:$) cannot, because computing the minimum of the two durations will not terminate as written above.

---

**Exercise 20.3** Define a version of ($/=:$) that shortens correctly when either one of its arguments is infinite in duration (but not both). (Hint: First define a function *minDur* that returns the minimum duration of two

*Music* values, even if one is infinite.) Harder: Define a version that works properly even when both arguments are infinite.

---

**Exercise 20.4** Prove that *dur* (*cut d m*) $<= d$, for all $d >= 0$.

### 20.2.7 Trills

A *trill* is an ornament that alternates rapidly between two (usually adjacent) pitches. The *Music* value *trill i d n* will be a trill beginning on the pitch of note *n*, with the alternate note being *i* semitones away, and with each trill note having duration *d*. The total duration of *trill i d n* should be the same as the duration of *n*.

*trill* :: *Int → Dur → Music → Music*

*trill i d n@*(*Note p nd*)
$$= \textbf{if } d >= nd \textbf{ then } n$$
$$\textbf{else } Note\ p\ d$$
$$\qquad :+: trill\ (negate\ i)\ d$$
$$\qquad\qquad (Note\ (trans\ i\ p)\ (nd - d))$$

*trill i d* (*Tempo a m*) = *Tempo a* (*trill i* (*d * a*) *m*)
*trill i d* (*Trans a m*) = *Trans a* (*trill i d m*)
*trill i d* (*Instr a m*) = *Instr a* (*trill i d m*)
*trill* _ _ _ = *error* "Trill input must be a single note"

It is simple to define a version of this function that starts on the alternate note rather than the start note:

*trill'* :: *Int → Dur → Music → Music*
*trill' i sDur m* = *trill* (*negate i*) *sDur* (*Trans i m*)

It is also convenient to define a function *roll* that generates a trill whose interval is zero. This feature is particularly useful for percussion.

*roll* :: *Dur → Music → Music*
*roll dur m* = *trill* 0 *dur m*

---

**Exercise 20.5** Define a function *trilln* :: *Int → Int → Music → Music* that is just like *trill* except that its second argument is the number of trill notes to be generated, rather than the duration of a single trill note. Also define: (a) *trilln'*, which is to *trilln* as *trill'* is to *trill*, and (b) *rolln*, which is to *roll* as *trilln* is to *trill*.

Here is a simple example of the use of *trill* and *trilln* in expressing the opening flute line in John Philip Sousa's *Stars and Stripes Forever*:

$$ssfMelody \;=\; m1 \;\text{:+:}\; m2 \;\text{:+:}\; m3 \;\text{:+:}\; m4$$

$$m1 \quad=\; trilln\;2\;5\;(bf\;6\;en)\;\text{:+:}$$
$$\qquad\qquad line\;[ef\;7\;en,\;ef\;6\;en,\;ef\;7\;en]$$

$$m2 \quad=\; line\;[bf\;6\;sn,\;c\;7\;sn,\;bf\;6\;sn,\;g\;6\;sn,\;ef\;6\;en,\;bf\;5\;en]$$

$$m3 \quad=\; line\;[ef\;6\;sn,\;f\;6\;sn,\;g\;6\;sn,\;af\;6\;sn,\;bf\;6\;en,\;ef\;7\;en]$$

$$m4 \quad=\; trill\;2\;tn\;(bf\;6\;qn)\;\text{:+:}\;bf\;6\;sn\;\text{:+:}\;denr$$

$$ssf \quad=\; Instr\;Flute\;(Tempo\;2\;(ssfMelody))$$

---

**Exercise 20.6**  Prove that $dur\;(trill\;i\;d\;n) = dur\;n$.

### 20.2.8  Percussion

Speaking of percussion, how do we express that in the MDL framework? Percussion is a difficult notion to represent in the abstract, because, in a way, a percussion instrument is just another instrument, so why should it be treated differently? On the other hand, even common practice notation treats it specially, even though it has much in common with nonpercussion notation. The MIDI standard is equally ambiguous about the treatment of percussion. On one hand, percussion sounds are chosen by specifying an octave and pitch, just like any other instrument. On the other hand, these notes have no tonal meaning whatsoever; they are just a convenient way to select from a large number of percussion sounds. Indeed, part of the General MIDI Standard is a set of names for commonly used percussion sounds.

Because MIDI is such a popular platform, we can at least define some handy functions for using the General MIDI Standard. We start by defining the data type shown in Fig. 20.4, which borrows its constructor names from the General MIDI standard. The comments reflecting the "MIDI Key" numbers will be explained later, but basically a MIDI Key is the equivalent of an absolute pitch in our terminology. So all we need is a way to convert these percussion sound names into a *Music* value (i.e., a *Note*):

$$perc \quad\text{::}\quad PercussionSound \rightarrow Dur \rightarrow Music$$
$$perc\;ps \;=\; Note\;(pitch\;(fromEnum\;ps + 35))$$

> **DETAILS**
> Recall that *fromEnum* is a method in the *Enum* class, and has type $(Ord\;a,\;Enum\;a) \Rightarrow a \rightarrow Int$ (see Chapter 24).

Because *PercussionSound* is a (derived) instance of *Enum*, *fromEnum* $ps$ returns $(n - 1)$ if percussion sound $ps$ is the $n$th constructor in the

```
data PercussionSound
   =   AcousticBassDrum      -- MIDI Key 35
   |   BassDrum1       -- MIDI Key 36
   |   SideStick    -- ...
   |   AcousticSnare | HandClap | ElectricSnare | LowFloorTom
   |   ClosedHiHat | HighFloorTom | PedalHiHat | LowTom
   |   OpenHiHat | LowMidTom | HiMidTom | CrashCymbal1
   |   HighTom | RideCymbal1 | ChineseCymbal | RideBell
   |   Tambourine | SplashCymbal | Cowbell | CrashCymbal2
   |   Vibraslap | RideCymbal2 | HiBongo | LowBongo
   |   MuteHiConga | OpenHiConga | LowConga | HighTimbale
   |   LowTimbale | HighAgogo | LowAgogo | Cabasa
   |   Maracas | ShortWhistle | LongWhistle | ShortGuiro
   |   LongGuiro | Claves | HiWoodBlock | LowWoodBlock
   |   MuteCuica | OpenCuica | MuteTriangle
   |   OpenTriangle      -- MIDI Key 82
       deriving (Show, Eq, Ord, Ix, Enum)
```

Figure 20.4: General MIDI Percussion Names

*PercussionSound* data type. Adding 35 to this yields the correct absolute pitch for this sound according to the General MIDI standard, and converting this into a pitch allows us to use the *Note* constructor.

For example, here are eight bars of a simple rock or "funk groove" that uses *perc* and *roll*:

```
funkGroove
   = let p1  =  perc LowTom qn
         p2  =  perc AcousticSnare en
     in Tempo 3 (Instr Percussion (cut 8 (repeatM
         ((p1 :+: qnr :+: p2 :+: qnr :+: p2 :+:
           p1 :+: p1 :+: qnr :+: p2 :+: enr)
          :=: roll en (perc ClosedHiHat 2))
     )))
```

**Exercise 20.7** Find a simple piece of music written by your favorite composer, and transcribe it into Haskell. In doing so, look for repeating patterns, transposed phrases, and so on, and reflect this in your code, thus revealing deeper structural aspects of the music than that found in common practice notation.

**Exercise 20.8** If you are familiar with the terms, define Haskell functions *invert*, *retro*, *retroInvert*, and *invertRetro* to implement the concepts of inversion, retrograde, retrograde inversion, and inverted retrograde, respectively, as used in twelve-tone music theory. You may assume that the input to these functions is created by an application of *line* above. Prove that "*retro . retro*," "*invert . invert*," and "*retroInvert . invertRetro*" are the identity function on values created by *line*.

---

**Exercise 20.9** A shortcoming of our current design of musical values is that there is no representation of *dynamics* (i.e., loudness, or volume). There are several ways we could deal with this; the most straightforward is to add a constructor to the *Music* data type that expressed volume. Explore some designs for this, including direct numerical representation of the volume, as well as more traditional notations such as *pianissimo*, *piano*, *mezzo piano*, *mezzo forte*, *forte*, and *fortissimo* (often abbreviated *pp*, *p*, *mp*, *mf*, *f*, and *ff*, respectively, and for which a Haskell data type could easily be defined).

Other notions of dynamics include *legato*, *staccato*, *slurring*, *crescendo*, and *diminuendo*. In addition, with respect to tempo, there are notions of *ritardando* and *accelerando*. If these notions are simply captured in the *Music* data type, then the most interesting aspect will be their *interpretation* in Chapter 22.

---

**Exercise 20.10** Define a data type *Mode* that enumerates the seven scale modes: ionian, dorian, phrygian, lydian, mixolydian, aeolian, and locrian. Then define a function *scale* that, given a mode and tonic (a start note), generates a scale in that mode starting on the tonic.

## 20.3 A Couple of Final Examples

In this section I will briefly explore two ideas for "algorithmic composition": the idea of writing fairly concise expressions that yield interesting (hopefully) music.

### 20.3.1 Cascades

Here is a function that recursively applies transformations $f$ (to elements in a sequence) and $g$ (to accumulated phrases) a total of $n$ times, playing everything in unison:

$$
\begin{aligned}
rep \quad &:: \quad (Music \rightarrow Music) \rightarrow (Music \rightarrow Music) \rightarrow Int \rightarrow Music \\
&\quad\quad \rightarrow Music \\
rep\ f\ g\ 0\ m \quad &= \quad Rest\ 0 \\
rep\ f\ g\ n\ m \quad &= \quad m :=: g\ (rep\ f\ g\ (n-1)\ (f\ m))
\end{aligned}
$$

For example, here is a rising arpeggio of perfect fourths beginning on middle C:

    *run* = *rep* (*Trans* 5) (*delay tn*) 8 (*c* 4 *tn*)

Now suppose we use this entire phrase as an argument to *rep*, transposing it a major third each time, and delaying each phrase by an eighth note:

    *cascade* = *rep* (*Trans* 4) (*delay en*) 8 *run*

Let's do this again, only repeating the phrase once, a few beats later:

    *cascades* = *rep id* (*delay sn*) 2 *cascade*

The result is a "cascade" of sound that has some interesting properties. All of this was generated from a single starting note. We can create a final result, a cascade palindrome that I call a "waterfall," played using a vibraphone as follows:

    *waterfall* = *Instr Vibraphone* (*cascades* :+: *revM cascades*)

---

**Exercise 20.11** Experiment with this idea futher, using other fragments to start the process, and other transformations.

## 20.3.2  Self-Similar (Fractal) Music

Fractal images were discussed briefly in Chapter 3. But what does it mean to have fractal *music*? There are actually several notions of what fractal music might be. My notion is as follows. Start with a very simple melody of *n* notes. Now duplicate this melody *n* times, playing each in succession, but first performing the following transformation: the *i*th melody is transposed by an amount proportional to the pitch of the *i*th note in the original melody, and is shifted in tempo by a factor proportional to the duration of the *i*th note. For example, Fig. 20.5 shows the result of

Figure 20.5: An Example of Self-Similar Music

applying this process once to a four-note melody. Now imagine that this process is repeated infinitely often, yielding an infinitely dense melody of infinitesimally shorter notes! To make the result playable, however, we will stop the process at some predetermined level.

How can this be represented in Haskell? A *tree* seems to be the logical choice, which I will call a *Cluster*:

> **data** *Cluster* = *Cluster SNote* [*Cluster*]
> **type** *SNote* = (*AbsPitch, Dur*)

This particular kind of tree happens to be called a *rose tree*. An *SNote* is just a "simple note."

The sequence of *SNotes* at each level of the cluster is the melodic fragment for that level. The very top cluster will contain a "dummy" note, the next level will contain the original melody, the next level will contain one iteration of the process described earlier (e.g., the melody in Fig. 20.5), and so forth.

To achieve this, I will define a function *selfSim*, which takes the initial melody as argument and generates an infinitely deep cluster:

> *selfSim* :: [*SNote*] → *Cluster*
> *selfSim pat* = *Cluster* (0, 0) (*map mkCluster pat*)
>     **where** *mkCluster note*
>         = *Cluster note* (*map* (*mkCluster . addmult note*) *pat*)
>
> *addmult* (*p0, d0*) (*p1, d1*) = (*p0 + p1, d0 ∗ d1*)

Note that *selfSim* itself is not recursive, but *mkCluster* is.

Next, I define a function to skim off the notes at the *n*th level, or *n*th "fringe," of a cluster:

> *fringe* :: *Int* → *Cluster* → [*SNote*]
> *fringe* 0 (*Cluster note cls*) = [*note*]
> *fringe n* (*Cluster note cls*) = *concat* (*map* (*fringe* (*n* − 1)) *cls*)

---

**DETAILS**
Recall that *concat* appends together a list of lists. It is defined in the Standard Prelude as:

> *concat* :: [[*a*]] → [*a*]
> *concat xss* = *foldr* (++) [ ] *xss*

All that is left to do is convert this into a *Music* value that we can convert to MIDI:

$$simToHask \quad :: \quad [SNote] \rightarrow Music$$
$$simToHask \; ss \quad = \quad \textbf{let} \; mkNote \; (p, d) \; = \; Note \; (pitch \; p) \; d$$
$$\textbf{in} \; line \; (map \; mkNote \; ss)$$

Putting it all together, below is a small composition whose seed is the four-note melody:

$$pat \;\; :: \;\; [SNote]$$
$$pat \;\; = \;\; [(3, 0.5), (4, 0.25), (0, 0.25), (6, 1.0)]$$

Note that the flute line and acoustic bass line are the reverse of one another. The result is rather interesting:

$$main$$
$$= \; \textbf{let} \; s \; = \; Trans \; 60$$
$$(Tempo \; 2$$
$$(simToHask \; (fringe \; 3 \; (selfSim \; pat))))$$
$$\textbf{in} \; Instr \; Flute \; s$$
$$:=: Instr \; AcousticBass \; (Trans \; (-24) \; (revM \; s))$$

---

**Exercise 20.12** Experiment with this idea futher, using other melodic seeds, exploring different depths of the clusters, and so on.

---

**Exercise 20.13** The function *fringe* is not very efficient, for the following reason: The function *concat* is defined as *foldr* (++) [ ], which means that it takes a number of steps proportional to the sum of the lengths of the lists being concatenated. We cannot do any better than this. (If *foldl* were used instead, the number of steps would be proportional to the number of lists times their average length.)

The problem is, *concat* is being used over and over again, like this:

$$concat \; [concat \; [\ldots], \; concat \; [\ldots], \; concat \; [\ldots]]$$

This causes a number of steps proportional to the depth of the tree times the length of the sublists; clearly not optimal.

Define a version of *fringe* that is linear in the total length of the final list.

# CHAPTER TWENTY-ONE

# Interpreting Functional Music

In Chapter 20 I defined a language called MDL for describing musical *structures*. The question now is, how do we actually *interpret* the structures; that is, how do we turn them into real music? (This is analogous to the question of how to draw a *Shape* or *Region* value in a graphics window.) The approach I will take will be to convert a *Music* value into a *Standard MIDI File*, which can then be played on your computer using any standard media player. I will do this, however, in three steps:

1. First I will convert a *Music* value into a value of type *Performance*, which is an abstract notion of what the music *means*.
2. Then I will convert this into a value of type *MidiFile*, a data type imported from the *Haskore* library,[1] which represents the structure of a Standard MIDI File.
3. Finally, I will use the *outputMidiFile* function, also imported from the *Haskore* library, to write this *MidiFile* value to an actual file.

Dividing the problem into separate steps like this allows us to separate two concerns: interpreting *Music* values as music, and the details of rendering that music as a MIDI file. It also facilitates readability by having a cleaner structuring of the code, aids debugging by allowing us to look at each intermediate result, and makes it easier to later add an interface to some computer music platform other than MIDI (there are several).

In this chapter I will describe only the first step above; steps two and three are described in the next (Chapter 22). Also in this chapter I will discuss how the abstract notion of a performance can be used to uncover

---

[1] See the Preface for instructions on how to obtain this module if it is not installed on your Haskell system.

*algebraic properties* of musical structures.

**module** *Perform* **where**

**import** *Music*

## 21.1  Interpreting Music: A *Performance*

Our first goal is to interpret a *Music* value as an abstract *performance*, which is a temporally ordered sequence of musical *events*:

**type** *Performance*  =  [*Event*]

**data** *Event*      =  *Event* {*eTime* :: *Time*, *eInst* :: *IName*,
                     *ePitch* :: *AbsPitch*, *eDur* :: *DurT*}
  **deriving** (*Eq*, *Ord*, *Show*)

**type** *Time*      = *Float*
**type** *DurT*      = *Float*

An event *Event s i p d* captures the fact that at start time *s* instrument *i* sounds pitch *p* for a duration *d* (where now duration and time is measured in seconds, rather than beats).

To generate a complete performance of (i.e., give an interpretation to) a musical structure expressed in MDL, we must know the time to begin the performance, the default instrument to use, and the proper key and tempo. We can thus model a "performer" as a function *perform*, which uses all of this information (called the *context*) to translate a musical structure into a performance. It can also be thought of as an interpeter for an MDL program:

*perform*  ::  *Context* → *Music* → *Performance*

**data** *Context*  =  *Context* {*cTime* :: *Time*, *cInst* :: *IName*,
                     *cDur* :: *DurT*, *cKey* :: *Key*}
  **deriving** *Show*

**type** *Key*      = *AbsPitch*

The *cDur* :: *DurT* component of the context is the duration, in seconds, of one whole note. To make it easier to compute this, we can define a "metronome" function that, given a standard metronome marking (in beats per minute) and the note type associated with one beat (quarter note, eighth note, and so forth), generates the duration of one whole note:

$$metro \qquad :: \quad Float \to Dur \to DurT$$
$$metro\ setting\ dur \quad = \quad 60/(setting * ratioToFloat\ dur)$$

For example, *metro* 96 *qn* creates a tempo of 96 quarter notes per minute.

The function *metro* uses the following coercion function, which will also be used several times later:

$$ratioToFloat \quad :: \ Ratio\ Int \to Float$$
$$ratioToFloat\ r\ =\ intToFloat\,(numerator\ r)/intToFloat\,(denominator\ r)$$

$$intToFloat \quad :: \ Int \to Float$$
$$intToFloat \quad = \ fromInteger\,.\,toInteger$$

---

**DETAILS**

*numerator* and *denominator* extract the numerator and denominator, respectively, from a *Ratio* value.

---

The definition of *perform* is relatively straightforward, so I will present it all at once:

```
perform c@(Context t i dt k) m  =
  case m of
    Note p d     →  let d' = ratioToFloat d * dt
                    in [Event t i (transpose p k i) d']
    Rest d       →  [ ]
    m1 :+: m2    →  perform c m1 ++
                    perform
                          (c{cTime = t + ratioToFloat(dur m1) * dt}) m2
    m1 :=: m2    →  merge (perform c m1) (perform c m2)
    Tempo a m    →  perform (c {cDur = dt/ratioToFloat a}) m
    Trans p m    →  perform (c {cKey = k + p}) m
    Instr nm m   →  perform (c {cInst = nm}) m
  where transpose p k Percussion  =  absPitch p
        transpose p k _           =  absPitch p + k
```

A single note is translated into a single-event performance. Note that the pitch is transposed to correspond to the key, with one catch: No transposition is done to *Percussion*, because the note corresponds to the actual percussion instrument. A rest translates into an empty performance. Note how the *Context* is used as the running "state" of the

$$
\begin{array}{lll}
perform & :: & Context \rightarrow Music \rightarrow Performance \\
perform\ c\ m & = & fst\ (perf\ c\ m)
\end{array}
$$

$$
\begin{array}{lll}
perf & :: & Context \rightarrow Music \rightarrow (Performance,\ DurT)
\end{array}
$$

$perf\ c@(Context\ t\ i\ dt\ k)\ m\ =$
  **case** $m$ **of**

| | | |
|---|---|---|
| *Note p d* | $\rightarrow$ | **let** $d' = ratioToFloat\ d * dt$ |
| | | **in** $([Event\ t\ i\ (transpose\ p\ k\ i)\ d'],\ d')$ |
| *Rest d* | $\rightarrow$ | $([\,],\ ratioToFloat\ d * dt)$ |
| $m1 :+: m2$ | $\rightarrow$ | **let** $(pf1, d1) = perf\ c\ m1$ |
| | | $\quad\ (pf2, d2) = perf\ (c\ \{cTime = t + d1\})\ m2$ |
| | | **in** $(pf1 \mathbin{+\!\!+} pf2,\ d1 + d2)$ |
| $m1 :=: m2$ | $\rightarrow$ | **let** $(pf1, d1) = perf\ c\ m1$ |
| | | $\quad\ (pf2, d2) = perf\ c\ m2$ |
| | | **in** $(merge\ pf1\ pf2,\ max\ d1\ d2)$ |
| *Tempo a m* | $\rightarrow$ | $perf\ (c\ \{cDur = dt/ratioToFloat\ a\})\ m$ |
| *Trans p m* | $\rightarrow$ | $perf\ (c\ \{cKey = k + p\})\ m$ |
| *Instr nm m* | $\rightarrow$ | $perf\ (c\ \{cInst = nm\})\ m$ |

  **where** $transpose\ p\ k\ Percussion = absPitch\ p$
            $transpose\ p\ k\ \_\quad\quad\quad = absPitch\ p + k$

Figure 21.1: An Efficient *perform* Function

performance, and gets updated in several different ways. For example, the interpretation of the *Tempo* constructor involves scaling $dt$ appropriately and updating the *cDur* field of the context.

In the treatment of (:+:), note that the subsequences are appended together, with the start time of the second argument delayed by the duration of the first. The function *dur* (defined in Section 20.2) is used to compute this duration. Unfortunately, this strategy generates a number of steps proportional to the square of the size of the *Music* value. A more efficient solution is to have *perform* compute the duration directly, returning it as part of its result. This version of *perform* is shown in Fig. 21.1.

In contrast, the subsequences derived from the arguments to (:=:) are merged into a time-ordered stream. The definition of *merge* is:

$$
merge\ ::\ Performance \rightarrow Performance \rightarrow Performance
$$

$merge\ a@(e1 : es1)\ b@(e2 : es2)\ =$
  **if** $e1 < e2$ **then** $e1 : merge\ es1\ b$
            **else** $e2 : merge\ a\ es2$

| | | |
|---|---|---|
| $merge\ [\,]\ es2$ | $=$ | $es2$ |
| $merge\ es1\ [\,]$ | $=$ | $es1$ |

Note that *merge* compares entire events rather than just start times. This is to ensure that it is commutative, a desirable condition for some of the proofs used in Section 21.2. Here is a more efficient version that will work just as well in practice:

$$
\begin{aligned}
&\textit{merge } a@(e1 : es1) \; b@(e2 : es2) \; = \\
&\quad \textbf{if } eTime \; e1 < eTime \; e2 \; \textbf{then } e1 : merge \; es1 \; b \\
&\quad\quad\quad\quad\quad\quad\quad\quad\quad\quad \textbf{else } e2 : merge \; a \; es2
\end{aligned}
$$

$$
\begin{aligned}
&\textit{merge } [\,] \; es2 \quad\quad\quad\quad\quad\quad = \; es2 \\
&\textit{merge } es1 \; [\,] \quad\quad\quad\quad\quad\quad = \; es1
\end{aligned}
$$

---

**Exercise 21.1**   Prove that the two versions of *perform* are equivalent.

## 21.2   An Algebra of Music

A *literal performance* is a performance in which no aesthetic interpretation is given to a musical object. The function *perform* in fact yields a literal performance for an MDL program.

There are many musical objects whose literal performances we expect to be *equivalent*. For example, the following two musical objects are certainly not equal as data structures, but we would expect their literal performances to be identical:

$$
\begin{aligned}
&(m1 \; \mathbin{:\!+\!:} \; m2) \; \mathbin{:\!+\!:} \; m3 \\
&m1 \; \mathbin{:\!+\!:} \; (m2 \; \mathbin{:\!+\!:} \; m3)
\end{aligned}
$$

Thus, I will define a formal notion of equivalence:

---

**Definition**   Two musical objects $m1$ and $m2$ are *equivalent*, written $m1 \; \equiv \; m2$, if and only if:

$$(\forall c) \; perform \; c \; m1 \; \Rightarrow \; perform \; c \; m2$$

(Note the similarity of this to the notion of equivalence of regions defined in Chapter 8.)

One of the most useful things we can do with this notion of equivalence is establish the validity of certain *transformations* on musical objects. A transformation is *valid* if the result of the transformation is equivalent (in the sense defined above) to the original musical object (i.e., it is "meaning preserving").

The most basic of these transformations we treat as *axioms* in an *algebra of music*. For example:

**Axiom 1**   For any $r1$, $r2$, and $m$:

$$Tempo \; r1 \; (Tempo \; r2 \; m) \; \equiv \; Tempo \; (r1 * r2) \; m$$

We can prove this axiom by calculation. For clarity I will simplify the context to just $dt$, the tempo duration, and will write $rtf$ as shorthand for $ratioToFloat$:

$perform \; dt \; (Tempo \; r1 \; (Tempo \; r2 \; m))$
 $\Rightarrow$  { unfold $perform$ }
$perform \; (dt/rtf \; r1) \; (Tempo \; r2 \; m)$
 $\Rightarrow$  { unfold $perform$ }
$perform \; ((dt/rtf \; r1)/(rtf \; r2)) \; m$
 $\Rightarrow$  { arithmetic }
$perform \; (dt/((rtf \; r1) * (rtf \; r2))) \; m$
 $\Rightarrow$  { lemma for $ratioToFLoat$ }
$perform \; (dt/(rtf \; (r1 * r2))) \; m$
 $\Rightarrow$  { fold $perform$ }
$perform \; dt \; (Tempo \; (r1 * r2) \; m)$

Here is another useful transformation and its validity proof (for clarity I will simplify the context to just $(t, dt)$, the start time and tempo):

**Axiom 2**   For any $r$, $m1$, and $m2$:

$$Tempo \; r \; (m1 \; {:\!+\!:} \; m2) \; \equiv \; Tempo \; r \; m1 \; {:\!+\!:} \; Tempo \; r \; m2$$

In other words, *tempo scaling distributes over sequential composition.*

**Proof:**

$perform \; (t, dt) \; (Tempo \; r \; (m1 \; {:\!+\!:} \; m2))$
 $\Rightarrow$  { unfold $perform$ }
$perform \; (t, dt/rtf \; r) \; (m1 \; {:\!+\!:} \; m2)$
 $\Rightarrow$  { unfold $perform$ }
$perform \; (t, dt/rtf \; r) \; m1 \; {+\!\!+} \; perform \; (t1, dt/rtf \; r) \; m2$
 $\Rightarrow$  { fold $perform$ }
$perform \; (t, dt) \; (Tempo \; r \; m1) \; {+\!\!+} \; perform \; (t1, dt) \; (Tempo \; r \; m2)$
 $\Rightarrow$  { arithmetic }
$perform \; (t, dt) \; (Tempo \; r \; m1) \; {+\!\!+} \; perform \; (t2, dt) \; (Tempo \; r \; m2)$
 $\Rightarrow$  { fold $dur$ }
$perform \; (t, dt) \; (Tempo \; r \; m1) \; {+\!\!+} \; perform \; (t3, dt) \; (Tempo \; r \; m2)$
 $\Rightarrow$  { fold $perform$ }

$$perform\ (t,\ dt)\ (Tempo\ r\ m1\ \mathbin{:\!+\!:}\ Tempo\ r\ m2)$$
$$\textbf{where}\ t1\ =\ t + rtf\ (dur\ m1) * (dt/rtf\ r)$$
$$t2\ =\ t + rtf\ (dur\ m1/r) * dt$$
$$t3\ =\ t + rtf\ (dur\ (Tempo\ r\ m1)) * dt$$

An even simpler axiom is given by:

---

**Axiom 3**  For any $m$:

$$Tempo\ 1\ m\ \equiv\ m$$

In other words, *unit tempo scaling is the identity function for type Music.*

**Proof:**

$$perform\ (t,\ dt)\ (Tempo\ 1\ m)$$
$$\Rightarrow\ \{\ \text{unfold } perform\ \}$$
$$perform\ (t,\ dt/rtf\ 1)\ m$$
$$\Rightarrow\ \{\ \text{arithmetic}\ \}$$
$$perform\ (t,\ dt)\ m$$

Note that the above proofs, being used to establish axioms, all involve the definition of *perform*. In contrast, we can also establish *theorems* whose proofs involve only the axioms. For example, Axioms 1, 2, and 3 are all needed to prove the following:

---

**Theorem 1**  For any $r$, $m1$, and $m2$:

$$Tempo\ r\ m1\ \mathbin{:\!+\!:}\ m2\ \equiv\ Tempo\ r\ (m1\ \mathbin{:\!+\!:}\ Tempo\ (1/r)\ m2)$$

**Proof:**

$$Tempo\ r\ (m1\ \mathbin{:\!+\!:}\ Tempo\ (1/r)\ m2)$$
$$\Rightarrow\ \{\ \text{by Axiom 2}\ \}$$
$$Tempo\ r\ m1\ \mathbin{:\!+\!:}\ Tempo\ r\ (Tempo\ (1/r)\ m2)$$
$$\Rightarrow\ \{\ \text{by Axiom 1}\ \}$$
$$Tempo\ r\ m1\ \mathbin{:\!+\!:}\ Tempo\ (r * (1/r))\ m2$$
$$\Rightarrow\ \{\ \text{arithmetic}\ \}$$
$$Tempo\ r\ m1\ \mathbin{:\!+\!:}\ Tempo\ 1\ m2$$
$$\Rightarrow\ \{\ \text{by Axiom 3}\ \}$$
$$Tempo\ r\ m1\ \mathbin{:\!+\!:}\ m2$$

Many other interesting transformations of MDL musical objects can be stated and proved correct via calculation. I leave as an exercise the proofs of the axioms listed below (which include the above axioms as special cases). In general, axioms such as these constitute a set of *domain-specific* properties that often capture the essence of the domain under consideration. Indeed, it is possible to start with these properties as the specification of the system being designed. This approach is commonly referred to as *algebraic semantics*, but I will not pursue the idea here.

---

**Axiom 4** *Tempo* is *multiplicative* and *Transpose* is *additive*. That is, for any $r1$, $r2$, $p1$, $p2$, and $m$:

> $Tempo\ r1\ (Tempo\ r2\ m) \;\equiv\; Tempo\ (r1 * r2)\ m$
> $Trans\ p1\ (Trans\ p2\ m) \;\equiv\; Trans\ (p1 + p2)\ m$

---

**Axiom 5** Function composition is *commutative* with respect to both tempo scaling and transposition. That is, for any $r1$, $r2$, $p1$ and $p2$:

> $Tempo\ r1 . Tempo\ r2 \;\equiv\; Tempo\ r2 . Tempo\ r1$
> $Trans\ p1 . Trans\ p2 \;\equiv\; Trans\ p2 . Trans\ p1$
> $Tempo\ r1 . Trans\ p1 \;\equiv\; Trans\ p1 . Tempo\ r1$

---

**Axiom 6** Tempo scaling and transposition are *distributive* over both sequential and parallel composition. That is, for any $r$, $p$, $m1$, and $m2$:

> $Tempo\ r\ (m1 :\!+: m2) \;\equiv\; Tempo\ r\ m1 :\!+: Tempo\ r\ m2$
> $Tempo\ r\ (m1 :\!=: m2) \;\equiv\; Tempo\ r\ m1 :\!=: Tempo\ r\ m2$
> $Trans\ p\ (m1 :\!+: m2) \;\equiv\; Trans\ p\ m1 :\!+: Trans\ p\ m2$
> $Trans\ p\ (m1 :\!=: m2) \;\equiv\; Trans\ p\ m1 :\!=: Trans\ p\ m2$

---

**Axiom 7** Sequential and parallel composition are *associative*. That is, for any $m0$, $m1$, and $m2$:

> $m0 :\!+: (m1 :\!+: m2) \;\equiv\; (m0 :\!+: m1) :\!+: m2$
> $m0 :\!=: (m1 :\!=: m2) \;\equiv\; (m0 :\!=: m1) :\!=: m2$

---

**Axiom 8** Parallel composition is *commutative*. That is, for any $m0$ and $m1$:

> $m0 :\!=: m1 \;\equiv\; m1 :\!=: m0$

---

**Axiom 9** *Rest* 0 is a *unit* for *Tempo* and *Trans*, and a *zero* for sequential and parallel composition. That is, for any $r$, $p$, and $m$:

> $Tempo\ r\ (Rest\ 0) \;\equiv\; Rest\ 0$
> $Trans\ p\ (Rest\ 0) \;\equiv\; Rest\ 0$

$$m \mathbin{:\!+\!:} Rest\ 0 \;\equiv\; m \;\equiv\; Rest\ 0 \mathbin{:\!+\!:} m$$
$$m \mathbin{:=:} Rest\ 0 \;\equiv\; m \;\equiv\; Rest\ 0 \mathbin{:=:} m$$

**Exercise 21.2**  Establish the validity of each of the above axioms.

**Exercise 21.3**  Prove that:

$$(m0 \mathbin{:\!+\!:} m1) \mathbin{:=:} (m2 \mathbin{:\!+\!:} m3) \;\equiv\; (m0 \mathbin{:=:} m2) \mathbin{:\!+\!:} (m1 \mathbin{:=:} m3)$$

if $dur\ m0 = dur\ m2$.

**Exercise 21.4**  Recall the function *revM* defined in Chapter 20, and note that, in general, *revM* (*revM m*) is not equal to *m*. However, the following is true:

$$revM\ (revM\ m) \;\equiv\; m$$

Prove this fact by calculation.

# CHAPTER TWENTY-TWO

# From Performance to MIDI

MIDI is shorthand for "Musical Instrument Digital Interface," and is a standard protocol for describing electronic music. In this chapter I will describe how to convert an abstract *performance* as defined in Chapter 21 into a *MIDI file* that can be played on any modern PC with a standard sound card.

> **module** *MDL* **where**
>
> **import** *Music*
> **import** *Perform*
> **import** *Haskore* (*MidiFile* (..), *MidiChannel*, *ProgNum*, *MEvent*,
>                   *MFType*, *Velocity*, *MEvent* (..), *MidiEvent* (..),
>                   *MetaEvent* (..), *Division* (..), *MTempo*,
>                   *outputMidiFile*)
> **import** *List* (*partition*)
> **import** *System* (*system*)

As mentioned in Chapter 20, *Haskore* is a library for computer music that is more extensive than MDL, and I will borrow much of the basic MIDI data types defined there, as well as the low-level function *outputMidiFile*, to be described later.

## 22.1 An Introduction to MIDI

MIDI is a standard adopted by most, if not all, manufacturers of electronic instruments. At its core is a protocol for communicating *musical events* (such as note on, note off, key press, pedal press) as well as so-called *meta events* (such as select synthesizer patch, change volume). Beyond the logical protocol, the MIDI standard also specifies electrical signal characteristics and cabling details. In addition, it specifies what is known as a *Standard MIDI File*, which any MIDI-compatible software package should be able to recognize.

Over the years musicians and manufacturers decided that they also wanted a standard way to refer to *common* or *general* instruments such as "acoustic grand piano," "electric piano," "violin," and "acoustic bass," as well as more exotic ones such as "chorus aahs," "voice oohs," "bird tweet," and "helicopter." A simple standard known as *General MIDI* was developed to fill this role. It is nothing more than an agreed-upon list of instrument names along with a *program patch number* for each, a parameter in the MIDI standard that is used to select a MIDI instrument's sound. The constructor names in the *IName* data type (see Fig. 20.1 in Chapter 20) come directly from this standard.

Most sound cards on conventional PCs know about MIDI and General MIDI. The sound generated by such modules, even through the typically-scrawny speakers on most PCs, is pretty good these days. For the best sound, an outboard keyboard or tone generator, attached to a computer via a MIDI cable at one end, and to a nice stereo system on the other, will provide the best sound. It is possible to connect several MIDI instruments to the same computer, with each assigned a different *channel*. Modern keyboards and tone generators are quite amazing little beasts. Not only is the sound quite good, they are also usually *multi-timbral*, which means they are able to generate many different sounds simultaneously, as well as *polyphonic*, meaning that simultaneous instantiations of the same sound are possible.

If you decide to use the General MIDI features of your sound card, you need to know about one other convention, namely that Channel 10 (9 in our 0-based numbering) is dedicated to *percussion*. I will use this assumption in this chapter.

## 22.2 The Conversion Process

Fig. 22.1 is a specification, imported from the *Haskore* library, that contains as much of the *MidiFile* datatype that we will need. The details of this datatype are unimportant, except for the following points:

1. There are three types of MIDI files; the value of *MFType* makes the distinction:
   (a) A Format 0 MIDI file stores its information in a single track of events, and is best used only for monophonic music.

```
data MidiFile      = MidiFile MFType Division [Track]
   deriving (Show, Eq)


type MFType        = Int
type Track         = [MEvent]


data Division      = Ticks Int | SMPTE Int Int
   deriving (Show, Eq)


data MEvent        = MidiEvent ElapsedTime MidiEvent
                   | MetaEvent ElapsedTime MetaEvent
                   | NoEvent
   deriving (Show, Eq)


type ElapsedTime   = Int

      -- Midi Events
data MidiEvent     = NoteOff MidiChannel MPitch Velocity
                   | NoteOn MidiChannel MPitch Velocity
                   | ProgChange MidiChannel ProgNum
                   | ...
   deriving (Show, Eq)
type MPitch        = Int
type Velocity      = Int
type ProgNum       = Int
type MidiChannel   = Int


      -- Meta Events
data MetaEvent     = SetTempo MTempo
                   | ...
   deriving (Show, Eq)
type MTempo        = Int
```

Figure 22.1: Partial Definition of *MidiFile* Data Type

(b) A Format 1 MIDI file stores its information in multiple tracks that are played simultaneously, and offers the advantage of being able to devote each track to one voice in a polyphonic piece.

(c) A Format 2 MIDI file also has multiple tracks, but they are temporally independent.

In this chapter we will only use Format 1, so the *MFType* field will always be 1.

2. The *Division* field refers to the "time-code division," or timing strategy, used by the MIDI file. We will always use 96 time divisions, or "ticks," per quarter-note, and thus this field will always be *Ticks 96*.

3. The main body of a MIDI file is a list of *Track*s, each of which in turn is a list of time-stamped (using the *ElapsedTime* field) *MEvent*s. There are two kinds of *MEvent*s: *MidiEvent*s and *MetaEvent*s. Fig. 22.1 shows just those instances of these events that we are interested in:

   (a) *NoteOn ch p v* turns on note (pitch) *p* with velocity (volume) *v* on MIDI channel *ch*. *NoteOff ch p v* performs a similar function in turning the note off. The volume is an integer in the range 0 to 127; we will always use the maximum volume 127.

   (b) *ProgChange ch pr* sets the program number for channel *ch* to *pr*. This is how an instrument is selected.

   (c) *SetTempo t* sets the tempo to *t*. For Format 1 MIDI files, *t* is the time, in microseconds, of one whole note. Using 120 beats per minute as the norm, or 2 beats per second, works out to 500,000 microseconds per beat, which is the default value that we will use.

With this structure in mind, our goal is to define a function *performToMidi* that converts a *Performance* into the *MidiFile* data type:

$$
\begin{array}{ll}
\textit{performToMidi} & :: \quad \textit{Performance} \rightarrow \textit{MidiFile} \\
\textit{performToMidi pf} & = \\
\multicolumn{2}{l}{\quad \textit{MidiFile mfType (Ticks division)}} \\
\multicolumn{2}{l}{\qquad\qquad\qquad (\textit{map performToMEvs (splitByInst pf)})}
\end{array}
$$

$$
\begin{array}{l}
\textit{mfType} \;=\; 1 :: \textit{Int} \\
\textit{division} \;=\; 96 :: \textit{Int}
\end{array}
$$

There are two yet-to-be-defined functions here: *performToMEvs* and *splitByInst*.

Because we are implementing Type 1 MIDI Files, we must associate each instrument with a separate track. That is the purpose of *splitByInst*, which takes a performance *pf* and returns a list of performances, one for each unique instrument in *pf*. As part of this process it also assigns a unique channel number to each instrument, along with the appropriate program number to select the proper instrument. Thus:

$$splitByInst :: Performance \rightarrow [(MidiChannel, ProgNum, Performance)]$$

Remember that channel 9 is reserved for percussion, so a special case is made for that: The other channels are selected sequentially in the range 0 to 15 (excluding 9). With this strategy, there can be at most 16 instruments (15 if percussion is not used), and thus an error is signaled if this number is exceeded:

```
splitByInst p
    =  aux 0 p where
          aux n [ ] = [ ]
          aux n pf = let i          = eInst (head pf)
                         (pf1, pf2)  = partition (\e → eInst e == i) pf
                         n'          = if n == 8 then 10 else n + 1
                     in if i == Percussion
                        then (9, 0, pf1) : aux n pf2
                        else if n > 15
                                then error "Too many instruments"
                                else (n, fromEnum i, pf1) : aux n' pf2
```

---

**DETAILS**

The function *partition* is imported from the *List* Standard Library module. It takes a predicate and a list and returns a pair of lists: those elements of the argument list that do and do not satisfy the predicate, respectively. *partition* is defined by:

```
partition      ::  (a → Bool) → [a] → ([a], [a])
partition p xs  =
  foldr select ([ ], [ ]) xs
     where select x (ts, fs) | p x         = (x : ts, fs)
                             | otherwise   = (ts, x : fs)
```

---

Note how *partition* is used to group into *pf*1 those events that use the same instrument as the first event in the performance. The rest of the events are collected into *pf*2, which is passed recursively to the next iteration of the *aux* loop.

The crux of the conversion process is *performToMEvs*, which converts a *Performance* into a stream of *MEvents* (i.e., a *Track*).

*performToMEvs* :: (*MidiChannel, ProgNum, Performance*) → [*MEvent*]

*performToMEvs* (*ch, pn, perf*)
    = **let** *setupInst*    = *MidiEvent* 0 (*ProgChange ch pn*)
           *setTempo*    = *MetaEvent* 0 (*SetTempo tempo*)
           *loop* [ ]     = [ ]
           *loop* (*e* : *es*)  = **let** (*mev1, mev2*)  = *mkMEvents ch e*
                               **in** *mev*1 : *insertMEvent mev2* (*loop es*)
      **in** *setupInst* : *setTempo* : *loop perf*

*tempo*  = 500000 :: *Int*    −− number of microseconds in one beat

An important source of incompatibilty between our abstract notion of a performance and that of MIDI is that in a performance a note is represented as one event with an onset and a duration, while in MIDI it is represented as two separate events, a note-on event and a note-off event. Thus, *MkMEvents* turns an *Event* into two *MEvents*, a *NoteOn* and a *NoteOff*.

*mkMEvents*  ::  *MidiChannel* → *Event* → (*MEvent, MEvent*)

*mkMEvents mChan* (*Event* {*eTime* = *t*, *ePitch* = *p*, *eDur* = *d*})
    = (*MidiEvent* (*toDelta t*) (*NoteOn mChan p* 127),
        *MidiEvent* (*toDelta* (*t* + *d*)) (*NoteOff mChan p* 127))

*toDelta t*  =  *round* (*t* ∗ 4.0 ∗ *intToFloat division*)

The time-stamp associated with an event in MIDI is called a *delta-time*, and is the time at which the event should occur expressed in time-code divisions since the beginning of the performance. Because there are 96 time-code divisions per quarter note, there are four times that many in a whole note; multiplying that by the time-stamp on one of our *Events* gives us the proper delta-time.

In the code for *performToMEvs*, note that the location of the first event returned from *mkMEvents* is obvious; it belongs just where it was created. However, the second event must be inserted into the proper place in the rest of the stream of events; there is no way to know of its proper

position ahead of time. The function *insertMEvent* is thus used to insert
an *MEvent* into an already time-ordered sequence of *MEvent*s.

*insertMEvent* :: *MEvent* → [*MEvent*] → [*MEvent*]

*insertMEvent ev*1 [ ]
   = [*ev*1]
*insertMEvent ev*1@(*MidiEvent t*1 _) *evs*@(*ev*2@(*MidiEvent t*2 _) : *evs*′)
   = **if** *t*1 <= *t*2 **then** *ev*1 : *evs*
                **else** *ev*2 : *insertMEvent ev*1 *evs*′

## 22.3 Putting It All Together

We are almost done. All that remains is to write the *MidiFile* value into
a real file. The details of this are surprisingly ugly, however, primarily
because MIDI files were invented at a time when disk space was precious,
and thus a compact bit-level representation was chosen. Fortunately,
there is a function in the *Haskore* library that solves this problem for
us:

*outputMidiFile* :: *String* → *MidiFile* → *IO* ()

To make this easier to use, let's define a function *test*, which converts a
*Music* value using a default *Context* into a *MidiFile* value, and then writes
that to a file "test.mid":

*test*     :: *Music* → *IO* ()
*test m*   = *outputMidiFile* "test.mid"
             (*performToMidi* (*perform defCon m*))

*defCon* :: *Context*
*defCon* = *Context* {*cTime* = 0,
                 *cInst* = *AcousticGrandPiano*,
                 *cDur* = *metro* 120 *qn*,
                 *cKey* = 0}

So if you type *test m* for some *Music* value *m*, it will be converted
to MIDI and written to the file "test.mid", which you can then play
using whatever MIDI-file player is supplied with your computer. If you
are running the Hugs implementation of Haskell on Windows 95/NT
or Linux, you can invoke the standard media player from Haskell by
defining one of the following functions (for these to work you must

also import *system* from the Hugs module *System*, via **import** *System* (*system*)):

$$testWin95, testNT, testLinux \ :: \ Music \rightarrow IO \ ()$$

$$
\begin{aligned}
testWin95 \ m \ = \ &\textbf{do } test \ m \\
&system \ \texttt{"mplayer test.mid"} \\
&return \ ()
\end{aligned}
$$

$$
\begin{aligned}
testNT \ m \quad = \ &\textbf{do } test \ m \\
&system \ \texttt{"mplay32 test.mid"} \\
&return \ ()
\end{aligned}
$$

$$
\begin{aligned}
testLinux \ m \ = \ &\textbf{do } test \ m \\
&system \ \texttt{"playmidi -rf test.mid"} \\
&return \ ()
\end{aligned}
$$

For example, typing:

$$testNT \ funkGroove$$

using Hugs on an NT system will write the *funkGroove* example from Chapter 20 into a MIDI file and then automatically fire up the media player so that you can hear the result. Try the above for other examples from Chapter 20, such as *cMajArp*, *cMajChd*, *pr*12, *waterfall*, and *main*.

# CHAPTER TWENTY-THREE

# A Tour of the PreludeList Module

The use of lists is particularly common when programming in Haskell, and thus, not surprisingly, there are many predefined polymorphic functions for lists. The list data type itself, plus some of the most useful functions on it, are contained in the Standard Prelude's *PreludeList* module, which I will cover in detail in this chapter. There is also a Standard Library module called *List* that has additional useful functions. It is a good idea to become familiar with both modules.

Although this chapter may feel like a long list of "Haskell features," the functions described here capture many common patterns of list usage that have been discovered by functional programmers over many years of trials and tribulations. In many ways higher-order declarative programming with lists takes the place of lower-level imperative control structures in more conventional languages. By becoming familiar with these list functions you will be able to more quickly and confidently develop your own applications using lists. Furthermore, if all of us do this, we will have a common vocabulary with which to understand each others' programs. Finally, by reading through the code in this module you will develop a good feel for how to write proper function definitions in Haskell.

It is not necessary for you to understand the details of every function, but you should try to get a sense for what is available so that you can return later when your programming needs demand it. In the long run, you are well-advised to read the rest of the Standard Prelude as well as the various Standard Libraries, to discover a host of other functions and data types that you might someday find useful in your own work.

## 23.1 The PreludeList Module

To get a feel for the *PreludeList* module, let's first look at its module declaration:

**module** *PreludeList* (
　　*map*, (++), *filter, concat,*
　　*head, last, tail, init, null, length,* (!!),
　　*foldl, foldl1, scanl, scanl1, foldr, foldr1, scanr, scanr1,*
　　*iterate, repeat, replicate, cycle,*
　　*take, drop, splitAt, takeWhile, dropWhile, span, break,*
　　*lines, words, unlines, unwords, reverse, and, or,*
　　*any, all, elem, notElem, lookup,*
　　*sum, product, maximum, minimum, concatMap,*
　　*zip, zip3, zipWith, zipWith3, unzip, unzip3* )
**where**

**import** *qualified Char* (*isSpace*)

**infixl**　9　!!
**infixr**　5　++
**infix**　　4　'*elem*', '*notElem*'

I will not cover all of the functions listed above, but will cover most of them (and some were covered in previous chapters).

## 23.2　Simple List Selector Functions

The functions *head* and *tail* extract the first element and remaining elements, respectively, from a list, which must be nonempty. The functions *last* and *init* are the dual functions that work from the end of a list, rather than from the beginning:

```
head         ::  [a] → a
head (x : _) =   x
head []      =   error "PreludeList.head: empty list"

last         ::  [a] → a
last [x]     =   x
last (_ : xs) =  last xs
last []      =   error "PreludeList.last: empty list"

tail          ::  [a] → [a]
tail (_ : xs) =   xs
tail []       =   error "PreludeList.tail: empty list"

init          ::  [a] → [a]
init [x]      =   []

init (x : xs) =   x : init xs
init []       =   error "PreludeList.init: empty list"
```

Although *head* and *tail* were previously discussed in Section 5.1, the definitions here include an equation describing their behaviors under erroneous situations – such as selecting the head of an empty list – in which case the *error* function is called. It is a good idea to include such an equation for any definition in which you have not covered every possible case in pattern-matching (i.e., if it is possible that the pattern-matching could "run off the end" of the set of equations). The string argument that you supply to the *error* function should be detailed enough that you can easily track down the precise location of the error in your program.

**DETAILS**

If such an error equation is omitted, and then during pattern-matching all equations fail, most Haskell systems will invoke the *error* function anyway, but most likely with a string that will be less informative than one you can supply on your own.

The *null* function tests to see if a list is empty.

$$null \qquad :: \quad [a] \to Bool$$
$$null\ [\ ] \quad = \quad True$$
$$null\ (\_:\_) \quad = \quad False$$

## 23.3 Index-Based Selector Functions

To select the *n*th element from a list, with the first element being the 0th element, we can use the indexing function (!!):

$$(!!) \qquad\qquad :: \quad [a] \to Int \to a$$
$$(x:\_)\ !!\ 0 \qquad = \quad x$$
$$(\_:xs)\ !!\ n\ |\ \ n > 0 \quad = \quad xs\ !!\ (n-1)$$
$$(\_:\_)\ !!\ \_ \qquad\qquad = \quad error\ \text{``PreludeList.!!: negative index''}$$
$$[\ ]\ !!\ \_ \qquad\qquad\quad = \quad error\ \text{``PreludeList.!!: index too large''}$$

**DETAILS**

Note the definition of two error conditions; be sure that you understand under what conditions these two equations would succeed. In particular, recall that equations are matched in top-down order: The first to match is the one that is chosen.

The value *take n xs* is the prefix of *xs* of length *n*, or *xs* itself if *n* > *length xs*. Similarly, *drop n xs* is the suffix of *xs* after the first *n* elements, or [ ] if *n* > *length xs*. Finally, *splitAt n xs* is equivalent to (*take n xs, drop n xs*).

$$
\begin{array}{lll}
take & :: & Int \rightarrow [a] \rightarrow [a] \\
take\ 0\ \_ & = & [\,] \\
take\ \_\ [\,] & = & [\,] \\
take\ n\ (x:xs)\quad |\ n > 0 & = & x:take\ (n-1)\ xs \\
take\ \_\ \_ & = & error\ \text{``PreludeList.take:} \\
& & \quad \text{negative argument''}
\end{array}
$$

$$
\begin{array}{lll}
drop & :: & Int \rightarrow [a] \rightarrow [a] \\
drop\ 0\ xs & = & xs \\
drop\ \_\ [\,] & = & [\,] \\
drop\ n\ (\_:xs)\quad |\ n > 0 & = & drop\ (n-1)\ xs \\
drop\ \_\ \_ & = & error\ \text{``PreludeList.drop:} \\
& & \quad \text{negative argument''}
\end{array}
$$

$$
\begin{array}{lll}
splitAt & :: & Int \rightarrow [a] \rightarrow ([a], [a]) \\
splitAt\ 0\ xs & = & ([\,], xs) \\
splitAt\ \_\ [\,] & = & ([\,], [\,]) \\
splitAt\ n\ (x:xs)\ |\ n > 0 & = & (x:xs', xs'') \\
& & \textbf{where}\ (xs', xs'')\ =\ splitAt\ (n-1)\ xs \\
splitAt\ \_\ \_ & = & error\ \text{``PreludeList.splitAt:} \\
& & \quad \text{negative argument''}
\end{array}
$$

$$
\begin{array}{lll}
length & :: & [a] \rightarrow Int \\
length\ [\,] & = & 0 \\
length\ (\_:l) & = & 1 + length\ l
\end{array}
$$

For example:

$$
\begin{array}{l}
take\ 3\ [0, 1..5]\ \Rightarrow\ [0, 1, 2] \\
drop\ 3\ [0, 1..5]\ \Rightarrow\ [3, 4, 5] \\
splitAt\ 3\ [0, 1..5]\ \Rightarrow\ ([0, 1, 2], [3, 4, 5])
\end{array}
$$

## 23.4 Predicate-Based Selector Functions

The value *takeWhile p xs* is the longest (possibly empty) prefix of *xs*, all of whose elements satisfy the predicate *p*. The value *dropWhile p xs* is the remaining suffix. Finally, *span p xs* is equivalent to (*takeWhile p xs*, *dropWhile p xs*), while *break p* uses the negation of *p*.

$$
\begin{array}{lll}
takeWhile & :: & (a \rightarrow Bool) \rightarrow [a] \rightarrow [a] \\
takeWhile\ p\ [\,] & = & [\,] \\
takeWhile\ p\ (x:xs) & & \\
\quad |\ p\ x & = & x:takeWhile\ p\ xs \\
\quad |\ otherwise & = & [\,]
\end{array}
$$

```
dropWhile        ::  (a → Bool) → [a] → [a]
dropWhile p [ ]  =   [ ]
dropWhile p xs@(x : xs')
  | p x          =   dropWhile p xs'
  | otherwise    =   xs

span, break      ::  (a → Bool) → [a] → ([a], [a])
span p [ ]       =   ([ ], [ ])
span p xs@(x : xs')
  | p x          =   (x : xs', xs'') where (xs', xs'')  =   span p xs
  | otherwise    =   (xs, [ ])

break p          =   span (not . p)
```

The function *filter* removes all elements of a list not satisfying a predicate:

```
filter                      ::  (a → Bool) → [a] → [a]
filter p [ ]                =   [ ]
filter p (x : xs) | p x     =   x : filter p xs
                | otherwise =   filter p xs
```

## 23.5  Fold-like Functions

The functions *foldl1* and *foldr1* are variants of *foldl* and *foldr* that have no starting value argument, and thus must be applied to nonempty lists.

```
foldl            ::  (a → b → a) → a → [b] → a
foldl f z [ ]    =   z
foldl f z (x : xs) =   foldl f (f z x) xs

foldl1           ::  (a → a → a) → [a] → a
foldl1 f (x : xs) =   foldl f x xs
foldl1 _ [ ]     =   error "PreludeList.foldl1: empty list"

foldr            ::  (a → b → b) → b → [a] → b
foldr f z [ ]    =   z
foldr f z (x : xs) =   f x (foldr f z xs)

foldr1           ::  (a → a → a) → [a] → a
foldr1 f [x]     =   x
foldr1 f (x : xs) =   f x (foldr1 f xs)
foldr1 _ [ ]     =   error "PreludeList.foldr1: empty list"
```

The functions *foldl*1 and *foldr*1 are best used in cases where an empty list makes no sense for the application. For example, computing the maximum or minimum element of a list does not make sense if the list is empty. Thus, *foldl*1 *max* is a proper function to compute the maximum element of a list.

The function *scanl* is similar to *foldl*, but returns a list of successive reduced values from the left:

$$scanl \; f \; z \; [x1, x2, \ldots] == [z, z \; `f` \; x1, (z \; `f` \; x1) \; `f` \; x2, \ldots]$$

For example:

$$scanl \; (+) \; 0 \; [1, 2, 3] \;\Rightarrow\; [0, 1, 3, 6]$$

Note that *last* (*scanl f z xs*) = *foldl f z xs*. *scanl*1 is similar, but without the starting element:

$$scanl1 \; f \; [x1, x2, \ldots] == [x1, x1 \; `f` \; x2, \ldots]$$

Here are the full definitions:

```
scanl          :: (a → b → a) → a → [b] → [a]
scanl f q xs   = q : (case xs of
                        []    → []
                        x : xs → scanl f (f q x) xs)
scanl1         :: (a → a → a) → [a] → [a]
scanl1 f (x : xs) = scanl f x xs
scanl1 _ []    = error "PreludeList.scanl1: empty list"

scanr          :: (a → b → b) → b → [a] → [b]
scanr f q0 []  = [q0]
scanr f q0 (x : xs) = f x q : qs
                 where qs@(q : _) = scanr f q0 xs

scanr1         :: (a → a → a) → [a] → [a]
scanr1 f [x]   = [x]
scanr1 f (x : xs) = f x q : qs
                 where qs@(q : _) = scanr1 f xs
scanr1 _ []    = error "PreludeList.scanr1: empty list"
```

## 23.6 List Generators

There are some functions that are very useful for generating lists from scratch in interesting ways. To start, *iterate f x* returns an *infinite list* of repeated applications of *f* to *x*. That is:

$$\text{iterate } f \ x \ \Rightarrow \ [x, f \ x, f \ (f \ x), \ldots]$$

It is defined by:

$$\text{iterate} \quad :: \ (a \rightarrow a) \rightarrow a \rightarrow [a]$$
$$\text{iterate } f \ x \ = \ x : \text{iterate } f \ (f \ x)$$

The value *repeat x* is an infinite list, with *x* the value of every element and *replicate n x* is a list of length *n* with *x* the value of every element. Also, *cycle* ties a finite list into a circular one, or equivalently, the infinite repetition of the original list:

$$\text{repeat} \quad :: \ a \rightarrow [a]$$
$$\text{repeat } x \quad = \ xs \ \textbf{where } xs \ = \ x : xs$$

$$\text{replicate} \quad :: \ Int \rightarrow a \rightarrow [a]$$
$$\text{replicate } n \ x \ = \ take \ n \ (repeat \ x)$$

$$\text{cycle} \quad :: \ [a] \rightarrow [a]$$
$$\text{cycle } [\,] \quad = \ error \ \text{``Prelude.cycle: empty list''}$$
$$\text{cycle } xs \quad = \ xs' \ \textbf{where } xs' \ = \ xs + xs'$$

## 23.7 String-Based Functions

Recall that strings in Haskell are just lists of characters. Manipulating strings (i.e., text) is a very common practice, so it makes sense that Haskell would have a few predefined functions to make this easier for you.

The function *lines* breaks a string at every newline character (written as '\n' in Haskell), thus yielding a *list* of strings, each of which contains no newline characters. Similarly, *words* breaks a string up into a list of words, which were delimited by white space. Finally, *unlines* and *unwords* are the inverse operations: *unlines* joins lines with terminating newline characters, and *unwords* joins words with separating spaces. (Because of the potential presence of multiple spaces and newline characters, however, these pairs of functions are not true inverses of each other.)

$$
\begin{array}{lll}
\textit{lines} & :: & \textit{String} \rightarrow [\textit{String}] \\
\textit{lines} \ \text{""} & = & [\,] \\
\textit{lines} \ s & = & \textbf{let} \ (l, s') \ = \ \textit{break} \ (==' \ \backslash n') \ s \\
& & \quad \textbf{in} \ l : \textbf{case} \ s' \ \textbf{of} \\
& & \qquad\qquad [\,] \qquad \rightarrow \quad [\,] \\
& & \qquad\qquad (\_: s'') \ \rightarrow \ \textit{lines} \ s''
\end{array}
$$

$$
\begin{array}{lll}
\textit{words} & :: & \textit{String} \rightarrow [\textit{String}] \\
\textit{words} \ s & = & \textbf{case} \ \textit{dropWhile} \ \textit{Char.isSpace} \ s \ \textbf{of} \\
& & \quad \text{""} \ \rightarrow \ [\,] \\
& & \quad s' \ \rightarrow \ w : \textit{words} \ s'' \\
& & \qquad\qquad \textbf{where} \ (w, s'') \ = \ \textit{break} \ \textit{Char.isSpace} \ s'
\end{array}
$$

$$
\begin{array}{lll}
\textit{unlines} & :: & [\textit{String}] \rightarrow \textit{String} \\
\textit{unlines} & = & \textit{concatMap} \ (+\!\!+ \ \text{"}\backslash n\text{"})
\end{array}
$$

$$
\begin{array}{lll}
\textit{unwords} & :: & [\textit{String}] \rightarrow \textit{String} \\
\textit{unwords} \ [\,] & = & \text{""} \\
\textit{unwords} \ ws & = & \textit{foldr}1 \ (\backslash w \ s \rightarrow w +\!\!+ '\,' : s) \ ws
\end{array}
$$

The function *reverse* reverses the elements in a finite list:

$$
\begin{array}{lll}
\textit{reverse} & :: & [a] \rightarrow [a] \\
\textit{reverse} & = & \textit{foldl} \ (\textit{flip} \ (:)) \ [\,]
\end{array}
$$

## 23.8 Boolean List Functions

The elements *and* and *or* compute the logical "and" and "or," respectively, of all the elements in a list of Boolean values:

$$
\begin{array}{lll}
\textit{and, or} & :: & [\textit{Bool}] \rightarrow \textit{Bool} \\
\textit{and} & = & \textit{foldr} \ (\&\&) \ \textit{True} \\
\textit{or} & = & \textit{foldr} \ (||) \ \textit{False}
\end{array}
$$

Applied to a predicate and a list, *any* determines if any element of the list satisfies the predicate. An analogous behavior holds for *all*:

$$
\begin{array}{lll}
\textit{any, all} & :: & (a \rightarrow \textit{Bool}) \rightarrow [a] \rightarrow \textit{Bool} \\
\textit{any} \ p & = & \textit{or} \,.\, \textit{map} \ p \\
\textit{all} \ p & = & \textit{and} \,.\, \textit{map} \ p
\end{array}
$$

## 23.9  List Membership Functions

The function *elem* is the list membership predicate, usually written in infix form, e.g., *x* '*elem*' *xs* (which is why it was given a fixity declaration at the beginning of the module). The function *notElem* is the negation of this function:

```
elem, notElem  ::  (Eq a) ⇒ a → [a] → Bool
elem x         =   any (== x)
notElem x      =   all (/= x)
```

It is common to store "key/value" pairs in a list, and to access the list by finding the value associated with a given key (for this reason the list is often called an *association list*). The function *lookup* looks up a key in an association list, returning *Nothing* if it is not found, or *Just y* if *y* is the value associated with the key:

```
lookup              ::  (Eq a) ⇒ a → [(a, b)] → Maybe b
lookup key []       =   Nothing
lookup key ((x, y) : xys)
    | key == x      =   Just y
    | otherwise     =   lookup key xys
```

## 23.10  Arithmetic on Lists

The functions *sum* and *product* compute the sum and product, respectively, of a finite list of numbers:

```
sum, product   ::  (Num a) ⇒ [a] → a
sum            =   foldl (+) 0
product        =   foldl (*) 1
```

The functions *maximum* and *minimum* return the maximum and minimum value, respectively, from a nonempty, finite list whose element type is ordered:

```
maximum, minimum  ::  (Ord a) ⇒ [a] → a
maximum []        =   error "Prelude.maximum: empty list"
maximum xs        =   foldl1 max xs

minimum []        =   error "Prelude.minimum: empty list"
minimum xs        =   foldl1 min xs
```

Note that even though *foldl*1 is used in the definition, a test is made for the empty list to give an error message that more accurately reflects the source of the problem.

## 23.11  List Combining Functions

The functions *map* and (++) were defined in previous chapters, but are repeated here for completeness:

$$
\begin{aligned}
map \quad &:: \ (a \to b) \to [a] \to [a] \\
map \ f \ [\,] \quad &= \ [\,] \\
map \ f \ (x : xs) \quad &= \ f \ x : map \ f \ xs
\end{aligned}
$$

$$
\begin{aligned}
(++) \quad &:: \ [a] \to [a] \to [a] \\
[\,] ++ ys \quad &= \ ys \\
(x : xs) ++ ys \quad &= \ x : (xs ++ ys)
\end{aligned}
$$

The function *concat* appends together a list of lists:

$$
\begin{aligned}
concat \quad &:: \ [[a]] \to [a] \\
concat \ xss \quad &= \ foldr \ (++) \ [\,] \ xss
\end{aligned}
$$

The function *concatMap* does what it says: It concatenates the result of mapping a function down a list:

$$
\begin{aligned}
concatMap \quad &:: \ (a \to [b]) \to [a] \to [b] \\
concatMap \ f \quad &= \ concat . map \ f
\end{aligned}
$$

The function *zip* takes two lists and returns a list of corresponding pairs. If one input list is short, excess elements of the longer list are discarded. And *zip3* takes three lists and returns a list of triples. ("Zips" for larger tuples are contained in the List Library.)

$$
\begin{aligned}
zip \quad &:: \ [a] \to [b] \to [(a, b)] \\
zip \quad &= \ zipWith \ (,)
\end{aligned}
$$

$$
\begin{aligned}
zip3 \quad &:: \ [a] \to [b] \to [c] \to [(a, b, c)] \\
zip3 \quad &= \ zipWith3 \ (,,)
\end{aligned}
$$

**DETAILS**

The functions (,) and (,,) are the pairing and tripling functions, respectively:

$$
\begin{aligned}
(,) \quad &\Rightarrow \ \backslash x \ y \to (x, y) \\
(,,) \quad &\Rightarrow \ \backslash x \ y \ z \to (x, y, z)
\end{aligned}
$$

The *zipWith* family generalizes the *zip* and *map* families (or, in a sense, combines them) by applying a function (given as the first argument) to each pair (or triple, etc.) of values. For example, *zipWith* $(+)$ is applied to two lists to produce the list of corresponding sums:

$$
\begin{aligned}
zipWith \quad &:: \quad (a \to b \to c) \to [a] \to [b] \to [c] \\
zipWith\ z\ (a:as)\ (b:bs) & \\
&= \quad z\ a\ b : zipWith\ z\ as\ bs \\
zipWith\ \_\ \_\ \_ \quad &= \quad [\,]
\end{aligned}
$$

$$
\begin{aligned}
zipWith3 \quad &:: \quad (a \to b \to c \to d) \to [a] \to [b] \to [c] \to [d] \\
zipWith3\ z\ (a:as)\ (b:bs)\ (c:cs) & \\
&= \quad z\ a\ b\ c : zipWith3\ z\ as\ bs\ cs \\
zipWith3\ \_\ \_\ \_\ \_ \quad &= \quad [\,]
\end{aligned}
$$

The following two functions perform the inverse operations of *zip* and *zip3*, respectively:

$$
\begin{aligned}
unzip \quad &:: \quad [(a,\ b)] \to ([a],\ [b]) \\
unzip \quad &= \quad foldr\ (\backslash(a,\ b)\ \tilde{}\ (as,\ bs) \to (a:as,\ b:bs))\ ([\,],\ [\,])
\end{aligned}
$$

$$
\begin{aligned}
unzip3 \quad &:: \quad [(a,\ b,\ c)] \to ([a],\ [b],\ [c]) \\
unzip3 \quad &= \quad foldr\ (\backslash(a,\ b,\ c)\ \tilde{}\ (as,\ bs,\ cs) \to (a:as,\ b:bs,\ c:cs)) \\
& \qquad\qquad ([\,],\ [\,],\ [\,])
\end{aligned}
$$

# CHAPTER TWENTY-FOUR

# A Tour of Haskell's Standard Type Classes

In this chapter I will give you a "tour" through the predefined standard type classes in Haskell, as I did for lists in Chapter 23. These classes have been simplified somewhat by omitting some of the less interesting methods. The Haskell Report and Standard Library Report contain more complete descriptions.

## 24.1 The Ordered Class

The equality class *Eq* was defined precisely in Chapter 12, along with a simplified version of the class *Ord*. Here is its full specification of class *Ord*; note the many default methods:

```
class (Eq a) ⇒ Ord a where
    compare              ::  a → a → Ordering
    (<), (<=), (>=), (>) ::  a → a → Bool
    max, min             ::  a → a → a

    compare x y
       | x == y          =  EQ
       | x <= y          =  LT
       | otherwise       =  GT

    x <= y               =  compare x y /= GT
    x < y                =  compare x y == LT
    x >= y               =  compare x y /= LT
    x > y                =  compare x y == GT

    max x y
       | x >= y          =  x
       | otherwise       =  y
```

$$min \ x \ y$$
$$| \ x < y \qquad = \ x$$
$$| \ otherwise \qquad = \ y$$
**data** *Ordering* $\qquad = \ LT \ | \ EQ \ | \ GT$
    **deriving** (*Eq, Ord, Enum, Read, Show, Bounded*)

Note that the default method for *compare* is defined in terms of (<=), and that the default method for (<=) is defined in terms of *compare*. This means that an instance of *Ord* should contain a method for at least one of these for everything to be well defined. (Using *compare* can be more efficient for complex types.) This is a common idea in designing a type class.

## 24.2 The Enumeration Class

Class *Enum* has a set of operations that underlie the syntactic sugar of *arithmetic sequences*; for example, the arithmetic sequence [1, 3..] is actually shorthand for *enumFromThen* 1 3. If this is true, then we should be able to generate arithmetic sequences for any type that is an instance of *Enum*. This includes not only most numeric types, but also *Char*, so that, for instance, [$'a'$..$'z'$] denotes the list of lower-case letters in alphabetical order. Furthermore, a user-defined enumerated type such as *Color*:

    **data** *Color* $=$ *Red* | *Orange* | *Yellow* | *Green* | *Blue* | *Indigo* | *Violet*

can easily be given an *Enum* instance declaration, after which we can calculate the following results:

    [*Red..Violet*] $\Rightarrow$ [*Red, Orange, Yellow, Green, Blue, Indigo, Violet*]
    [*Red, Yellow..*] $\Rightarrow$ [*Red, Yellow, Blue, Violet*]
    *fromEnum Green* $\Rightarrow$ 3
    *toEnum* 5 :: *Color* $\Rightarrow$ *Indigo*

Indeed, the derived instance will give this result. Note that the sequences are still *arithmetic* in the sense that the increment between values is constant, even though the values are not numbers.

The complete definition of the *Enum* class is given below:

    **class** *Enum a* **where**
      *succ, pred* $\qquad\qquad$ :: $a \to a$
      *toEnum* $\qquad\qquad\quad$ :: $Int \to a$
      *fromEnum* $\qquad\qquad$ :: $a \to Int$
      *enumFrom* $\qquad\qquad$ :: $a \to [a] \qquad$ -- [n..]
      *enumFromThen* $\qquad\;$ :: $a \to a \to [a] \qquad$ -- [n,n'..]
      *enumFromTo* $\qquad\quad$ :: $a \to a \to [a] \qquad$ -- [n..m]
      *enumFromThenTo* $\quad$ :: $a \to a \to a \to [a] \qquad$ -- [n,n'..m]

$$-- \text{ Minimal complete definition: toEnum, fromEnum}$$

$$
\begin{aligned}
succ &= toEnum \,.\, (+1) \,.\, fromEnum \\
pred &= toEnum \,.\, (subtract\ 1) \,.\, fromEnum \\
enumFrom\ x &= map\ toEnum\ [fromEnum\ x..] \\
enumFromThen\ x\ y &= map\ toEnum\ [fromEnum\ x,\ fromEnum\ y..] \\
enumFromTo\ x\ y &= map\ toEnum\ [fromEnum\ x..fromEnum\ y] \\
enumFromThenTo\ x\ y\ z &= \\
\end{aligned}
$$
$$map\ toEnum\ [fromEnum\ x,\ fromEnum\ y..fromEnum\ z]$$

The six default methods are sufficient for most applications, so when writing your own instance declaration, it is usually sufficient to only provide methods for the remaining two operations: *toEnum* and *fromEnum*.

In terms of arithmetic sequences, the expressions on the left below are equivalent to those on the right:

$$
\begin{aligned}
enumFrom\ n &\quad [n..] \\
enumFromThen\ n\ n' &\quad [n,\ n'..] \\
enumFromTo\ n\ m &\quad [n..m] \\
enumFromThenTo\ n\ n'\ m &\quad [n,\ n'..m]
\end{aligned}
$$

## 24.3  The Bounded Class

The class *Bounded* captures data types that are linearly bounded in some way (i.e., they have both a minimum value and a maximum value):

```
class Bounded a where
    minBound  ::  a
    maxBound  ::  a
```

## 24.4  The Show Class

Instances of the class *Show* are those types that can be converted to character strings. This is useful, for example, when writing a representation of a value to the standard output area or to a file. The class *Read* works in the other direction: It provides operations for parsing character strings to obtain the values that they represent. In this section, we will look at the *Show* class; in the next we will look at *Read*.

For efficiency reasons, the primitive operations in these classes are somewhat esoteric, but they provide good lessons in both algorithm and software design, so we will look at them in some detail.

First, let's look at one of the higher-level functions that are defined in terms of the lower-level primitives:

*show* :: (*Show a*) ⇒ *a* → *String*

Naturally enough, *show* takes a value of any type that is a member of *Show*, and returns its representation as a string. For example, *show* (2 + 2) yields the string "4", as does *show* (6 − 2), as well as *show* applied to any other expression whose value is 4.

Furthermore, we can construct strings such as:

"The sum of " ++ *show x* ++ " and " ++ *show y* ++ " is "
  ++ *show* (*x* + *y*) ++ "."

with no difficulty. In particular, because (++) is right associative, the number of steps to construct this string is directly proportional to its total length, and we can't expect to do any better than that. (Because (++) needs to reconstruct its left argument, if it were left associative the above expression would repeatedly reconstruct the same substring on each application of (++). If the total string length were *n*, then in the worst case, the number of steps needed to do this would be proportional to $n^2$, instead of proportional to *n* in the case where (++) is right associative.)

Unfortunately, this strategy breaks down when construction of the list is nested. A particularly nasty version of this problem arises for tree-shaped data structures. Consider a function *showTree* that converts a value of type *Tree* into a string, as in:

*showTree* (*Branch* (*Branch* (*Leaf* 2) (*Leaf* 3)) (*Leaf* 4))
  ⟹ "<<2|3>|4>"

We can define this behavior straightforwardly as follows:

*showTree* :: (*Show a*) ⇒ *Tree a* → *String*
*showTree* (*Leaf x*)
        = *show x*
*showTree* (*Branch l r*)
        = "<" ++ *showTree l* ++ "|" ++ *showTree r* ++ ">"

Each of the recursive calls to *showTree* introduces more applications of (++), but because they are nested, a large amount of list reconstruction takes place (similar to the problem that would arise if (++) were left associative). If the tree being converted has size *n*, then in the worst case, the number of steps needed to perform this conversion is proportional to $n^2$. This is no good!

To restore linear complexity, suppose we had a function *shows*:

$$shows \;\; :: \;\; (Show\ a) \Rightarrow a \to String \to String$$

which takes a showable value and a string and returns that string with the value's representation concatenated at the front. For example, we would expect *shows* $(2 + 2)$ "`hello`" to return the string "`4hello`". The string argument should be thought of as an "accumulator" for the final result.

Using *shows* we can define a more efficient version of *showTree* which, like *shows*, has a string accumulator argument. Let's call this function *showsTree*:

$$showsTree \;\; :: \;\; (Show\ a) \Rightarrow Tree\ a \to String \to String$$
$$showsTree\ (Leaf\ x)\ s$$
$$= \;\; shows\ x\ s$$
$$showsTree\ (Branch\ l\ r)\ s$$
$$= \;\; \text{``<''} + showsTree\ l\ (\text{``|''} + showsTree\ r\ (\text{``>''} + s))$$

This function requires a number of steps directly proportional to the size of the tree, thus solving our efficiency problem. To see why this is so, note that the accumulator argument $s$ is never reconstructed. It is simply passed as an argument in one recursive call to *shows* or *showsTree*, and is incrementally extended to its left using $(+\!\!+)$.

The function *showTree* can now be redefined in terms of *showsTree* using an empty accumulator:

$$showTree\ t \;\; = \;\; showsTree\ t\ \text{``''}$$

---

**Exercise 24.1**    Prove that this version of *showTree* is equivalent to the old.

Although this solves our efficiency problem, the presentation of this function (and others like it) can be improved somewhat. First, let's create a type synonym (part of the Standard Prelude):

$$\textbf{type}\ ShowS \;\; = \;\; String \to String$$

Second, we can avoid carrying accumulators around, and also avoid amassing parentheses at the right end of long sequences of concatenations, by using functional composition:

$showsTree \ :: \ (Show \ a) \Rightarrow Tree \ a \rightarrow ShowS$
$showsTree \ (Leaf \ x)$
$\quad\quad = \ shows \ x$
$showsTree \ (Branch \ l \ r)$
$\quad\quad = \ (\text{``<''} +\!+) \ . \ showsTree \ l \ . \ (\text{``|''} +\!+) \ . \ showsTree \ r \ . \ (\text{``>''} +\!+)$

**DETAILS**

This can be simplified slightly more by noting that (**"c"** +\!+) is equivalent to
(`'c'` :) for any character $c$.

Something more important than just tidying up the code has come
about by this transformation: We have raised the presentation from an
*object level* (in this case, strings) to a *function level*. You can read the
type signature of *showsTree* as saying that *showsTree* maps a tree into a
*showing function*. Functions like (**"<"** +\!+) and (**"a string"** +\!+) are primitive showing functions, and we build up more complex ones by function
composition.

The actual *Show* class in Haskell has two additional levels of complexity (and functionality): (1) the ability to specify the *precedence* of a string
being generated, which is important when *show*ing a data type that has
infix constructors, because it determines when parentheses are needed,
and (2) a function for *show*ing a *list* of values of the type under consideration, because lists have special syntax in Haskell and are so commonly
used that they deserve special treatment. The full definition of the *Show*
class is given by:

**class** *Show a* **where**
$\quad showsPrec \ :: \ Int \rightarrow a \rightarrow ShowS$
$\quad showList \ \ :: \ [a] \rightarrow ShowS$

$showList \ [\,]$
$\quad = \ showString \ \text{``[]''}$
$showList \ (x : xs)$
$\quad = \ showChar \ '[' \ . \ shows \ x \ . \ showl \ xs$
$\quad\quad\quad \textbf{where} \ showl \ [\,] \quad\quad = \ showChar \ ']'$
$\quad\quad\quad\quad\quad\quad showl \ (x : xs) \ = \ showString \ \text{``, ''} \ . \ shows \ x \ . \ showl \ xs$

Note the default method for *showList*, and its "function level" style of
definition.

In addition to this class declaration, the Standard Prelude defines the
following functions, which return us to where we started our journey in

this section:

$$shows \quad :: \quad (Show\ a) \Rightarrow a \rightarrow ShowS$$
$$shows \quad = \quad showsPrec\ 0$$

$$show \quad :: \quad (Show\ a) \Rightarrow a \rightarrow String$$
$$show\ x \quad = \quad shows\ x\ \text{""}$$

Some details about *showsPrec* can be found in the Haskell Report, but if you are not displaying constructors in infix notation, the precedence can be ignored. Furthermore, the default method for *showList* is perfectly good for most uses of lists that you will encounter. Thus, for example, we can finish our *Tree* example by declaring it to be an instance of the class *Show* very simply as:

**instance** $(Show\ a) \Rightarrow Show\ (Tree\ a)$ **where**
$\qquad showsPrec\ n \quad = \quad showsTree$

## 24.5 The Read Class

Now that we can convert trees into strings, let's turn to the inverse problem: converting strings into trees. The basic idea is to define a *parser* for a type *a*, which at first glance seems as if it should be a function of type *String* → *a*. However, this simple approach has two problems: (1) it's possible that the string is ambiguous, leading to more than one way to interpret it as a value of type *a*, and (2) it's possible that only a prefix of the string will parse correctly. Thus, we choose instead to return a list of (*a*, *String*) pairs as the result of a parse. If all goes well, we will always get a singleton list, such as [(*v*, "")], as the result of a parse, but we cannot count on it (in fact, when recursively parsing substrings, we will expect a singleton list with a *nonempty* trailing string).

The Standard Prelude provides a type synonym for parsers of the kind just described:

**type** $ReadS\ a \quad = \quad String \rightarrow [(a,\ String)]$

and also defines a function *reads* that by analogy is similar to *shows*:

$$reads \quad :: \quad (Read\ a) \Rightarrow ReadS\ a$$

We will return later to the precise definition of this function, but for now let's use it to define a parser for the *Tree* data type, whose string representation is as described in the previous section. List comprehensions give us a convenient idiom for constructing such parsers:[1]

$$readsTree \quad :: \quad (Read\ a) \Rightarrow ReadS\ (Tree\ a)$$
$$readsTree\ ('<':s) = [(Branch\ l\ r,\ u)\ |\ (l,\ '|':t) \leftarrow readsTree\ s,$$
$$(r,\ '>':u) \leftarrow readsTree\ t]$$
$$readsTree\ s \quad\quad = [(Leaf\ x,\ t)\ |\ (x,\ t) \leftarrow reads\ s]$$

Let's take a moment to examine this function definition in detail. There are two main cases to consider: If the string has the form $'<':s$, we should have the representation of a branch, in which case parsing $s$ as a tree should yield a left branch $l$ followed by a string of the form $'|':t$; parsing $t$ as a tree should then yield the right branch $r$ followed by a string of the form $'>':u$. The resulting tree *Branch l r* is then returned, along with the trailing string $u$. Note the expressive power we get from the combination of pattern matching and list comprehension.

If the initial string is not of the form $'<':s$, then we must have a leaf, in which case the string is parsed using the generic *reads* function, and the result is directly returned.

If we accept on faith for the moment that there is a *Read* instance for *Int* that behaves as one would expect, for example:

(*reads* "5 golden rings") :: [(*Int, String*)]
⟹ [(5, " golden rings")]

then you should be able to verify the following calculations:

*readsTree* "< <1|2>|3>"
⟹ [(*Branch* (*Branch* (*Leaf* 1) (*Leaf* 2)) (*Leaf* 1)), "")]

*readsTree* "<1|2" ⟹ []

There are a couple of shortcomings, however, in our definition of *readsTree*. One is that the parser is quite rigid in that it allows no "white space" (such as extra spaces, tabs, or line feeds) before or between the elements of the tree representation. The other is that the way we parse our punctuation symbols ($'<'$, $'|'$, and $'>'$) is quite different from the way we parse leaf values and subtrees. This lack of uniformity makes the function definition harder to read.

We can address both of these problems by using a *lexical analyzer*, which parses a string into primitive "lexemes" defined by some rules

---

[1] An even more elegant approach to parsing uses monads and parser combinators. These are part of a standard parsing library distributed with most Haskell systems.

about the string construction. The Standard Prelude defines a lexical analyzer:

$$lex \ :: \ ReadS \ String$$

whose lexical rules are those of the Haskell language, which can be found in the Haskell Report. For our purposes, an informal explanation is sufficient. *lex* normally returns a singleton list containing a pair of strings: The first string is the first lexeme in the input string, and the second string is the remainder of the input. White space, including Haskell comments, is completely ignored. If the input string is empty or contains only white space and comments, *lex* returns [("", "")]. If the input is not empty in this sense, but also does not begin with a valid lexeme after any leading white space, *lex* returns [ ].

Using this lexical analyzer, our tree parser can be rewritten as:

$$
\begin{aligned}
readsTree \quad &:: \quad (Read \ a) \Rightarrow ReadS \ (Tree \ a) \\
readsTree \ s \quad &= \quad [(Branch \ l \ r, \ x) \mid (\text{``<''}, \ t) \leftarrow lex \ s, \\
& \qquad\qquad\qquad\qquad (l, \ u) \leftarrow readsTree \ t, \\
& \qquad\qquad\qquad\qquad (\text{``|''}, \ v) \leftarrow lex \ u, \\
& \qquad\qquad\qquad\qquad (r, \ w) \leftarrow readsTree \ v, \\
& \qquad\qquad\qquad\qquad (\text{``>''}, \ x) \leftarrow lex \ w] \\
& \quad +\!\!+ \\
& \quad [(Leaf \ x, \ t) \mid (x, \ t) \leftarrow reads \ s]
\end{aligned}
$$

This definition solves both problems mentioned earlier: White space is suitably ignored, and parsing of substrings has a more uniform structure.

To tie all of this together, let's first look at the definition of the class *Read* in the Standard Prelude:

```
class Read a where
    readsPrec  ::  Int → ReadS a
    readList   ::  ReadS [a]

    readList   =  readParen False (\r → [pr | ("[", s) ← lex r,
                                              pr ← readl s])
                    where readl s   =  [([ ], t) | ("]", t) ← lex s] ++
                                       [(x : xs, u) | (x, t) ← reads s,
                                                      (xs, u) ← readl' t]
                          readl' s  =  [([ ], t) | ("]", t) ← lex s] ++
                                       [(x : xs, v) | (",", t) ← lex s,
                                                      (x, u) ← reads t,
                                                      (xs, v) ← readl' u]
```

$$readParen \quad :: \quad Bool \to ReadS\ a \to ReadS\ a$$
$$readParen\ b\ g \quad = \quad \textbf{if}\ b\ \textbf{then}\ mandatory\ \textbf{else}\ optional$$
$$\qquad \textbf{where}\ optional\ r \quad = g\ r + \!\!+ mandatory\ r$$
$$\qquad mandatory\ r = [(x,\ u)\ |\ (\text{``(''},\ s) \leftarrow lex\ r,$$
$$\qquad\qquad (x,\ t) \leftarrow optional\ s,$$
$$\qquad\qquad (\text{``)''},\ u) \leftarrow lex\ t]$$

The default method for *readList* is rather tedious, but otherwise straightforward. The function *reads* can now be defined, along with an even higher-level function, *read*:

$$reads \quad :: \quad (Read\ a) \Rightarrow ReadS\ a$$
$$reads \quad = \quad readsPrec\ 0$$

$$read \quad :: \quad (Read\ a) \Rightarrow String \to a$$
$$read\ s \quad = \quad \textbf{case}\ [x\ |\ (x,\ t) \leftarrow reads\ s,\ (\text{``''},\ \text{``''}) \leftarrow lex\ t]\ \textbf{of}$$
$$\qquad [x] \quad \to \quad x$$
$$\qquad [\,] \quad \to \quad error\ \text{``PreludeText.read: no parse''}$$
$$\qquad \_ \quad \to \quad error\ \text{``PreludeText.read: ambiguous parse''}$$

The definition of *reads* (like *shows*) should not be surprising. The definition of *read* assumes that exactly one parse is expected, and thus causes a run-time error if there is no unique parse or if the input contains anything more than a representation of exactly one value of type *a* (and possibly comments and white space).

You can test that the *Read* and *Show* instances for a particular type are working correctly by applying (*read . show*) to a value in that type, which in most situations should be the identity function.

## 24.6 The Index Class

The Standard Prelude defines a type class of array indices:

$$\textbf{class}\ (Ord\ a) \Rightarrow Ix\ a\ \textbf{where}$$
$$range \quad :: \quad (a,\ a) \to [a]$$
$$index \quad :: \quad (a,\ a) \to a \to Int$$
$$inRange \quad :: \quad (a,\ a) \to a \to Bool$$

Arrays are defined elsewhere, but the index class is useful for other things besides arrays, so I will describe it here.

Instance declarations are provided for *Int*, *Integer*, *Char*, *Bool*, and tuples of *Ix* types; in addition, instances may be automatically derived for

```
class (Eq a, Show a) ⇒ Num a where
  (+), (−), (∗)  ::  a → a → a
  negate          ::  a → a
  abs, signum    ::  a → a
  fromInteger    ::  Integer → a

class (Num a, Ord a) ⇒ Real a where
  toRational  ::  a → Rational

class (Real a, Enum a) ⇒ Integral a where
  quot, rem, div, mod  ::  a → a → a
  quotRem, divMod      ::  a → a → (a, a)
  toInteger            ::  a → Integer

class (Num a) ⇒ Fractional a where
  (/)          ::  a → a → a
  recip        ::  a → a
  fromRational ::  Rational → a

class (Fractional a) ⇒ Floating a where
  pi                    ::  a
  exp, log, sqrt        ::  a → a
  (∗∗), logBase         ::  a → a → a
  sin, cos, tan         ::  a → a
  asin, acos, atan      ::  a → a
  sinh, cosh, tanh      ::  a → a
  asinh, acosh, atanh   ::  a → a

class (Real a, Fractional a) ⇒ RealFrac a where
  properFraction  ::  (Integral b) ⇒ a → (b, a)
  truncate, round ::  (Integral b) ⇒ a → b
  ceiling, floor  ::  (Integral b) ⇒ a → b

class (RealFrac a, Floating a) ⇒ RealFloat a where
  floatRadix   ::  a → Integer
  floatDigits  ::  a → Int
  floatRange   ::  a → (Int, Int)
  decodeFloat  ::  a → (Integer, Int)
  encodeFloat  ::  Integer → Int → a
  exponent     ::  a → Int
  significand  ::  a → a
  scaleFloat   ::  Int → a → a
  isNaN, isInfinite, isDenormalized, isNegativeZero, isIEEE
               ::  a → Bool
```

Figure 24.1: Standard Numeric Classes

enumerated and tuple types. You should think of the primitive types as vector indices, and tuple types as indices of multidimensional rectangular arrays. Note that the first argument of each operation of class *Ix* is a pair of indices; these are typically the *bounds* (first and last indices) of an array. For example, the bounds of a 10-element, zero-origin vector with *Int* indices would be (0, 9), while a 100 by 100 1-origin matrix might have the bounds ((1, 1), (100, 100)). (In many other languages, such bounds would be written in a form like 1 : 100, 1 : 100, but the present form fits the type system better, because each bound is of the same type as a general index.)

The *range* operation takes a bounds pair and produces the list of indices lying between those bounds, in index order. For example,

*range* (0, 4)  ⟹  [0, 1, 2, 3, 4]
*range* ((0, 0), (1, 2))  ⟹  [(0, 0), (0, 1), (0, 2), (1, 0), (1, 1), (1, 2)]

The *inRange* predicate determines whether an index lies between a given pair of bounds. (For a tuple type, this test is performed componentwise, and then combined with (&&).) Finally, the *index* operation determines the (zero-based) position of an index within a bounded range; for example:

*index* (1, 9) 2  ⟹  1
*index* ((0, 0), (1, 2)) (1, 1)  ⟹  4

## 24.7  The Numeric Classes

The *Num* class and the numeric class hierarchy were briefly described in Section 12.4. Fig. 24.1 gives the full class declarations.

# APPENDIX A

# Built-in Types Are Not Special

Throughout this text we have introduced many "built-in" types such as lists, tuples, integers, and characters. We have also shown how new user-defined types can be defined. Aside from special syntax, you might be wondering if the built-in types are in any way more special than the user-defined ones. The answer is *no*. The special syntax is for convenience and for consistency with historical convention, but has no semantic consequence.

We can emphasize this point by considering what the type declarations would look like for these built-in types if in fact we were allowed to use the special syntax in defining them. For example, the *Char* type might be written as:

```
data Char  =  'a' |' b' |' c' | ...      -- This is not valid
           |  'A' |' B' |' C' | ...      -- Haskell code!
           |  '1' |' 2' |' 3' | ...
```

These constructor names are not syntactically valid; to fix them we would have to write something like:

```
data Char  =  Ca | Cb | Cc | ...
           |  CA | CB | CC | ...
           |  C1 | C2 | C3 | ...
```

Even though these constructors are actually more concise, they are quite unconventional for representing characters, and thus, the special syntax is used instead.

In any case, writing "pseudo-Haskell" code in this way helps us to see through the special syntax. We see now that *Char* is just a data type consisting of a large number of nullary (meaning they take no arguments) constructors. Thinking of *Char* in this way makes it clear why, for example, we can pattern-match against characters (i.e., we would expect to be able to do so for any of a data type's constructors).

Similarly, using pseudo-Haskell, we could define *Int* and *Integer* by:

```
-- more pseudo-code:
data Int     = (-2^29) | ... | -1 | 0 | 1 | ... | (2^29 - 1)
data Integer = ... - 2 | -1 | 0 | 1 | 2 ...
```

(Recall that $-2\hat{\ }29$ to $2\hat{\ }29 - 1$ is the minimum range for the *Int* data type.) *Int* is clearly a much larger enumeration than *Char*, but it's still finite! In contrast, the pseudo-code for *Integer* (the type of arbitrary precision integers) is intended to convey an *infinite* enumeration (and in that sense only, the *Integer* data type *is* somewhat special).

Haskell has a data type called *unit*, which has exactly one value: (). The name of this data type is also written (). This is trivially expressed in Haskell pseudo-code:

```
data () = ()    -- more pseudo-code
```

Tuples are also easy to define playing this game:

```
data (a, b)       = (a, b)     -- more pseudo-code
data (a, b, c)    = (a, b, c)
data (a, b, c, d) = (a, b, c, d)
```

and so on. Each declaration above defines a tuple type of a particular length, with parentheses playing a role in both the expression syntax (as data constructor) and type-expression syntax (as type constructor). By "and so on" we mean that there are an infinite number of such declarations, reflecting the fact that tuples of all finite lengths are allowed in Haskell.

The list data type is also easily handled in pseudo-Haskell, and more interestingly, it is recursive:

```
data [a] = [] | a : [a]    -- more pseudo-code
infixr   5 :
```

We can now see clearly what we described about lists earlier: [ ] is the empty list, and (:) is the infix list constructor; thus [1, 2, 3] must be equivalent to the list $1 : 2 : 3 : [\ ]$. (Note that (:) is right associative.) The type of [ ] is [a], and the type of (:) is $a \rightarrow [a] \rightarrow [a]$.

> **DETAILS**
> The way (:) is defined here is actually legal syntax. Infix constructors are permitted in **data** declarations, and are distinguished from infix operators (for pattern-matching purposes) by the fact that they must begin with a colon (a property trivially satisfied by ":").

At this point the reader should note carefully the differences between tuples and lists, which the above definitions make abundantly clear. In particular, note the recursive nature of the list type whose elements are homogeneous and of arbitrary length, and the nonrecursive nature of a (particular) tuple type whose elements are heterogeneous and of fixed length. The typing rules for tuples and lists should now also be clear: For $(e1, e2, \ldots, en)$, $n \geq 2$, if $Ti$ is the type of $ei$, then the type of the tuple is $(T1, T2, \ldots, Tn)$. For $[e1, e2, \ldots, en]$, $n \geq 0$, each $ei$ must have the same type $T$, and the type of the list is $[T]$.

# APPENDIX B

# Pattern-Matching Details

In this section Haskell's pattern-matching process will be explained in greater detail. Haskell defines a fixed set of patterns for use in case expressions and function definitions. Pattern matching is permitted using the constructors of any type, whether user-defined or predefined in Haskell. This includes tuples, strings, numbers, characters, and so on. For example, here's a contrived function that matches against a tuple of "constants:"

> *contrived* :: ([*a*], *Char*, (*Int*, *Float*), *String*, *Bool*) → *Bool*
> *contrived* ([ ], '*b*', (1, 2.0), "hi", *True*)
>          = *False*

This example also demonstrates that *nesting* of patterns is permitted (to arbitrary depth).

Technically speaking, *formal parameters* to functions are also patterns – it's just that they *never fail to match a value*. As a "side effect" of a successful match, the formal parameter is bound to the value it is being matched against. For this reason, patterns in any one equation are not allowed to have more than one occurrence of the same formal parameter.

A pattern that may fail to match is said to be *refutable*; for example, the empty list [ ] is refutable. Patterns such as formal parameters that never fail to match are said to be *irrefutable*. There are three other kinds of irrefutable patterns, which are summarized below.

The first pattern is referred to as an *as-pattern*. Sometimes it is convenient to name a pattern for use on the right-hand side of an equation. For example, a function that duplicates the first element in a list might be written as:

> *f* (*x* : *xs*) = *x* : *x* : *xs*

Note that *x* : *xs* appears both as a pattern on the left-hand side, and as an expression on the right-hand side. To improve readability, we might prefer to write $x : xs$ just once, which we can achieve using an *as-pattern* as follows:[1]

$$f \ s@(x : xs) \ = \ x : s$$

Technically speaking, as-patterns always result in a successful match, although the subpattern (in this case $x : xs$) could, of course, fail.

The second pattern is known as a *wildcard*. Another common situation is matching against a value we really care nothing about. For example, the functions *head* and *tail* can be written as:

$$head \ (x : \_) \ = \ x$$
$$tail \ (\_ : xs) \ = \ xs$$

in which we have "advertised" the fact that we don't care what a certain part of the input is. Each wildcard will independently match anything, but in contrast to a formal parameter, each will bind nothing; for this reason more than one are allowed in an equation.

The third kind of pattern allowed in Haskell is called a *lazy pattern*, and has the form ~*pat*. Lazy patterns are *irrefutable*: matching a value $v$ against ~*pat* always succeeds, regardless of *pat*. Operationally speaking, if an identifier in *pat* is later "used" on the right-hand side, it will be bound to that portion of the value that would result if $v$ were to successfully match *pat*, and $\perp$ otherwise.

Lazy patterns are useful in contexts where infinite data structures are being defined recursively. For example, infinite lists are an excellent vehicle for writing *simulation* programs, and in this context, the infinite lists are often called *streams*. Streams were discussed at length in Chapter 14.

## Pattern-Matching Semantics

So far we have discussed how individual patterns are matched, how some are refutable, some are irrefutable, and so forth. But what drives the overall process? In what order are the matches attempted? What if none succeed? This section addresses these questions.

Pattern matching can either *fail*, *succeed*, or *diverge*. A successful match binds the formal parameters in the pattern. Divergence occurs when a value needed by the pattern diverges (i.e., is nonterminating) or

---

[1] Another advantage to doing this is that a naive implementation might otherwise completely reconstruct $x : xs$ rather than re-use the value being matched against.

results in an error (⊥). The matching process itself occurs "top-down, left-to-right." Failure of a pattern anywhere in one equation results in failure of the whole equation, and the next equation is then tried. If all equations fail, the value of the function application is ⊥, and results in a run-time error.

For example, if *bot* is a divergent or erroneous computation, and if [1, 2] is matched against [0, *bot*], then 1 fails to match 0, so the result is a failed match. But if [1, 2] is matched against [*bot*, 0], then matching 1 against *bot* causes divergence (i.e., ⊥).

The only other twist to this set of rules is that top-level patterns may also have a boolean *guard*, as in this definition of a function that forms an abstract version of a number's sign:

$$sign\ x\ |\ x > 0\ \ =\ 1$$
$$|\ x == 0\ =\ 0$$
$$|\ x < 0\ \ =\ -1$$

Note here that a sequence of guards is given for a single pattern; as with patterns, these guards are evaluated top-down, and the first that evaluates to *True* results in a successful match.

The pattern-matching rules can have subtle effects on the meaning of functions. For example, consider this definition of *take*:

$$take\ 0\ \_\ \ \ \ \ \ =\ [\ ]$$
$$take\ \_\ [\ ]\ \ \ \ \ =\ [\ ]$$
$$take\ n\ (x : xs)\ =\ x : take\ (n - 1)\ xs$$

and this slightly different version (the first two equations have been reversed):

$$take1\ \_\ [\ ]\ \ \ \ \ =\ [\ ]$$
$$take1\ 0\ \_\ \ \ \ \ \ =\ [\ ]$$
$$take1\ n\ (x : xs)\ =\ x : take1\ (n - 1)\ xs$$

Now note the following:

$$take\ 0\ bot\ \ \ \ \Longrightarrow\ \ [\ ]$$
$$take1\ 0\ bot\ \ \ \Longrightarrow\ \ \bot$$

$$take\ bot\ [\ ]\ \ \ \Longrightarrow\ \ \bot$$
$$take1\ bot\ [\ ]\ \ \Longrightarrow\ \ [\ ]$$

We see that *take* is "more defined" with respect to its second argument, whereas *take1* is more defined with respect to its first. It is difficult to say in this case which definition is better. Just remember that in certain applications, it may make a difference. (The Standard Prelude includes a definition corresponding to *take*.)

## Case Expressions

Pattern matching provides a way to "dispatch control" based on structural properties of a value. However, in many circumstances we don't wish to define a *function* every time we need to do this. Haskell's *case expression* provides a way to solve this problem. Indeed, the meaning of pattern matching in function definitions is specified in the Haskell Report in terms of case expressions, which are considered more primitive.

In particular, a function definition of the form:

$$f\,p_{11}...p_{1k} = e_1$$

...

$$f\,p_{n1}...p_{nk} = e_n$$

where each $p_{ij}$ is a pattern, is semantically equivalent to:

$$f\ x1\ x2\ ...\ xk = \textbf{case}\ (x1, \ldots, xk)\ \textbf{of}\ (p_{11}, ..., p_{1k}) \rightarrow e_1$$
$$...$$
$$(p_{n1}, ..., p_{nk}) \rightarrow e_n$$

where the *xi* are new identifiers. For example, the definition of *take* given earlier is equivalent to:

$$
\begin{aligned}
take\ m\ ys = \ &\textbf{case}\ (m,\ ys)\ \textbf{of} \\
&(0, \_)\quad \rightarrow [\,] \\
&(\_, [\,])\quad \rightarrow [\,] \\
&(n, x : xs) \rightarrow x : take\ (n-1)\ xs
\end{aligned}
$$

For type correctness, the types of the right-hand sides of a case expression or set of equations comprising a function definition must all be the same; more precisely, they must all share a common principal type.

The pattern-matching rules for case expressions are the same as we have given for function definitions.

# Bibliography

Rationale for the design of the Ada programming language, United States Department of Defense, ACM Sigplan Notices, Vol. 14, No. 6, June 1979.

Arya, K. 1986. A functional approach to animation. *Computer Graphics Forum*, 5:297–311.

———. 1989. Processes in a functional animation system. In *Proceedings of the Conference on Functional Programming Languages and Computer Architecture*, 382–395. New York: ACM/IFIP.

Augustsson, L., D. Barton, B. Boutel, W. Burton, J. Fasel, K. Hammond, R. Hinze, P. Hudak, T. Johnsson, M. Jones, J. Launchbury, E. Meijer, J. Peterson, A. Reid, C. Runciman, P. Walder. 1999. Haskell 98: A nonstrict, purely functional language. Technical Report YALEU/DCS/RR-1106, Department of Computer Science, J. Hughes and S. Peyton Jones, (eds.), Yale University.

Backus, J. 1978. The history of FORTRAN I, II, and III. *ACM Sigplan Notices*, 13(8):165–180.

Barnsley, M. 1993. *Fractals Everywhere*. New York: Academic Press.

Bird, R. 1998. *Introduction to functional programming using Haskell*. 2d ed. London: Prentice Hall.

Bird, R. and P. Wadler. 1988. *Introduction to functional programming*. New York: Prentice Hall.

Church, A. 1941. *The calculi of lambda conversion*. Princeton, NJ: Princeton University Press.

American National Standard COBOL (ANS X3.23-1968), 1968.

Dannenberg, R.B., C.L. Fraley, and P. Velikonja. 1992. A functional language for sound synthesis with behavioral abstraction and lazy evaluation. In *Computer generated music*, ed. D. Baggi, IEEE Computer Society Press.

Dijkstra, E.W. 1976. *A Discipline of Programming*. New York: Prentice-Hall.

de Morgan, R.M., I.D. Hill, and B.A. Wichmann. 1976. Modified report on the algorithmic language ALGOL 60. *Computer Journal*, 19:364–379.

Elliott, C. 1997. Modeling interactive 3D and multimedia animation with an embedded language. In *Proceedings of the first conference on Domain-Specific Languages*, 285–296. USENIX.

Elliott, C., and P. Hudak. 1997. Functional reactive animation. In *International Conference on Functional Programming*, 163–173.

Finne, S. and S. Peyton Jones. 1995. Pictures: A simple structured graphics model. In *Proceedings of Glasgow Functional Programming Workshop*. Glasgow, Scotland: Glasgow University.

Foley, J.D., A. van Dam, S.K. Feiner, and J.F. Hughes. 1996. *Computer Graphics – Principles and Practice*. 2d ed. Reading, MA: Addison-Wesley.

Gosling, J., B. Joy, and G. Steele. 1996. *The Java Language Specification*. Reading, MA: Addison-Wesley.

Henderson, P. 1982. Functional geometry. In *Proceedings of the 1982 ACM Symposium on Lisp and Functional Programming*, 179–187. New York: ACM.

Hindley, R., 1969. The principal type scheme of an object in combinatory logic. *Transactions of the American Mathematical Society*, 146:29–60.

Hofstadter, D.R. 1979. *Gödel, Escher, Bach: an Eternal Golden Braid*. New York: Vintage.

Hudak, P. 1989. Conception, evolution, and application of functional programming languages. *ACM Computing Surveys*, 21:359–411.

———. 1996. Haskore music tutorial. In *Second International School on Advanced Functional Programming*, 38–68. Springer Verlag, LNCS 1129.

Hudak, P., and P. Wadler, eds. 1988. Report on the functional programming language Haskell. Technical Report YALEU/DCS/RR666, Yale University, Department of Computer Science.

Hudak, P., and J. Fasel. 1992. A gentle introduction to Haskell. *ACM SIGPLAN Notices*, 27(5): T1–T53.

Hudak, P., T. Makucevich, S. Gadde, and B. Whong. 1996. Haskore music notation – an algebra of music. *Journal of Functional Programming*, 6:465–483.

Kernighan, B.W., and Ritchie, D.M. 1978. *The C Programming Language*. New York: Prentice Hall.

Lucas, P., and S.N. Zilles. 1987. Graphics in an applicative context. Technical report, IBM Almaden Research Center.

McCarthy, J. 1978. History of Lisp. *ACM Sigplan Notices*, 13:217–223.

Milner, R.A. 1978. A theory of type polymorphism in programming. *Journal of Computer and System Sciences*, 17:348–375.

Milner, R., M. Tofte, and R. Harper. 1990. *The Definition of Standard ML*. Cambridge, MA: The MIT Press.

Moggi, E. 1989. Computational lambda-calculus and monads. In *Proceedings of Symposium on Logic in Computer Science*, 14–23. IEEE. Washington D.C.: Computer Society Press.

Orlarey, O., D. Fober, S. Letz, and M. Bilton. 1994. Lambda calculus and music calculi. In *Proceedings of International Computer Music Conference*. San Francisco: International Computer Music Association.

Pappert, S. 1980. *Mindstorms: Children, computers and powerful ideas.* New York: Basic Books.

Pattis, R.E. 1981. *Karel the Robot – A Gentle Introduction to the Art of Programming with Pascal.* New York: John Wiley.

Peterson, J., G. Hager, and P. Hudak. 1999. A language for declarative robotic programming. In *International Conference on Robotics and Automation.* Washington, D.C.: IEEE.

Peterson, J., P. Hudak, and C. Elliott. 1999. Lambda in motion: Controlling robots with Haskell. In *First International Workshop on Practical Aspects of Declarative Languages.* SIGPLAN. New York: ACM.

Peyton Jones, S., and P. Wadler. 1993. Imperative functional programming. In *Proceedings 20th Symposium on Principles of Programming Languages.* New York: ACM. 71–84.

Pierce, B. 1991. *Basic Category Theory for Computer Scientists.* Cambridge, MA: MIT Press. 1991.

Quine, W.V.O. 1966. *The Ways of Paradox, and Other Essays.* New York: Random House.

Rees, J., and W. Clinger. 1986. Revised[3] report on the algorithmic language Scheme. *SIGPLAN Notices,* 21:37–79.

Schechter, G., C. Elliott, R. Yeung, and S. Abi-Ezzi. 1994. Functional 3D graphics in C++ – with an object-oriented, multiple dispatching implementation. In *Proceedings of the 1994 Eurographics Object-Oriented Graphics Workshop.* Eurographics, Berlin: Springer-Verlag.

Schönfinkel, M., 1924. Über die bausteine der mathematischen logik. *Mathematische Annalen,* 92:305.

Turner, D.A. 1976. SASL language manual. Technical report, St. Andrews, Scotland: University of St. Andrews.

———. 1985. Miranda: a non-strict functional language with polymorphic types. In *Functional Programming Languages and Computer Architecture,* 1–16. Berlin: Springer-Verlag LNCS 201.

Wadler, P. 1992. The essence of functional programming. In *Proceedings 19th Symposium on Principles of Programming Languages,* 1–14. New York: ACM.

Wiitala, S.A. 1987. *Discrete Mathematics – A Unified Approach.* New York: McGraw-Hill.

Zilles, S.N., P. Lucas, T.M. Linden, J.B. Lotspiech, and A.R. Harbury. 1998. The Escher document imaging model. In *Proceedings of the ACM Conference on Document Processing Systems,* 159–168. New York: ACM.

# Index